THE FURNACE

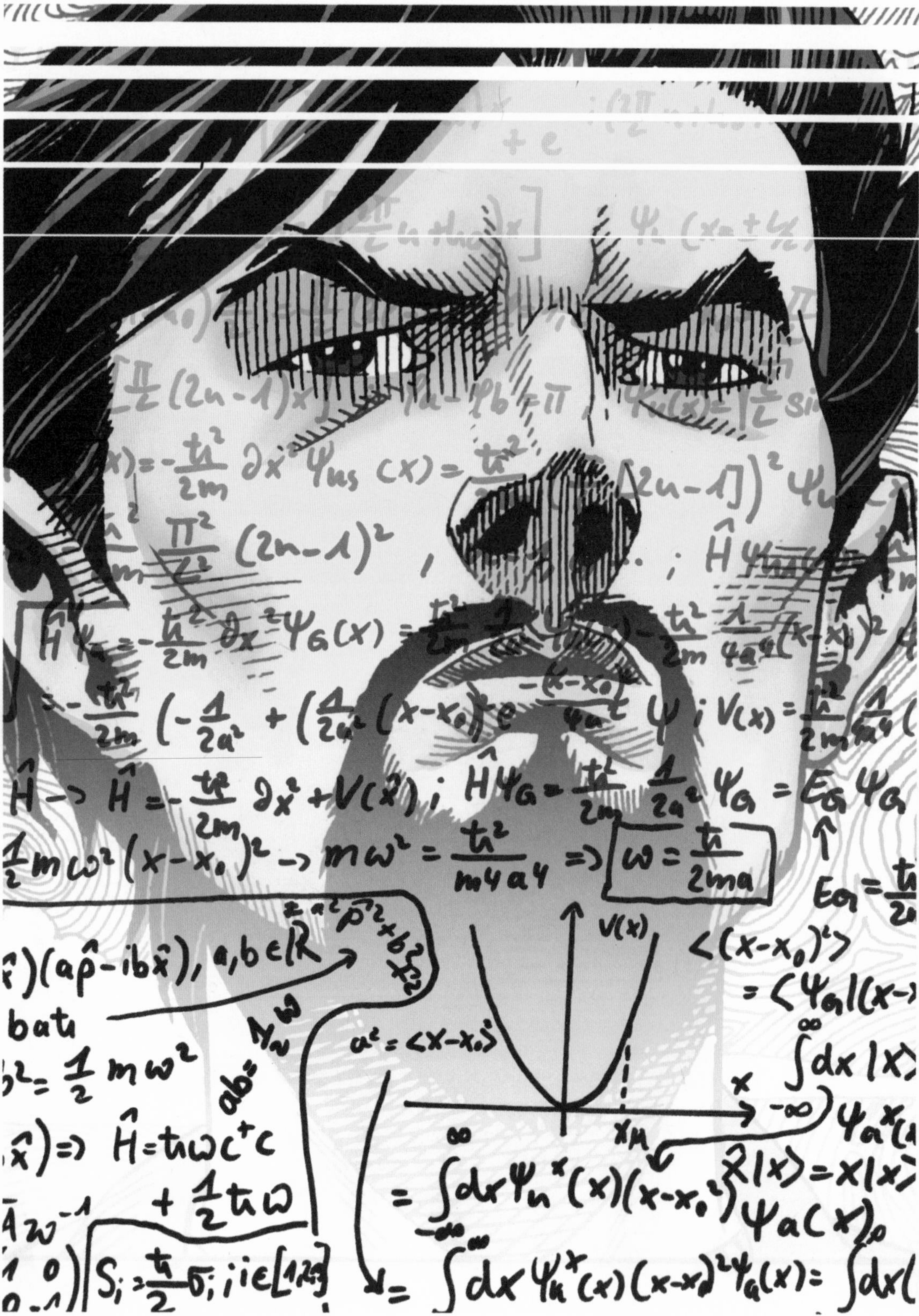

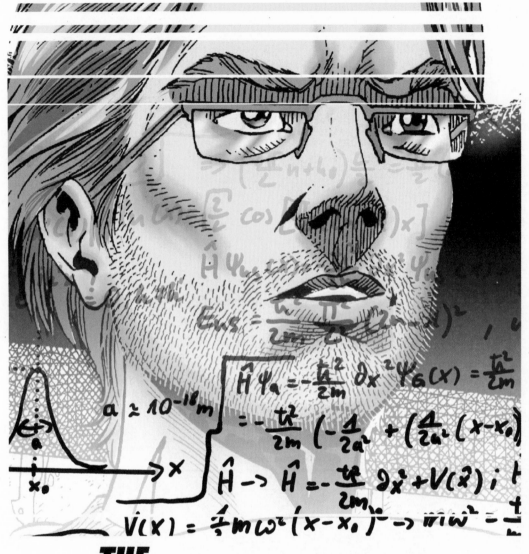

THE
FURNACE

PRENTIS ROLLINS

TOR

TOM DOHERTY ASSOCIATES / NEW YORK, NY

THE FURNACE

A TOR BOOK

PUBLISHED BY TOM DOHERTY ASSOCIATES
175 FIFTH AVENUE
NEW YORK, NY 10010

WWW. TOR-FORGE.COM

TOR ® IS A REGISTERED TRADEMARK OF MACMILLAN PUBLISHING GROUP, LLC.

ISBN 978-0-7653-9868-0 (TRADE PAPERBACK)
ISBN 978-0-7653-9867-3 (EBOOK)

OUR BOOKS MAY BE PURCHASED IN BULK FOR PROMOTIONAL, EDUCATIONAL, OR BUSINESS USE. PLEASE CONTACT YOUR LOCAL BOOKSELLER OR THE MACMILLAN CORPORATE AND PREMIUM SALES DEPARTMENT AT 1-800-221-7945, EXTENSION 5442, OR BY E-MAIL AT
MACMILLANSPECIALMARKETS@MACMILLAN.COM

FIRST EDITION: JULY 2018

PRINTED IN CHINA

0 9 8 7 6 5 4 3 2 1

For Dagny

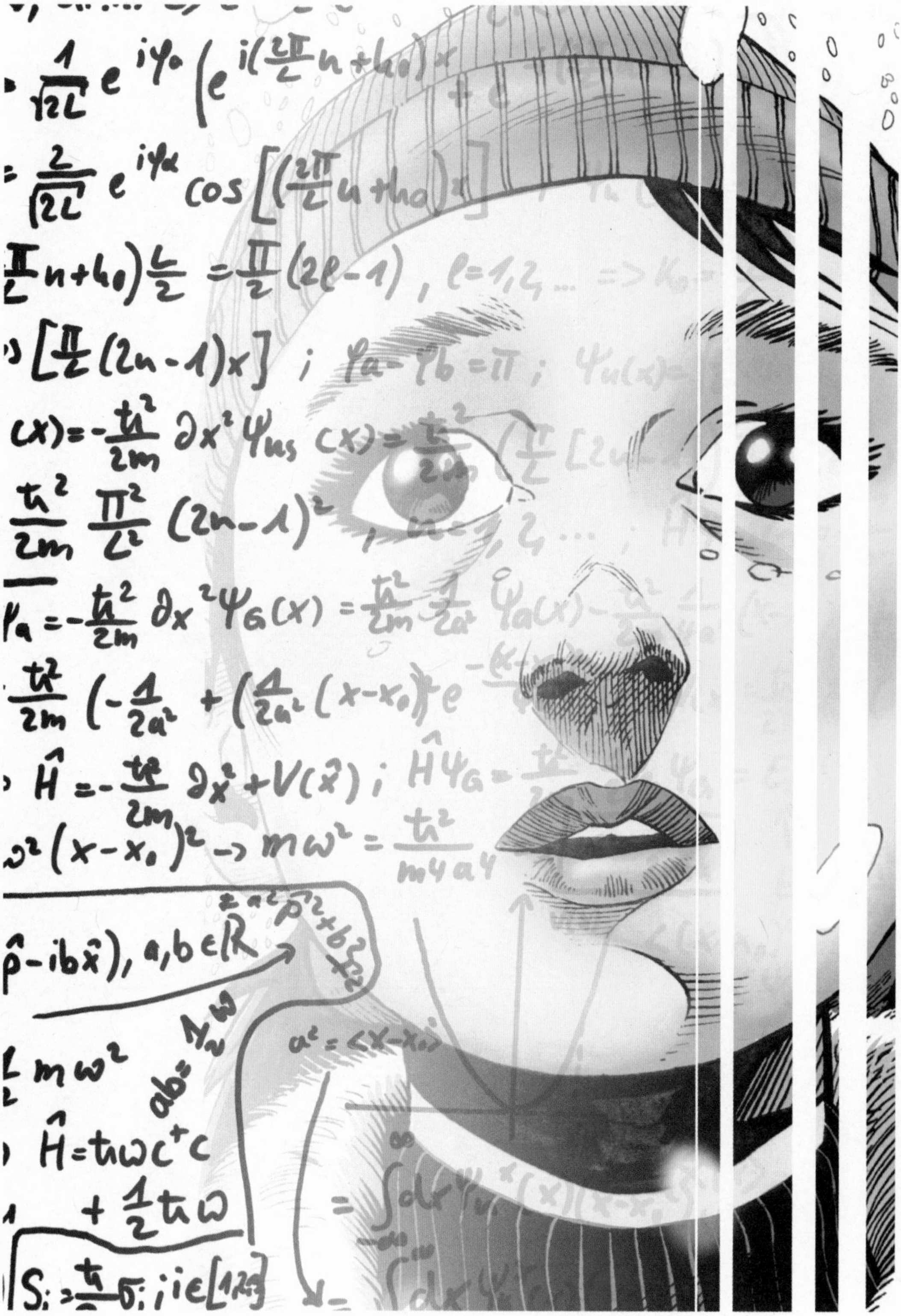

$$= \frac{1}{\sqrt{2L}} e^{i\psi_\alpha} \left(e^{i\left(\frac{2\pi}{L}n + h\alpha\right)x} \right.$$

$$= \frac{2}{\sqrt{2L}} e^{i\psi_\alpha} \cos\left[\left(\frac{2\pi}{L}n + h\alpha\right)x\right]$$

$$\left(\frac{\pi}{L}n + h\alpha\right)\frac{L}{2} = \frac{\pi}{2}(2\ell - 1), \quad \ell = 1,2,\dots \Rightarrow K_0 =$$

$$\left[\frac{\pi}{L}(2n-1)x\right] ; \quad \psi_a - \psi_b = \pi ; \quad \psi_u(x) =$$

$$(x) = -\frac{\hbar^2}{2m} \partial_x^2 \psi_{us}(x) = \frac{\hbar^2}{2m}\left(\frac{\pi}{L}[2u\right.$$

$$\frac{\hbar^2}{2m} \frac{\pi^2}{L^2}(2n-1)^2 , \quad$$

$$\psi_a = -\frac{\hbar^2}{2m} \partial_x^2 \psi_G(x) = \frac{\hbar^2}{2m}\frac{1}{2a^2}\psi_a(x) -$$

$$\frac{\hbar^2}{2m}\left(-\frac{1}{2a^2} + \left(\frac{1}{2a^2}(x-x_0)\right)e^{-\frac{\hbar}{2}}\right.$$

$$\hat{H} = -\frac{\hbar^2}{2m} \partial_x^2 + V(\hat{x}) ; \quad \hat{H}\psi_G =$$

$$\omega^2(x-x_0)^2 \to m\omega^2 = \frac{\hbar^2}{m^4 a^4}$$

$$\hat{p} - ib\hat{x}), \ a,b \in \mathbb{R} \quad = a^2\hat{p}^2 + b^2\hat{x}^2$$

$$\frac{L}{2}m\omega^2 \quad abs \quad \frac{1}{2}\sqrt{\frac{\omega}{\omega}} \quad a^2 = \langle x - x_0 \rangle$$

$$\hat{H} = \hbar\omega c^+ c$$

$$+ \frac{1}{2}\hbar\omega \qquad = \int_{-\infty}^{\infty} dx' \psi_u^*(x)(x-x_0)$$

$$S_i = \frac{\hbar}{2}\sigma_i ; \ i \in [1,2,3] \qquad = \int_{-\infty}^{\infty} dx' \psi_a$$

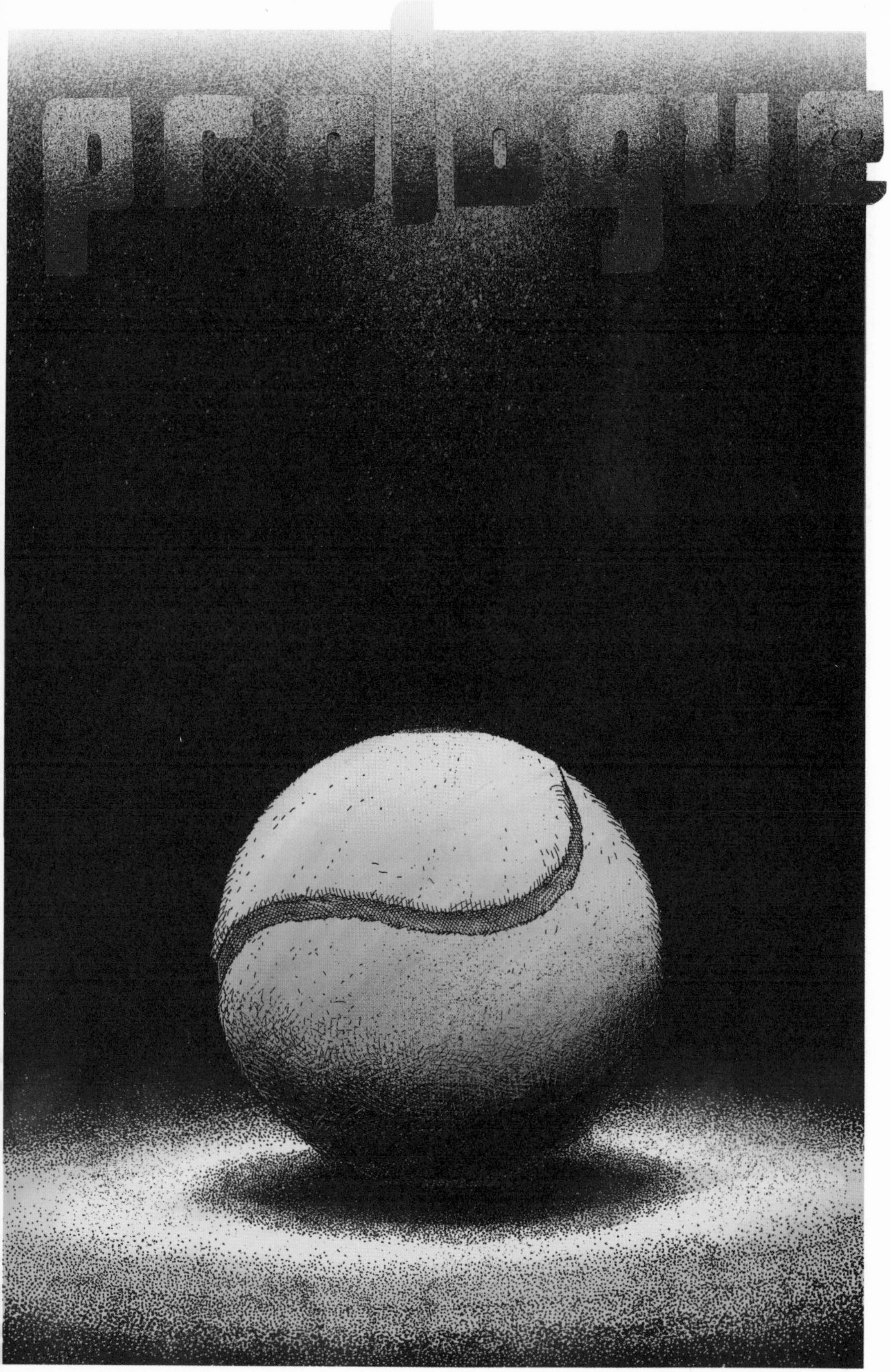
prologue

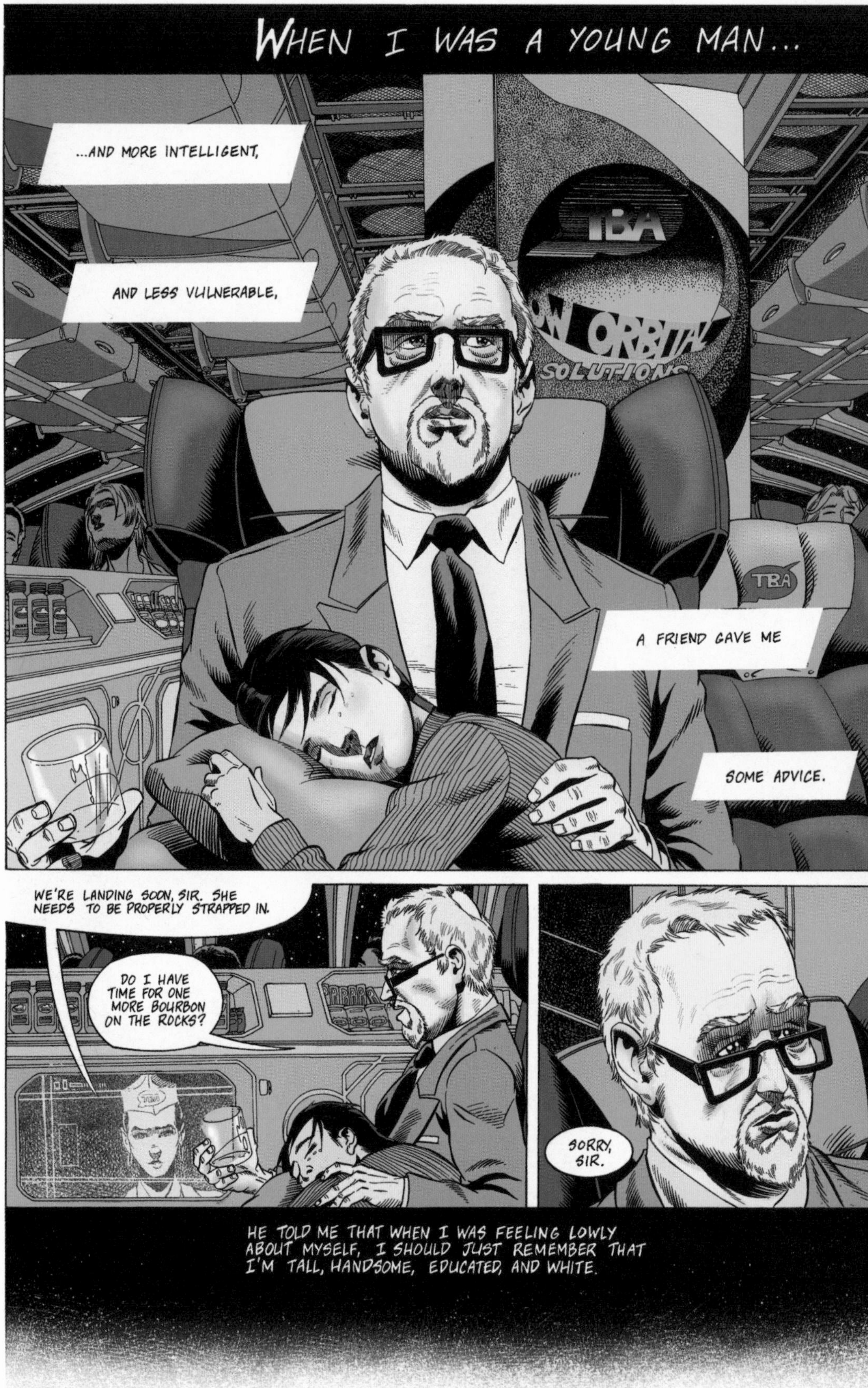

WHEN I WAS A YOUNG MAN...
...AND MORE INTELLIGENT,
AND LESS VULNERABLE,
TBA
ON ORBITAL SOLUTIONS
A FRIEND GAVE ME
SOME ADVICE.
WE'RE LANDING SOON, SIR. SHE NEEDS TO BE PROPERLY STRAPPED IN.
DO I HAVE TIME FOR ONE MORE BOURBON ON THE ROCKS?
SORRY, SIR.
HE TOLD ME THAT WHEN I WAS FEELING LOWLY ABOUT MYSELF, I SHOULD JUST REMEMBER THAT I'M TALL, HANDSOME, EDUCATED, AND WHITE.

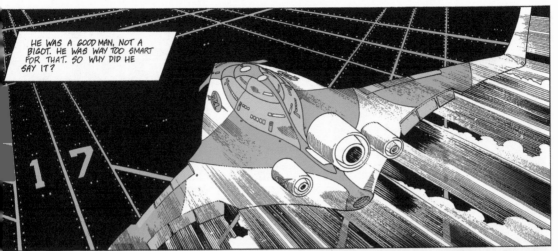

HE WAS A GOOD MAN, NOT A BIGOT. HE WAS WAY TOO SMART FOR THAT. SO WHY DID HE SAY IT?

I GUESS HE JUST MEANT THAT THE WORLD IS WHAT IT IS AND WE SHOULD BE THANKFUL FOR WHATEVER ADVANTAGES WE'RE GIVEN FROM THE START.

I'M FORTY-EIGHT NOW, AND VULNERABLE. I DRINK TOO MUCH, MY KNEES ARE SHOT, AND I HAVE A DAUGHTER. I KNOW, THAT SOUNDS AWFUL.

DON'T MISUNDERSTAND--I LOVE MY GIRL AS MUCH AS ANY PARENT EVER LOVED A CHILD. I KNOW I SHOULD BE THANKING GOD FOR ALL I'VE GOT.

IT'S JUST THAT TO BE A PARENT IS TO LIVE IN FEAR-- CONSTANT, ENDLESS FEAR.

BECAUSE...THE WORLD IS WHAT IT IS.

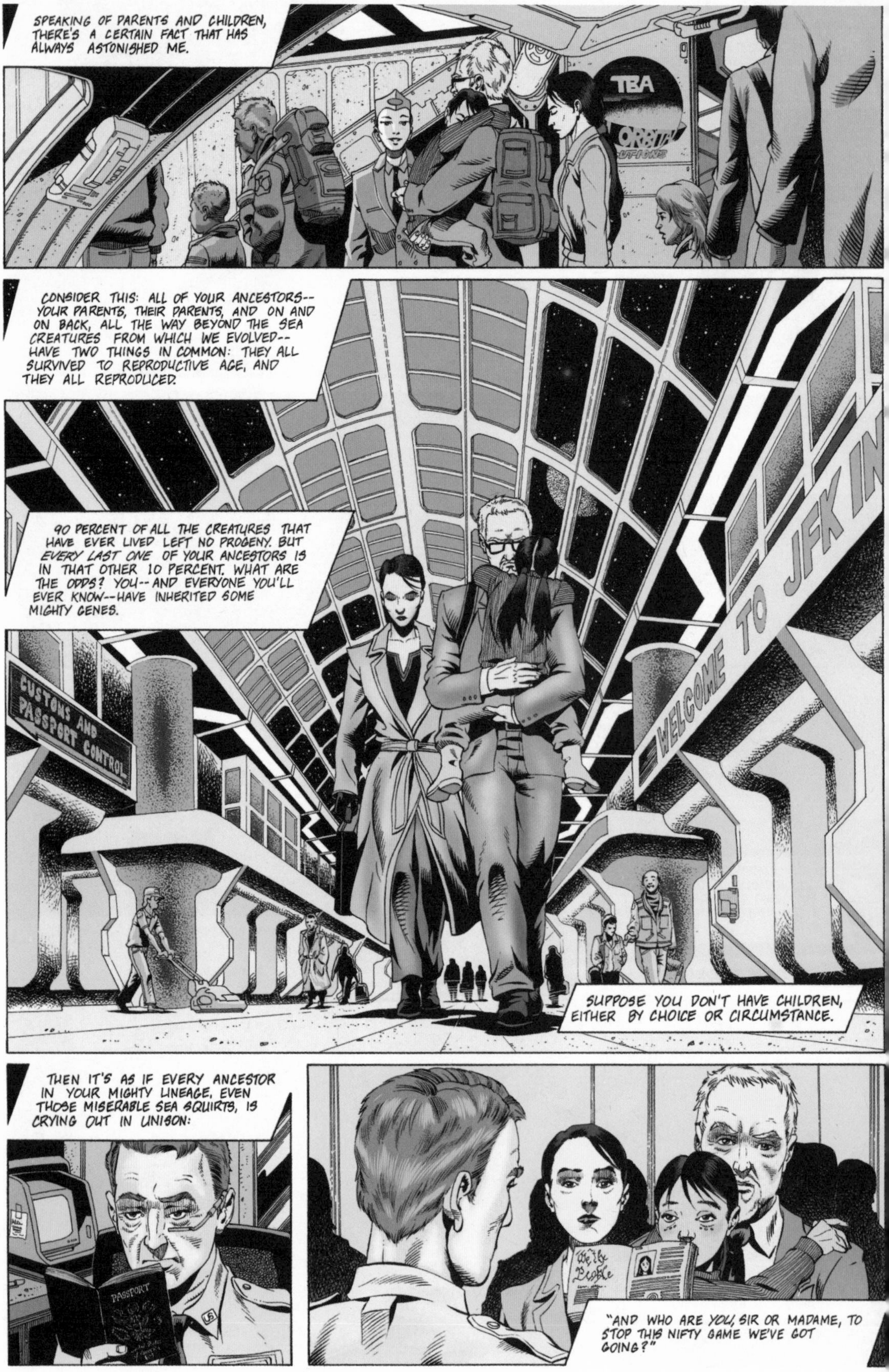
SPEAKING OF PARENTS AND CHILDREN, THERE'S A CERTAIN FACT THAT HAS ALWAYS ASTONISHED ME.
TBA
CONSIDER THIS: ALL OF YOUR ANCESTORS-- YOUR PARENTS, THEIR PARENTS, AND ON AND ON BACK, ALL THE WAY BEYOND THE SEA CREATURES FROM WHICH WE EVOLVED-- HAVE TWO THINGS IN COMMON: THEY ALL SURVIVED TO REPRODUCTIVE AGE, AND THEY ALL REPRODUCED.
90 PERCENT OF ALL THE CREATURES THAT HAVE EVER LIVED LEFT NO PROGENY. BUT EVERY LAST ONE OF YOUR ANCESTORS IS IN THAT OTHER 10 PERCENT. WHAT ARE THE ODDS? YOU--AND EVERYONE YOU'LL EVER KNOW--HAVE INHERITED SOME MIGHTY GENES.
CUSTOMS AND PASSPORT CONTROL
WELCOME TO JFK IN
SUPPOSE YOU DON'T HAVE CHILDREN, EITHER BY CHOICE OR CIRCUMSTANCE.
THEN IT'S AS IF EVERY ANCESTOR IN YOUR MIGHTY LINEAGE, EVEN THOSE MISERABLE SEA SQUIRTS, IS CRYING OUT IN UNISON:
PASSPORT
"AND WHO ARE YOU, SIR OR MADAME, TO STOP THIS NIFTY GAME WE'VE GOT GOING?"

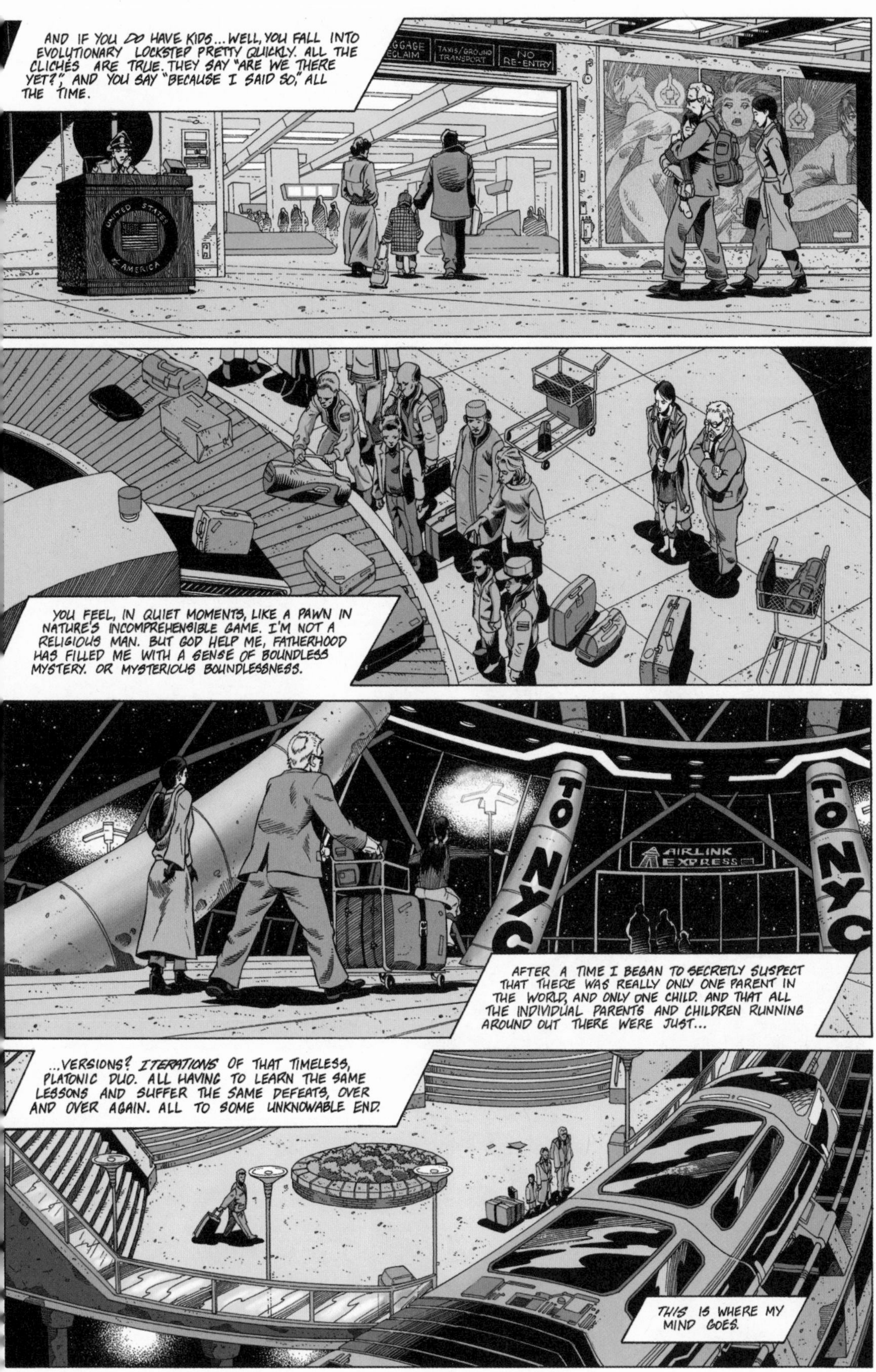
AND IF YOU DO HAVE KIDS... WELL, YOU FALL INTO EVOLUTIONARY LOCKSTEP PRETTY QUICKLY. ALL THE CLICHÉS ARE TRUE. THEY SAY "ARE WE THERE YET?," AND YOU SAY "BECAUSE I SAID SO," ALL THE TIME.
GGAGE
ECLAIM
TAXIS/GROUND TRANSPORT
NO RE-ENTRY
UNITED STATES OF AMERICA
YOU FEEL, IN QUIET MOMENTS, LIKE A PAWN IN NATURE'S INCOMPREHENSIBLE GAME. I'M NOT A RELIGIOUS MAN. BUT GOD HELP ME, FATHERHOOD HAS FILLED ME WITH A SENSE OF BOUNDLESS MYSTERY. OR MYSTERIOUS BOUNDLESSNESS.
TO NYC
AIRLINK EXPRESS
TO NYC
AFTER A TIME I BEGAN TO SECRETLY SUSPECT THAT THERE WAS REALLY ONLY ONE PARENT IN THE WORLD, AND ONLY ONE CHILD. AND THAT ALL THE INDIVIDUAL PARENTS AND CHILDREN RUNNING AROUND OUT THERE WERE JUST...
...VERSIONS? ITERATIONS OF THAT TIMELESS, PLATONIC DUO. ALL HAVING TO LEARN THE SAME LESSONS AND SUFFER THE SAME DEFEATS, OVER AND OVER AGAIN. ALL TO SOME UNKNOWABLE END.
THIS IS WHERE MY MIND GOES.

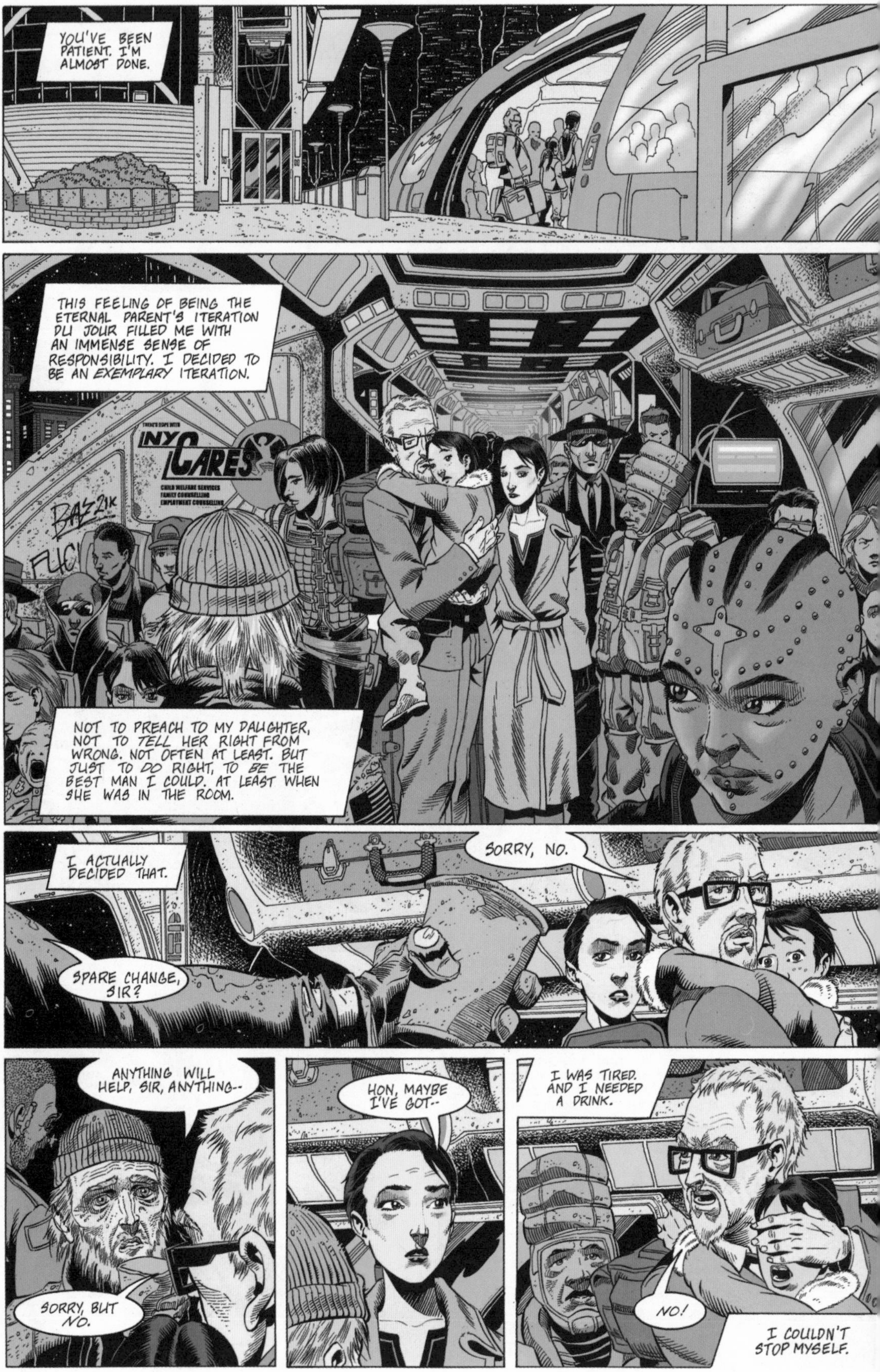

YOU'VE BEEN PATIENT. I'M ALMOST DONE.
THIS FEELING OF BEING THE ETERNAL PARENT'S ITERATION DU JOUR FILLED ME WITH AN IMMENSE SENSE OF RESPONSIBILITY. I DECIDED TO BE AN *EXEMPLARY* ITERATION.
NOT TO PREACH TO MY DAUGHTER, NOT TO *TELL* HER RIGHT FROM WRONG. NOT OFTEN AT LEAST. BUT JUST TO *DO* RIGHT, TO *BE* THE BEST MAN I COULD. AT LEAST WHEN SHE WAS IN THE ROOM.
I ACTUALLY DECIDED THAT.
SORRY, NO.
SPARE CHANGE, SIR?
ANYTHING WILL HELP, SIR, ANYTHING--
SORRY, BUT *NO*.
HON, MAYBE I'VE GOT--
I WAS TIRED. AND I NEEDED A DRINK.
NO!
I COULDN'T STOP MYSELF.

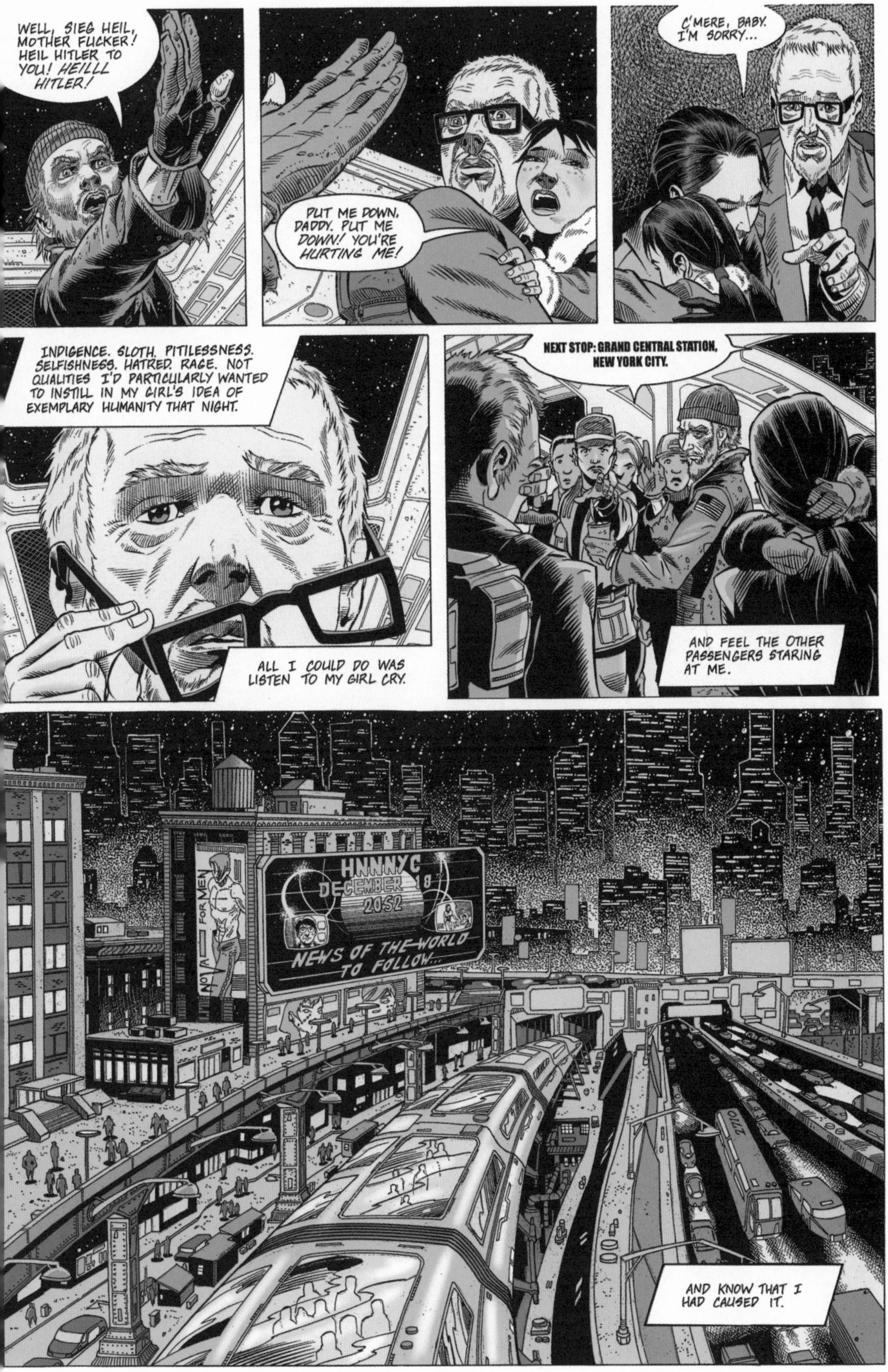
WELL, SIEG HEIL, MOTHER FUCKER! HEIL HITLER TO YOU! HEILLL HITLER!
PUT ME DOWN, DADDY. PUT ME DOWN! YOU'RE HURTING ME!
C'MERE, BABY. I'M SORRY...
INDIGENCE. SLOTH. PITILESSNESS. SELFISHNESS. HATRED. RAGE. NOT QUALITIES I'D PARTICULARLY WANTED TO INSTILL IN MY GIRL'S IDEA OF EXEMPLARY HUMANITY THAT NIGHT.
ALL I COULD DO WAS LISTEN TO MY GIRL CRY.
NEXT STOP: GRAND CENTRAL STATION, NEW YORK CITY.
AND FEEL THE OTHER PASSENGERS STARING AT ME.
HNNNYC
DECEMBER 18
2052
NEWS OF THE WORLD TO FOLLOW...
FOR MEN
AND KNOW THAT I HAD CAUSED IT.

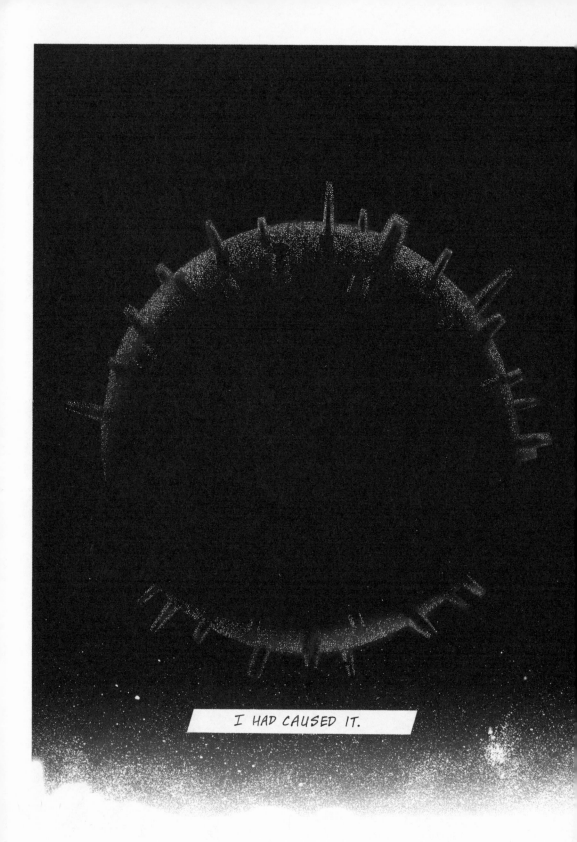

I HAD CAUSED IT.

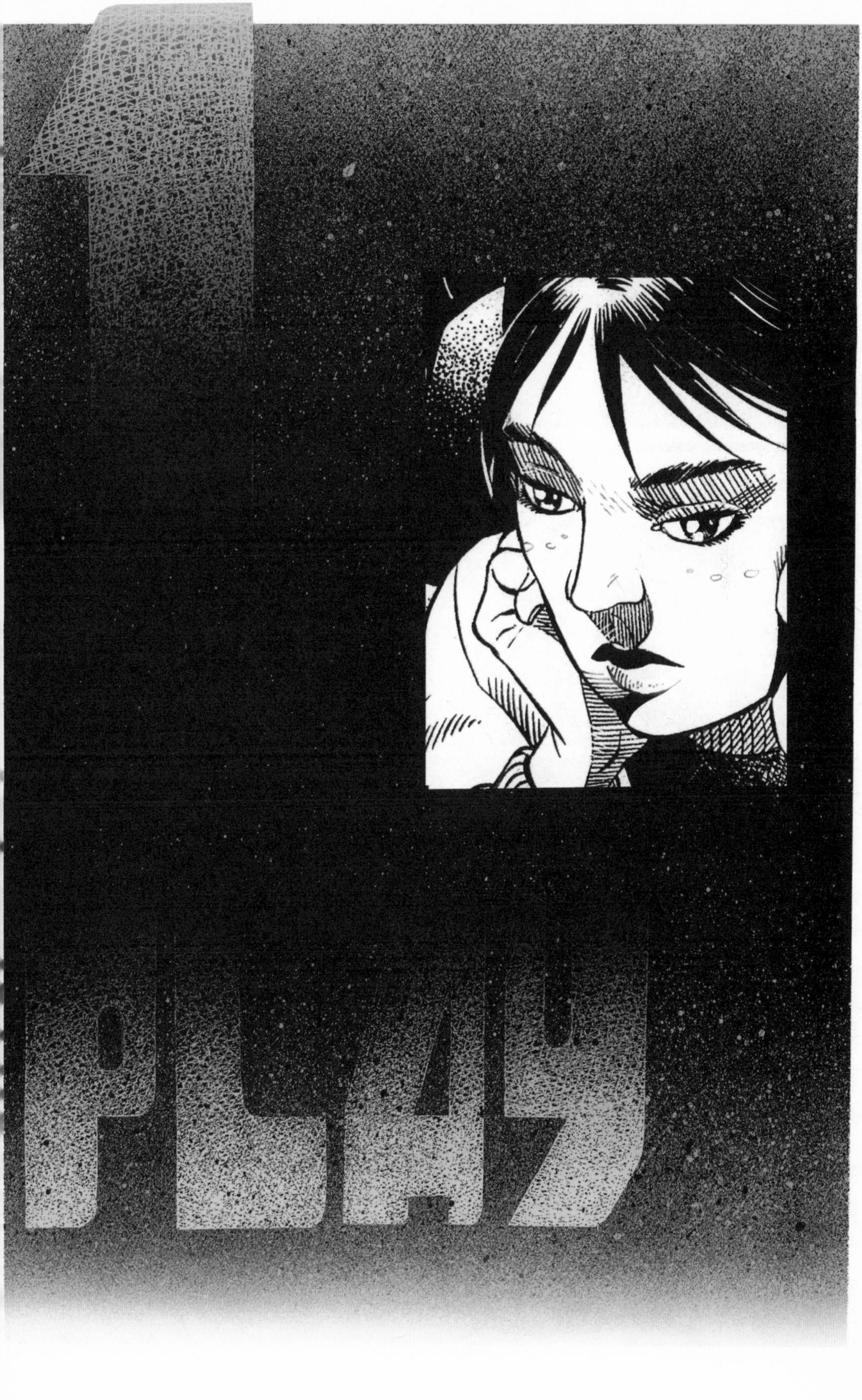
1
PLAY

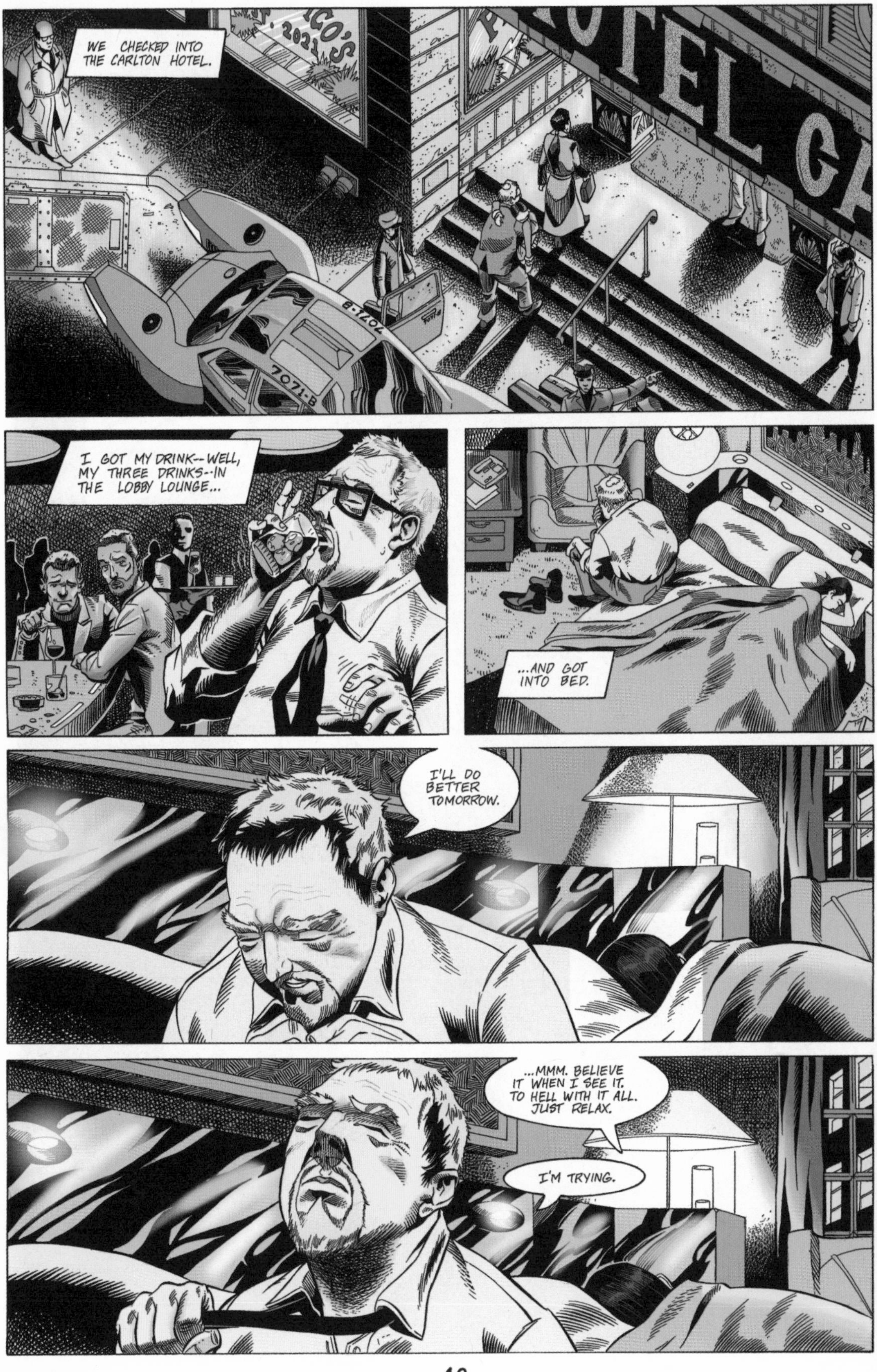
WE CHECKED INTO THE CARLTON HOTEL.
7071-B
I GOT MY DRINK--WELL, MY THREE DRINKS--IN THE LOBBY LOUNGE...
...AND GOT INTO BED.
I'LL DO BETTER TOMORROW.
...MMM. BELIEVE IT WHEN I SEE IT. TO HELL WITH IT ALL. JUST RELAX.
I'M TRYING.

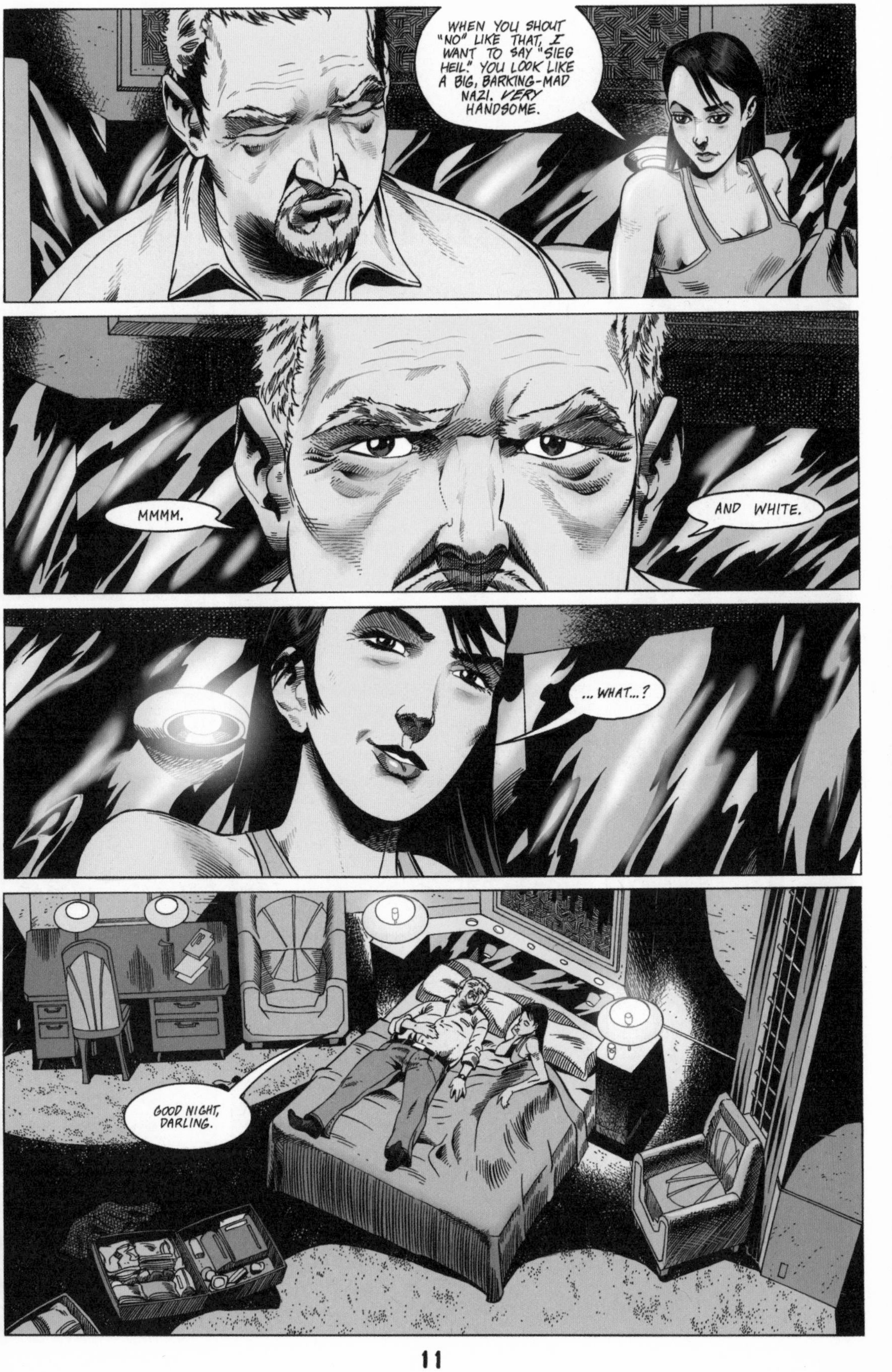
WHEN YOU SHOUT "NO" LIKE THAT, I WANT TO SAY "SIEG HEIL." YOU LOOK LIKE A BIG, BARKING-MAD NAZI. VERY HANDSOME.
MMMM.
AND WHITE.
...WHAT...?
GOOD NIGHT, DARLING.

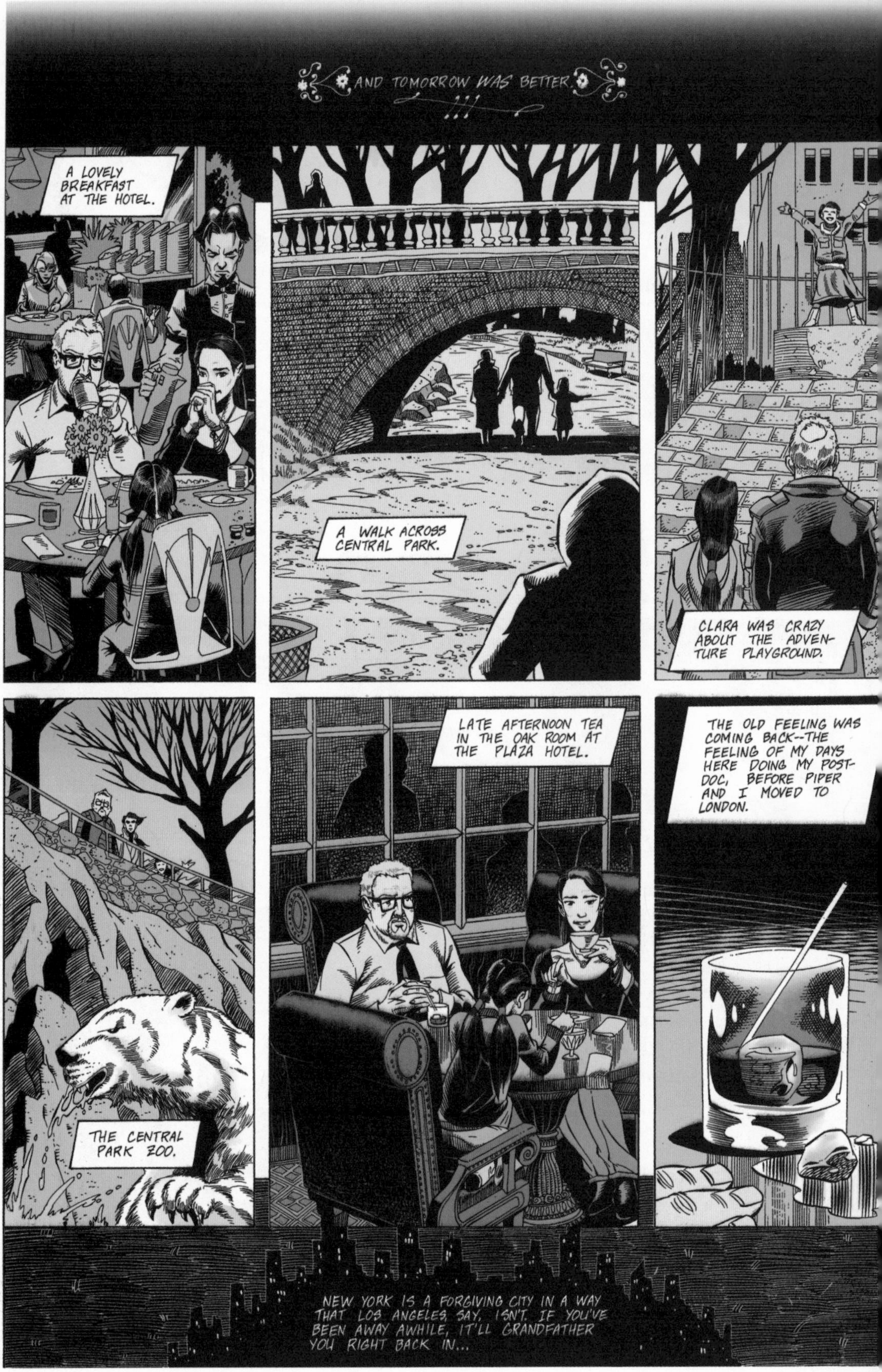
AND TOMORROW WAS BETTER
A LOVELY BREAKFAST AT THE HOTEL.
A WALK ACROSS CENTRAL PARK.
CLARA WAS CRAZY ABOUT THE ADVENTURE PLAYGROUND.
THE CENTRAL PARK ZOO.
LATE AFTERNOON TEA IN THE OAK ROOM AT THE PLAZA HOTEL.
THE OLD FEELING WAS COMING BACK--THE FEELING OF MY DAYS HERE DOING MY POST-DOC, BEFORE PIPER AND I MOVED TO LONDON.
NEW YORK IS A FORGIVING CITY IN A WAY THAT LOS ANGELES, SAY, ISN'T. IF YOU'VE BEEN AWAY AWHILE, IT'LL GRANDFATHER YOU RIGHT BACK IN...

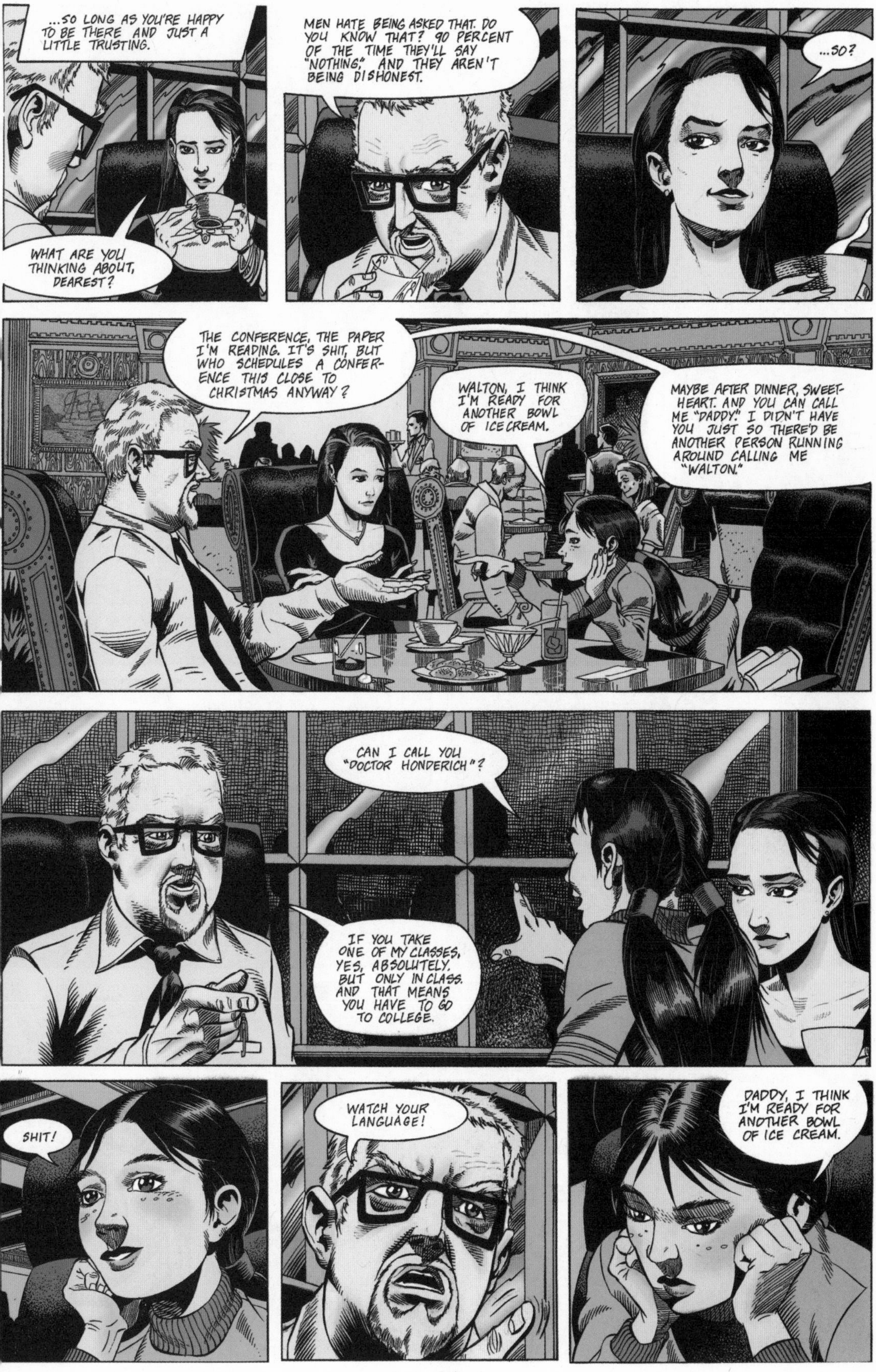
...SO LONG AS YOU'RE HAPPY TO BE THERE AND JUST A LITTLE TRUSTING.
WHAT ARE YOU THINKING ABOUT, DEAREST?
MEN HATE BEING ASKED THAT. DO YOU KNOW THAT? 90 PERCENT OF THE TIME THEY'LL SAY "NOTHING," AND THEY AREN'T BEING DISHONEST.
...SO?
THE CONFERENCE, THE PAPER I'M READING. IT'S SHIT, BUT WHO SCHEDULES A CONFERENCE THIS CLOSE TO CHRISTMAS ANYWAY?
WALTON, I THINK I'M READY FOR ANOTHER BOWL OF ICE CREAM.
MAYBE AFTER DINNER, SWEETHEART. AND YOU CAN CALL ME "DADDY." I DIDN'T HAVE YOU JUST SO THERE'D BE ANOTHER PERSON RUNNING AROUND CALLING ME "WALTON."
CAN I CALL YOU "DOCTOR HONDERICH"?
IF YOU TAKE ONE OF MY CLASSES, YES, ABSOLUTELY. BUT ONLY IN CLASS. AND THAT MEANS YOU HAVE TO GO TO COLLEGE.
SHIT!
WATCH YOUR LANGUAGE!
DADDY, I THINK I'M READY FOR ANOTHER BOWL OF ICE CREAM.

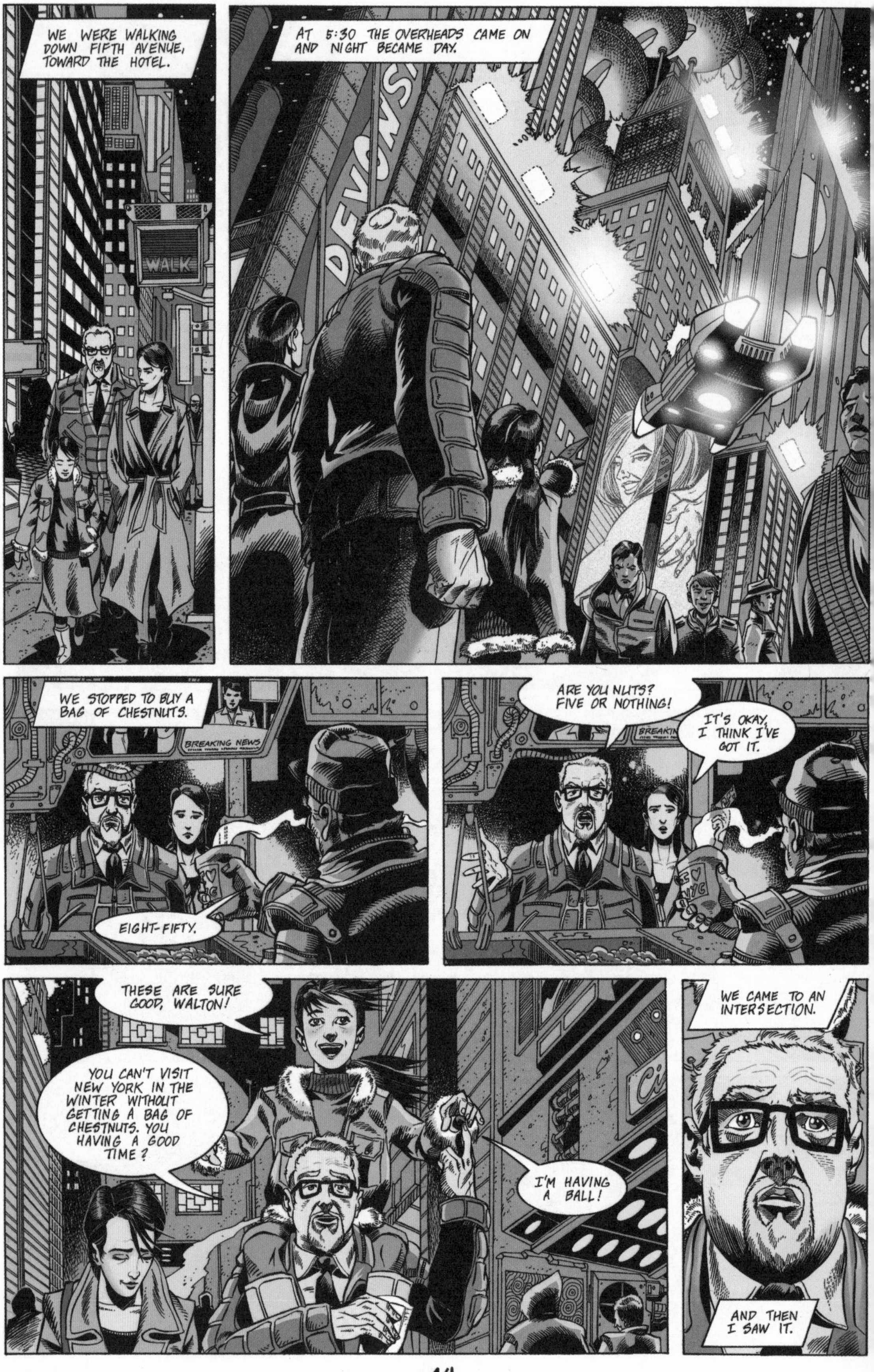
WE WERE WALKING DOWN FIFTH AVENUE, TOWARD THE HOTEL.
WALK
AT 5:30 THE OVERHEADS CAME ON AND NIGHT BECAME DAY.
WE STOPPED TO BUY A BAG OF CHESTNUTS.
BREAKING NEWS
EIGHT-FIFTY.
ARE YOU NUTS? FIVE OR NOTHING!
IT'S OKAY, I THINK I'VE GOT IT.
THESE ARE SURE GOOD, WALTON!
YOU CAN'T VISIT NEW YORK IN THE WINTER WITHOUT GETTING A BAG OF CHESTNUTS. YOU HAVING A GOOD TIME?
I'M HAVING A BALL!
WE CAME TO AN INTERSECTION.
AND THEN I SAW IT.

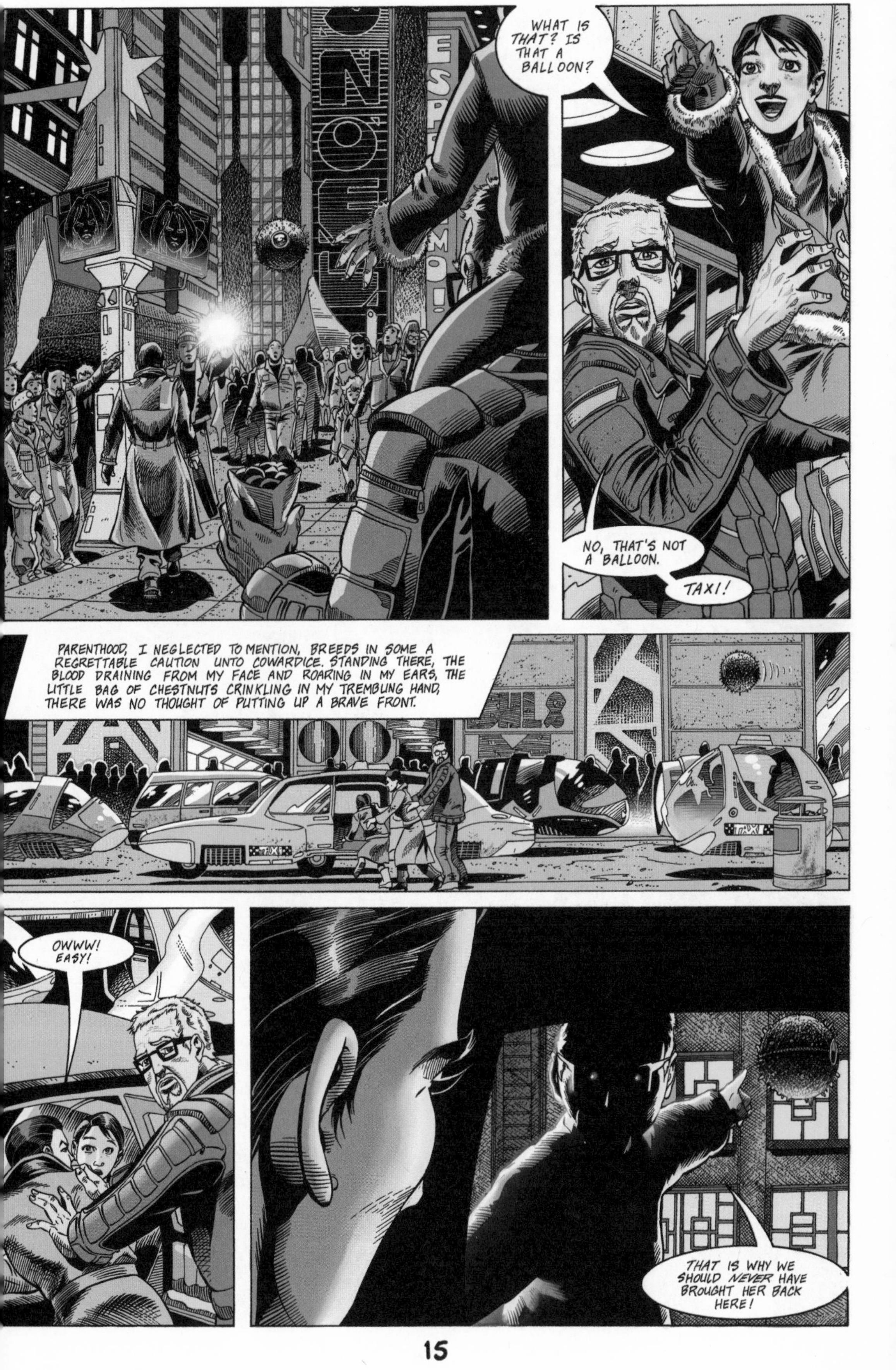
WHAT IS THAT? IS THAT A BALLOON?
NO, THAT'S NOT A BALLOON.
TAXI!
PARENTHOOD, I NEGLECTED TO MENTION, BREEDS IN SOME A REGRETTABLE CAUTION UNTO COWARDICE. STANDING THERE, THE BLOOD DRAINING FROM MY FACE AND ROARING IN MY EARS, THE LITTLE BAG OF CHESTNUTS CRINKLING IN MY TREMBLING HAND, THERE WAS NO THOUGHT OF PUTTING UP A BRAVE FRONT.
OWWW! EASY!
THAT IS WHY WE SHOULD NEVER HAVE BROUGHT HER BACK HERE!

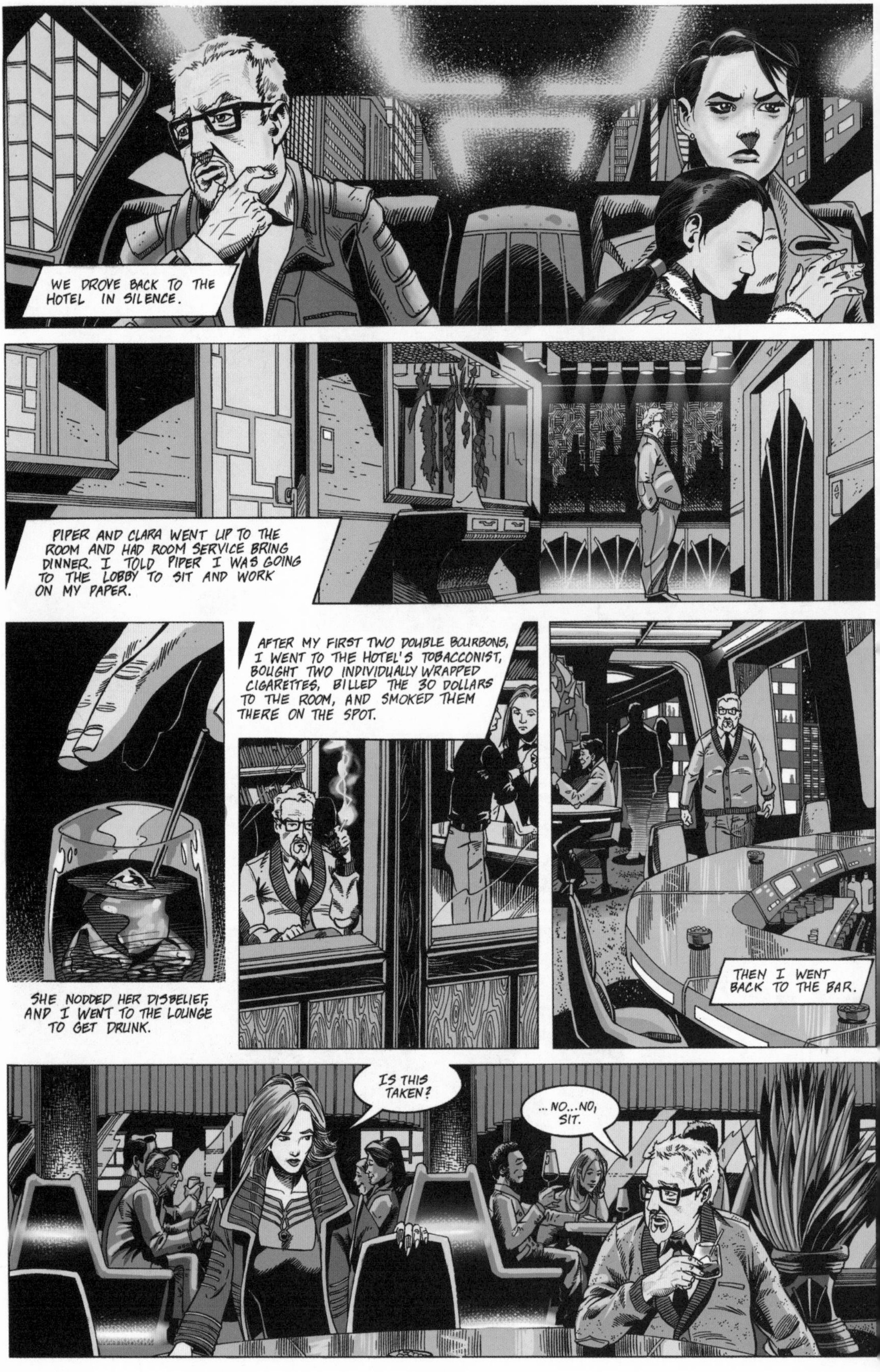
WE DROVE BACK TO THE HOTEL IN SILENCE.
PIPER AND CLARA WENT UP TO THE ROOM AND HAD ROOM SERVICE BRING DINNER. I TOLD PIPER I WAS GOING TO THE LOBBY TO SIT AND WORK ON MY PAPER.
SHE NODDED HER DISBELIEF, AND I WENT TO THE LOUNGE TO GET DRUNK.
AFTER MY FIRST TWO DOUBLE BOURBONS, I WENT TO THE HOTEL'S TOBACCONIST, BOUGHT TWO INDIVIDUALLY WRAPPED CIGARETTES, BILLED THE 30 DOLLARS TO THE ROOM, AND SMOKED THEM THERE ON THE SPOT.
THEN I WENT BACK TO THE BAR.
IS THIS TAKEN?
...NO...NO, SIT.

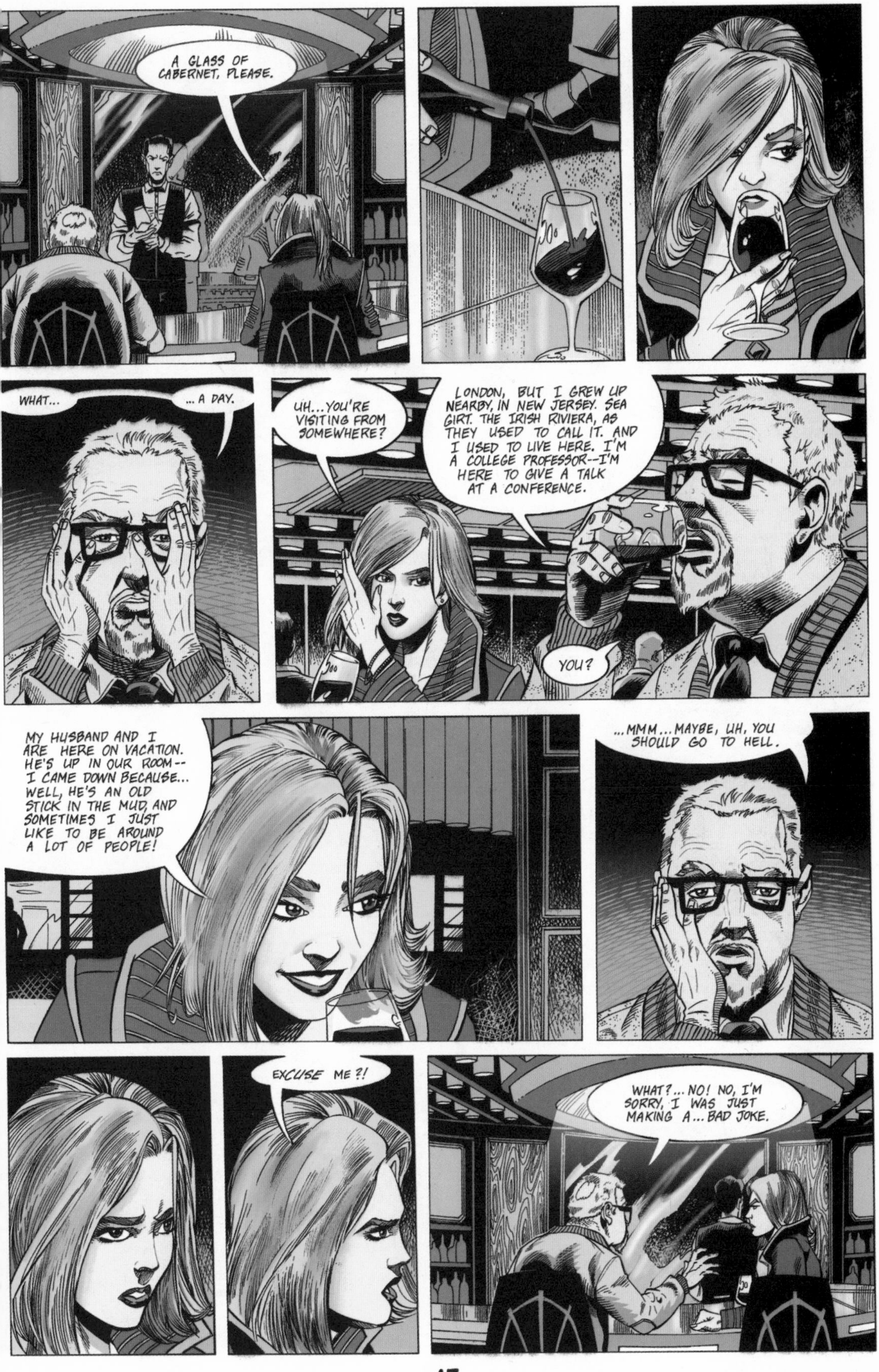
A GLASS OF CABERNET, PLEASE.
WHAT...
...A DAY.
UH...YOU'RE VISITING FROM SOMEWHERE?
LONDON, BUT I GREW UP NEARBY, IN NEW JERSEY. SEA GIRT. THE IRISH RIVIERA, AS THEY USED TO CALL IT. AND I USED TO LIVE HERE. I'M A COLLEGE PROFESSOR--I'M HERE TO GIVE A TALK AT A CONFERENCE.
YOU?
MY HUSBAND AND I ARE HERE ON VACATION. HE'S UP IN OUR ROOM-- I CAME DOWN BECAUSE... WELL, HE'S AN OLD STICK IN THE MUD, AND SOMETIMES I JUST LIKE TO BE AROUND A LOT OF PEOPLE!
...MMM...MAYBE, UH, YOU SHOULD GO TO HELL.
EXCUSE ME?!
WHAT?...NO! NO, I'M SORRY, I WAS JUST MAKING A...BAD JOKE.

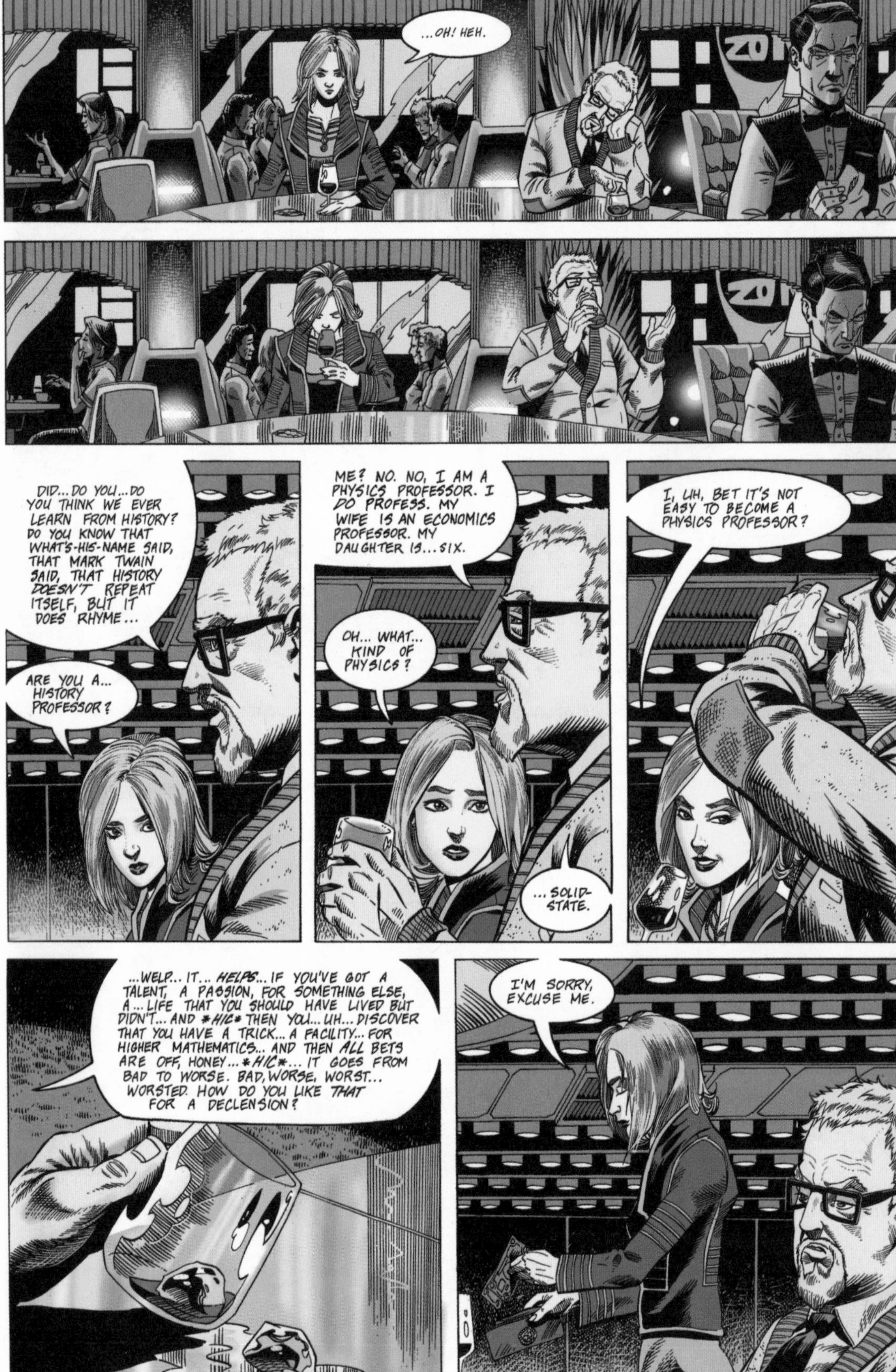

...OH! HEH.
DID...DO YOU...DO YOU THINK WE EVER LEARN FROM HISTORY? DO YOU KNOW THAT WHAT'S-HIS-NAME SAID, THAT MARK TWAIN SAID, THAT HISTORY DOESN'T REPEAT ITSELF, BUT IT DOES RHYME...
ARE YOU A... HISTORY PROFESSOR?
ME? NO. NO, I AM A PHYSICS PROFESSOR. I DO PROFESS. MY WIFE IS AN ECONOMICS PROFESSOR. MY DAUGHTER IS... SIX.
OH... WHAT... KIND OF PHYSICS?
...SOLID-STATE.
I, UH, BET IT'S NOT EASY TO BECOME A PHYSICS PROFESSOR?
...WELP... IT... HELPS... IF YOU'VE GOT A TALENT, A PASSION, FOR SOMETHING ELSE, A... LIFE THAT YOU SHOULD HAVE LIVED BUT DIDN'T... AND *HIC* THEN YOU... UH... DISCOVER THAT YOU HAVE A TRICK... A FACILITY... FOR HIGHER MATHEMATICS... AND THEN ALL BETS ARE OFF, HONEY... *HIC*... IT GOES FROM BAD TO WORSE. BAD, WORSE, WORST... WORSTED. HOW DO YOU LIKE THAT FOR A DECLENSION?
I'M SORRY, EXCUSE ME.

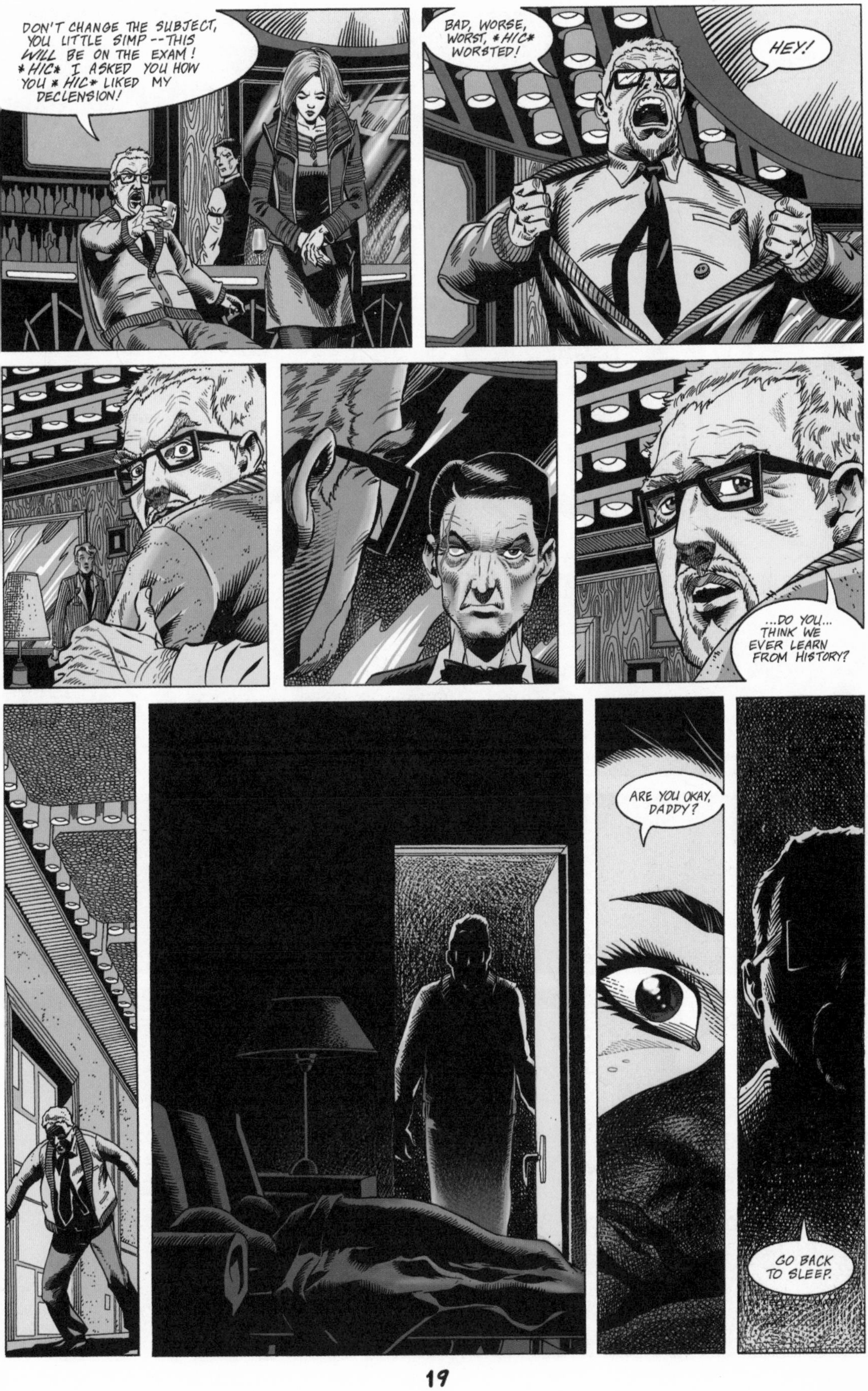
DON'T CHANGE THE SUBJECT, YOU LITTLE SIMP--THIS WILL BE ON THE EXAM! *HIC* I ASKED YOU HOW YOU *HIC* LIKED MY DECLENSION!
BAD, WORSE, WORST, *HIC* WORSTED!
HEY!
...DO YOU... THINK WE EVER LEARN FROM HISTORY?
ARE YOU OKAY, DADDY?
GO BACK TO SLEEP.

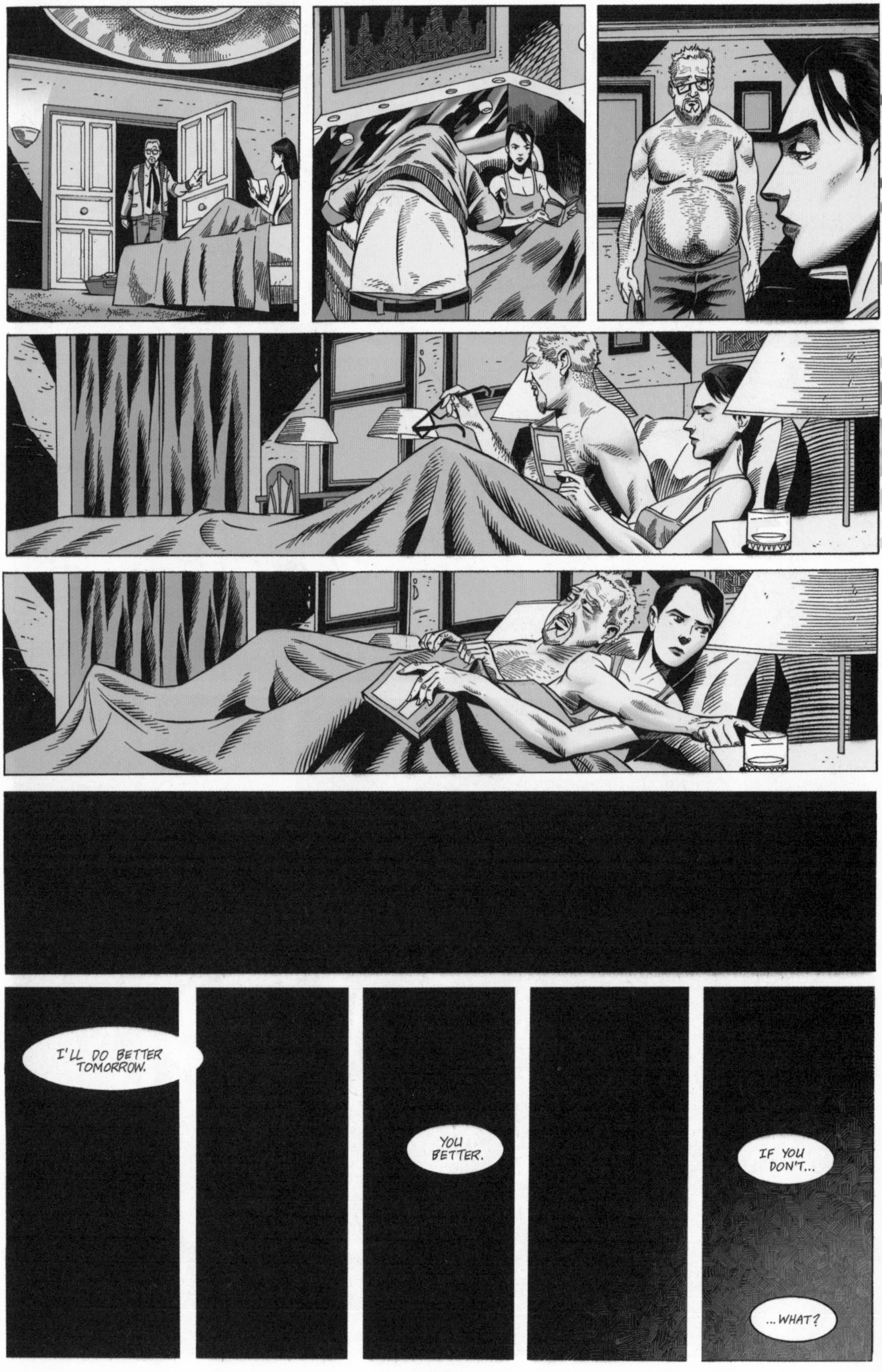
I'LL DO BETTER TOMORROW.
YOU BETTER.
IF YOU DON'T...
...WHAT?

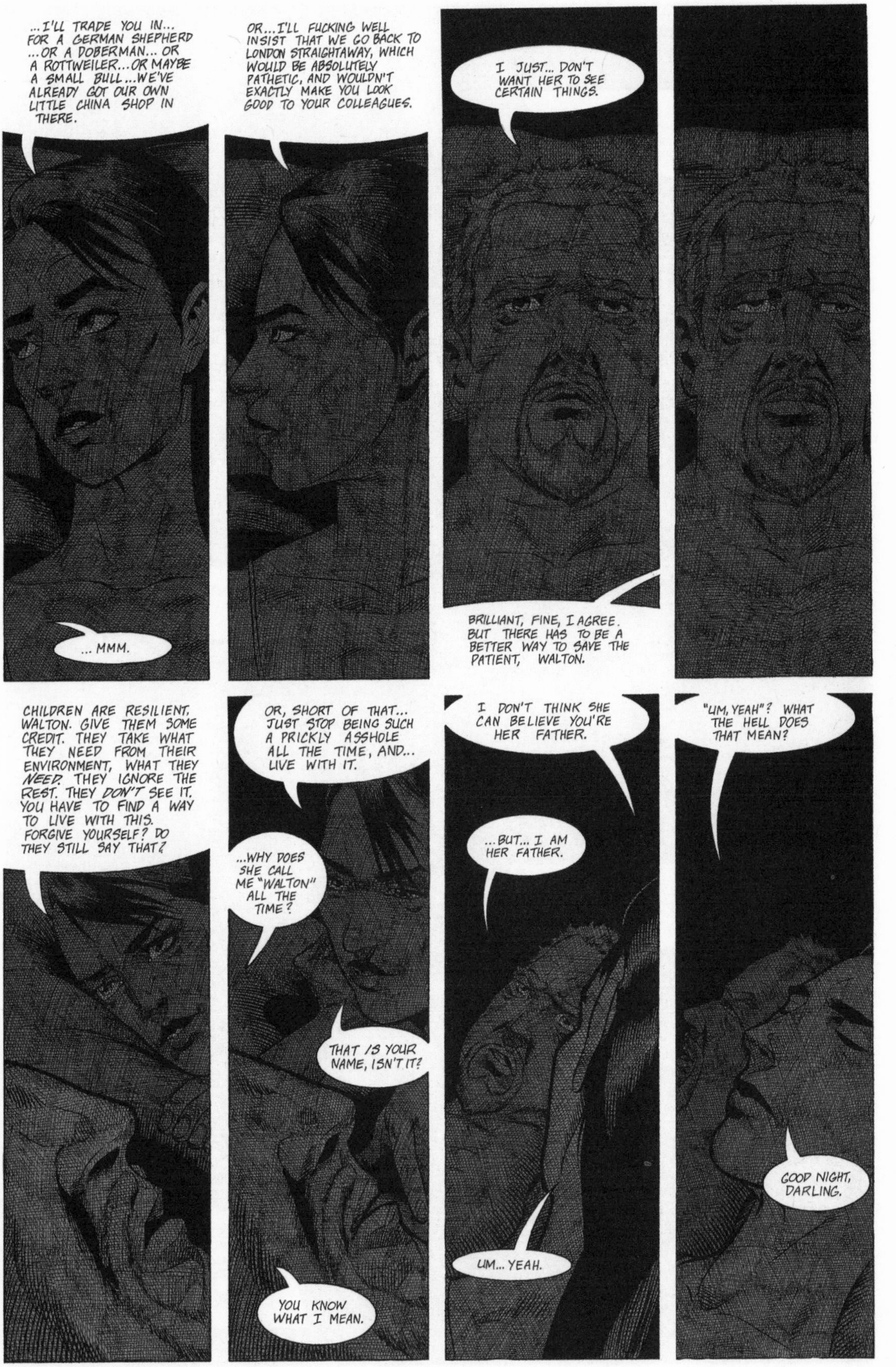
...I'LL TRADE YOU IN... FOR A GERMAN SHEPHERD ...OR A DOBERMAN... OR A ROTTWEILER...OR MAYBE A SMALL BULL...WE'VE ALREADY GOT OUR OWN LITTLE CHINA SHOP IN THERE.
...MMM.
OR...I'LL FUCKING WELL INSIST THAT WE GO BACK TO LONDON STRAIGHTAWAY, WHICH WOULD BE ABSOLUTELY PATHETIC, AND WOULDN'T EXACTLY MAKE YOU LOOK GOOD TO YOUR COLLEAGUES.
I JUST... DON'T WANT HER TO SEE CERTAIN THINGS.
BRILLIANT, FINE, I AGREE. BUT THERE HAS TO BE A BETTER WAY TO SAVE THE PATIENT, WALTON.
CHILDREN ARE RESILIENT, WALTON. GIVE THEM SOME CREDIT. THEY TAKE WHAT THEY NEED FROM THEIR ENVIRONMENT, WHAT THEY *NEED*. THEY IGNORE THE REST. THEY *DON'T* SEE IT. YOU HAVE TO FIND A WAY TO LIVE WITH THIS. FORGIVE YOURSELF? DO THEY STILL SAY THAT?
OR, SHORT OF THAT... JUST STOP BEING SUCH A PRICKLY ASSHOLE ALL THE TIME, AND... LIVE WITH IT.
...WHY DOES SHE CALL ME "WALTON" ALL THE TIME?
THAT *IS* YOUR NAME, ISN'T IT?
YOU KNOW WHAT I MEAN.
I DON'T THINK SHE CAN BELIEVE YOU'RE HER FATHER.
...BUT... I AM HER FATHER.
UM... YEAH.
"UM, YEAH"? WHAT THE HELL DOES THAT MEAN?
GOOD NIGHT, DARLING.

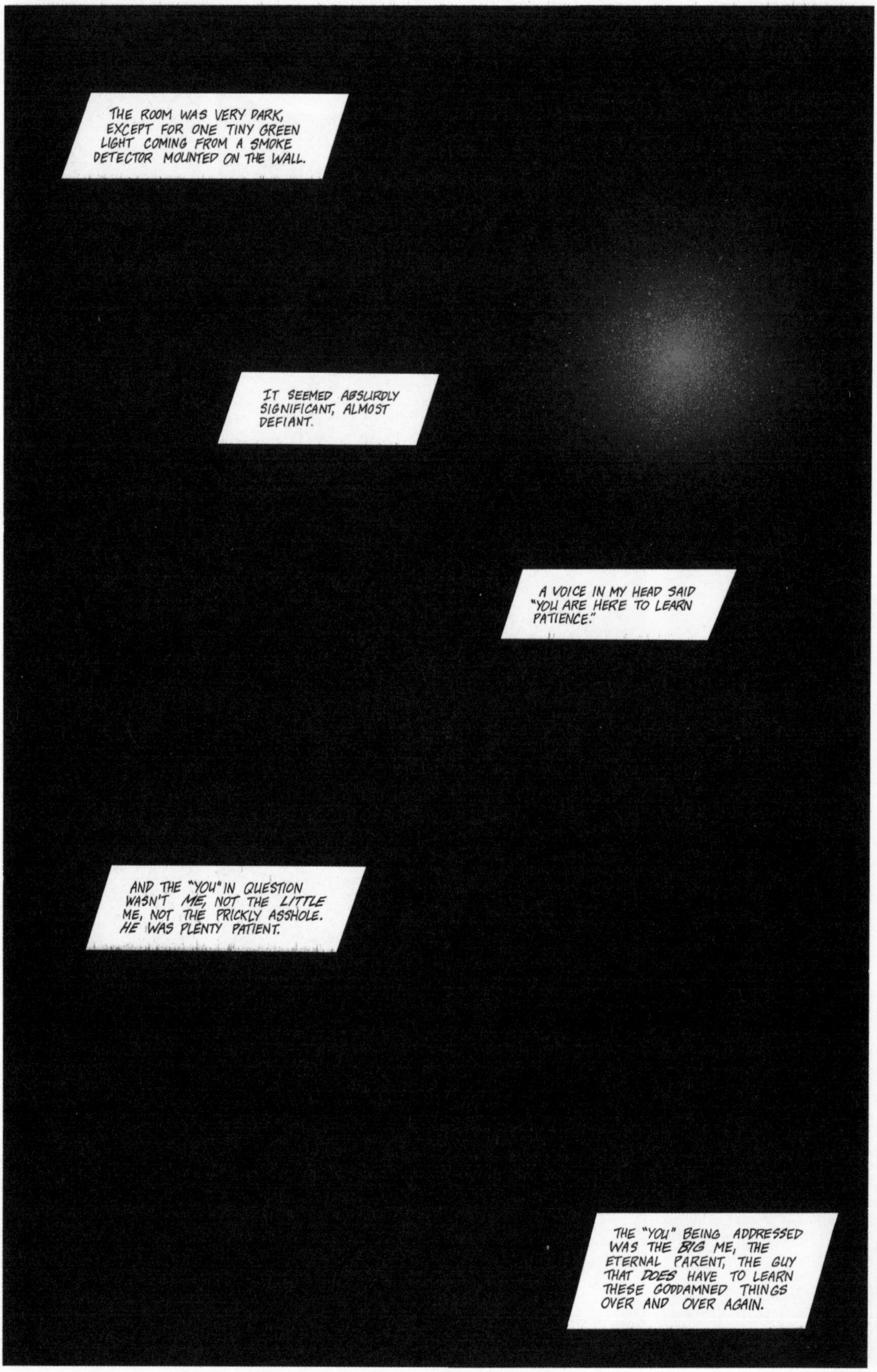
THE ROOM WAS VERY DARK, EXCEPT FOR ONE TINY GREEN LIGHT COMING FROM A SMOKE DETECTOR MOUNTED ON THE WALL.
IT SEEMED ABSURDLY SIGNIFICANT, ALMOST DEFIANT.
A VOICE IN MY HEAD SAID "YOU ARE HERE TO LEARN PATIENCE."
AND THE "YOU" IN QUESTION WASN'T *ME*, NOT THE *LITTLE* ME, NOT THE PRICKLY ASSHOLE. *HE* WAS PLENTY PATIENT.
THE "YOU" BEING ADDRESSED WAS THE *BIG* ME, THE ETERNAL PARENT, THE GUY THAT *DOES* HAVE TO LEARN THESE GODDAMNED THINGS OVER AND OVER AGAIN.

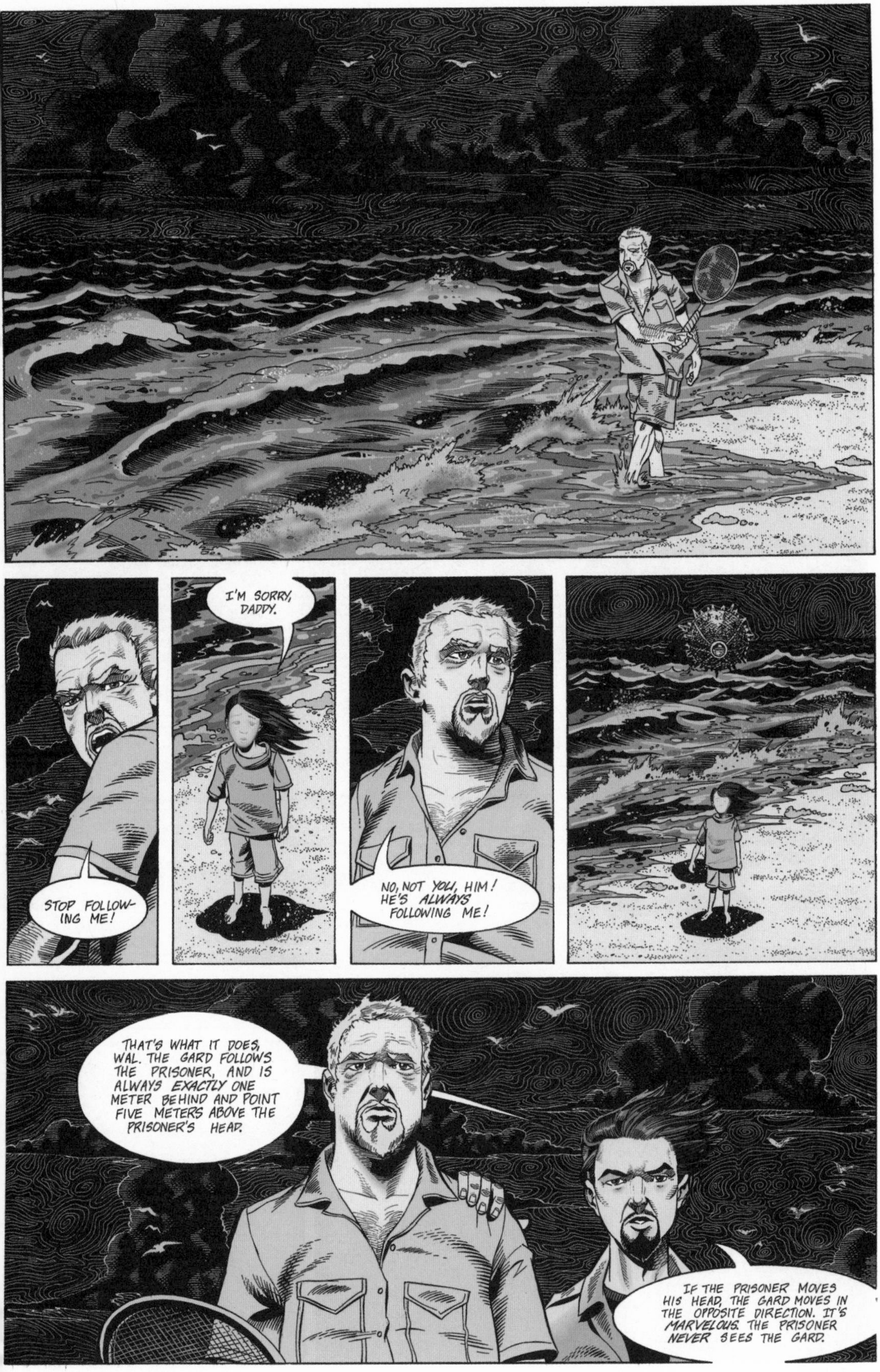
STOP FOLLOW-ING ME!
I'M SORRY, DADDY.
NO, NOT YOU, HIM! HE'S ALWAYS FOLLOWING ME!
THAT'S WHAT IT DOES, WAL. THE GARD FOLLOWS THE PRISONER, AND IS ALWAYS EXACTLY ONE METER BEHIND AND POINT FIVE METERS ABOVE THE PRISONER'S HEAD.
IF THE PRISONER MOVES HIS HEAD, THE GARD MOVES IN THE OPPOSITE DIRECTION. IT'S MARVELOUS. THE PRISONER NEVER SEES THE GARD.

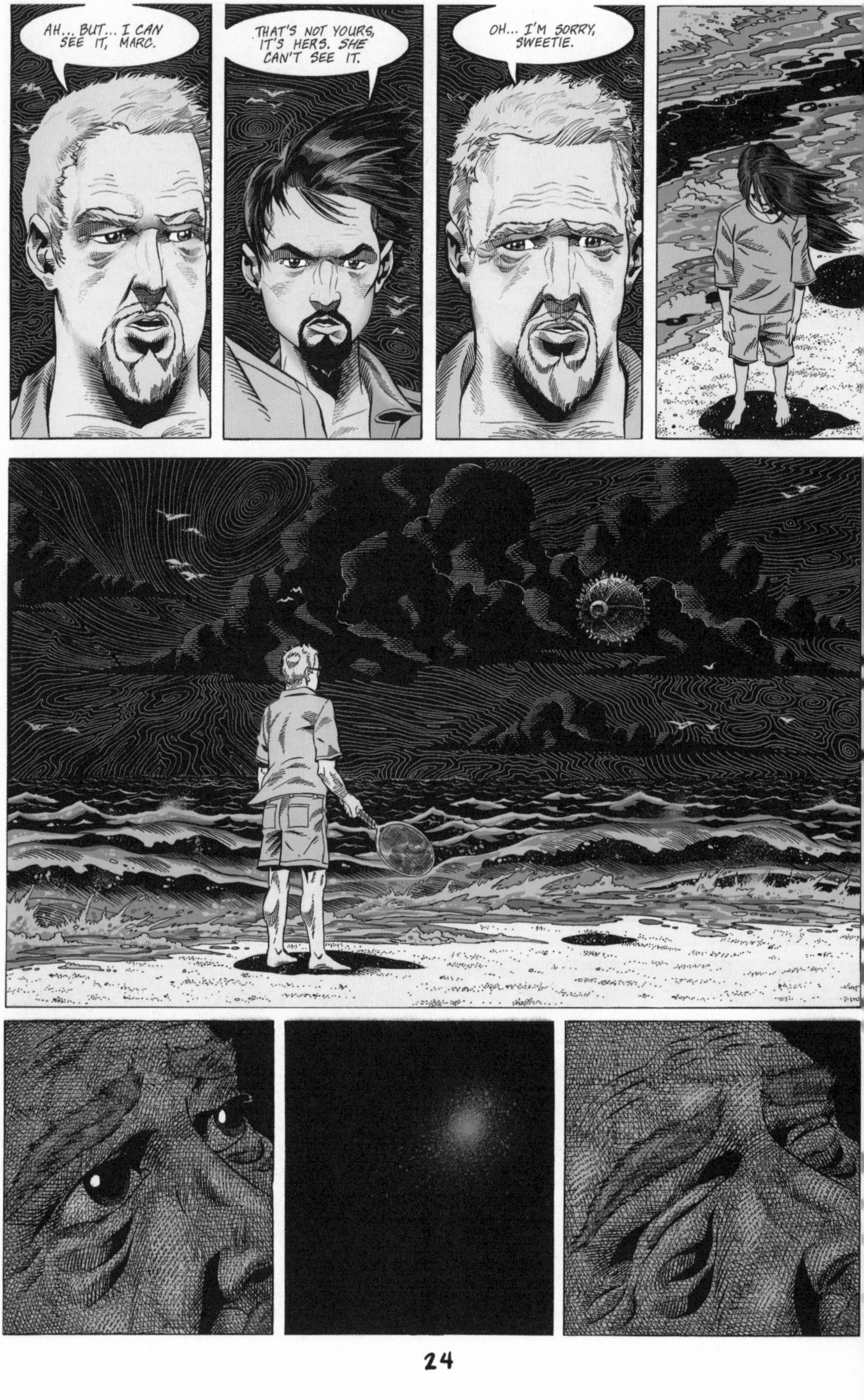
AH... BUT... I CAN SEE IT, MARC.
THAT'S NOT YOURS, IT'S HERS. SHE CAN'T SEE IT.
OH... I'M SORRY, SWEETIE.

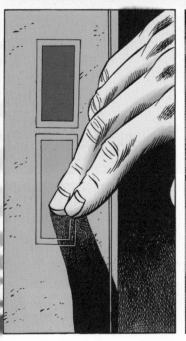

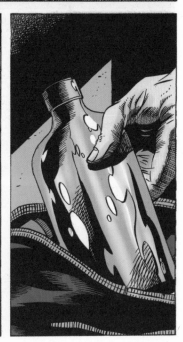

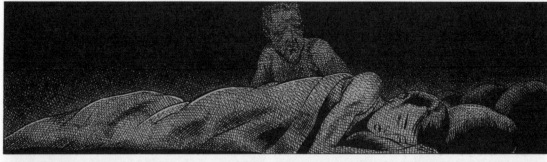

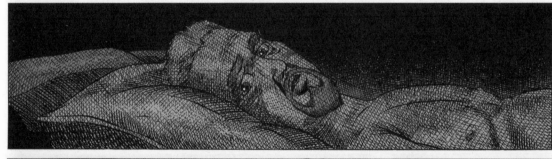

2:20 A.M.

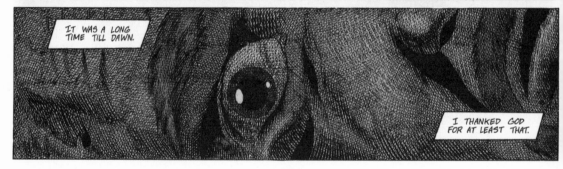

IT WAS A LONG
TIME TILL DAWN.

I THANKED GOD
FOR AT LEAST THAT.

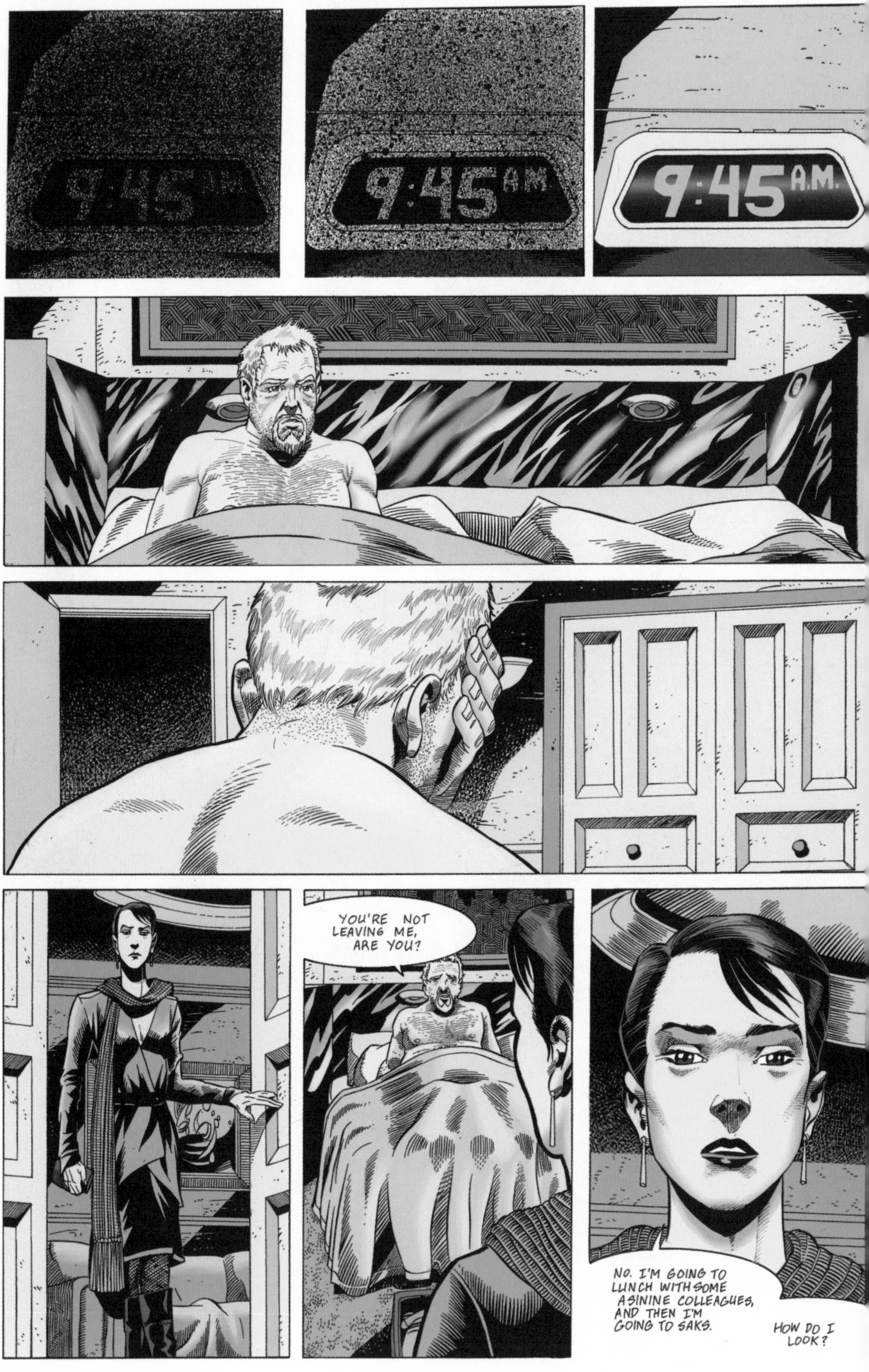
9:45 A.M.
9:45 A.M.
9:45 A.M.
YOU'RE NOT LEAVING ME, ARE YOU?
NO. I'M GOING TO LUNCH WITH SOME ASININE COLLEAGUES, AND THEN I'M GOING TO SAKS.
HOW DO I LOOK?

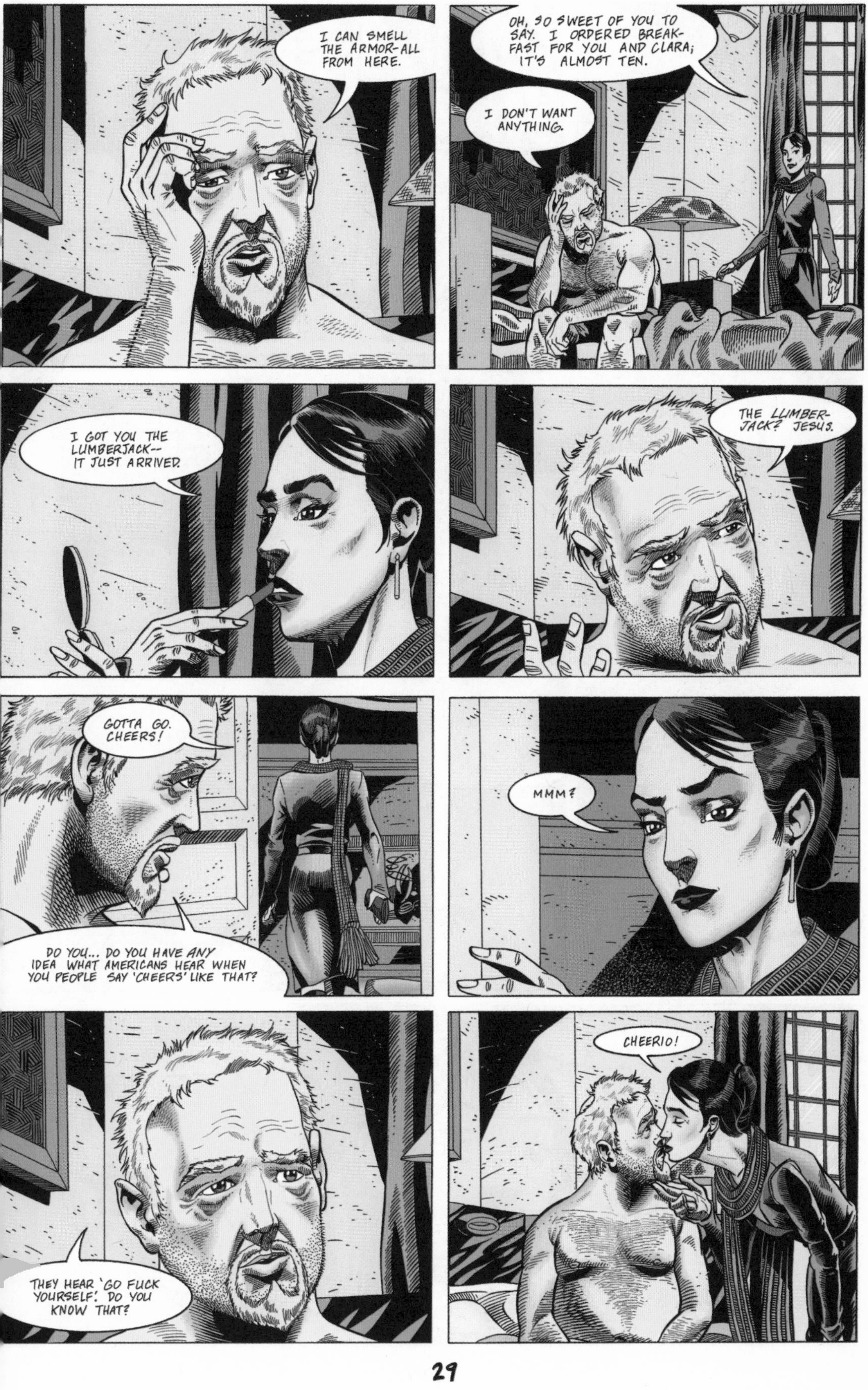
I CAN SMELL THE ARMOR-ALL FROM HERE.
OH, SO SWEET OF YOU TO SAY. I ORDERED BREAKFAST FOR YOU AND CLARA; IT'S ALMOST TEN.
I DON'T WANT ANYTHING.
I GOT YOU THE LUMBERJACK-- IT JUST ARRIVED.
THE LUMBERJACK? JESUS.
GOTTA GO. CHEERS!
DO YOU... DO YOU HAVE ANY IDEA WHAT AMERICANS HEAR WHEN YOU PEOPLE SAY 'CHEERS' LIKE THAT?
MMM?
THEY HEAR 'GO FUCK YOURSELF.' DO YOU KNOW THAT?
CHEERIO!

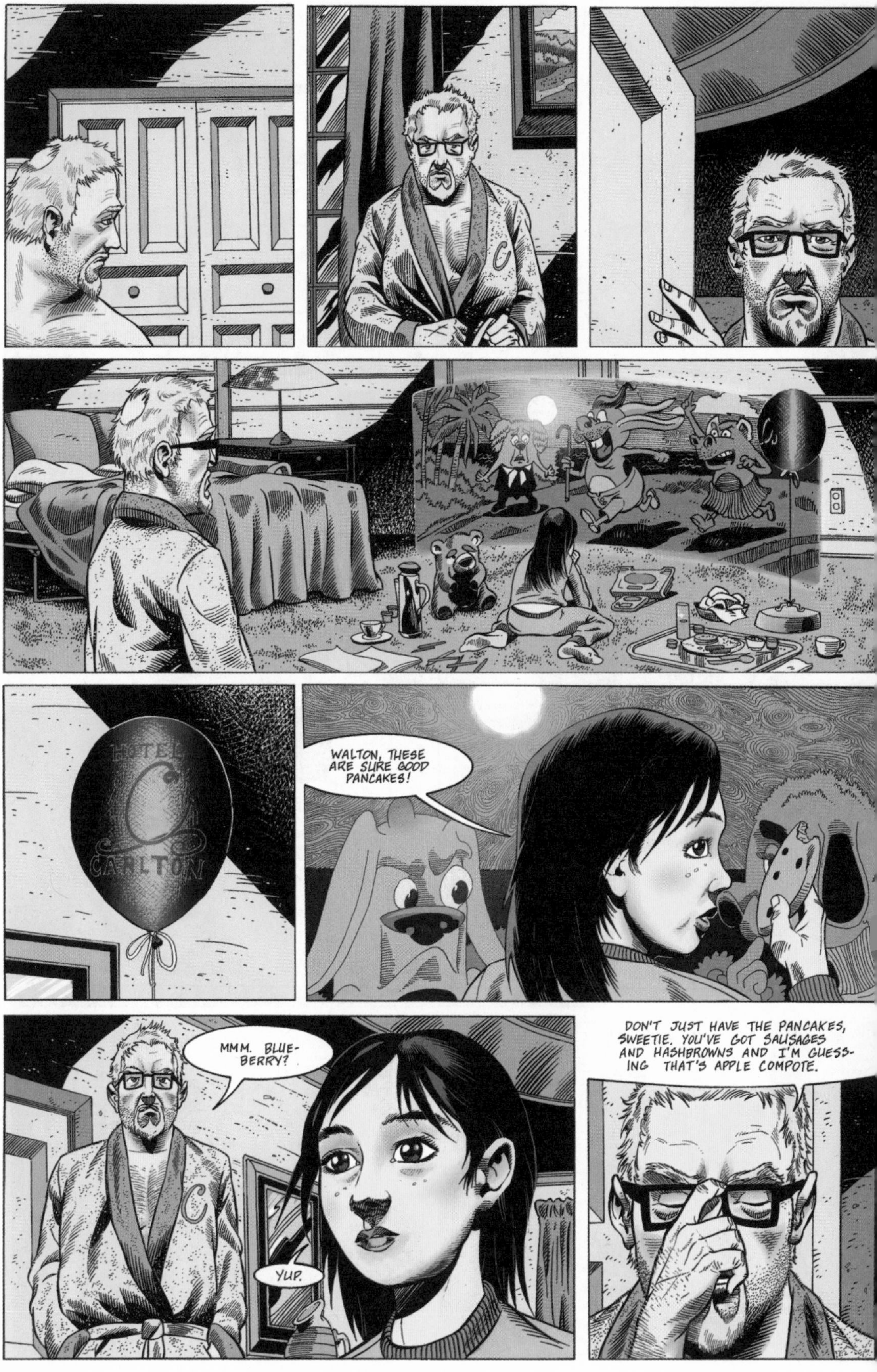
HOTEL
CARLTON
WALTON, THESE ARE SURE GOOD PANCAKES!
MMM. BLUE-BERRY?
YUP.
DON'T JUST HAVE THE PANCAKES, SWEETIE. YOU'VE GOT SAUSAGES AND HASHBROWNS AND I'M GUESS-ING THAT'S APPLE COMPOTE.

IT'S THE LUMBERJACK!

MMM.

WHAT'S APPLE COMPOTE, WALTON?

NOBODY KNOWS, SWEETIE.

ALL THIS WEEK KRYPTONITE

SON THE ALTM ME

HEY, YOU GOT A BALLOON, TOO.

HOTEL CARLTON

MMM-HMMM. WHAT'S A LUMBERJACK, WALTON?

WELL, SWEETIE, LUMBERJACKS WERE GUYS AND GALS WHO CUT DOWN TREES TO MAKE PAPER WITH. WHEN WE USED LOTS OF PAPER.

I GUESS YOU'D HAVE TO EAT ABOUT THIS MUCH IF YOU WERE GONNA GO OUT AND CHOP DOWN TREES ALL DAY, OR HUNT BEAR, OR SOMETHING... BUT PROBABLY NOT... TO GO LOOK AT ART IN A MUSEUM, OR SOMETHING LIKE THAT...

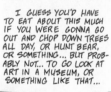

31

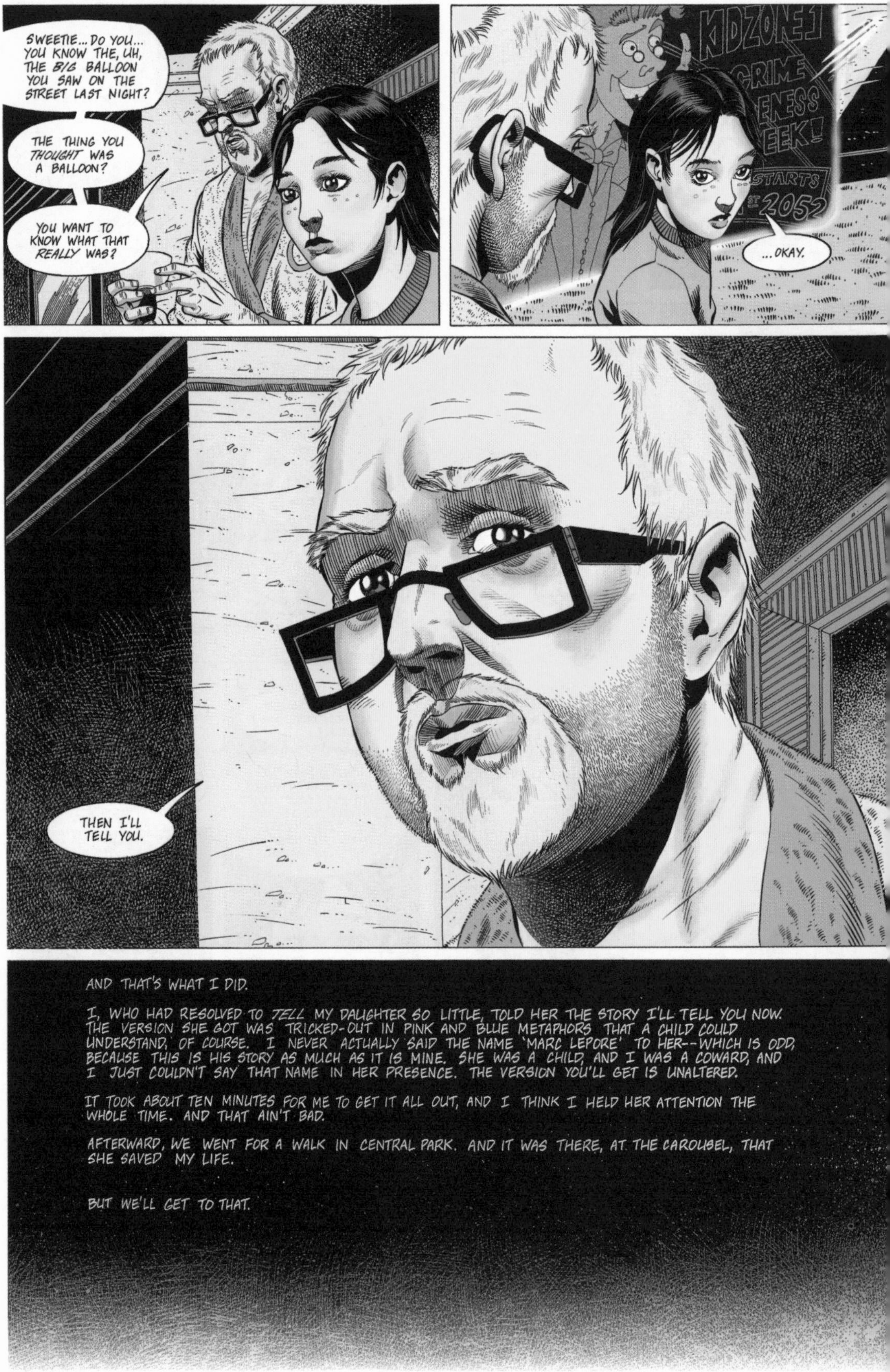
SWEETIE... DO YOU... YOU KNOW THE, UH, THE *BIG* BALLOON YOU SAW ON THE STREET LAST NIGHT?
THE THING YOU *THOUGHT* WAS A BALLOON?
YOU WANT TO KNOW WHAT THAT *REALLY* WAS?
...OKAY.
THEN I'LL TELL YOU.
AND THAT'S WHAT I DID.
I, WHO HAD RESOLVED TO *TELL* MY DAUGHTER SO LITTLE, TOLD HER THE STORY I'LL TELL YOU NOW. THE VERSION SHE GOT WAS TRICKED-OUT IN PINK AND BLUE METAPHORS THAT A CHILD COULD UNDERSTAND, OF COURSE. I NEVER ACTUALLY SAID THE NAME 'MARC LEPORE' TO HER--WHICH IS ODD, BECAUSE THIS IS HIS STORY AS MUCH AS IT IS MINE. SHE WAS A CHILD, AND I WAS A COWARD, AND I JUST COULDN'T SAY THAT NAME IN HER PRESENCE. THE VERSION YOU'LL GET IS UNALTERED.
IT TOOK ABOUT TEN MINUTES FOR ME TO GET IT ALL OUT, AND I THINK I HELD HER ATTENTION THE WHOLE TIME. AND THAT AIN'T BAD.
AFTERWARD, WE WENT FOR A WALK IN CENTRAL PARK. AND IT WAS THERE, AT THE CAROUSEL, THAT SHE SAVED MY LIFE.
BUT WE'LL GET TO THAT.

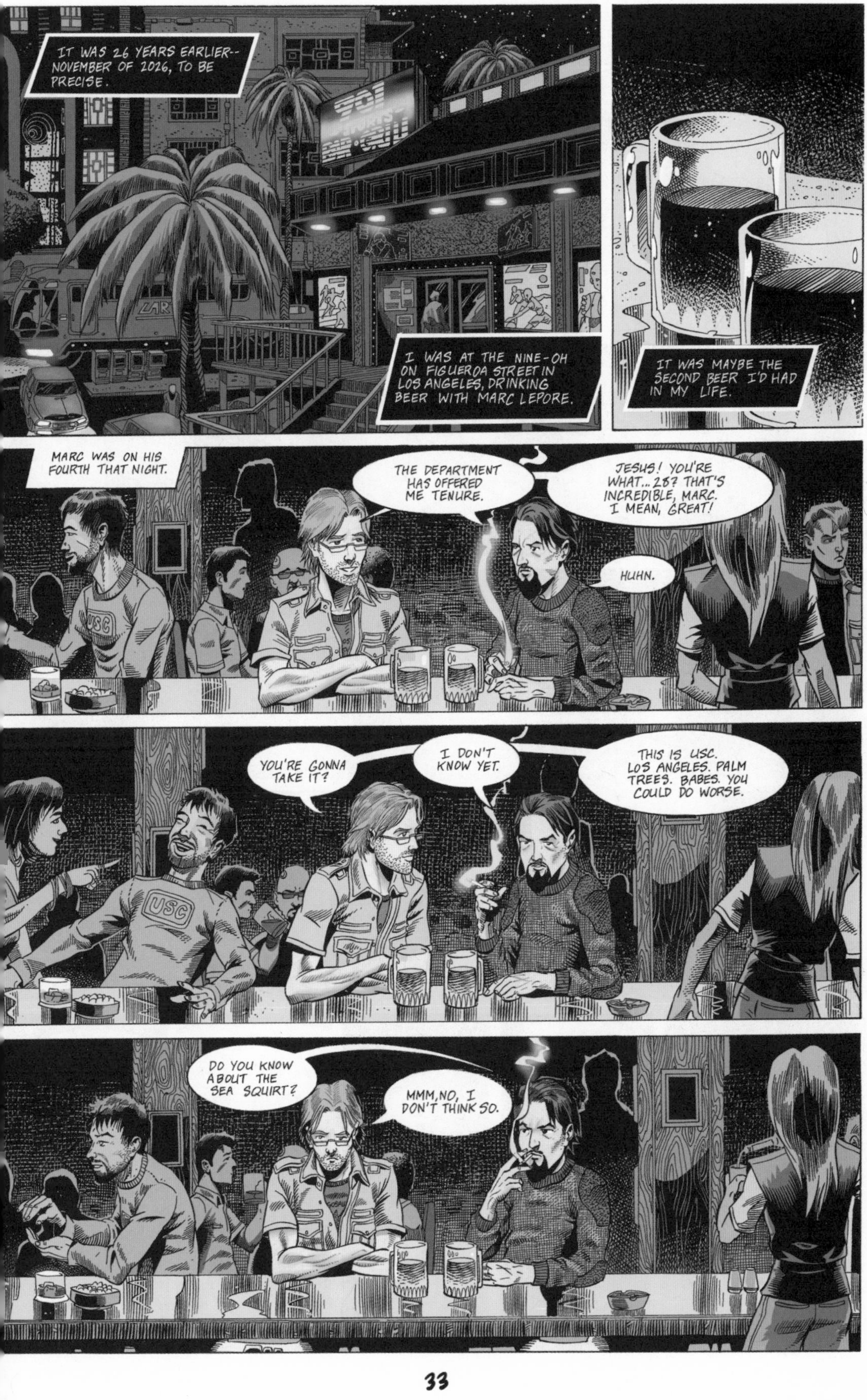
IT WAS 26 YEARS EARLIER--NOVEMBER OF 2026, TO BE PRECISE.
I WAS AT THE NINE-OH ON FIGUEROA STREET IN LOS ANGELES, DRINKING BEER WITH MARC LEPORE.
IT WAS MAYBE THE SECOND BEER I'D HAD IN MY LIFE.
MARC WAS ON HIS FOURTH THAT NIGHT.
THE DEPARTMENT HAS OFFERED ME TENURE.
JESUS! YOU'RE WHAT... 28? THAT'S INCREDIBLE, MARC. I MEAN, GREAT!
HUHN.
YOU'RE GONNA TAKE IT?
I DON'T KNOW YET.
THIS IS USC. LOS ANGELES. PALM TREES. BABES. YOU COULD DO WORSE.
DO YOU KNOW ABOUT THE SEA SQUIRT?
MMM, NO, I DON'T THINK SO.

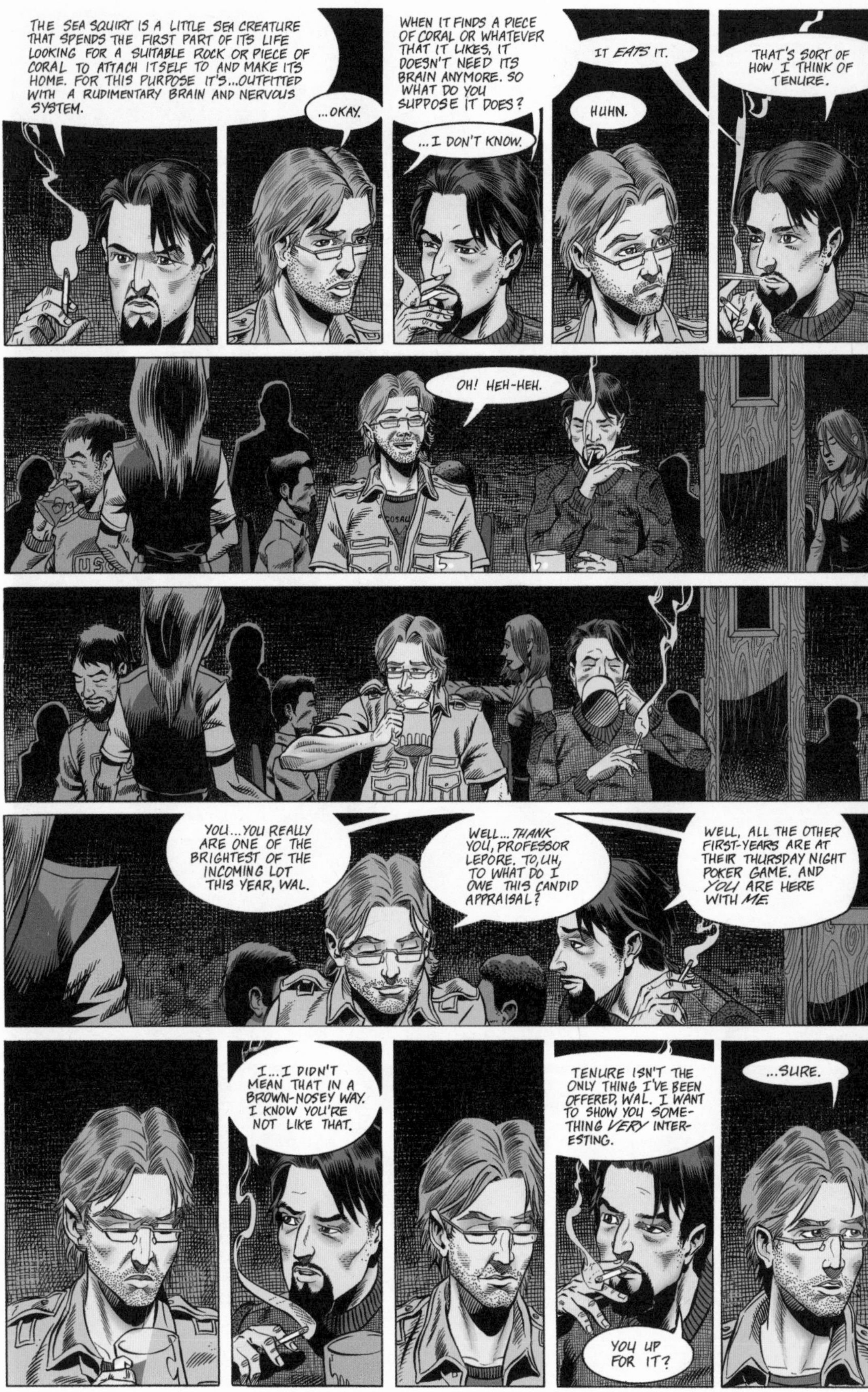
THE SEA SQUIRT IS A LITTLE SEA CREATURE THAT SPENDS THE FIRST PART OF ITS LIFE LOOKING FOR A SUITABLE ROCK OR PIECE OF CORAL TO ATTACH ITSELF TO AND MAKE ITS HOME. FOR THIS PURPOSE IT'S...OUTFITTED WITH A RUDIMENTARY BRAIN AND NERVOUS SYSTEM.
...OKAY.
WHEN IT FINDS A PIECE OF CORAL OR WHATEVER THAT IT LIKES, IT DOESN'T NEED ITS BRAIN ANYMORE. SO WHAT DO YOU SUPPOSE IT DOES?
...I DON'T KNOW.
IT EATS IT.
HUHN.
THAT'S SORT OF HOW I THINK OF TENURE.
OH! HEH-HEH.
YOU...YOU REALLY ARE ONE OF THE BRIGHTEST OF THE INCOMING LOT THIS YEAR, WAL.
WELL... THANK YOU, PROFESSOR LEPORE. TO, UH, TO WHAT DO I OWE THIS CANDID APPRAISAL?
WELL, ALL THE OTHER FIRST-YEARS ARE AT THEIR THURSDAY NIGHT POKER GAME. AND YOU ARE HERE WITH ME.
I...I DIDN'T MEAN THAT IN A BROWN-NOSEY WAY. I KNOW YOU'RE NOT LIKE THAT.
TENURE ISN'T THE ONLY THING I'VE BEEN OFFERED, WAL. I WANT TO SHOW YOU SOMETHING VERY INTERESTING.
YOU UP FOR IT?
...SURE.

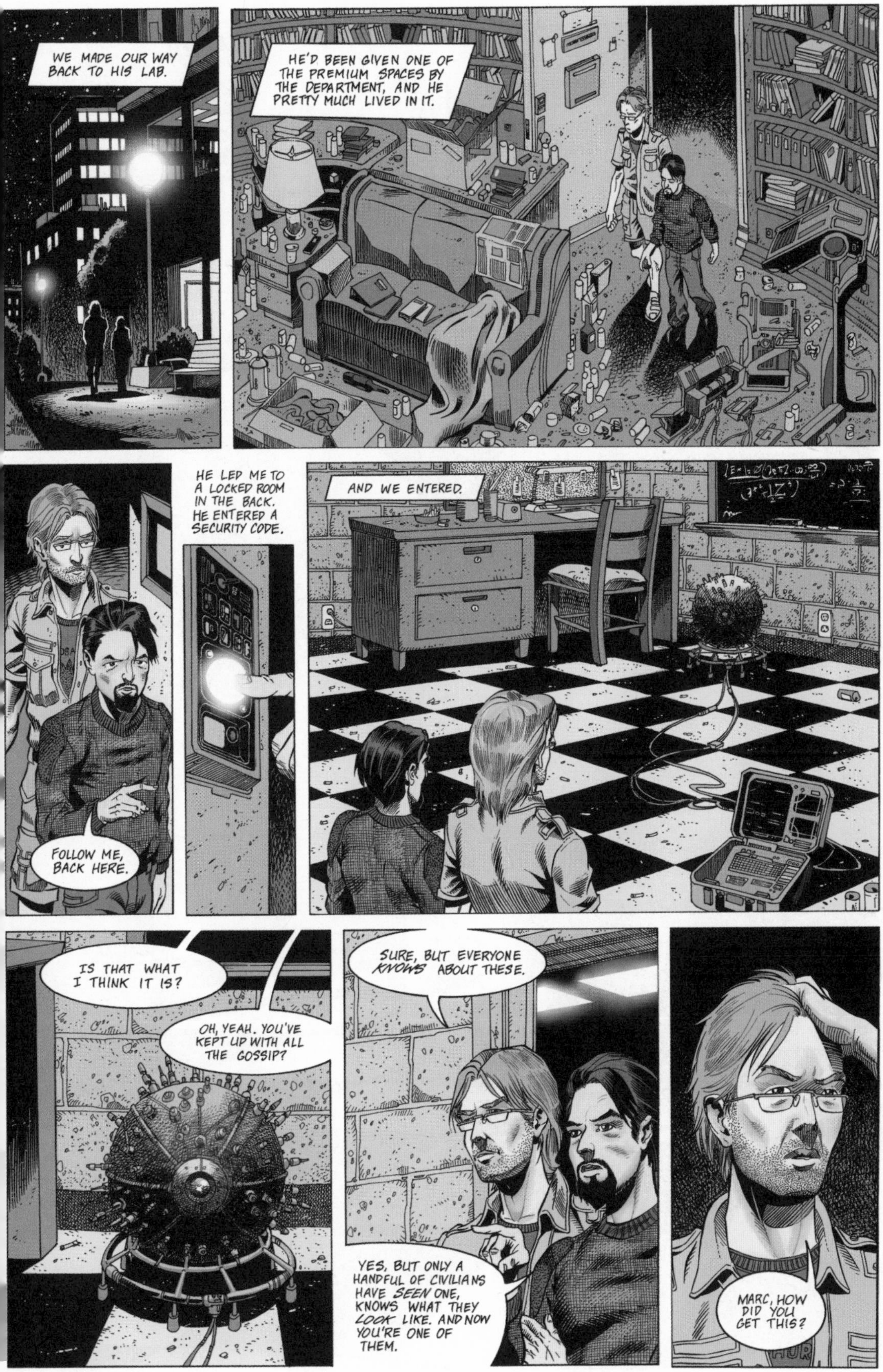
WE MADE OUR WAY BACK TO HIS LAB.
HE'D BEEN GIVEN ONE OF THE PREMIUM SPACES BY THE DEPARTMENT, AND HE PRETTY MUCH LIVED IN IT.
FOLLOW ME, BACK HERE.
HE LED ME TO A LOCKED ROOM IN THE BACK. HE ENTERED A SECURITY CODE.
AND WE ENTERED.
IS THAT WHAT I THINK IT IS?
OH, YEAH. YOU'VE KEPT UP WITH ALL THE GOSSIP?
SURE, BUT EVERYONE *KNOWS* ABOUT THESE.
YES, BUT ONLY A HANDFUL OF CIVILIANS HAVE *SEEN* ONE, KNOWS WHAT THEY *LOOK* LIKE. AND NOW YOU'RE ONE OF THEM.
MARC, HOW DID YOU GET THIS?

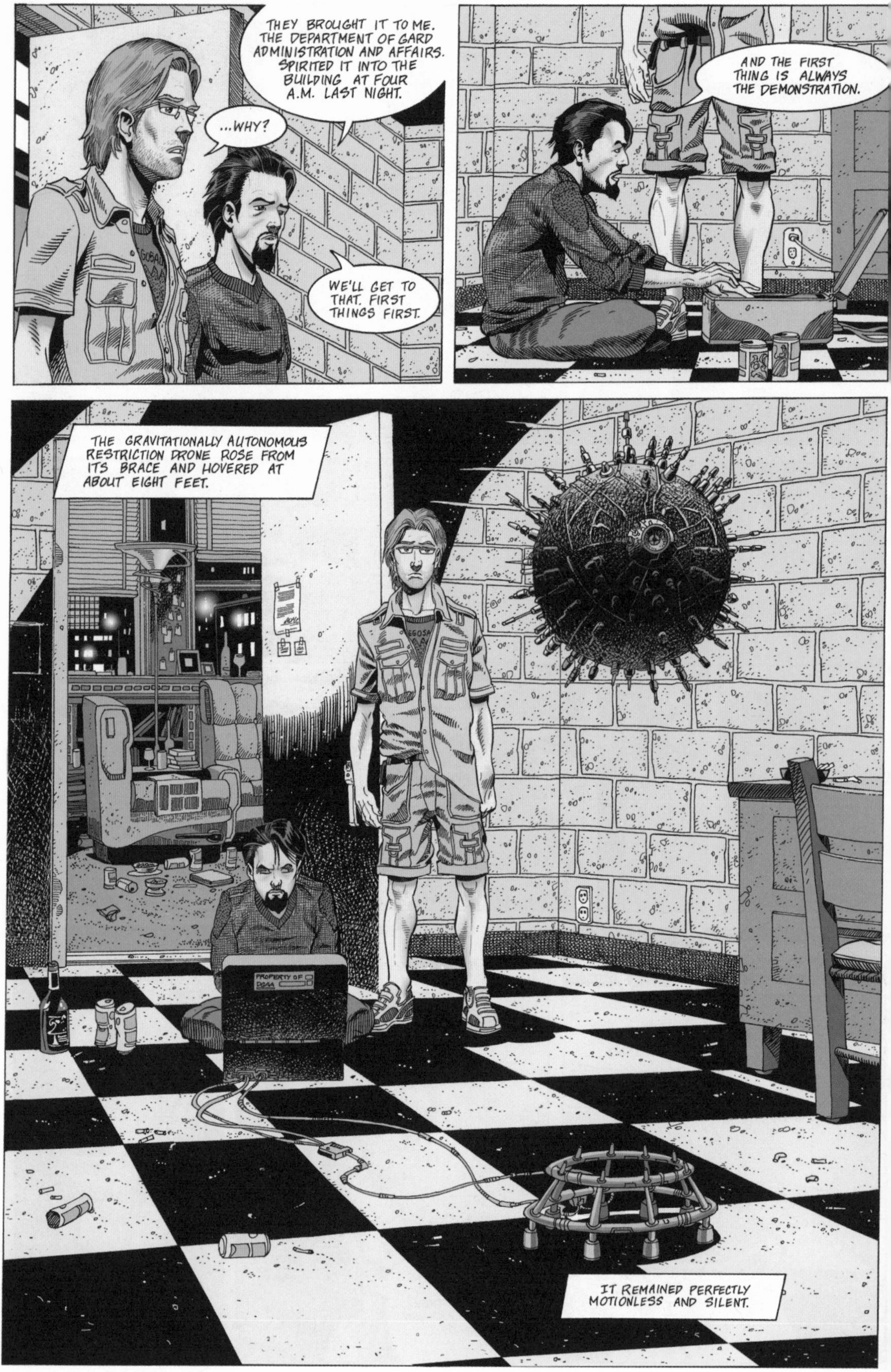
THEY BROUGHT IT TO ME. THE DEPARTMENT OF GARD ADMINISTRATION AND AFFAIRS. SPIRITED IT INTO THE BUILDING AT FOUR A.M. LAST NIGHT.
...WHY?
WE'LL GET TO THAT. FIRST THINGS FIRST.
AND THE FIRST THING IS ALWAYS THE DEMONSTRATION.
THE GRAVITATIONALLY AUTONOMOUS RESTRICTION DRONE ROSE FROM ITS BRACE AND HOVERED AT ABOUT EIGHT FEET.
PROPERTY OF DGAA
IT REMAINED PERFECTLY MOTIONLESS AND SILENT.

ALRIGHT, I'VE GOT IT IN *STATIONARY* MODE. THAT MEANS ONCE I GO INSIDE, I CAN'T COME OUT UNLESS *YOU* DISABLE IT. COME HERE.

PROPERTY OF DSAA

I'M GONNA GO IN. YOU WAIT A MINUTE OR SO, THEN JUST SELECT THIS.

THAT WAY I CAN COME OUT AGAIN. GOT IT?

PROPERTY OF DSAA

YEAH.

YOU'RE SURE.

SURE I'M SURE.

CHEERS!

HE STEPPED BENEATH THE GARD.

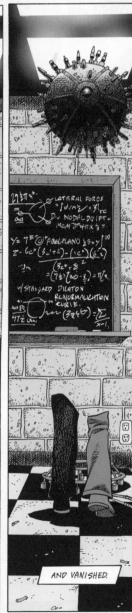

AND VANISHED.

EGOSA

IT WAS ASTONISHING.

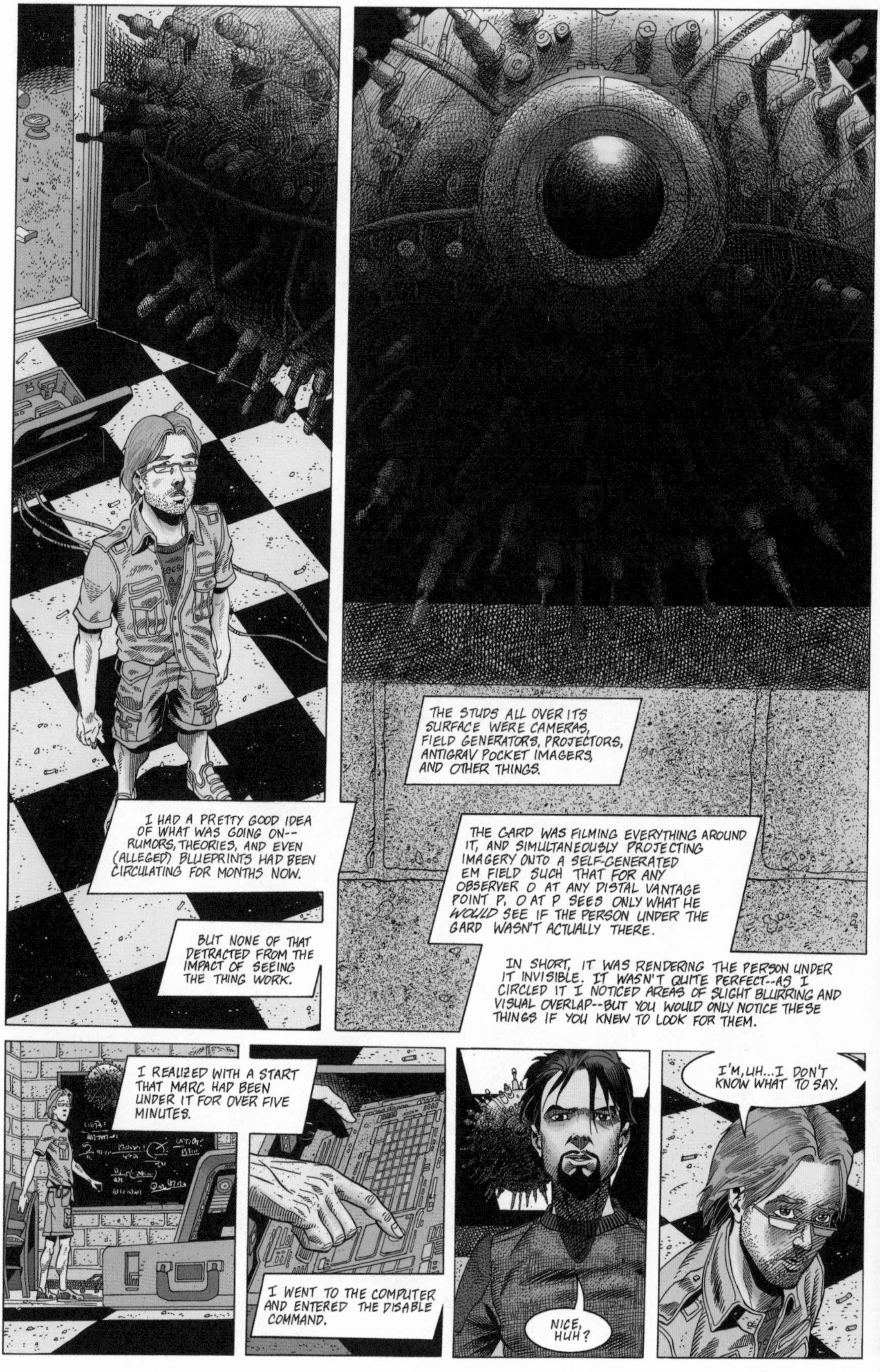
I HAD A PRETTY GOOD IDEA OF WHAT WAS GOING ON--RUMORS, THEORIES, AND EVEN (ALLEGED) BLUEPRINTS HAD BEEN CIRCULATING FOR MONTHS NOW.
BUT NONE OF THAT DETRACTED FROM THE IMPACT OF SEEING THE THING WORK.
THE STUDS ALL OVER ITS SURFACE WERE CAMERAS, FIELD GENERATORS, PROJECTORS, ANTIGRAV POCKET IMAGERS, AND OTHER THINGS.
THE GARD WAS FILMING EVERYTHING AROUND IT, AND SIMULTANEOUSLY PROJECTING IMAGERY ONTO A SELF-GENERATED EM FIELD SUCH THAT FOR ANY OBSERVER O AT ANY DISTAL VANTAGE POINT P, O AT P SEES ONLY WHAT HE *WOULD* SEE IF THE PERSON UNDER THE GARD WASN'T ACTUALLY THERE.
IN SHORT, IT WAS RENDERING THE PERSON UNDER IT INVISIBLE. IT WASN'T QUITE PERFECT--AS I CIRCLED IT I NOTICED AREAS OF SLIGHT BLURRING AND VISUAL OVERLAP--BUT YOU WOULD ONLY NOTICE THESE THINGS IF YOU KNEW TO LOOK FOR THEM.
I REALIZED WITH A START THAT MARC HAD BEEN UNDER IT FOR OVER FIVE MINUTES.
I WENT TO THE COMPUTER AND ENTERED THE DISABLE COMMAND.
NICE, HUH?
I'M, UH...I DON'T KNOW WHAT TO SAY.

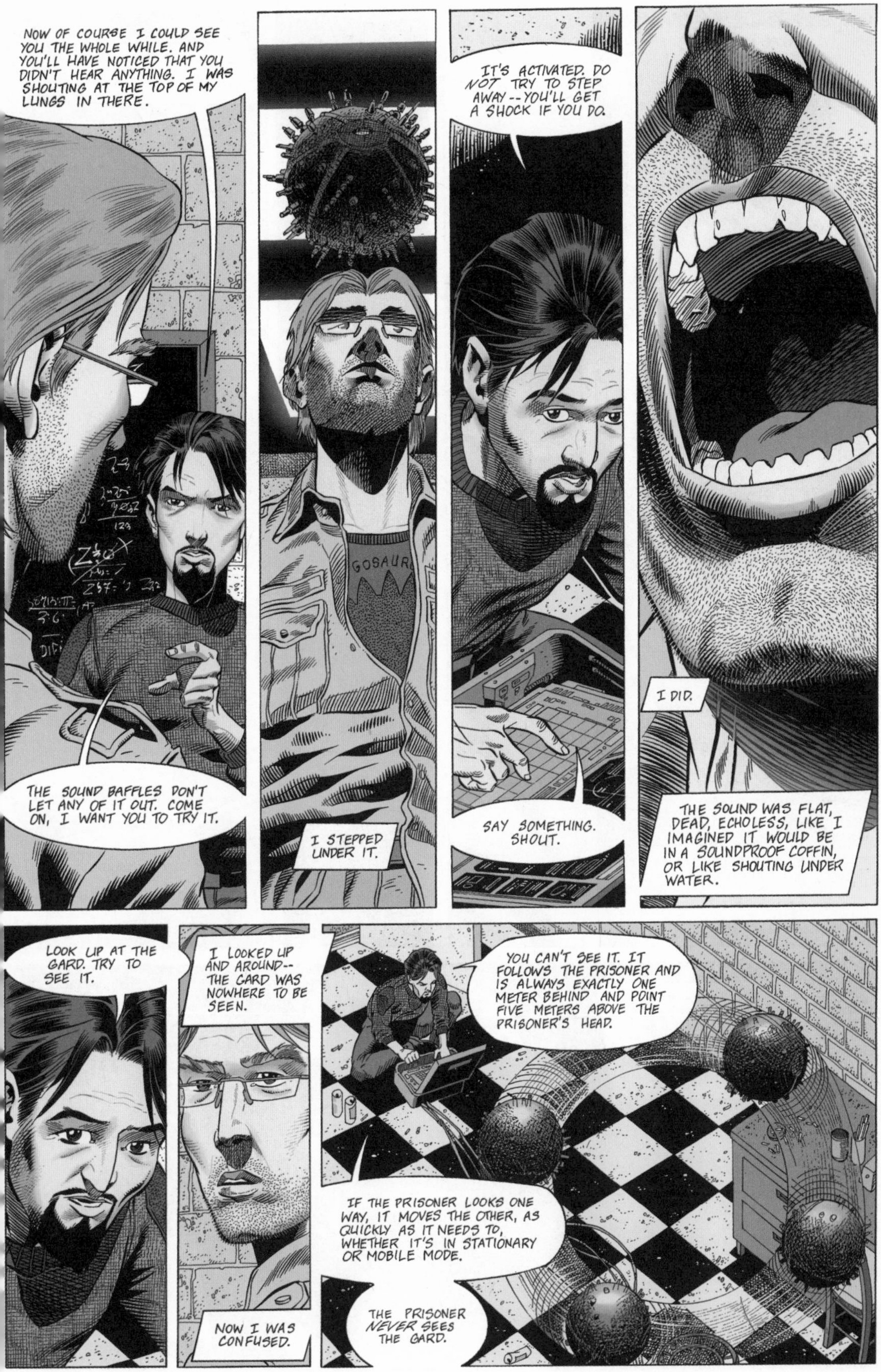
NOW OF COURSE I COULD SEE YOU THE WHOLE WHILE. AND YOU'LL HAVE NOTICED THAT YOU DIDN'T HEAR ANYTHING. I WAS SHOUTING AT THE TOP OF MY LUNGS IN THERE.
THE SOUND BAFFLES DON'T LET ANY OF IT OUT. COME ON, I WANT YOU TO TRY IT.
GOSAUR
I STEPPED UNDER IT.
IT'S ACTIVATED. DO *NOT* TRY TO STEP AWAY--YOU'LL GET A SHOCK IF YOU DO.
SAY SOMETHING. SHOUT.
I DID.
THE SOUND WAS FLAT, DEAD, ECHOLESS, LIKE I IMAGINED IT WOULD BE IN A SOUNDPROOF COFFIN, OR LIKE SHOUTING UNDER WATER.
LOOK UP AT THE GARD. TRY TO SEE IT.
I LOOKED UP AND AROUND-- THE GARD WAS NOWHERE TO BE SEEN.
NOW I WAS CONFUSED.
YOU CAN'T SEE IT. IT FOLLOWS THE PRISONER AND IS ALWAYS EXACTLY ONE METER BEHIND AND POINT FIVE METERS ABOVE THE PRISONER'S HEAD.
IF THE PRISONER LOOKS ONE WAY, IT MOVES THE OTHER, AS QUICKLY AS IT NEEDS TO, WHETHER IT'S IN STATIONARY OR MOBILE MODE.
THE PRISONER *NEVER* SEES THE GARD.

I KEPT LOOKING UP AND AROUND, TO NO AVAIL.

MY BREATH WAS COMING SHORT AND MY HEART WAS RACING.

MARC...TURN IT OFF NOW!

I FELT LIKE AN IDIOT. I KNEW HE WOULDN'T HEAR IT EVEN BEFORE I SAID IT.

THIS, BY THE WAY, IS AN EARLY PROTOTYPE, A COUPLE OF YEARS OLD.

IMPROVEMENTS IN THE IMAGING SYSTEMS HAVE BEEN MADE.

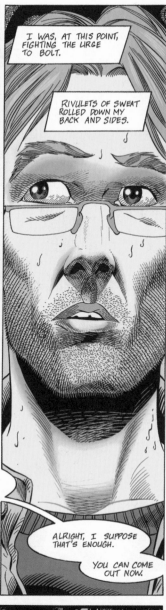

I WAS, AT THIS POINT, FIGHTING THE URGE TO BOLT.

RIVULETS OF SWEAT ROLLED DOWN MY BACK AND SIDES.

ALRIGHT, I SUPPOSE THAT'S ENOUGH.

YOU CAN COME OUT NOW.

I STEPPED FORWARD AND FELT THE GREATEST PAIN I'VE EVER FELT. GREATER THAN WHEN MY APPENDIX BURST AT AGE FIFTEEN. GREATER THAN WHEN MY PATELLA DETACHED AT AGE SEVENTEEN.

IT SEEMED AS IF A GREAT, COOL HAND HAD REACHED *INTO* MY BACK, GRABBED MY LUMBAR VERTEBRAE, AND LIFTED.

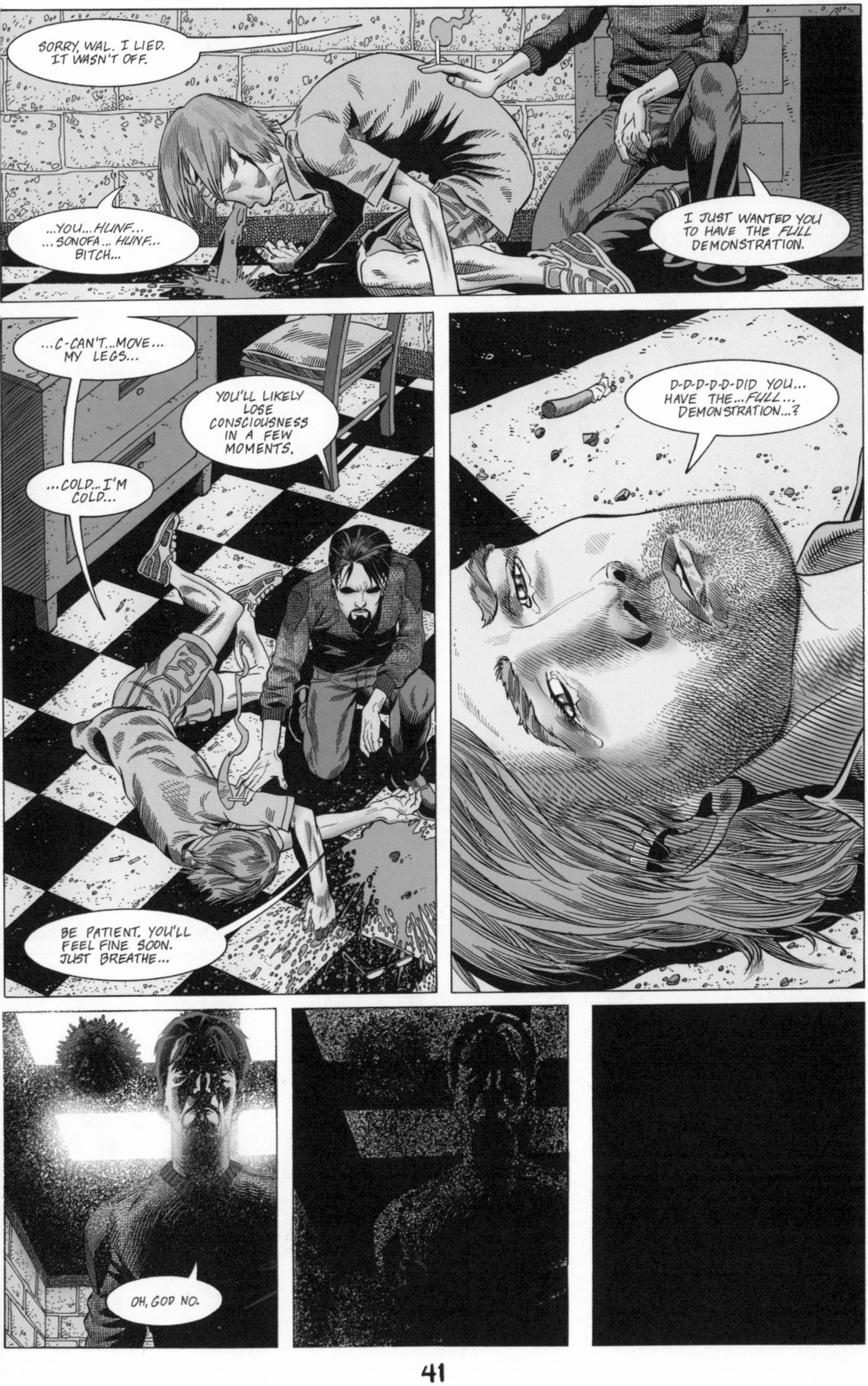
SORRY, WAL. I LIED. IT WASN'T OFF.
...YOU...HUNF... ...SONOFA... HUNF... BITCH...
I JUST WANTED YOU TO HAVE THE FULL DEMONSTRATION.
...C-CAN'T...MOVE... MY LEGS...
YOU'LL LIKELY LOSE CONSCIOUSNESS IN A FEW MOMENTS.
...COLD...I'M COLD...
BE PATIENT. YOU'LL FEEL FINE SOON. JUST BREATHE...
D-D-D-D-D-DID YOU... HAVE THE...FULL... DEMONSTRATION...?
OH, GOD NO.

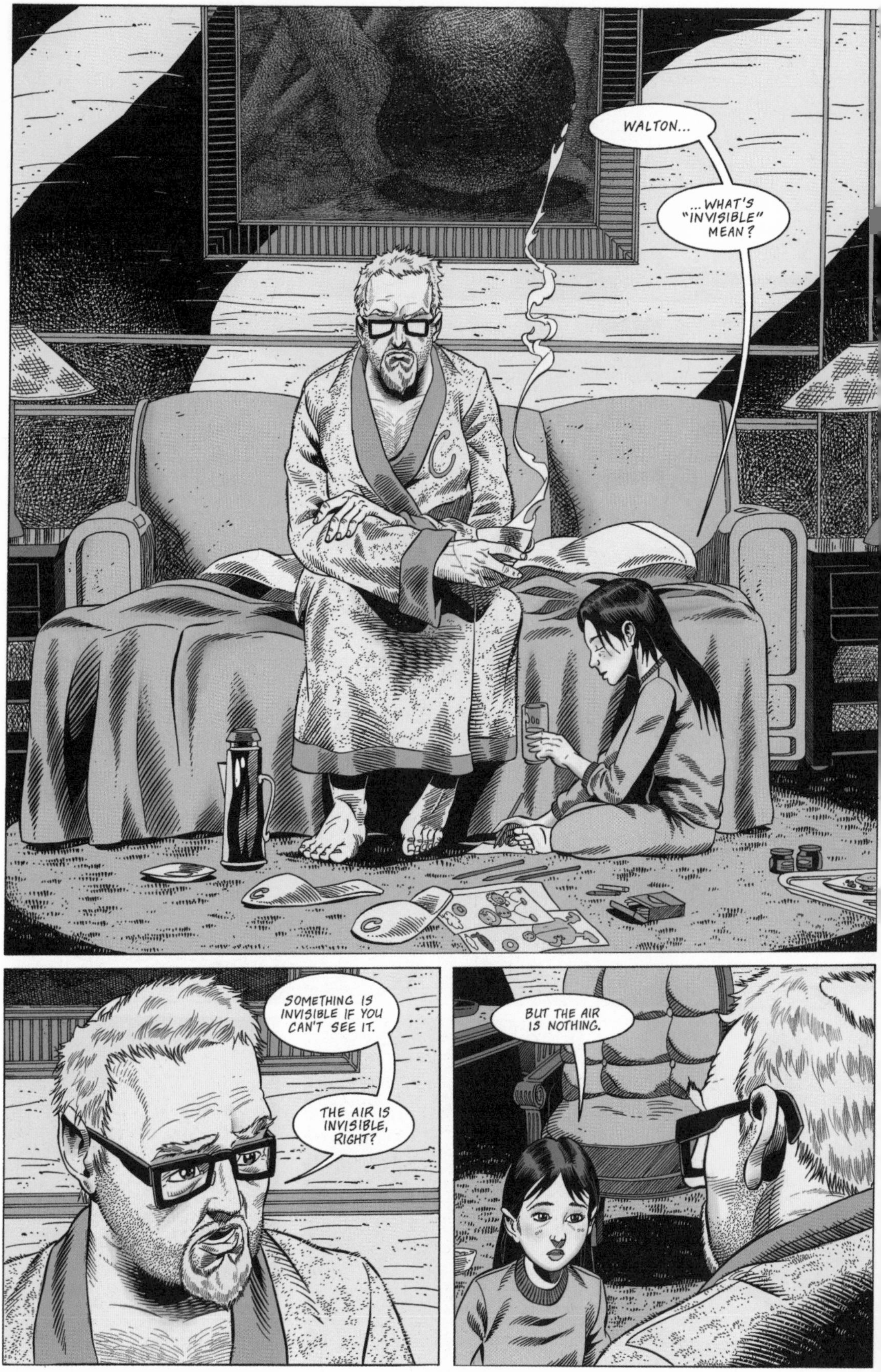
WALTON...
...WHAT'S "INVISIBLE" MEAN?
SOMETHING IS INVISIBLE IF YOU CAN'T SEE IT.
THE AIR IS INVISIBLE, RIGHT?
BUT THE AIR IS NOTHING.

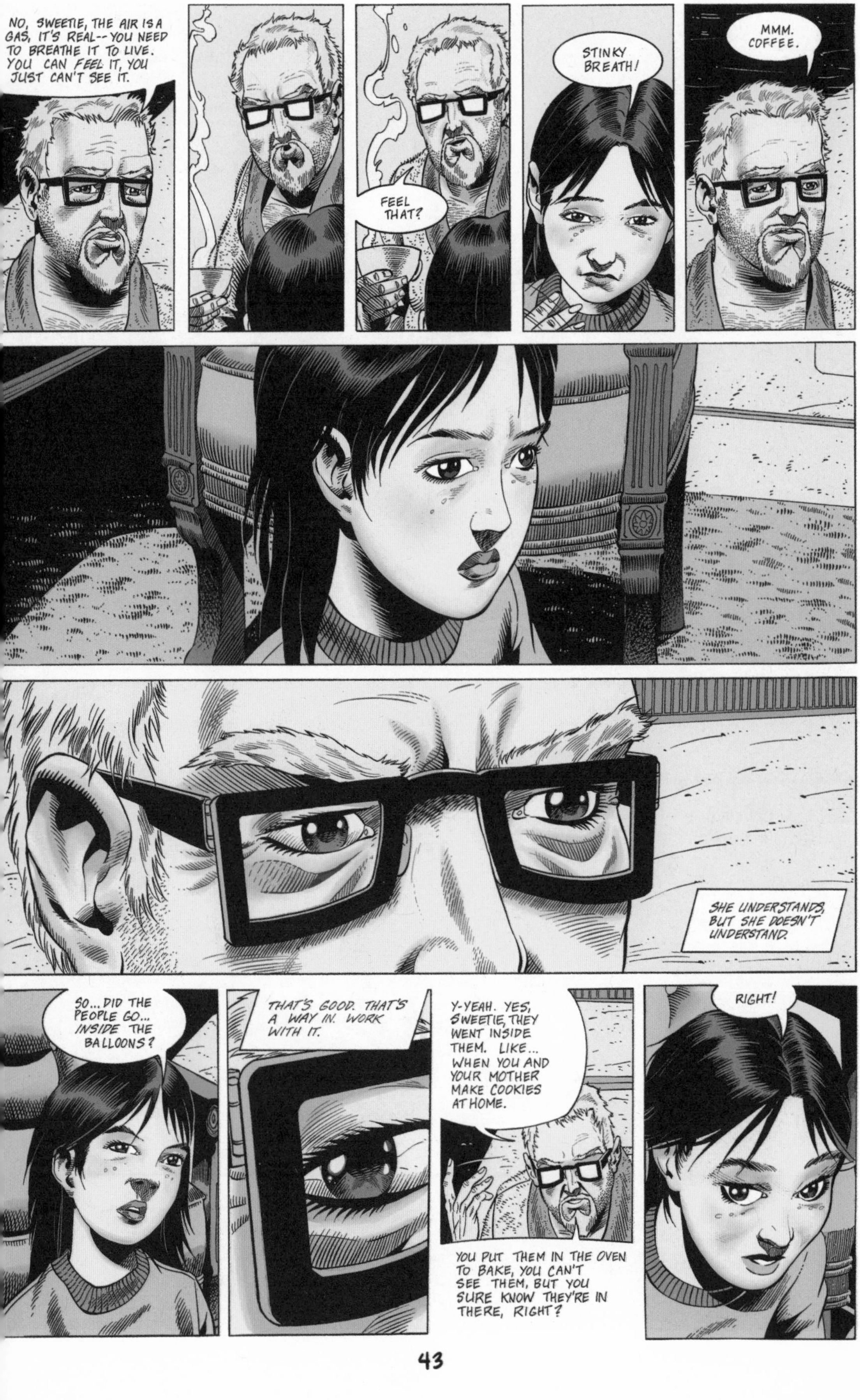
NO, SWEETIE, THE AIR IS A GAS, IT'S REAL-- YOU NEED TO BREATHE IT TO LIVE. YOU CAN FEEL IT, YOU JUST CAN'T SEE IT.
FEEL THAT?
STINKY BREATH!
MMM. COFFEE.
SHE UNDERSTANDS, BUT SHE DOESN'T UNDERSTAND.
SO... DID THE PEOPLE GO... INSIDE THE BALLOONS?
THAT'S GOOD. THAT'S A WAY IN. WORK WITH IT.
Y-YEAH. YES, SWEETIE, THEY WENT INSIDE THEM. LIKE... WHEN YOU AND YOUR MOTHER MAKE COOKIES AT HOME.
YOU PUT THEM IN THE OVEN TO BAKE, YOU CAN'T SEE THEM, BUT YOU SURE KNOW THEY'RE IN THERE, RIGHT?
RIGHT!

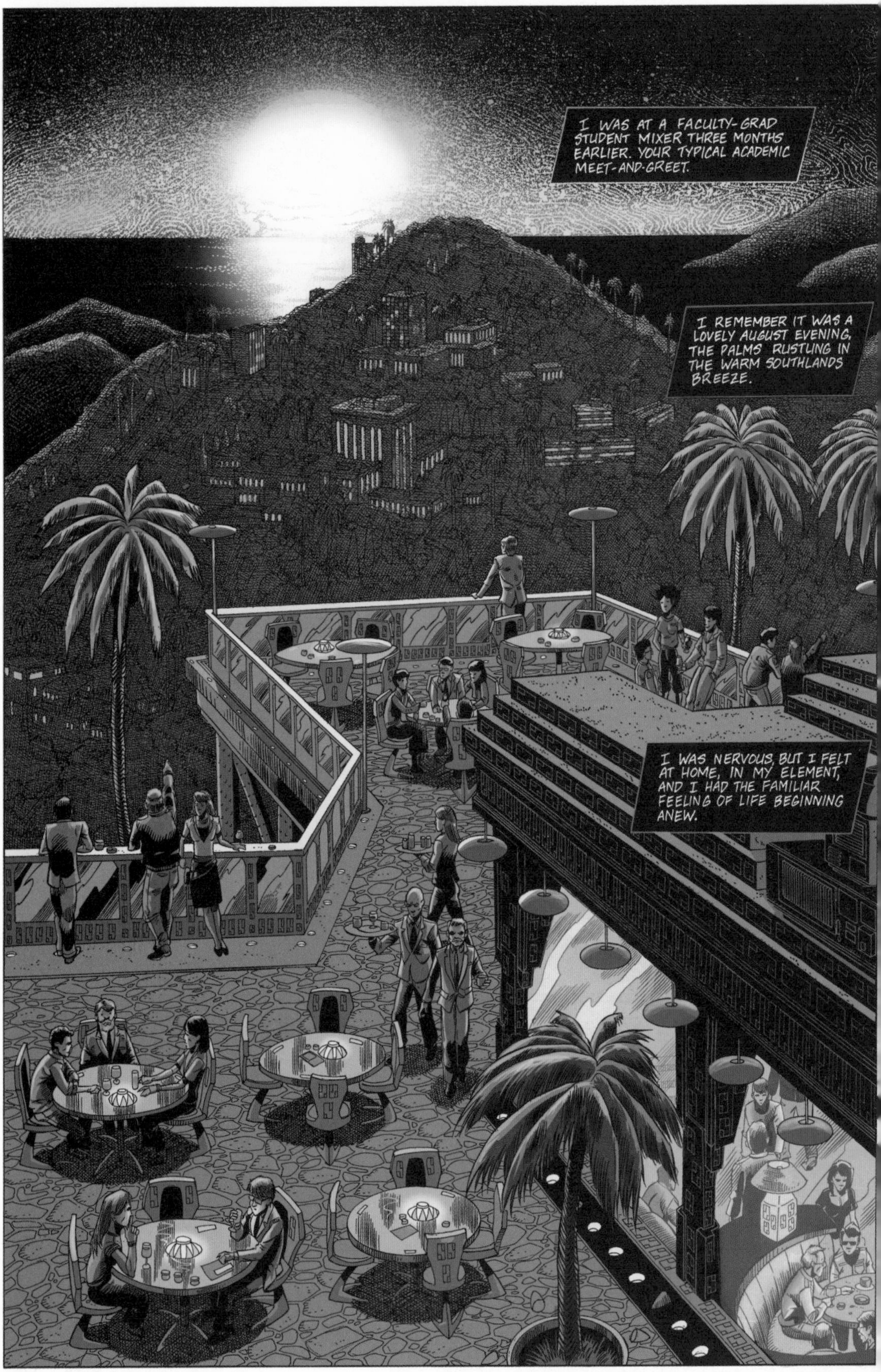
I WAS AT A FACULTY-GRAD STUDENT MIXER THREE MONTHS EARLIER. YOUR TYPICAL ACADEMIC MEET-AND-GREET.
I REMEMBER IT WAS A LOVELY AUGUST EVENING, THE PALMS RUSTLING IN THE WARM SOUTHLANDS BREEZE.
I WAS NERVOUS, BUT I FELT AT HOME, IN MY ELEMENT, AND I HAD THE FAMILIAR FEELING OF LIFE BEGINNING ANEW.

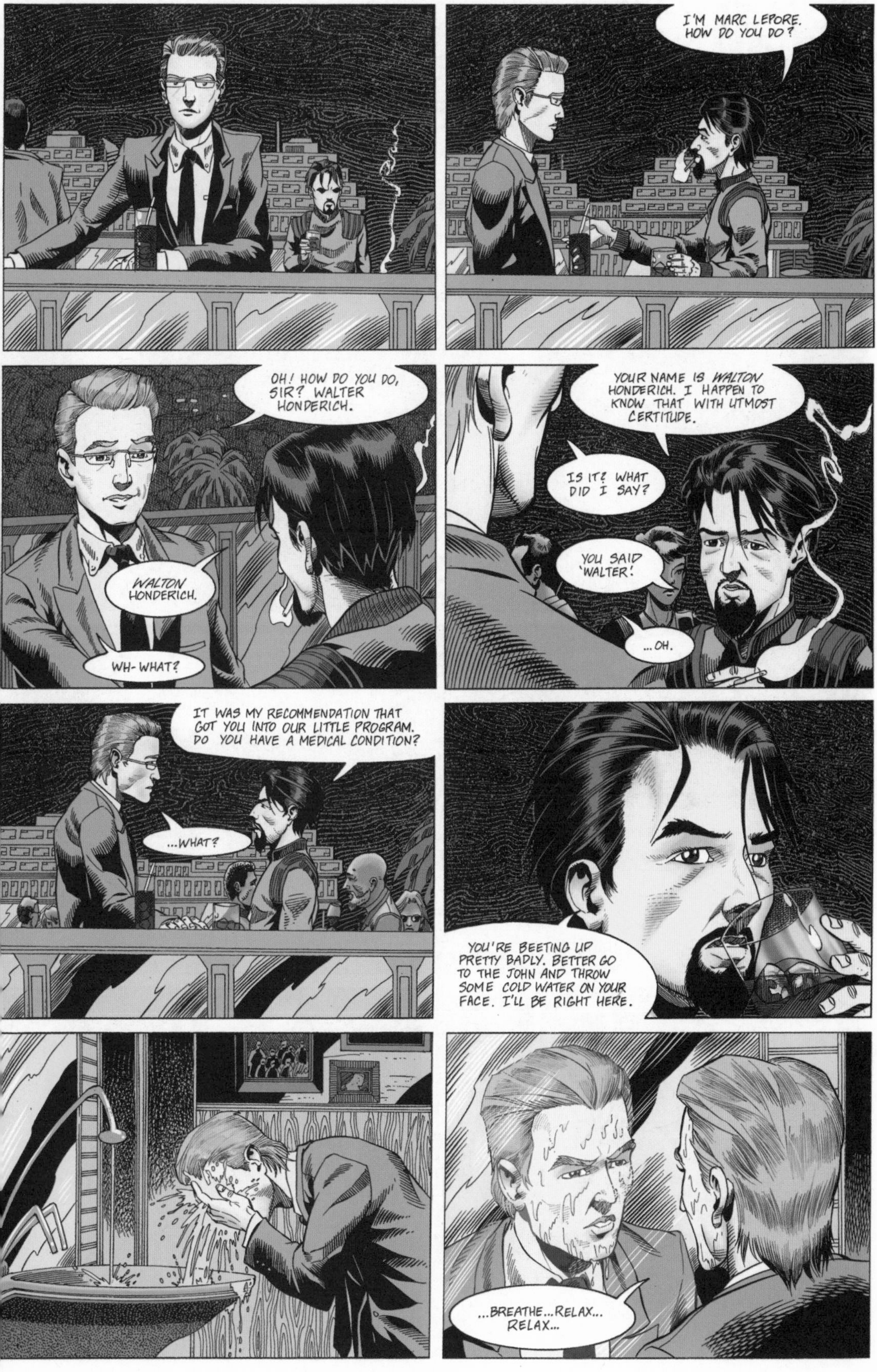
I'M MARC LEPORE. HOW DO YOU DO?
OH! HOW DO YOU DO, SIR? WALTER HONDERICH.
WALTON HONDERICH.
WH-WHAT?
YOUR NAME IS WALTON HONDERICH. I HAPPEN TO KNOW THAT WITH UTMOST CERTITUDE.
IS IT? WHAT DID I SAY?
YOU SAID 'WALTER.'
...OH.
IT WAS MY RECOMMENDATION THAT GOT YOU INTO OUR LITTLE PROGRAM. DO YOU HAVE A MEDICAL CONDITION?
...WHAT?
YOU'RE BEETING UP PRETTY BADLY. BETTER GO TO THE JOHN AND THROW SOME COLD WATER ON YOUR FACE. I'LL BE RIGHT HERE.
...BREATHE...RELAX... RELAX...

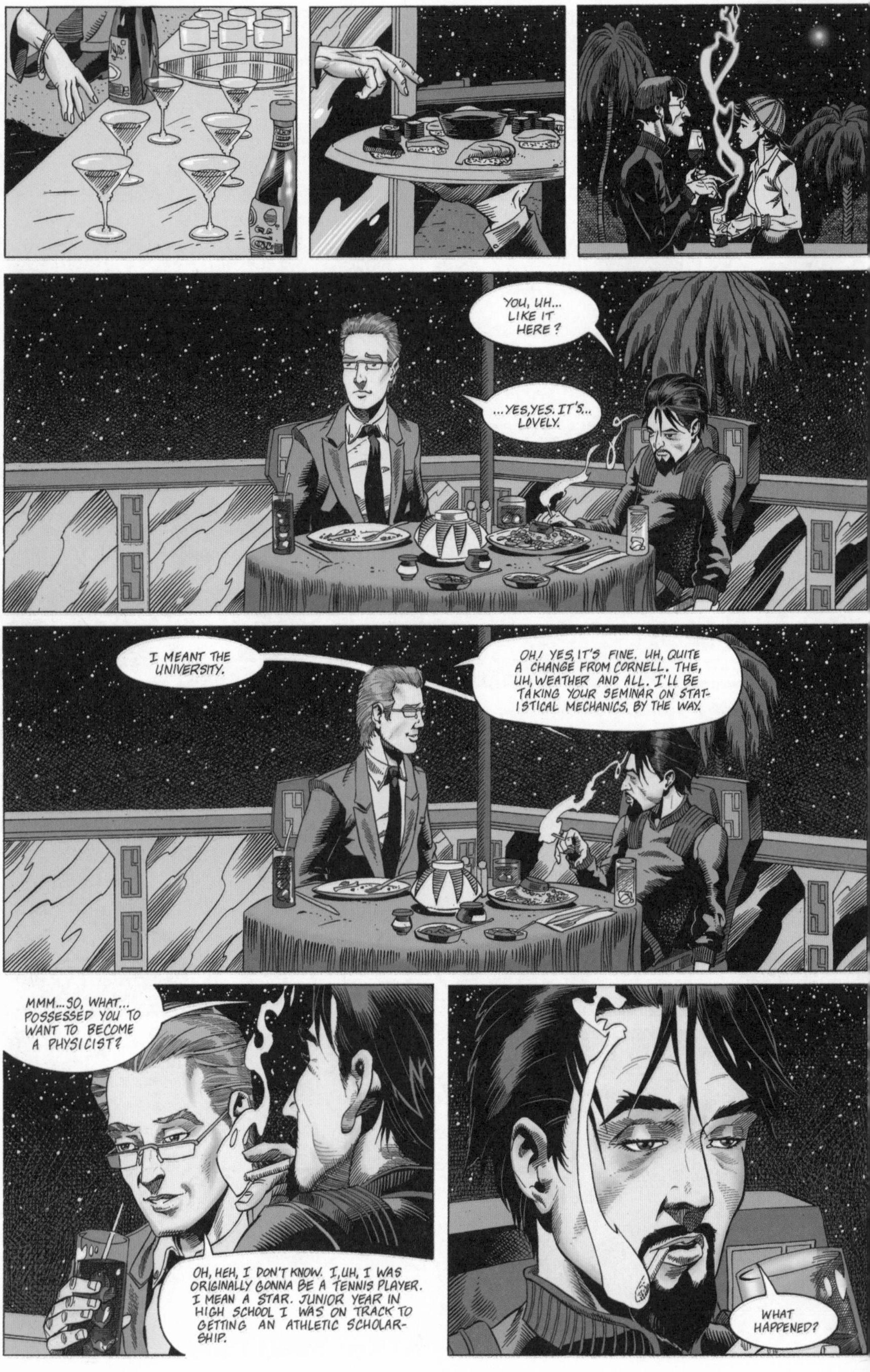
YOU, UH... LIKE IT HERE?
...YES,YES. IT'S... LOVELY.
I MEANT THE UNIVERSITY.
OH! YES, IT'S FINE. UH, QUITE A CHANGE FROM CORNELL. THE, UH, WEATHER AND ALL. I'LL BE TAKING YOUR SEMINAR ON STATISTICAL MECHANICS, BY THE WAY.
MMM...SO, WHAT... POSSESSED YOU TO WANT TO BECOME A PHYSICIST?
OH, HEH, I DON'T KNOW. I, UH, I WAS ORIGINALLY GONNA BE A TENNIS PLAYER. I MEAN A STAR. JUNIOR YEAR IN HIGH SCHOOL I WAS ON TRACK TO GETTING AN ATHLETIC SCHOLARSHIP.
WHAT HAPPENED?

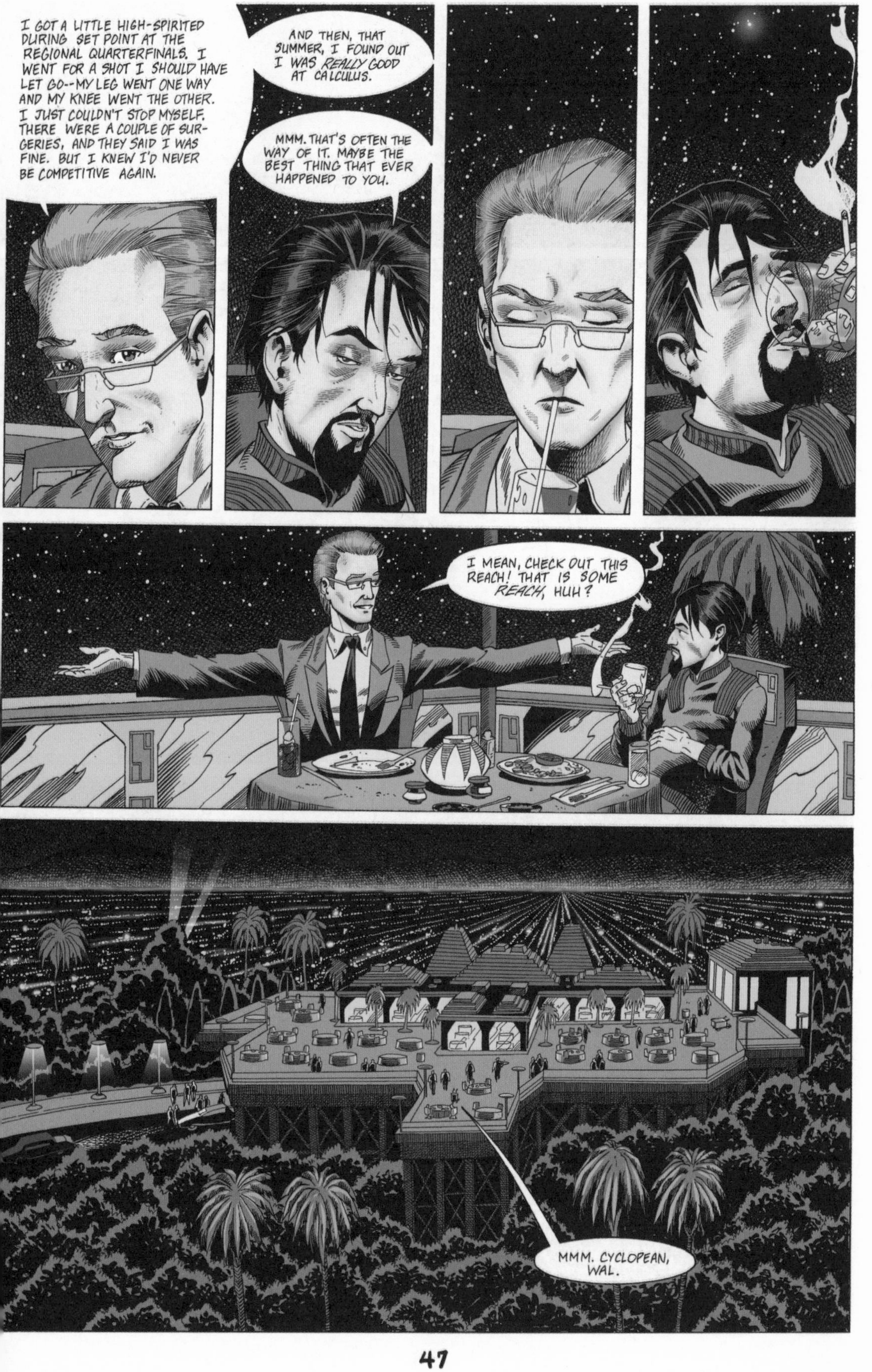
I GOT A LITTLE HIGH-SPIRITED DURING SET POINT AT THE REGIONAL QUARTERFINALS. I WENT FOR A SHOT I SHOULD HAVE LET GO--MY LEG WENT ONE WAY AND MY KNEE WENT THE OTHER. I JUST COULDN'T STOP MYSELF. THERE WERE A COUPLE OF SURGERIES, AND THEY SAID I WAS FINE. BUT I KNEW I'D NEVER BE COMPETITIVE AGAIN.
AND THEN, THAT SUMMER, I FOUND OUT I WAS *REALLY* GOOD AT CALCULUS.
MMM. THAT'S OFTEN THE WAY OF IT. MAYBE THE BEST THING THAT EVER HAPPENED TO YOU.
I MEAN, CHECK OUT THIS REACH! THAT IS SOME *REACH*, HUH?
MMM. CYCLOPEAN, WAL.

I GUESS IT WAS ABOUT SIX MONTHS EARLIER THAT WE'D ALL STARTED HEARING WHISPERINGS ABOUT THE GARD PROGRAM.

APPARENTLY IT HAD BEEN IN THE WORKS FOR SOME TIME.

IT WAS IN 2023 THAT THERE HAD BEEN A SPATE OF BOMBINGS AT SUPERMAX PENITENTIARIES IN THE WESTERN U.S. THERE WERE EXPLOSIONS AT FOUR PRISONS-- ALL TOLD, 57 PRISONERS AND 22 GUARDS DIED, AND OVER 100 PRISONERS ESCAPED. SOME ARE AT LARGE TODAY.

THE FEDERAL GOVERNMENT ACCUSED A RADICAL ANARCHIST TERRORIST NETWORK THAT WANTED TO END THE INHUMANE TREATMENT OF PRISONERS AT SUPERMAX PENS.

THE ANARCHISTS ACCUSED THE GOVERNMENT OF BOMBING THE PRISONS ITSELF, MAYBE TO THIN THE PRISON RANKS, OR TO DEMONSTRATE THE NEED FOR EVEN TOUGHER PRISONS, OR TO FOMENT FEAR AT LARGE, OR AS A PRETEXT TO LAUNCH SOME NEFARIOUS NEW PROGRAM.

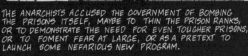

WHO KNOWS.

48

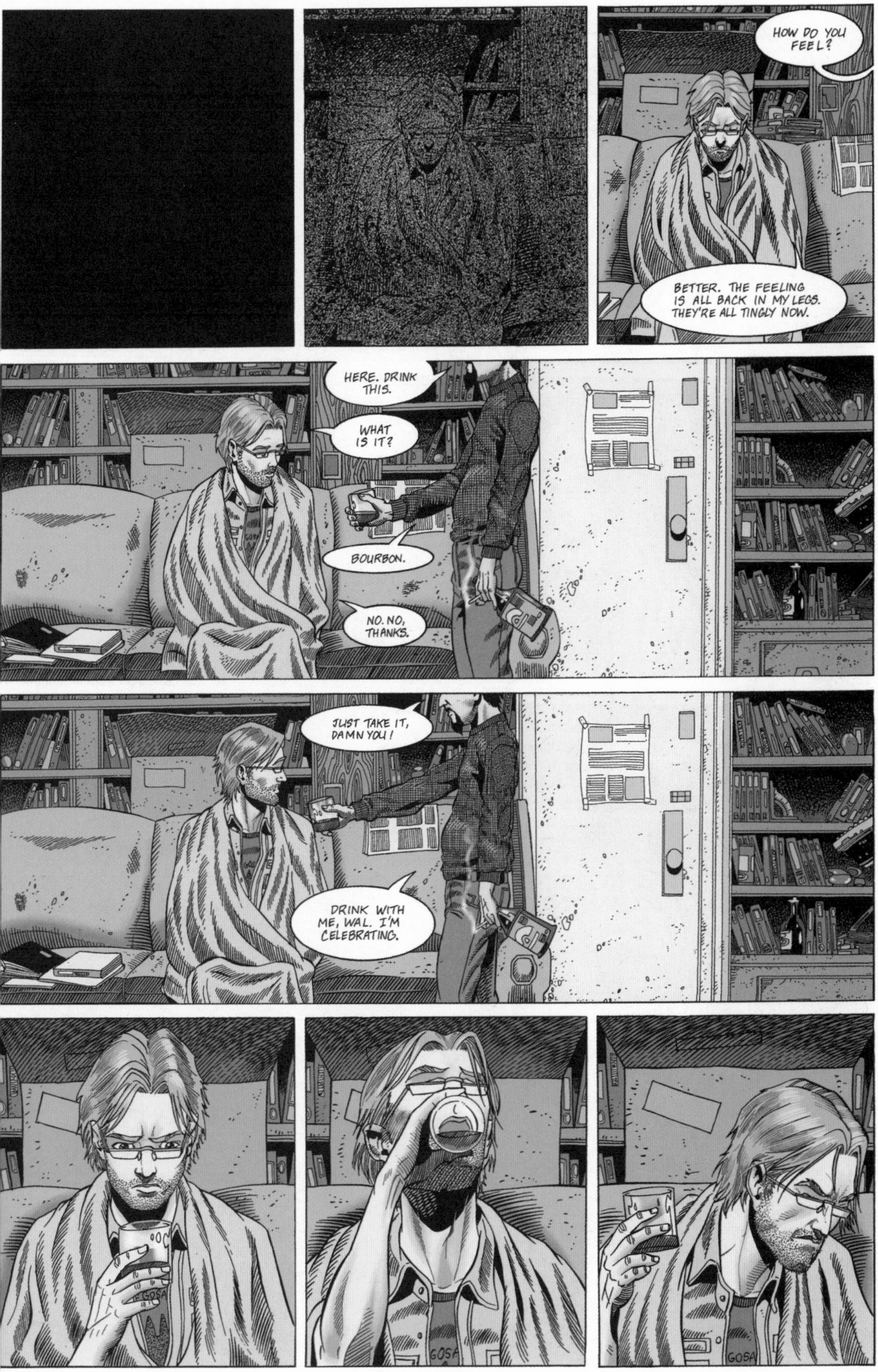
HOW DO YOU FEEL?
BETTER. THE FEELING IS ALL BACK IN MY LEGS. THEY'RE ALL TINGLY NOW.
HERE. DRINK THIS.
WHAT IS IT?
BOURBON.
NO. NO, THANKS.
JUST TAKE IT, DAMN YOU!
DRINK WITH ME, WAL. I'M CELEBRATING.

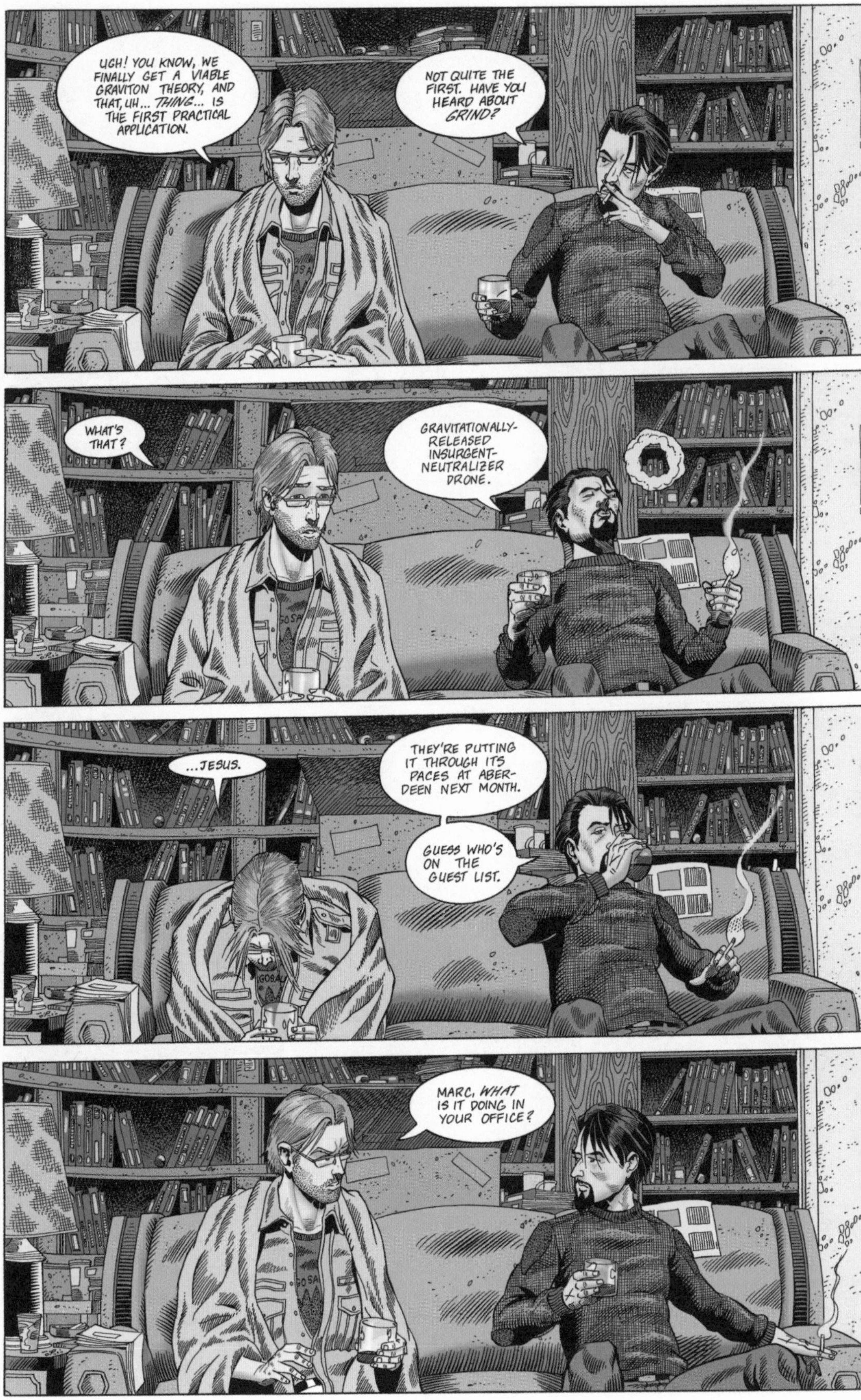
UGH! YOU KNOW, WE FINALLY GET A VIABLE GRAVITON THEORY, AND THAT, UH... *THING*... IS THE FIRST PRACTICAL APPLICATION.
NOT QUITE THE FIRST. HAVE YOU HEARD ABOUT *GRIND?*
WHAT'S THAT?
GRAVITATIONALLY-RELEASED INSURGENT-NEUTRALIZER DRONE.
...JESUS.
THEY'RE PUTTING IT THROUGH ITS PACES AT ABERDEEN NEXT MONTH.
GUESS WHO'S ON THE GUEST LIST.
MARC, *WHAT* IS IT DOING IN YOUR OFFICE?

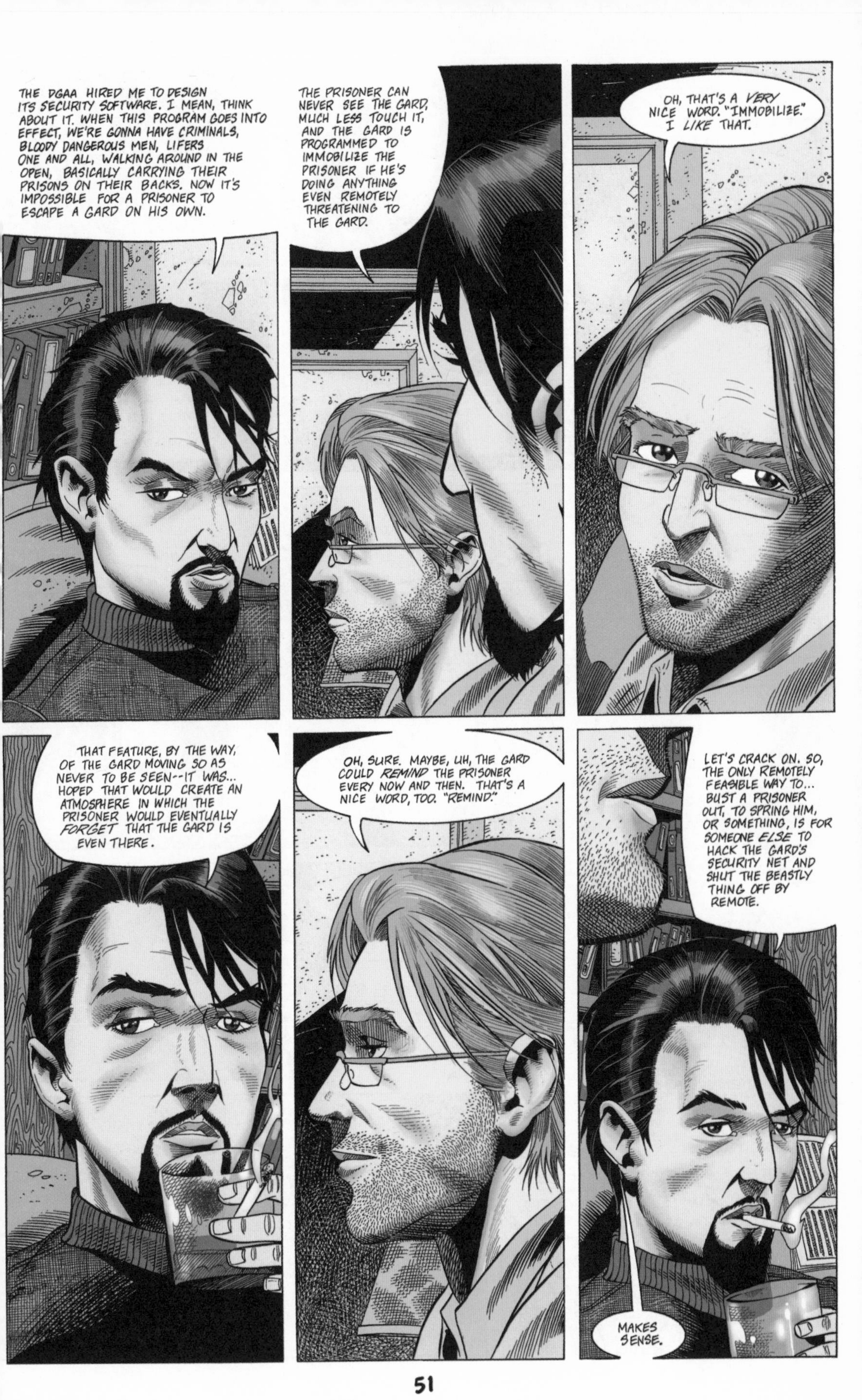
THE DGAA HIRED ME TO DESIGN ITS SECURITY SOFTWARE. I MEAN, THINK ABOUT IT. WHEN THIS PROGRAM GOES INTO EFFECT, WE'RE GONNA HAVE CRIMINALS, BLOODY DANGEROUS MEN, LIFERS ONE AND ALL, WALKING AROUND IN THE OPEN, BASICALLY CARRYING THEIR PRISONS ON THEIR BACKS. NOW IT'S IMPOSSIBLE FOR A PRISONER TO ESCAPE A GARD ON HIS OWN.
THE PRISONER CAN NEVER SEE THE GARD, MUCH LESS TOUCH IT, AND THE GARD IS PROGRAMMED TO IMMOBILIZE THE PRISONER IF HE'S DOING ANYTHING EVEN REMOTELY THREATENING TO THE GARD.
OH, THAT'S A VERY NICE WORD. "IMMOBILIZE." I LIKE THAT.
THAT FEATURE, BY THE WAY, OF THE GARD MOVING SO AS NEVER TO BE SEEN--IT WAS... HOPED THAT WOULD CREATE AN ATMOSPHERE IN WHICH THE PRISONER WOULD EVENTUALLY FORGET THAT THE GARD IS EVEN THERE.
OH, SURE. MAYBE, UH, THE GARD COULD REMIND THE PRISONER EVERY NOW AND THEN. THAT'S A NICE WORD, TOO. "REMIND."
LET'S CRACK ON. SO, THE ONLY REMOTELY FEASIBLE WAY TO... BUST A PRISONER OUT, TO SPRING HIM, OR SOMETHING, IS FOR SOMEONE ELSE TO HACK THE GARD'S SECURITY NET AND SHUT THE BEASTLY THING OFF BY REMOTE.
MAKES SENSE.

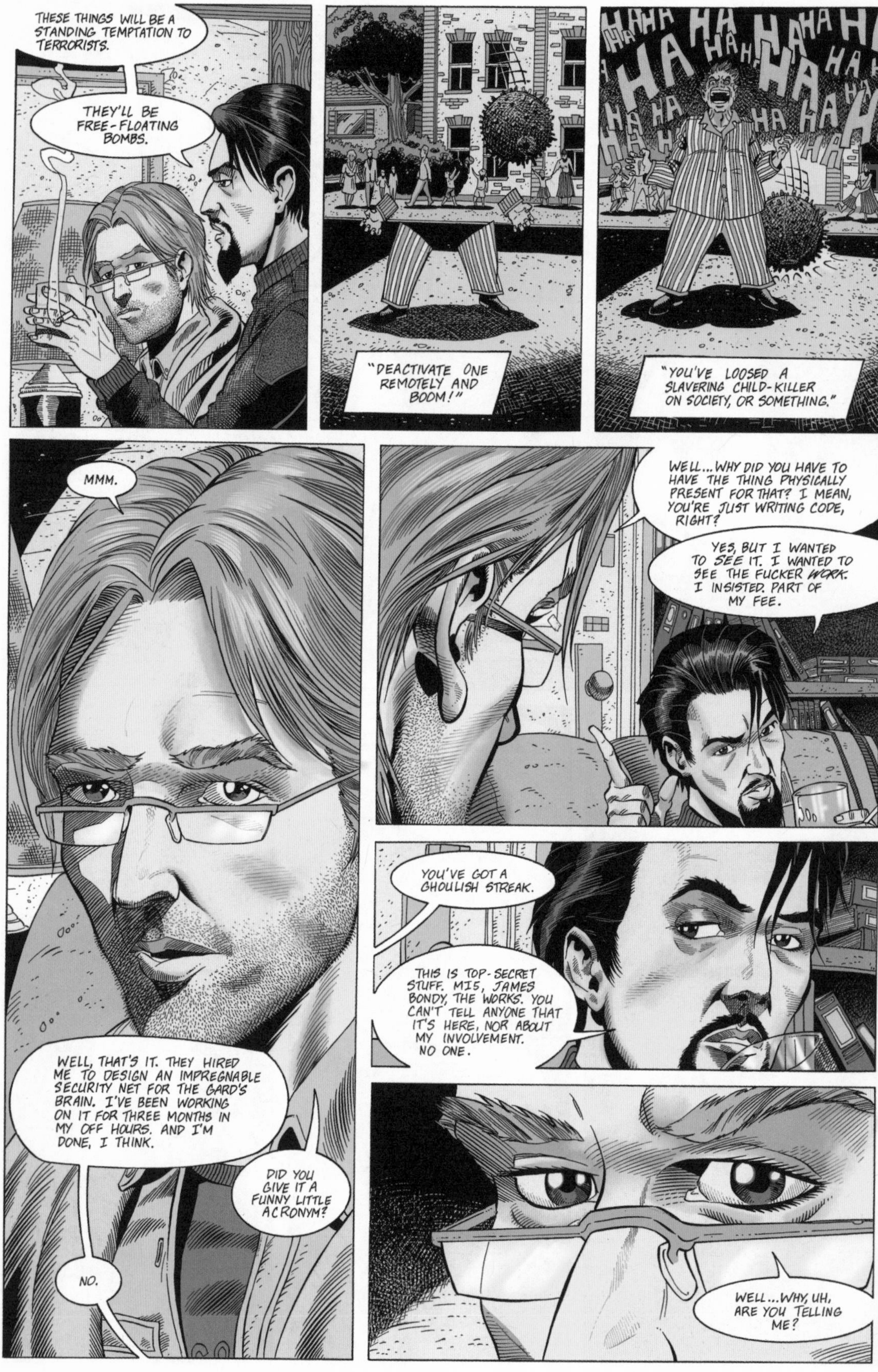
THESE THINGS WILL BE A STANDING TEMPTATION TO TERRORISTS.
THEY'LL BE FREE-FLOATING BOMBS.
"DEACTIVATE ONE REMOTELY AND BOOM!"
HA HA HA
"YOU'VE LOOSED A SLAVERING CHILD-KILLER ON SOCIETY, OR SOMETHING."
MMM.
WELL... WHY DID YOU HAVE TO HAVE THE THING PHYSICALLY PRESENT FOR THAT? I MEAN, YOU'RE JUST WRITING CODE, RIGHT?
YES, BUT I WANTED TO SEE IT. I WANTED TO SEE THE FUCKER WORK. I INSISTED. PART OF MY FEE.
YOU'VE GOT A GHOULISH STREAK.
THIS IS TOP-SECRET STUFF. MI5, JAMES BONDY, THE WORKS. YOU CAN'T TELL ANYONE THAT IT'S HERE, NOR ABOUT MY INVOLVEMENT. NO ONE.
WELL, THAT'S IT. THEY HIRED ME TO DESIGN AN IMPREGNABLE SECURITY NET FOR THE GARD'S BRAIN. I'VE BEEN WORKING ON IT FOR THREE MONTHS IN MY OFF HOURS. AND I'M DONE, I THINK.
DID YOU GIVE IT A FUNNY LITTLE ACRONYM?
NO.
WELL... WHY, UH, ARE YOU TELLING ME?

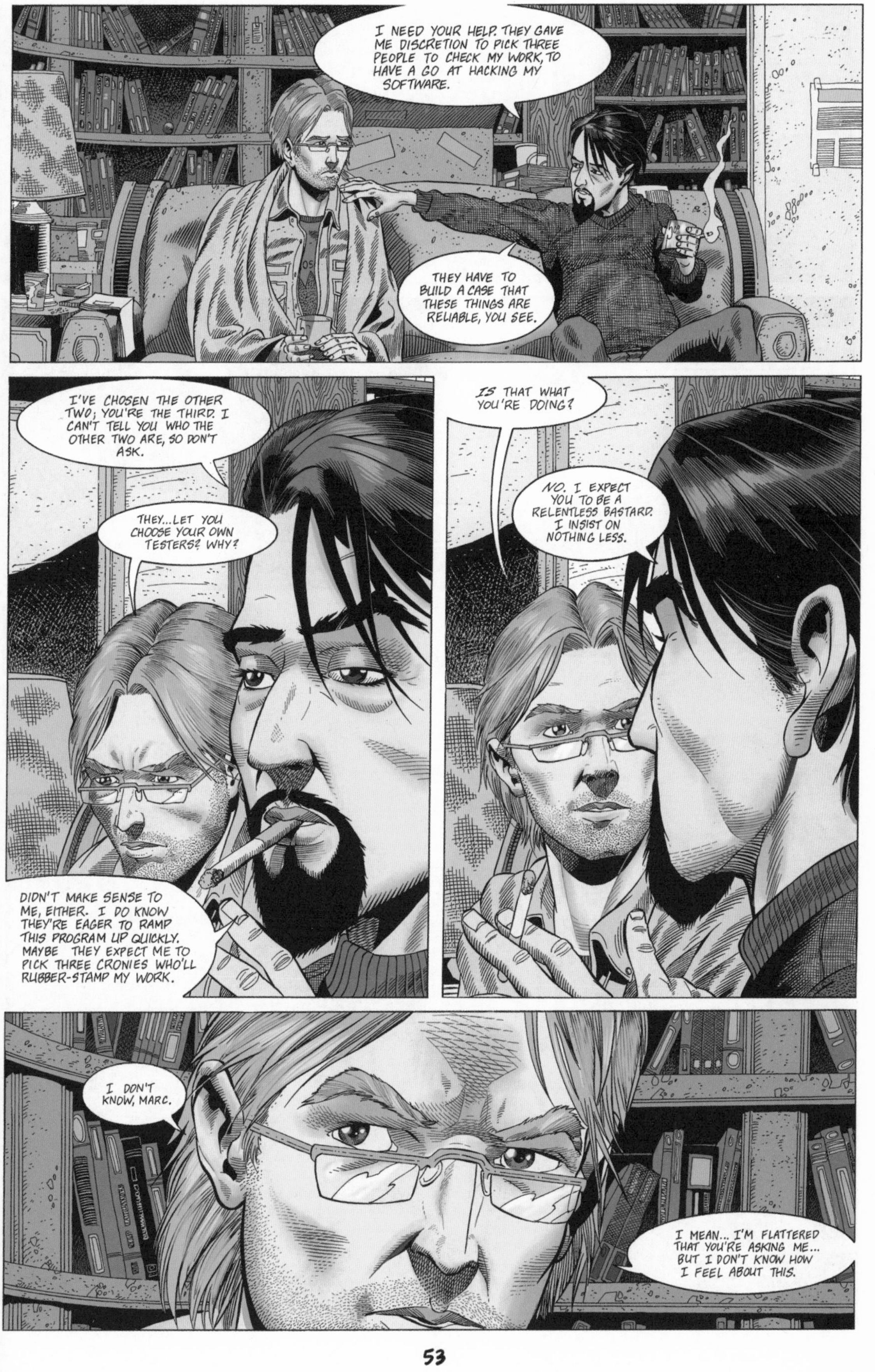
I NEED YOUR HELP. THEY GAVE ME DISCRETION TO PICK THREE PEOPLE TO CHECK MY WORK, TO HAVE A GO AT HACKING MY SOFTWARE.
THEY HAVE TO BUILD A CASE THAT THESE THINGS ARE RELIABLE, YOU SEE.
I'VE CHOSEN THE OTHER TWO; YOU'RE THE THIRD. I CAN'T TELL YOU WHO THE OTHER TWO ARE, SO DON'T ASK.
THEY...LET YOU CHOOSE YOUR OWN TESTERS? WHY?
DIDN'T MAKE SENSE TO ME, EITHER. I DO KNOW THEY'RE EAGER TO RAMP THIS PROGRAM UP QUICKLY. MAYBE THEY EXPECT ME TO PICK THREE CRONIES WHO'LL RUBBER-STAMP MY WORK.
IS THAT WHAT YOU'RE DOING?
NO. I EXPECT YOU TO BE A RELENTLESS BASTARD. I INSIST ON NOTHING LESS.
I DON'T KNOW, MARC.
I MEAN... I'M FLATTERED THAT YOU'RE ASKING ME... BUT I DON'T KNOW HOW I FEEL ABOUT THIS.

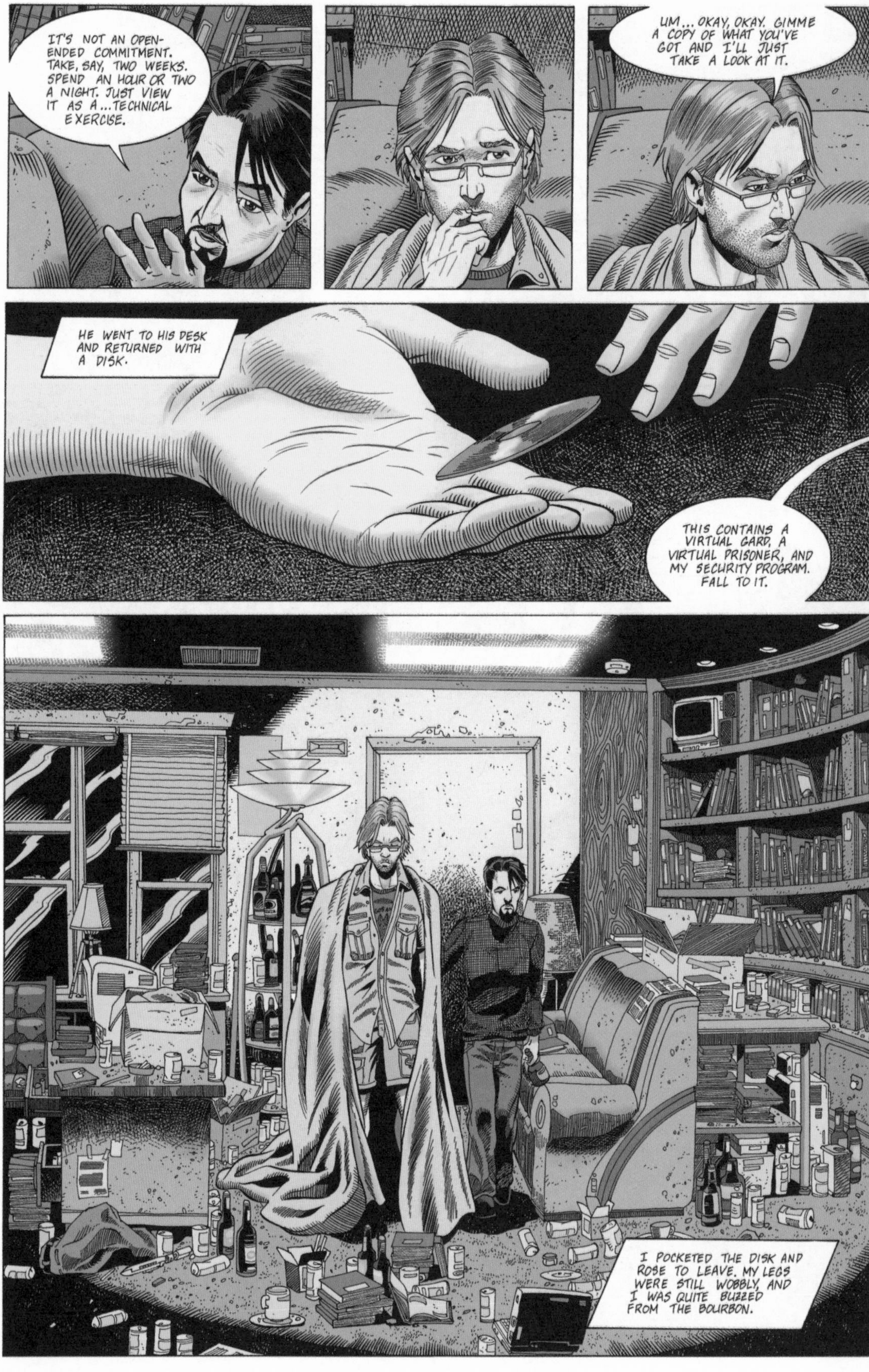
IT'S NOT AN OPEN-ENDED COMMITMENT. TAKE, SAY, TWO WEEKS. SPEND AN HOUR OR TWO A NIGHT. JUST VIEW IT AS A...TECHNICAL EXERCISE.
UM... OKAY, OKAY. GIMME A COPY OF WHAT YOU'VE GOT AND I'LL JUST TAKE A LOOK AT IT.
HE WENT TO HIS DESK AND RETURNED WITH A DISK.
THIS CONTAINS A VIRTUAL GARD, A VIRTUAL PRISONER, AND MY SECURITY PROGRAM. FALL TO IT.
I POCKETED THE DISK AND ROSE TO LEAVE. MY LEGS WERE STILL WOBBLY, AND I WAS QUITE BUZZED FROM THE BOURBON.

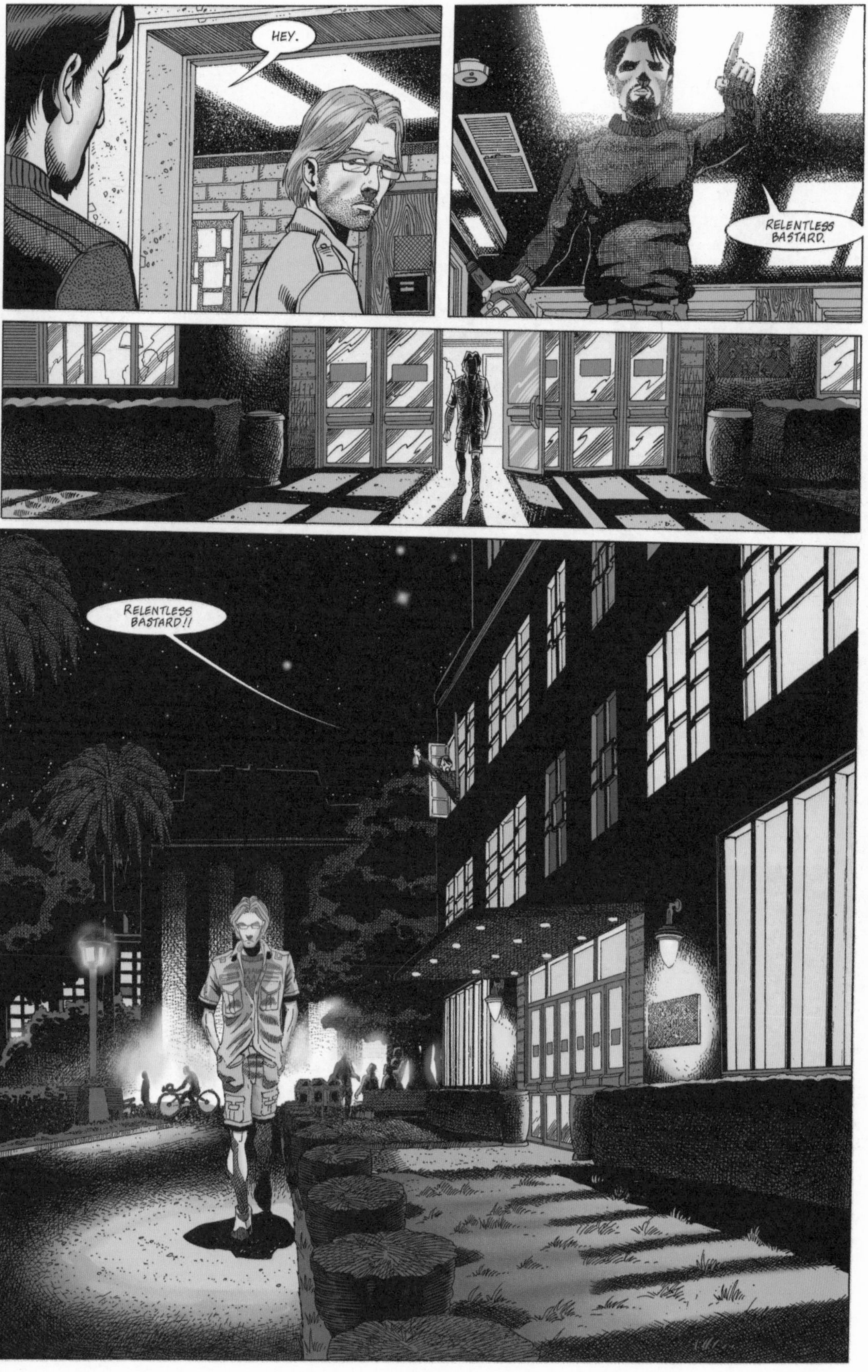
HEY.
RELENTLESS BASTARD.
RELENTLESS BASTARD!!

3

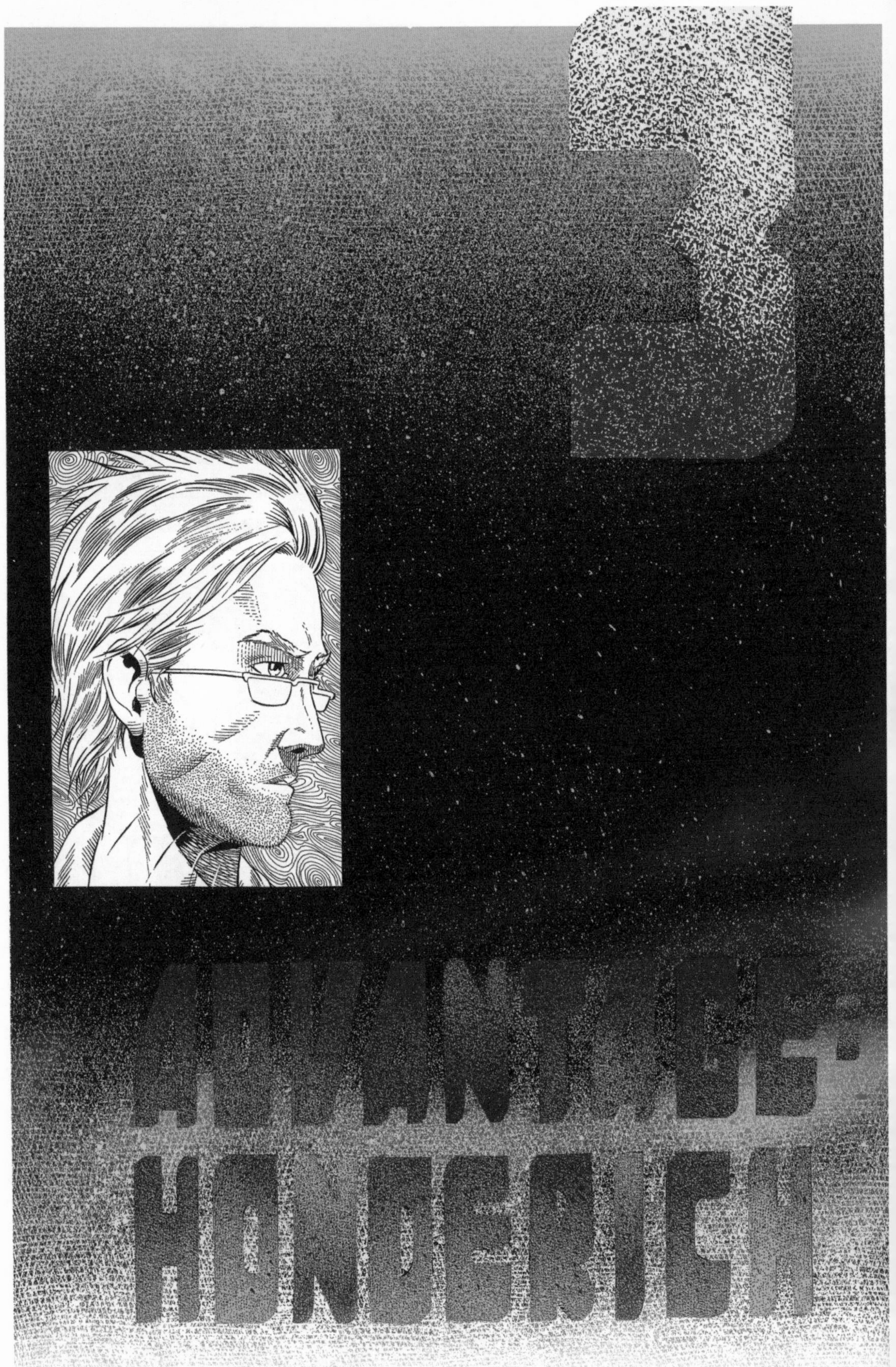

ADVANTAGE: HONDERICH

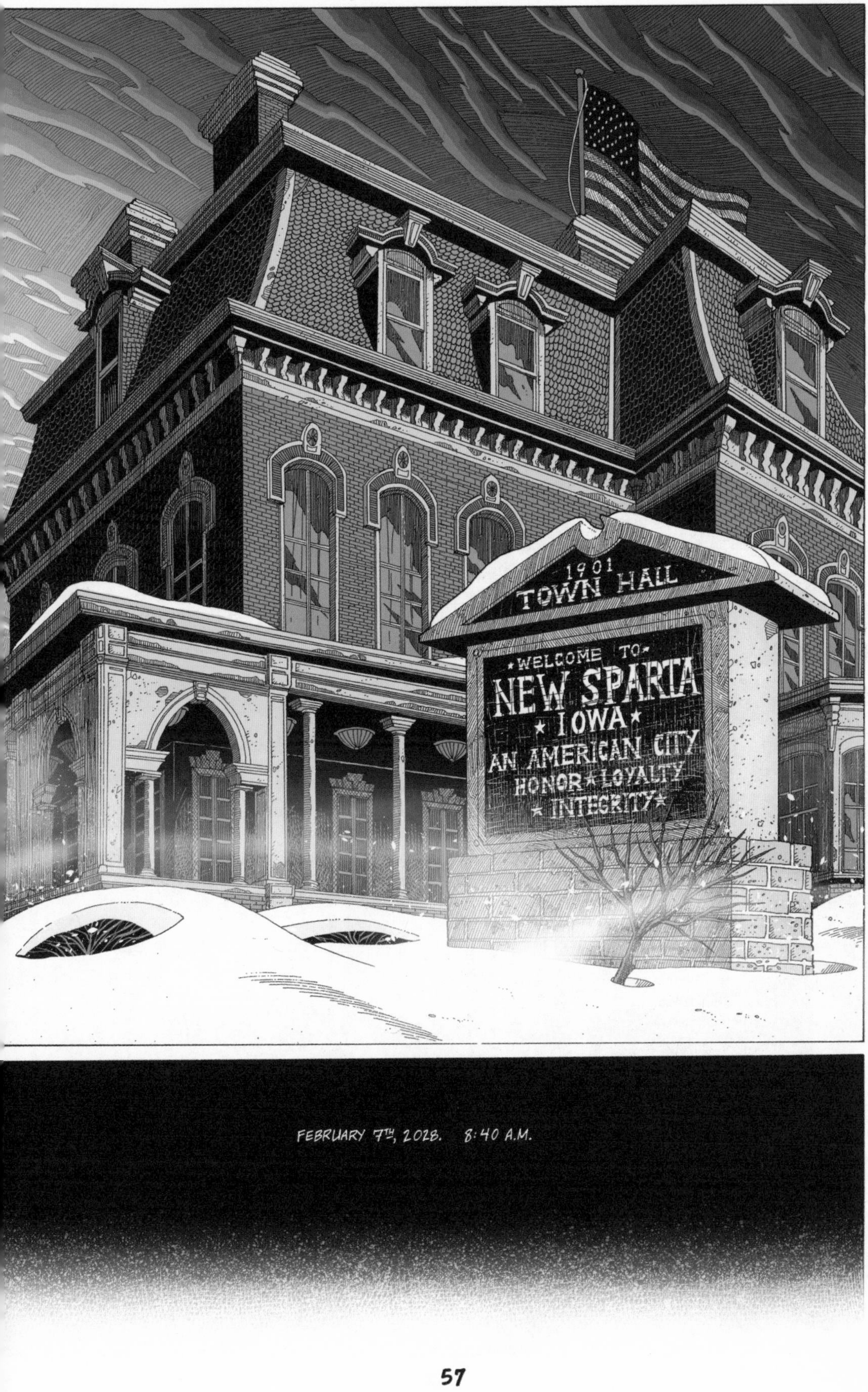
1901
TOWN HALL
WELCOME TO
NEW SPARTA
IOWA
AN AMERICAN CITY
HONOR LOYALTY
INTEGRITY

FEBRUARY 7TH, 2028. 8:40 A.M.

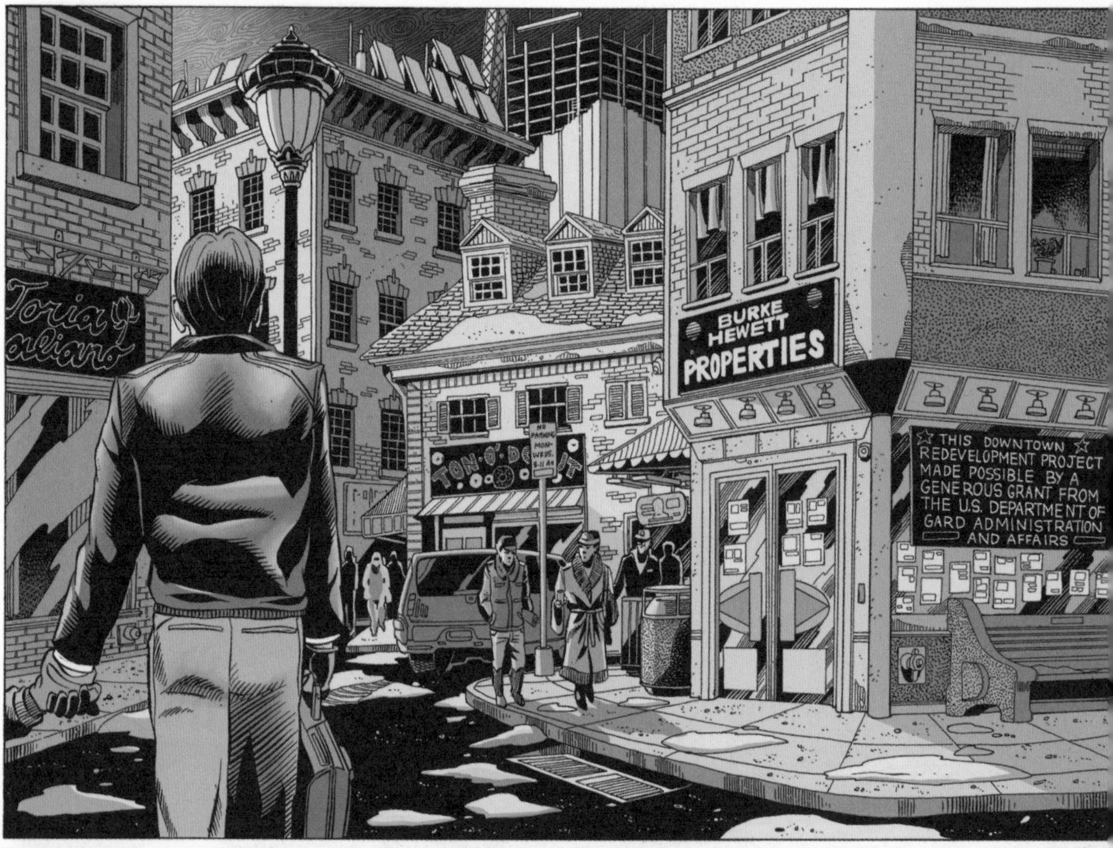
BURKE HEWETT PROPERTIES
THIS DOWNTOWN REDEVELOPMENT PROJECT MADE POSSIBLE BY A GENEROUS GRANT FROM THE U.S. DEPARTMENT OF GARD ADMINISTRATION AND AFFAIRS

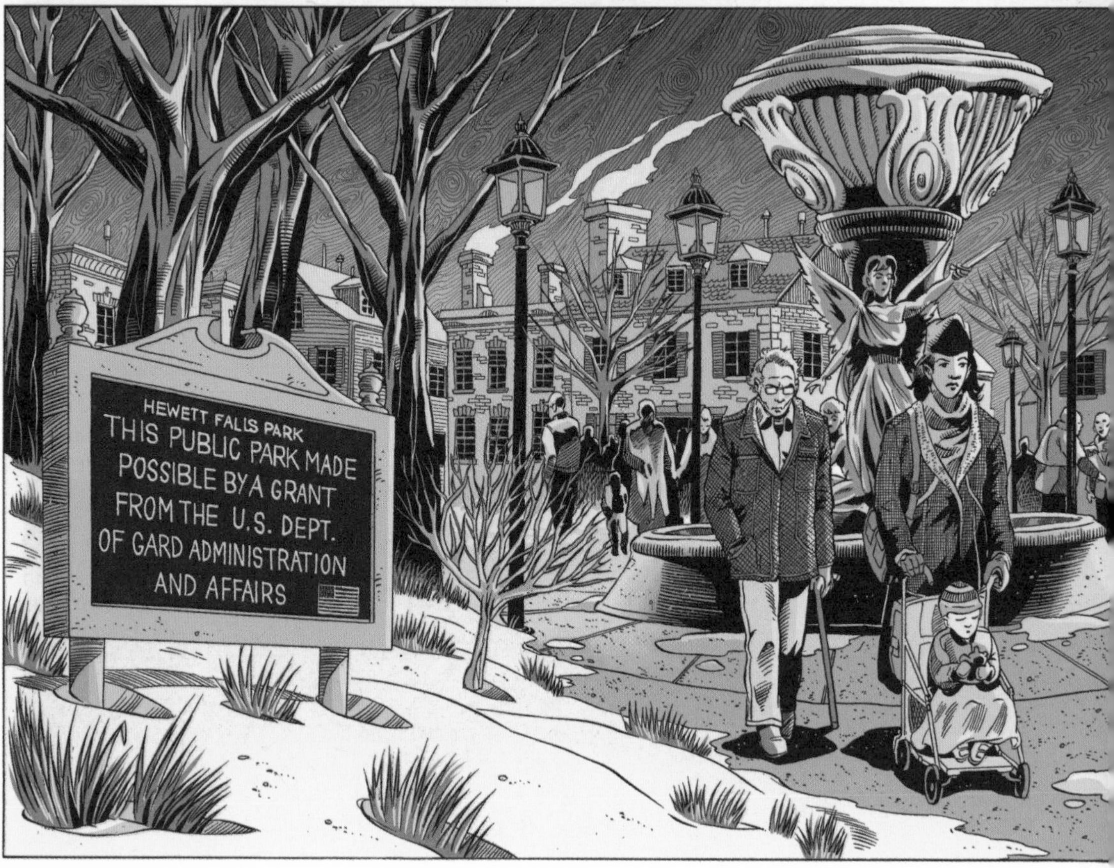
HEWETT FALLS PARK
THIS PUBLIC PARK MADE POSSIBLE BY A GRANT FROM THE U.S. DEPT. OF GARD ADMINISTRATION AND AFFAIRS

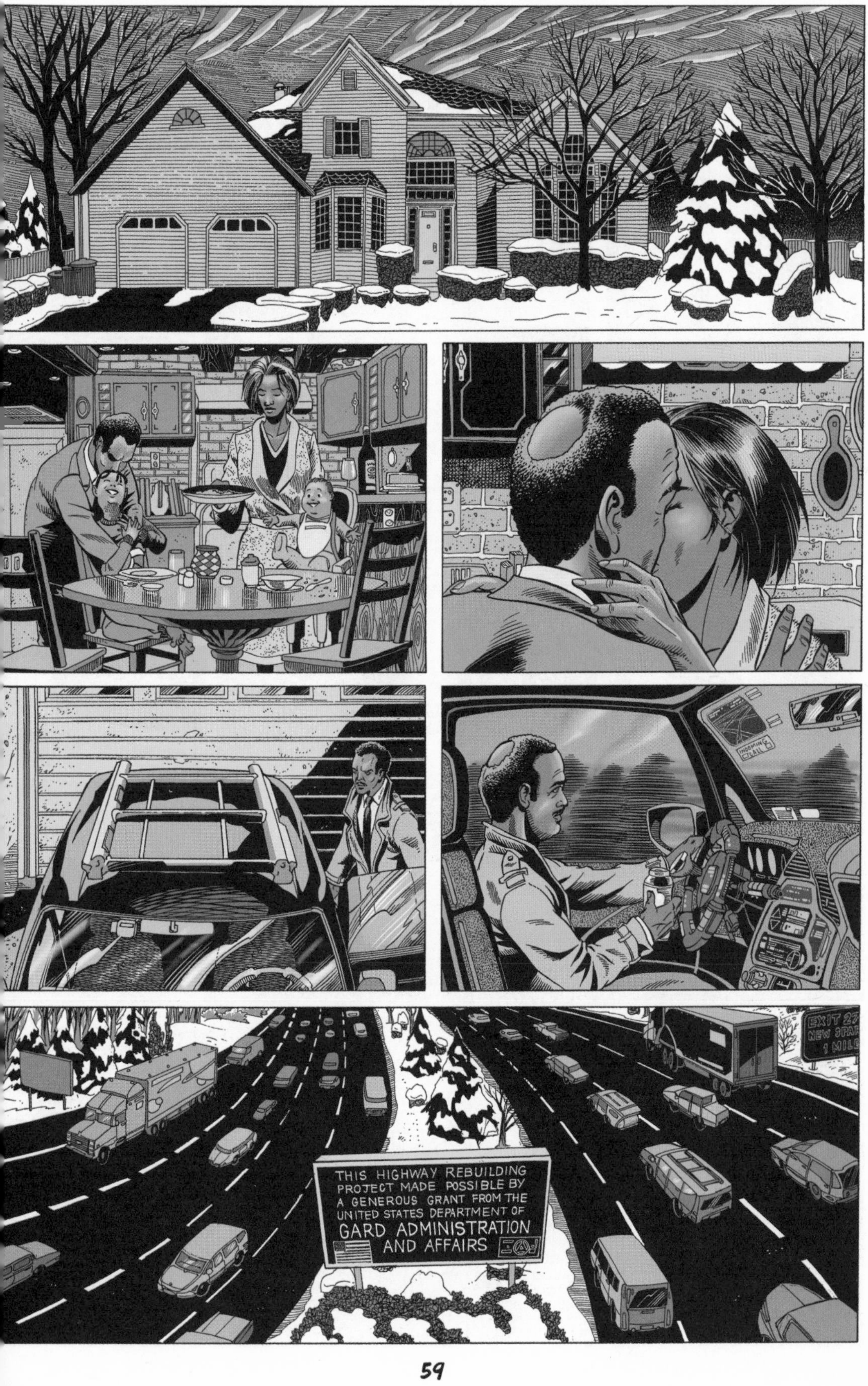
INCOMING CALL
THIS HIGHWAY REBUILDING PROJECT MADE POSSIBLE BY A GENEROUS GRANT FROM THE UNITED STATES DEPARTMENT OF
GARD ADMINISTRATION AND AFFAIRS

LITTLE RAINBOWS DAYCARE CENTER

227

PAULI

LITTLE RAINBOWS
IS MADE POSSIBLE
WITH THE GENEROUS
SUPPORT OF THE
U.S. DEPARTMENT OF
GARD ADMINISTRATION
AND AFFAIRS

IOWA
DKC3303

PAULI
PIT
& SU

DEPENDABLE,
LOVING NANNY
SEEKING PART-
TIME WORK.

PARENTING
SEMINAR:

VIOLIN
LESSONS
SUZUKI

LITTLE
Rainbo
NEWS

60

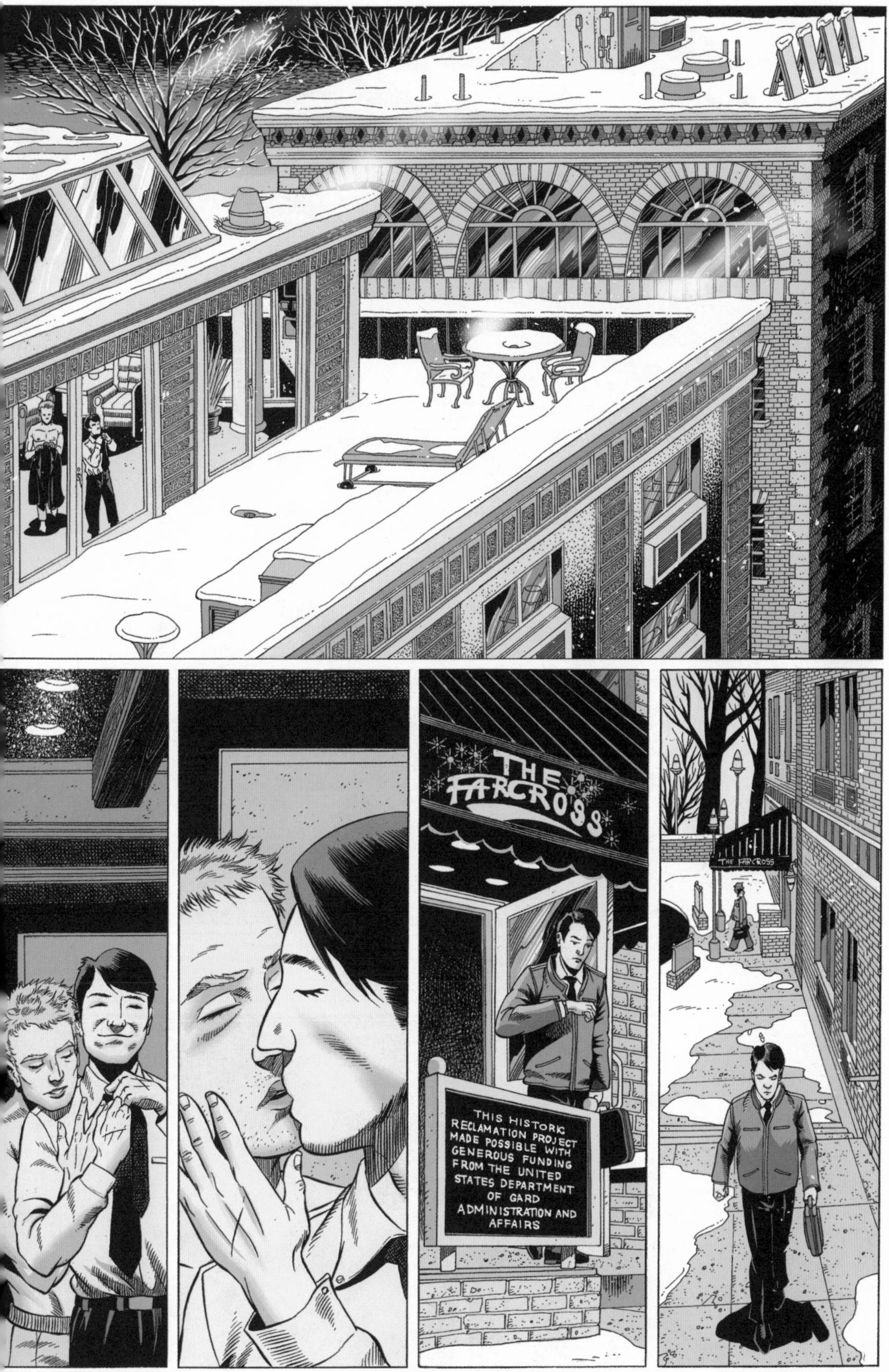
THE FARCROSS
THIS HISTORIC RECLAMATION PROJECT MADE POSSIBLE WITH GENEROUS FUNDING FROM THE UNITED STATES DEPARTMENT OF GARD ADMINISTRATION AND AFFAIRS
THE FARCROSS

PARKING DECK 7B

IOTA CLASS PERMITS ONLY

ALPHA CLASS PERMITS ONLY

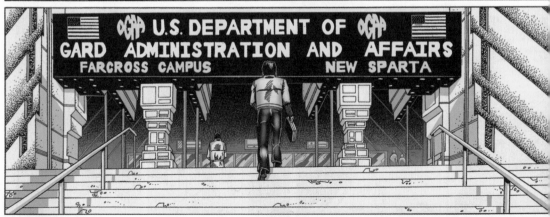

U.S. DEPARTMENT OF GARD ADMINISTRATION AND AFFAIRS

FARCROSS CAMPUS   NEW SPARTA

B WING
CAFETERIA
C LABS

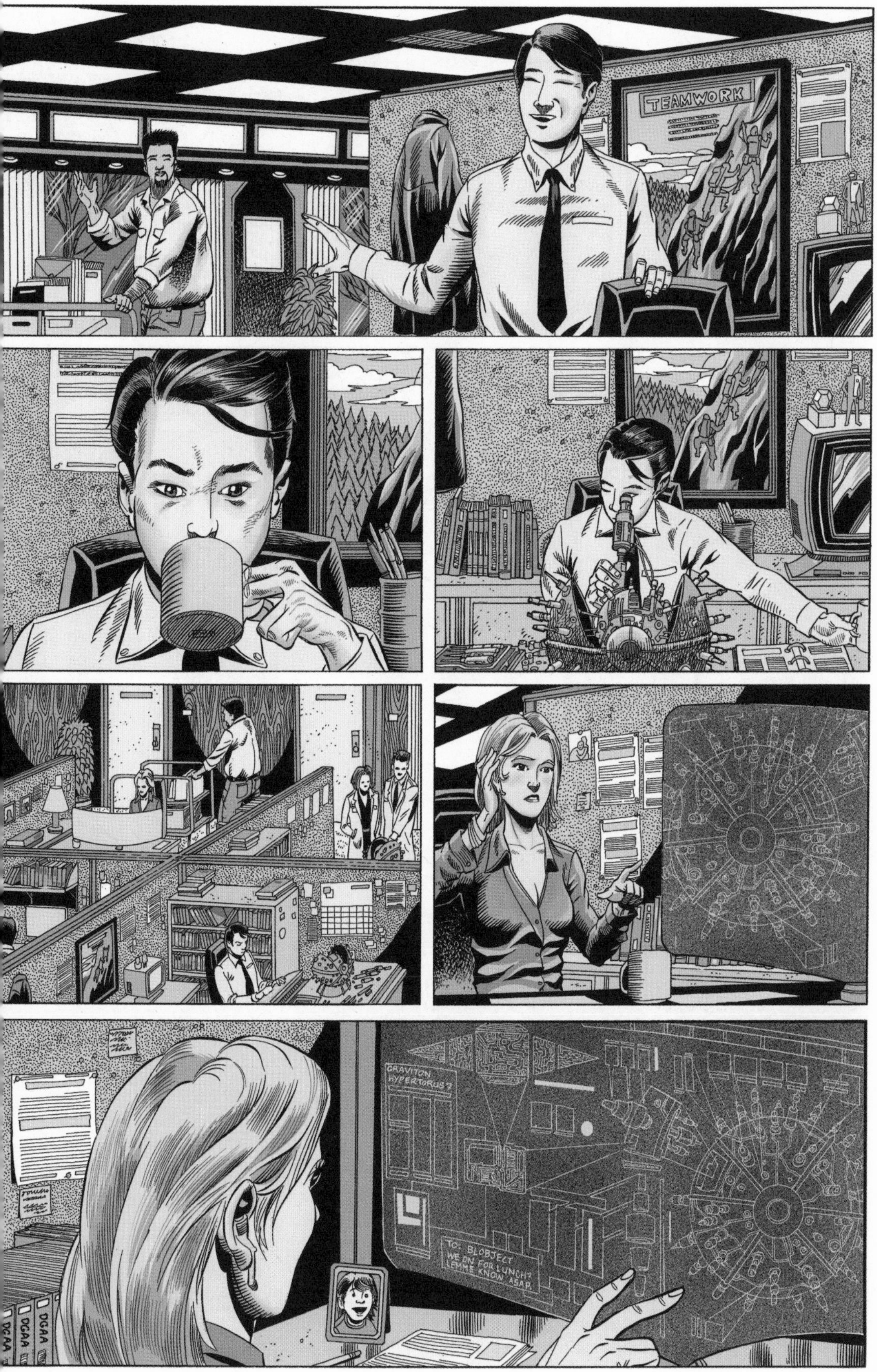
TEAMWORK
GRAVITON HYPERTORUS?
TO: BLOBJECT
WE ON FOR LUNCH?
LEMME KNOW ASAP.
DGAA
DGAA
DGAA

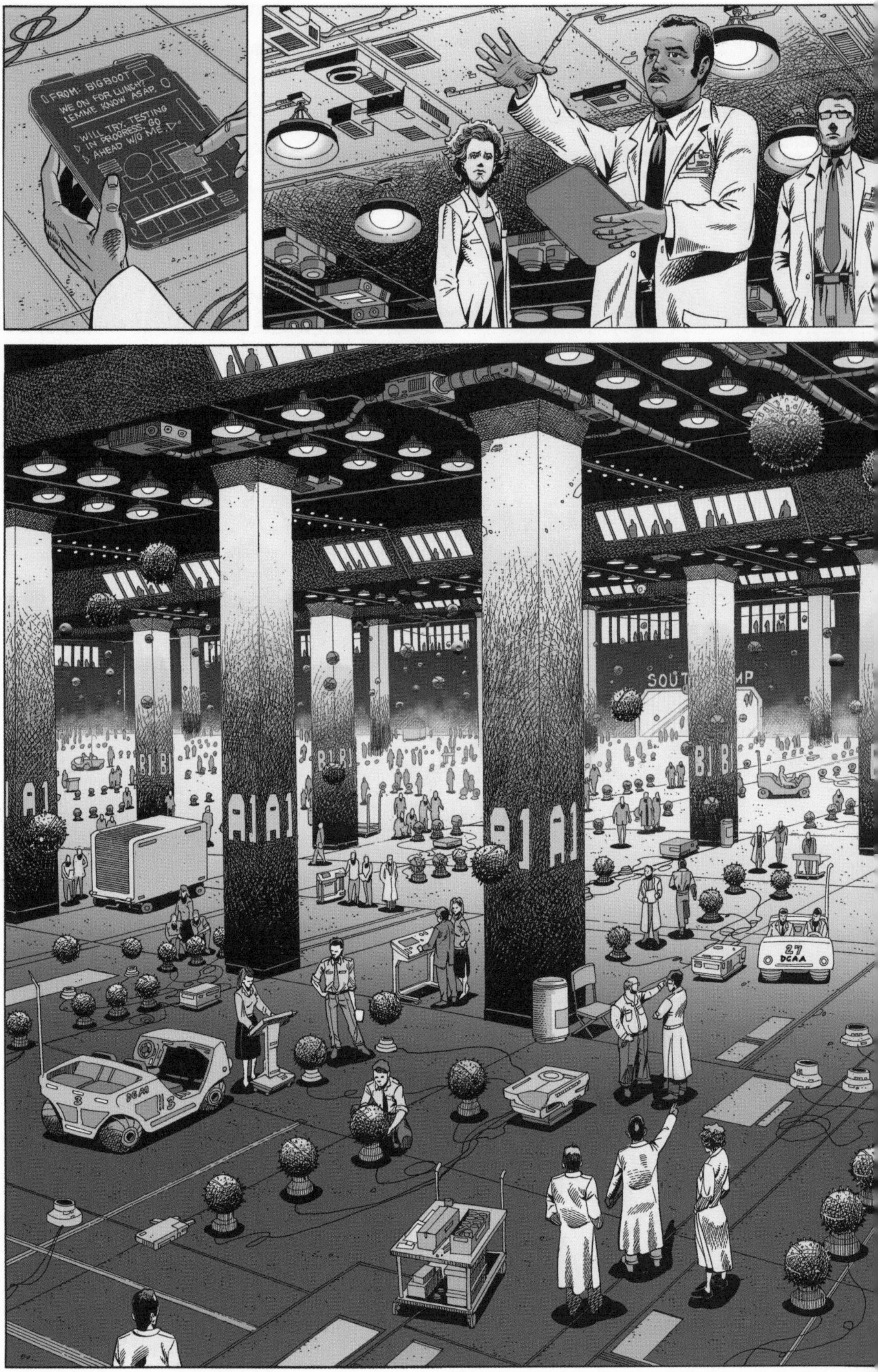
FROM: BIGBOOT
WE ON FOR LUNCH? LEMME KNOW ASAP.
WILL TRY. TESTING IN PROGRESS. GO AHEAD W/O ME.
SOUT
MP
B1 B1
A1 A1
27 DGAA
DGAA 3

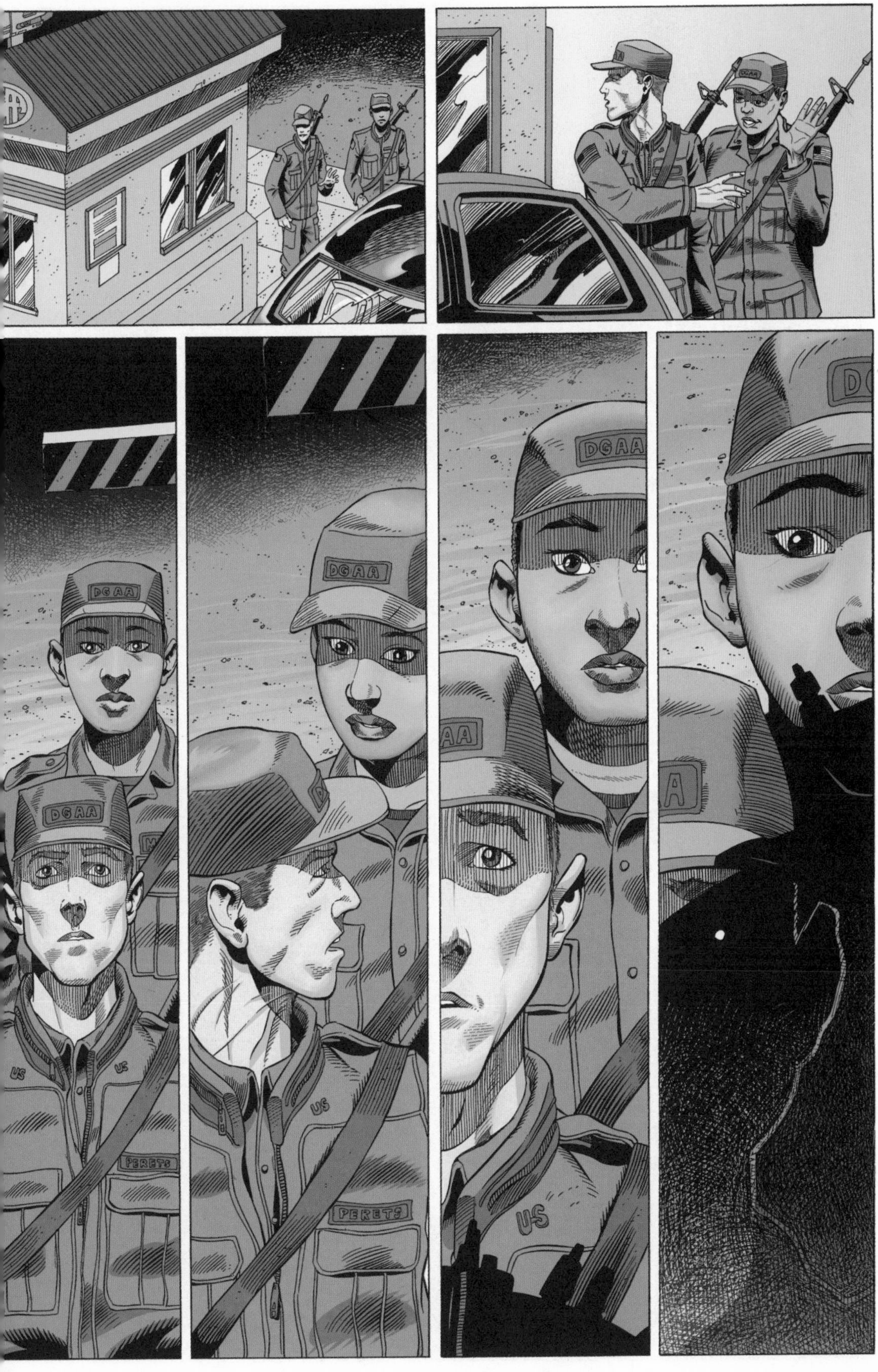
DGAA
PERETS
US

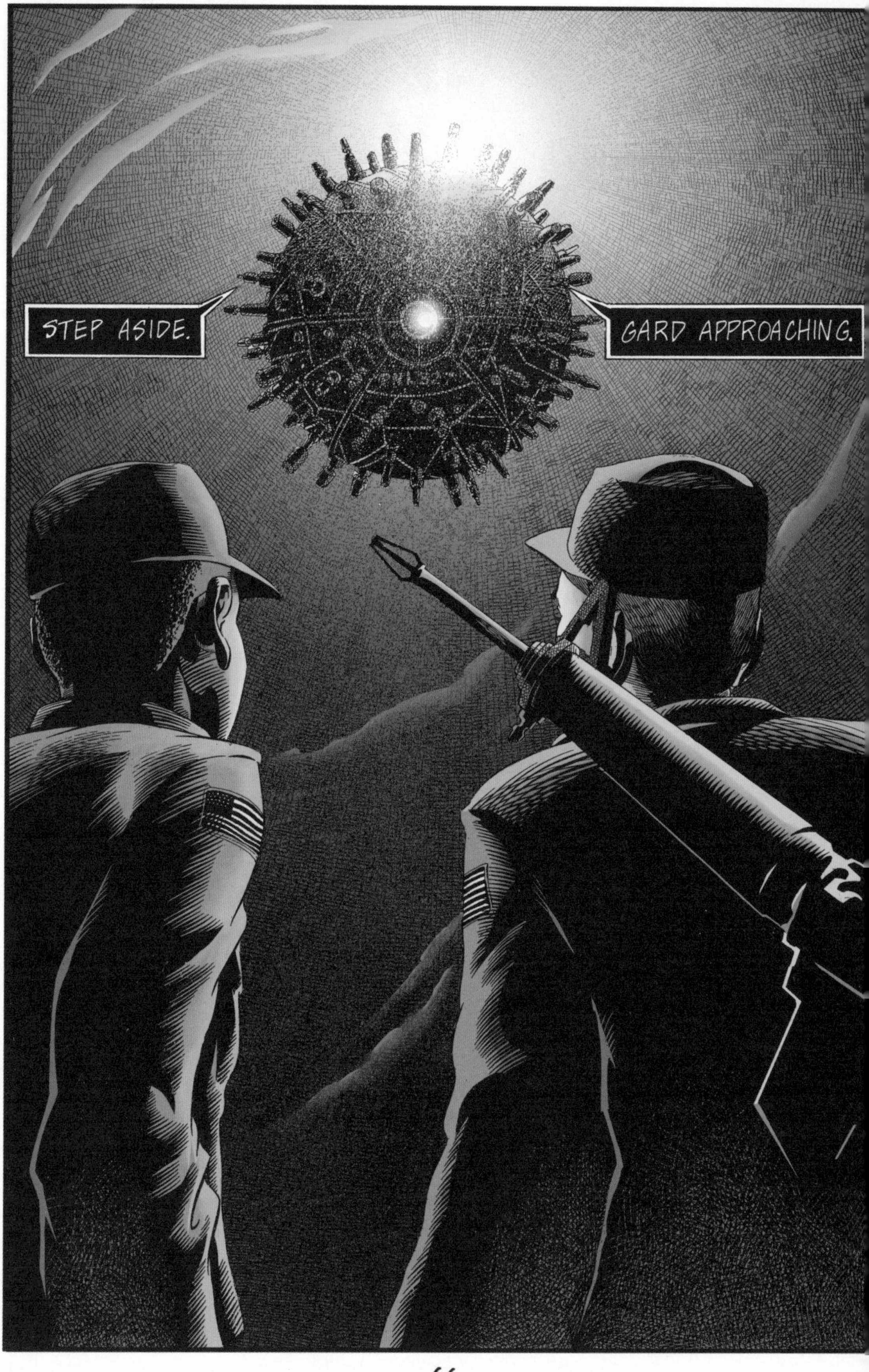
STEP ASIDE.
GARD APPROACHING.

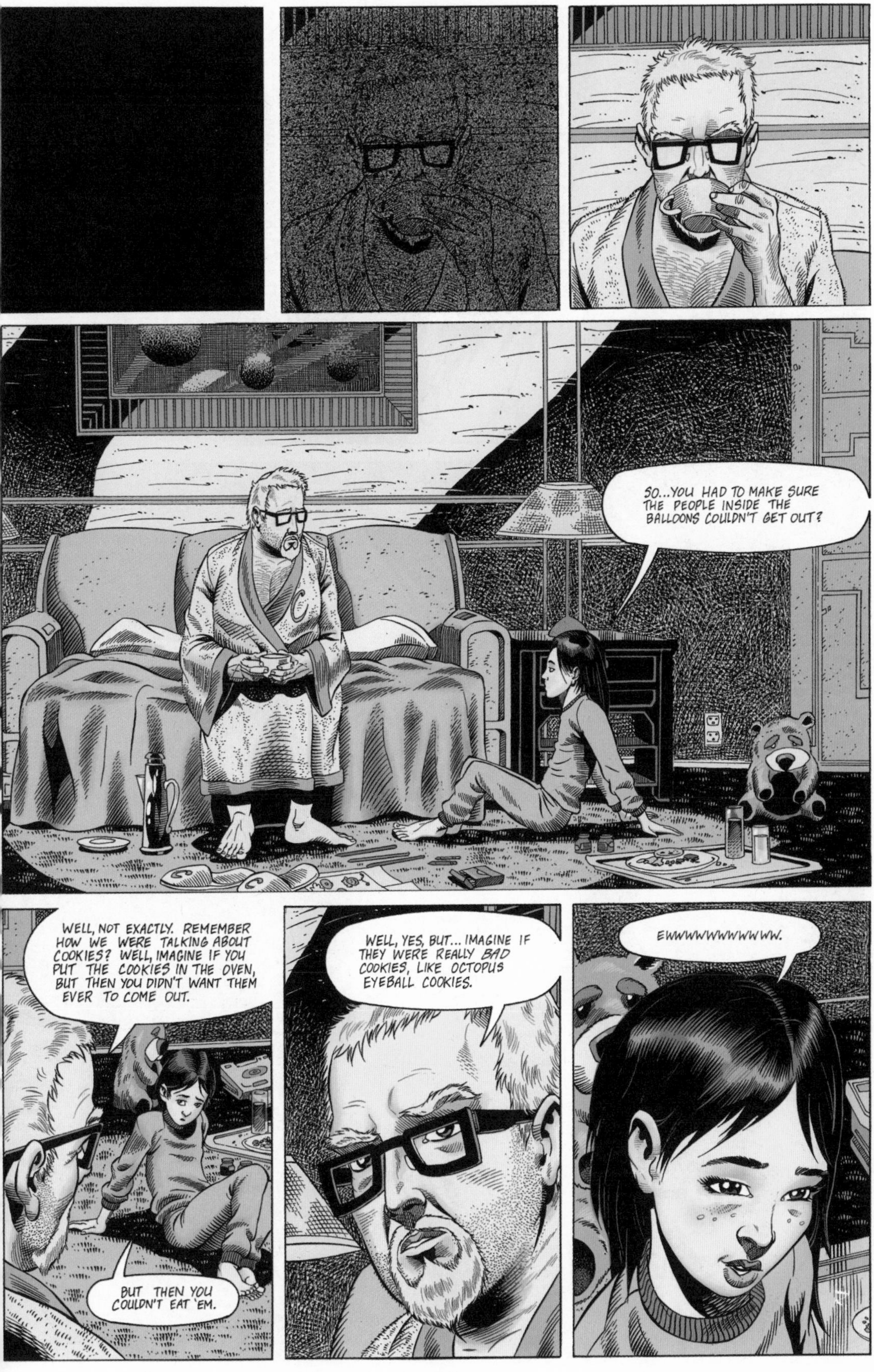
SO...YOU HAD TO MAKE SURE THE PEOPLE INSIDE THE BALLOONS COULDN'T GET OUT?
WELL, NOT EXACTLY. REMEMBER HOW WE WERE TALKING ABOUT COOKIES? WELL, IMAGINE IF YOU PUT THE COOKIES IN THE OVEN, BUT THEN YOU DIDN'T WANT THEM EVER TO COME OUT.
BUT THEN YOU COULDN'T EAT 'EM.
WELL, YES, BUT... IMAGINE IF THEY WERE REALLY *BAD* COOKIES, LIKE OCTOPUS EYEBALL COOKIES.
EWWWWWWWWWWW.

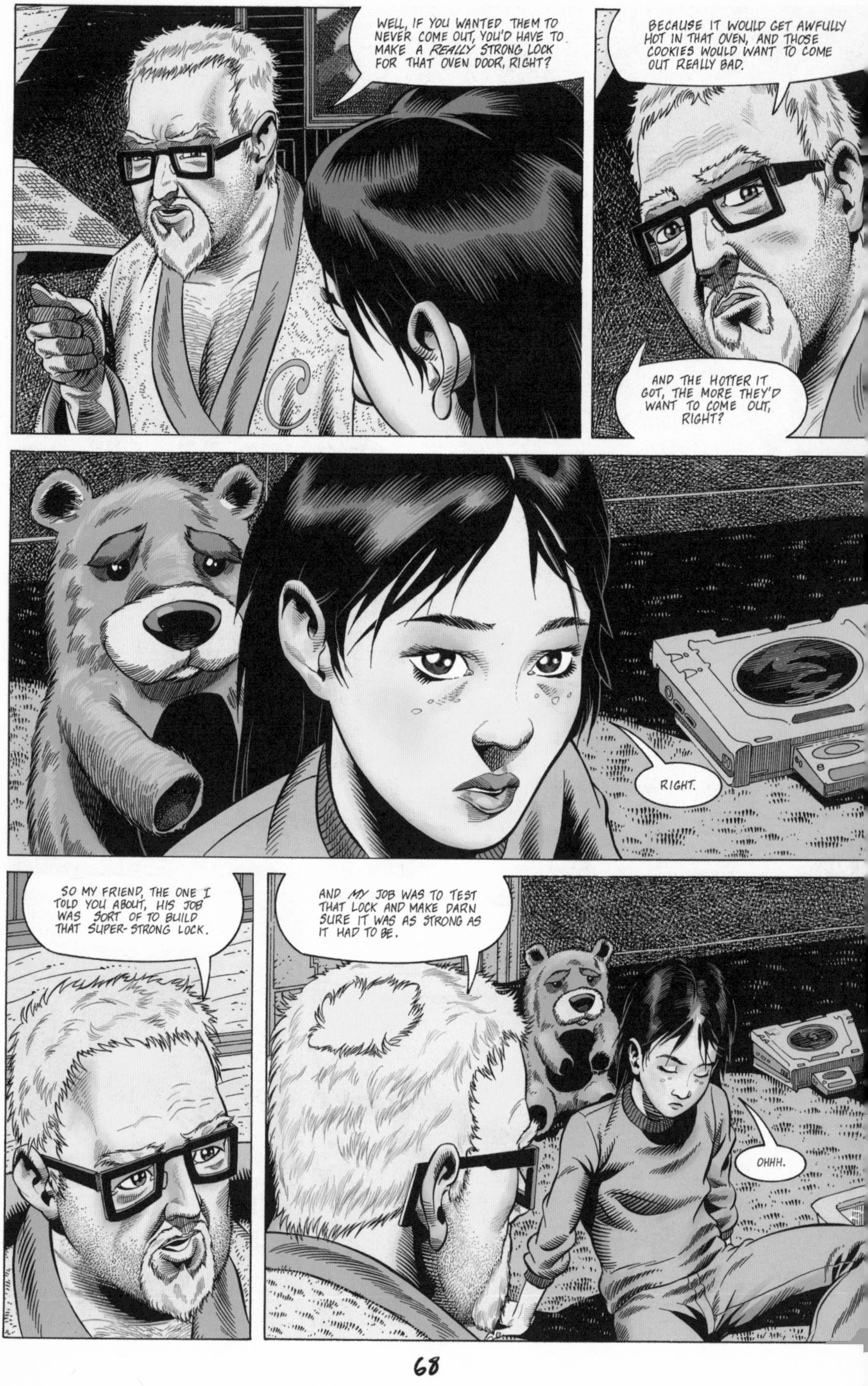
WELL, IF YOU WANTED THEM TO NEVER COME OUT, YOU'D HAVE TO MAKE A *REALLY* STRONG LOCK FOR THAT OVEN DOOR, RIGHT?
BECAUSE IT WOULD GET AWFULLY HOT IN THAT OVEN, AND THOSE COOKIES WOULD WANT TO COME OUT REALLY BAD.
AND THE HOTTER IT GOT, THE MORE THEY'D WANT TO COME OUT, RIGHT?
RIGHT.
SO MY FRIEND, THE ONE I TOLD YOU ABOUT, HIS JOB WAS SORT OF TO BUILD THAT SUPER-STRONG LOCK.
AND *MY* JOB WAS TO TEST THAT LOCK AND MAKE DARN SURE IT WAS AS STRONG AS IT HAD TO BE.
OHHH.

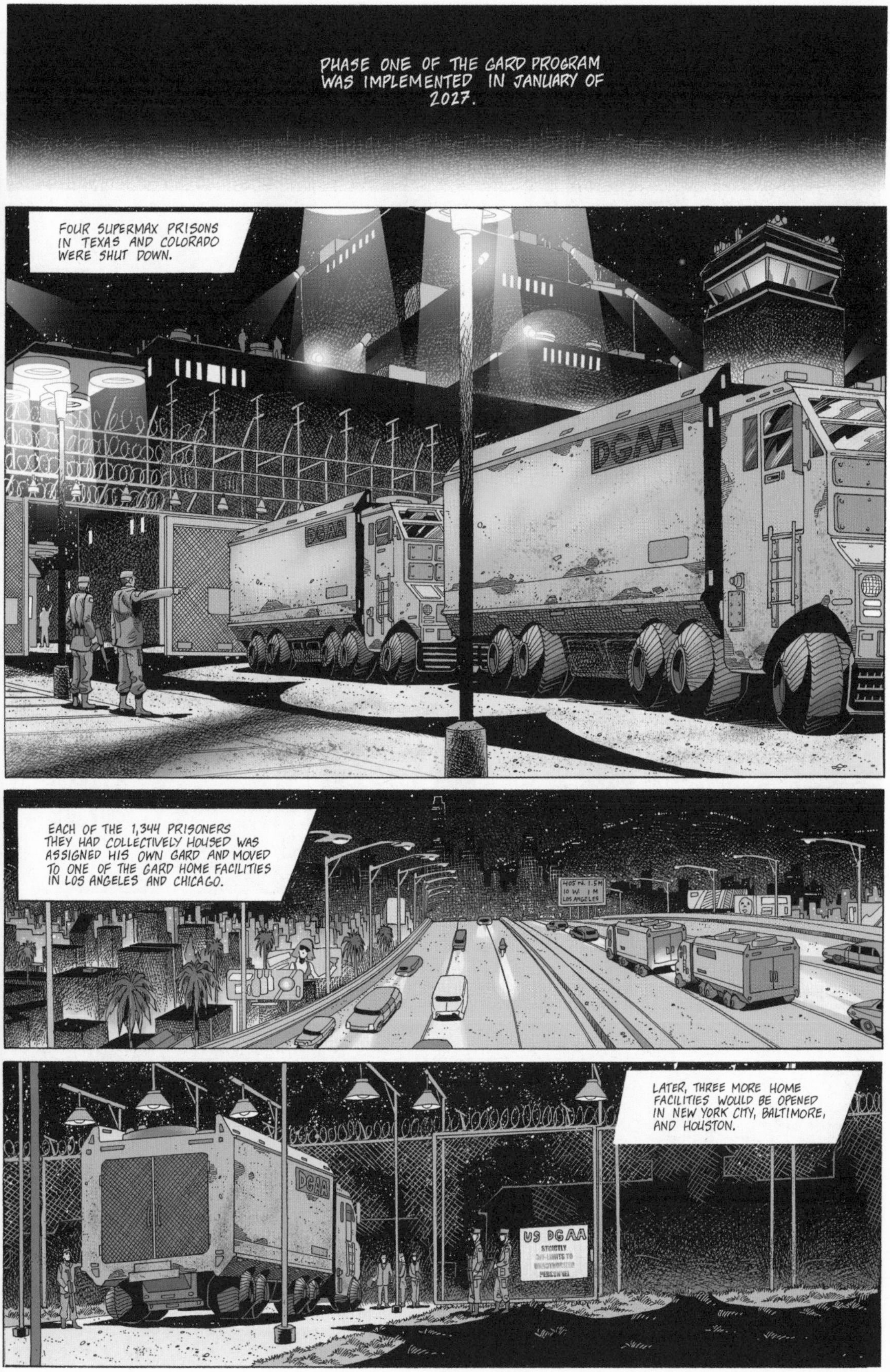
PHASE ONE OF THE GARD PROGRAM WAS IMPLEMENTED IN JANUARY OF 2027.
FOUR SUPERMAX PRISONS IN TEXAS AND COLORADO WERE SHUT DOWN.
DGAA
DGAA
EACH OF THE 1,344 PRISONERS THEY HAD COLLECTIVELY HOUSED WAS ASSIGNED HIS OWN GARD AND MOVED TO ONE OF THE GARD HOME FACILITIES IN LOS ANGELES AND CHICAGO.
LATER, THREE MORE HOME FACILITIES WOULD BE OPENED IN NEW YORK CITY, BALTIMORE, AND HOUSTON.
DGAA
US DGAA
STRICTLY

THE DENIZENS OF THESE TOWNS (AND TO A LESSER EXTENT OF THE ENTIRE NATION) WERE TREATED TO A MASSIVE ELECTRONIC AND PRINT AD CAMPAIGN EXPLAINING WHAT THE GARDS WERE, HOW THEIR POWER CELLS WERE AMPLE TO OUTLAST ANY LIFE SENTENCE, AND WHY THEY AND THE PRISONERS THEY WERE CHARGED WITH WERE OF NO POSSIBLE DANGER TO ORDINARY CITIZENS.

NATI (THE NEW APPROACH TO INCARCERATION) WAS HAILED AS A MARKED IMPROVEMENT, FISCALLY AND MORALLY, OVER THE OLD SYSTEM.

OVER THE COURSE OF YEARS, IT WAS VASTLY LESS EXPENSIVE TO HOUSE PRISONERS IN THIS WAY.

AND THE PRISONERS WOULD ACTUALLY BE ABLE TO MOVE ABOUT IN SOCIETY, TO WORK AND BETTER THEMSELVES.

AND THERE WAS VASTLY LESS DANGER OF HUMAN GUARDS AND PRISON PERSONNEL BEING HURT OR KILLED IN PRISON RIOTS OR OTHER EPISODES -- THE HUMAN PERSONNEL WERE SIMPLY BEING PHASED OUT ALTOGETHER.

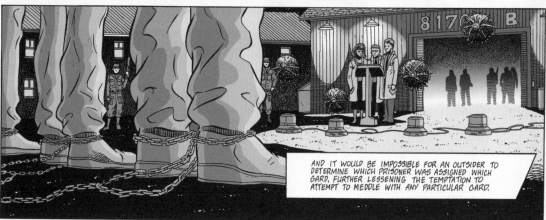

AND IT WOULD BE IMPOSSIBLE FOR AN OUTSIDER TO DETERMINE WHICH PRISONER WAS ASSIGNED WHICH GARD, FURTHER LESSENING THE TEMPTATION TO ATTEMPT TO MEDDLE WITH ANY PARTICULAR GARD.

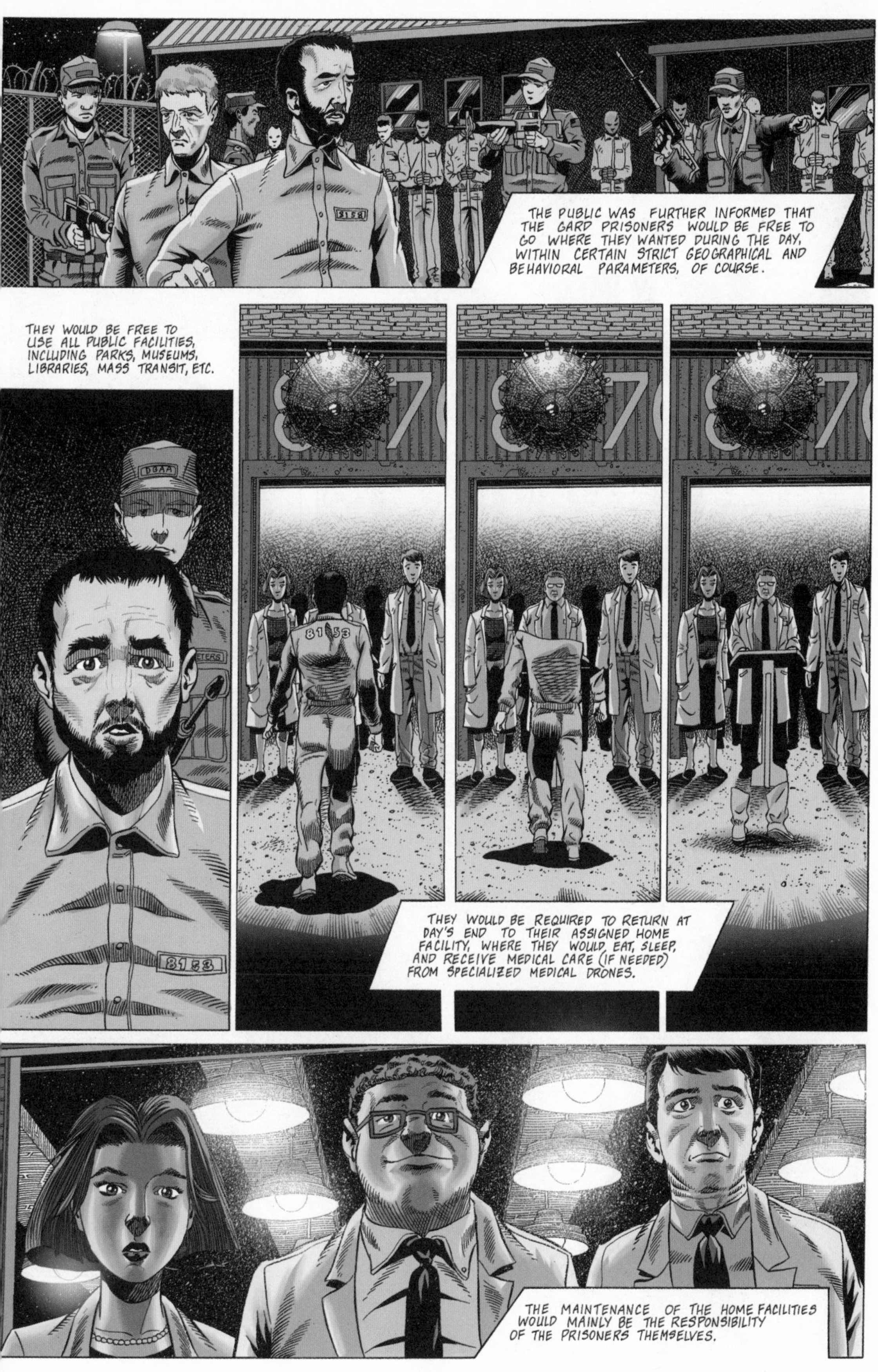
THE PUBLIC WAS FURTHER INFORMED THAT THE GARD PRISONERS WOULD BE FREE TO GO WHERE THEY WANTED DURING THE DAY, WITHIN CERTAIN STRICT GEOGRAPHICAL AND BEHAVIORAL PARAMETERS, OF COURSE.
THEY WOULD BE FREE TO USE ALL PUBLIC FACILITIES, INCLUDING PARKS, MUSEUMS, LIBRARIES, MASS TRANSIT, ETC.
THEY WOULD BE REQUIRED TO RETURN AT DAY'S END TO THEIR ASSIGNED HOME FACILITY, WHERE THEY WOULD EAT, SLEEP, AND RECEIVE MEDICAL CARE (IF NEEDED) FROM SPECIALIZED MEDICAL DRONES.
THE MAINTENANCE OF THE HOME FACILITIES WOULD MAINLY BE THE RESPONSIBILITY OF THE PRISONERS THEMSELVES.

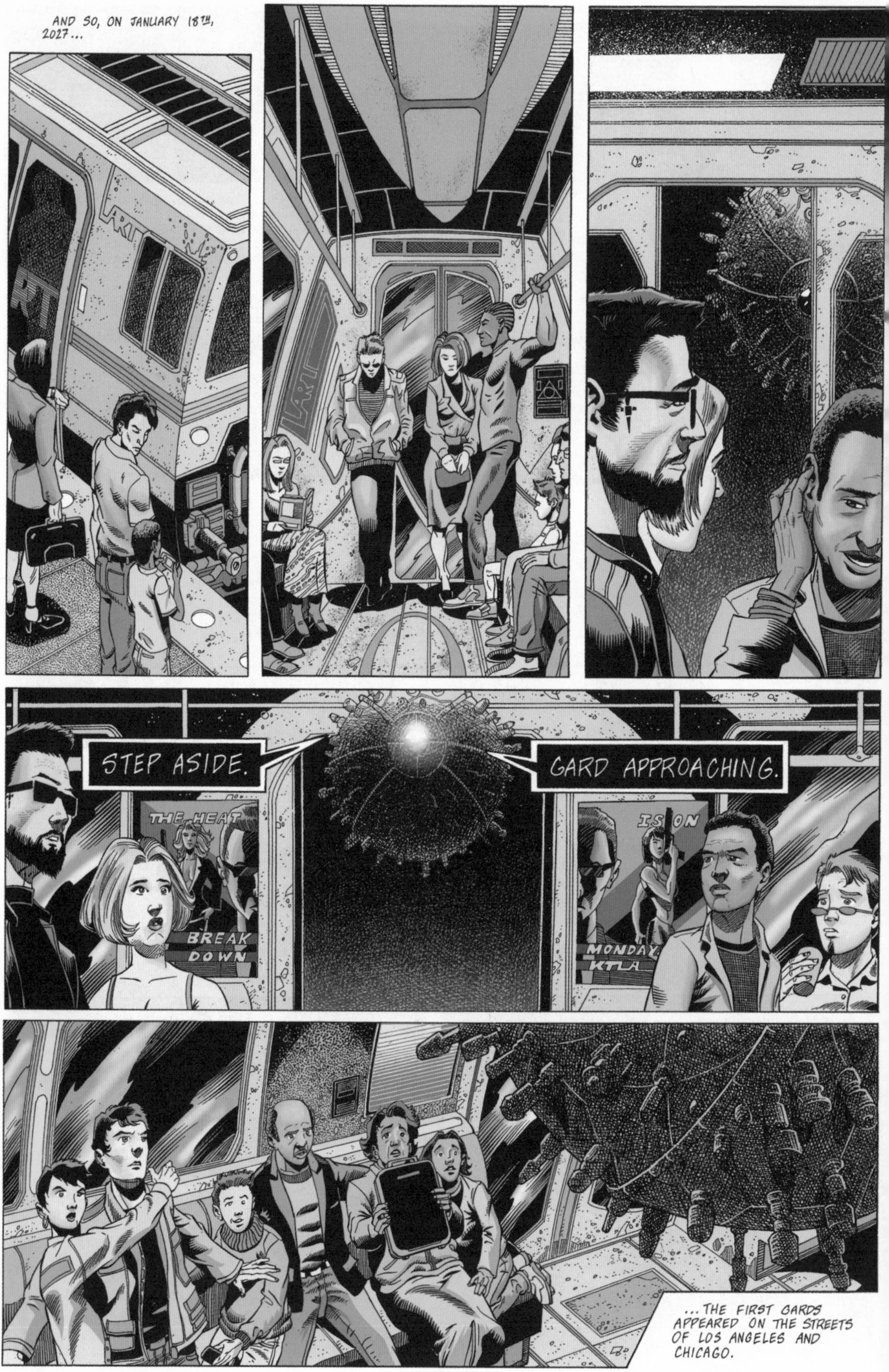
AND SO, ON JANUARY 18TH, 2027...
STEP ASIDE.
GARD APPROACHING.
THE HEAT
IS ON
BREAK DOWN
MONDAY
KTLA
...THE FIRST GARDS APPEARED ON THE STREETS OF LOS ANGELES AND CHICAGO.

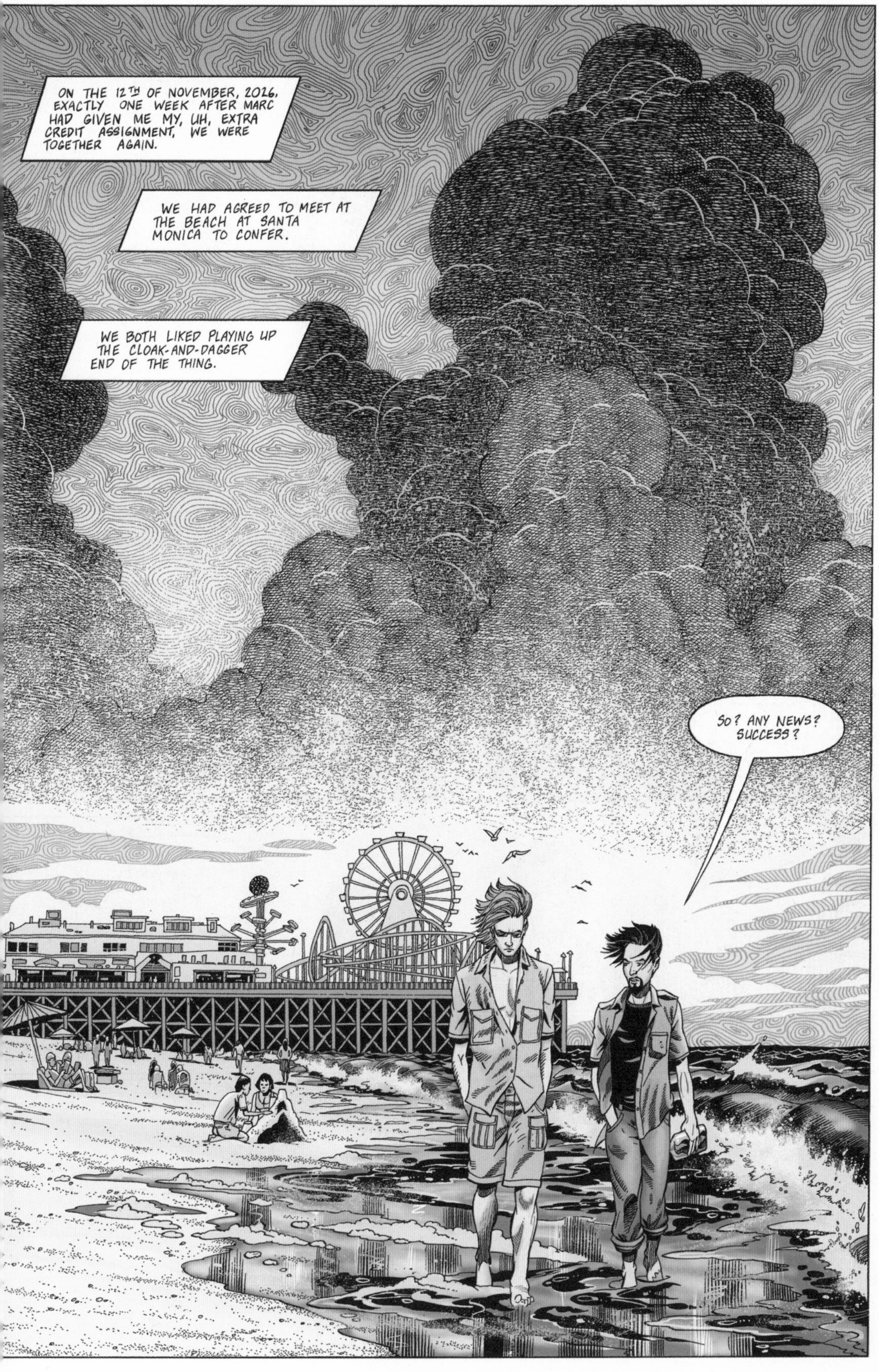
ON THE 12TH OF NOVEMBER, 2016, EXACTLY ONE WEEK AFTER MARC HAD GIVEN ME MY, UH, EXTRA CREDIT ASSIGNMENT, WE WERE TOGETHER AGAIN.
WE HAD AGREED TO MEET AT THE BEACH AT SANTA MONICA TO CONFER.
WE BOTH LIKED PLAYING UP THE CLOAK-AND-DAGGER END OF THE THING.
SO? ANY NEWS? SUCCESS?

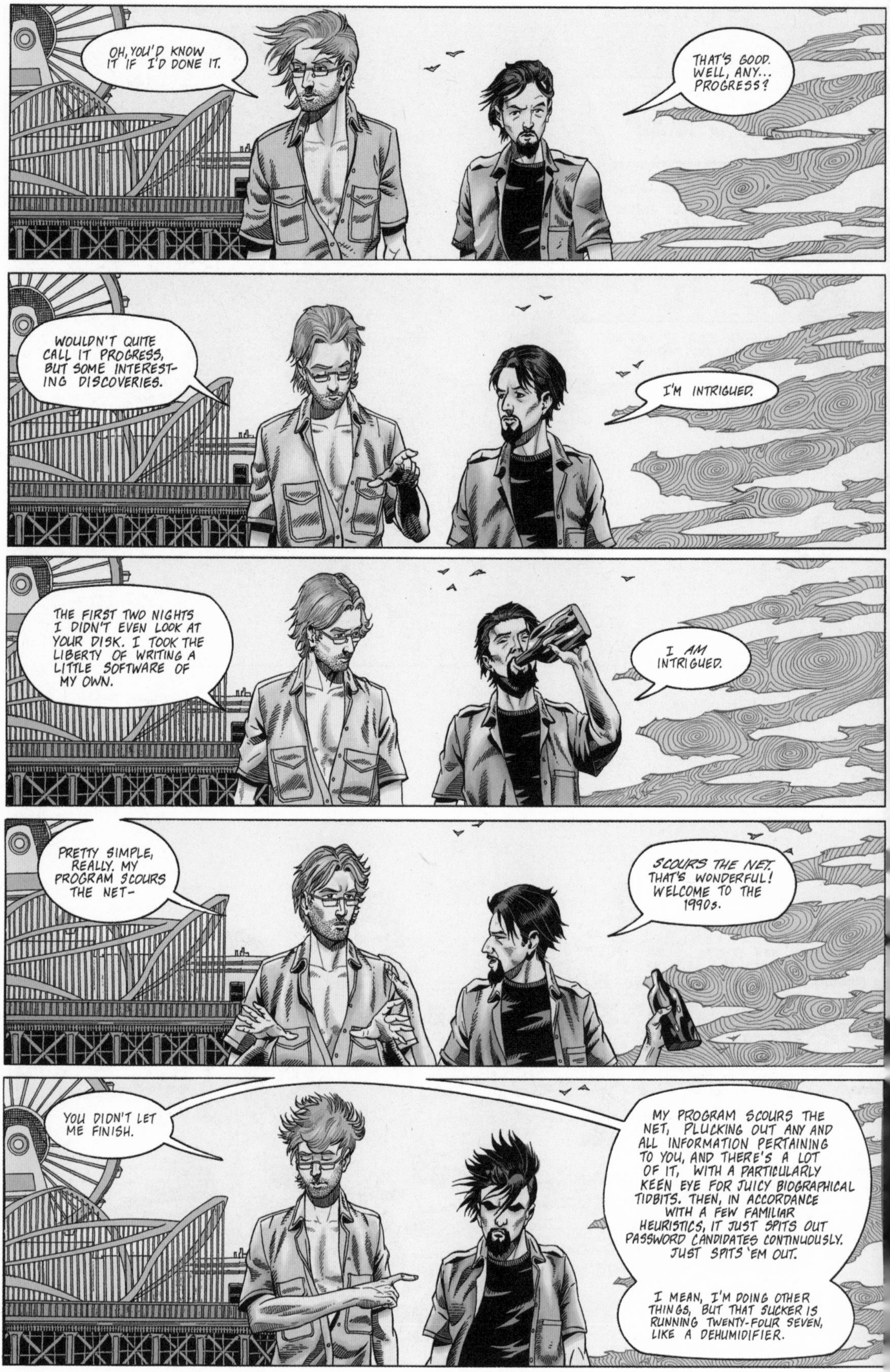
OH, YOU'D KNOW IT IF I'D DONE IT.
THAT'S GOOD. WELL, ANY... PROGRESS?
WOULDN'T QUITE CALL IT PROGRESS, BUT SOME INTERESTING DISCOVERIES.
I'M INTRIGUED.
THE FIRST TWO NIGHTS I DIDN'T EVEN LOOK AT YOUR DISK. I TOOK THE LIBERTY OF WRITING A LITTLE SOFTWARE OF MY OWN.
I AM INTRIGUED.
PRETTY SIMPLE, REALLY. MY PROGRAM SCOURS THE NET-
SCOURS THE NET. THAT'S WONDERFUL! WELCOME TO THE 1990s.
YOU DIDN'T LET ME FINISH.
MY PROGRAM SCOURS THE NET, PLUCKING OUT ANY AND ALL INFORMATION PERTAINING TO YOU, AND THERE'S A LOT OF IT, WITH A PARTICULARLY KEEN EYE FOR JUICY BIOGRAPHICAL TIDBITS. THEN, IN ACCORDANCE WITH A FEW FAMILIAR HEURISTICS, IT JUST SPITS OUT PASSWORD CANDIDATES CONTINUOUSLY. JUST SPITS 'EM OUT.
I MEAN, I'M DOING OTHER THINGS, BUT THAT SUCKER IS RUNNING TWENTY-FOUR SEVEN, LIKE A DEHUMIDIFIER.

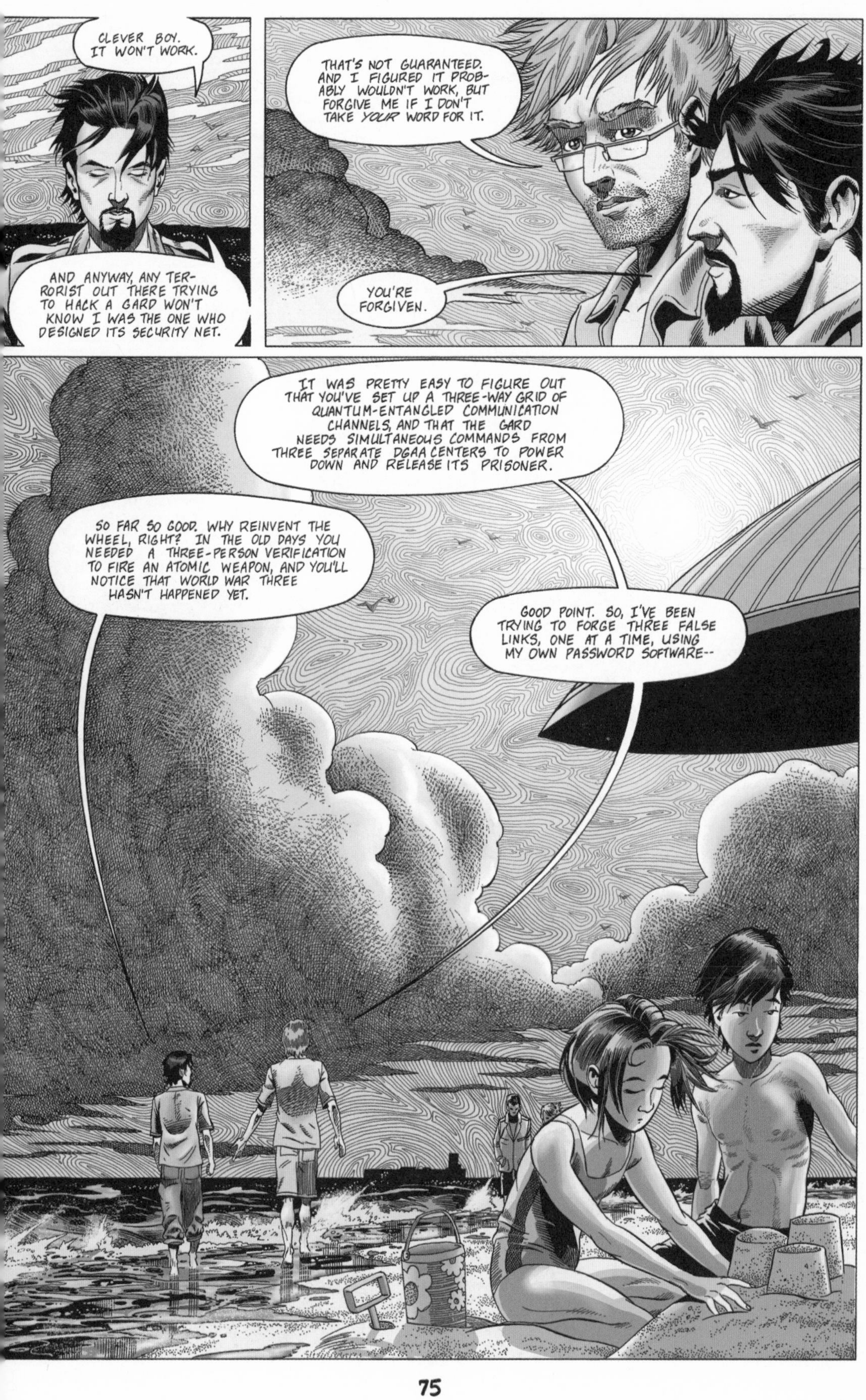
CLEVER BOY. IT WON'T WORK.
THAT'S NOT GUARANTEED. AND I FIGURED IT PROBABLY WOULDN'T WORK, BUT FORGIVE ME IF I DON'T TAKE YOUR WORD FOR IT.
AND ANYWAY, ANY TERRORIST OUT THERE TRYING TO HACK A GARD WON'T KNOW I WAS THE ONE WHO DESIGNED ITS SECURITY NET.
YOU'RE FORGIVEN.
IT WAS PRETTY EASY TO FIGURE OUT THAT YOU'VE SET UP A THREE-WAY GRID OF QUANTUM-ENTANGLED COMMUNICATION CHANNELS, AND THAT THE GARD NEEDS SIMULTANEOUS COMMANDS FROM THREE SEPARATE DGAA CENTERS TO POWER DOWN AND RELEASE ITS PRISONER.
SO FAR SO GOOD. WHY REINVENT THE WHEEL, RIGHT? IN THE OLD DAYS YOU NEEDED A THREE-PERSON VERIFICATION TO FIRE AN ATOMIC WEAPON, AND YOU'LL NOTICE THAT WORLD WAR THREE HASN'T HAPPENED YET.
GOOD POINT. SO, I'VE BEEN TRYING TO FORGE THREE FALSE LINKS, ONE AT A TIME, USING MY OWN PASSWORD SOFTWARE--

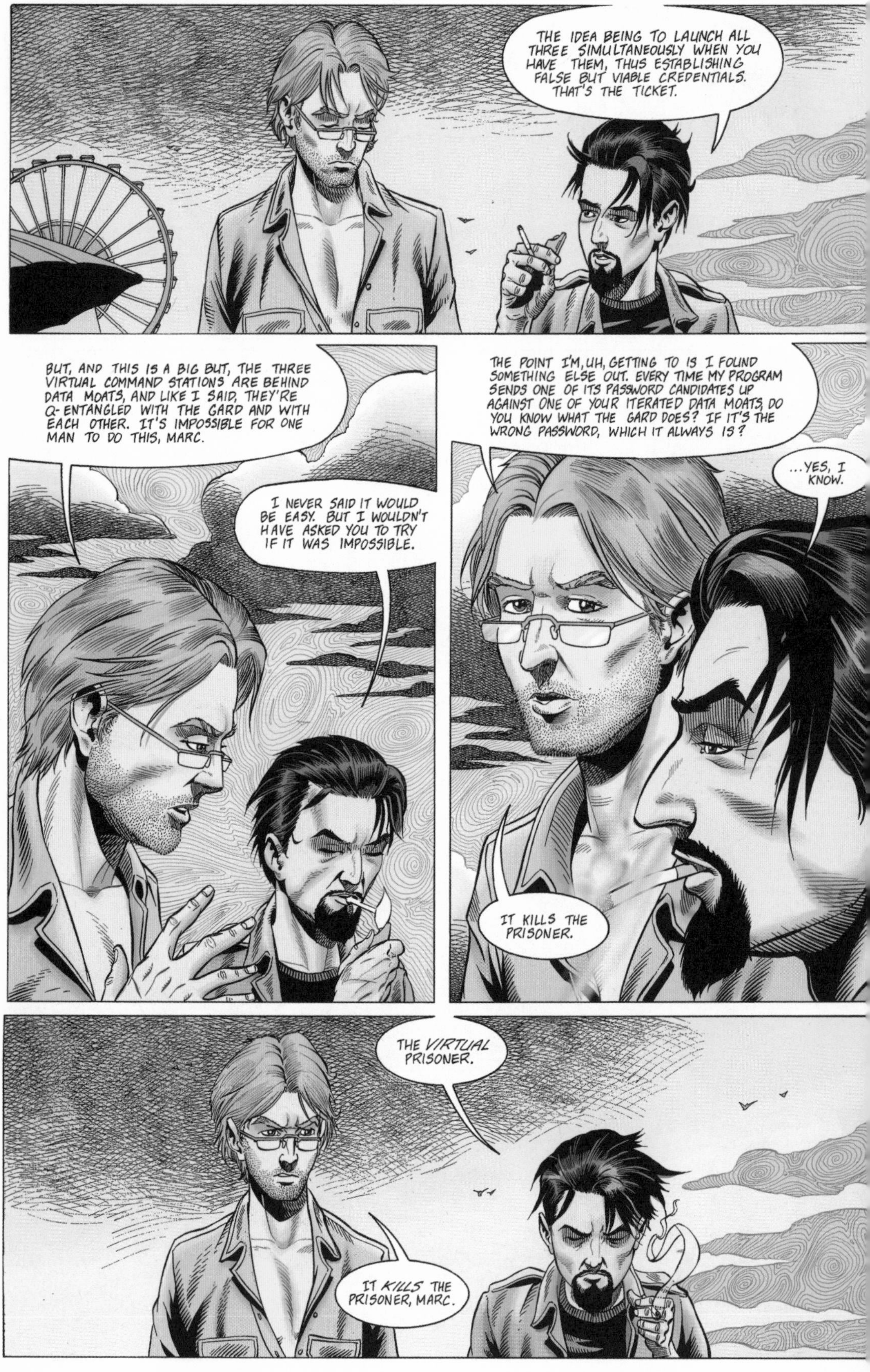
THE IDEA BEING TO LAUNCH ALL THREE SIMULTANEOUSLY WHEN YOU HAVE THEM, THUS ESTABLISHING FALSE BUT VIABLE CREDENTIALS. THAT'S THE TICKET.
BUT, AND THIS IS A BIG BUT, THE THREE VIRTUAL COMMAND STATIONS ARE BEHIND DATA MOATS, AND LIKE I SAID, THEY'RE Q-ENTANGLED WITH THE GARD AND WITH EACH OTHER. IT'S IMPOSSIBLE FOR ONE MAN TO DO THIS, MARC.
I NEVER SAID IT WOULD BE EASY. BUT I WOULDN'T HAVE ASKED YOU TO TRY IF IT WAS IMPOSSIBLE.
THE POINT I'M, UH, GETTING TO IS I FOUND SOMETHING ELSE OUT. EVERY TIME MY PROGRAM SENDS ONE OF ITS PASSWORD CANDIDATES UP AGAINST ONE OF YOUR ITERATED DATA MOATS, DO YOU KNOW WHAT THE GARD DOES? IF IT'S THE WRONG PASSWORD, WHICH IT ALWAYS IS?
...YES, I KNOW.
IT KILLS THE PRISONER.
THE *VIRTUAL* PRISONER.
IT *KILLS* THE PRISONER, MARC.

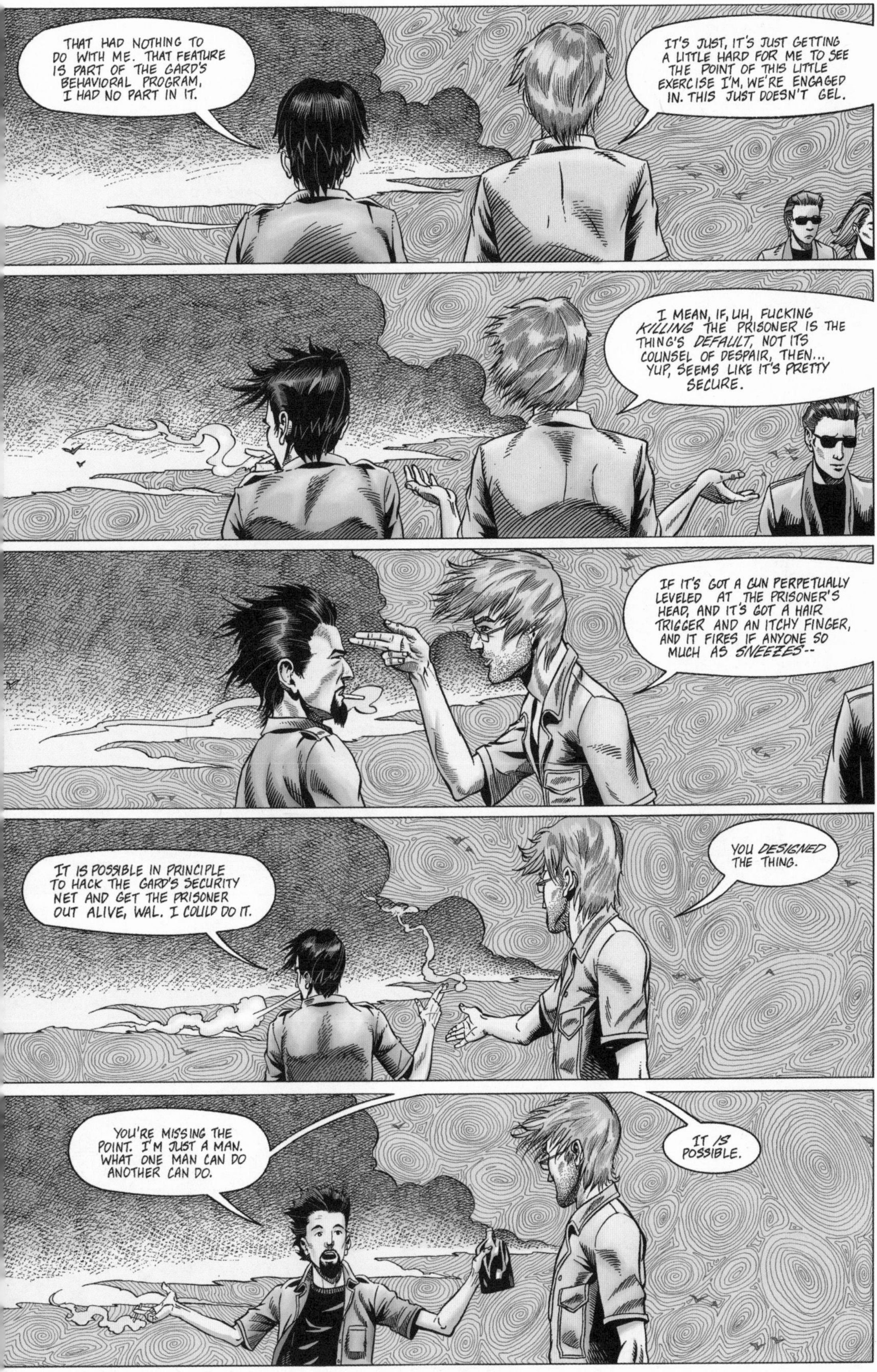
THAT HAD NOTHING TO DO WITH ME. THAT FEATURE IS PART OF THE GARD'S BEHAVIORAL PROGRAM, I HAD NO PART IN IT.
IT'S JUST, IT'S JUST GETTING A LITTLE HARD FOR ME TO SEE THE POINT OF THIS LITTLE EXERCISE I'M, WE'RE ENGAGED IN. THIS JUST DOESN'T GEL.
I MEAN, IF, UH, FUCKING *KILLING* THE PRISONER IS THE THING'S *DEFAULT*, NOT ITS COUNSEL OF DESPAIR, THEN... YUP, SEEMS LIKE IT'S PRETTY SECURE.
IF IT'S GOT A GUN PERPETUALLY LEVELED AT THE PRISONER'S HEAD, AND IT'S GOT A HAIR TRIGGER AND AN ITCHY FINGER, AND IT FIRES IF ANYONE SO MUCH AS *SNEEZES*--
IT IS POSSIBLE IN PRINCIPLE TO HACK THE GARD'S SECURITY NET AND GET THE PRISONER OUT ALIVE, WAL. I COULD DO IT.
YOU *DESIGNED* THE THING.
YOU'RE MISSING THE POINT. I'M JUST A MAN. WHAT ONE MAN CAN DO ANOTHER CAN DO.
IT *IS* POSSIBLE.

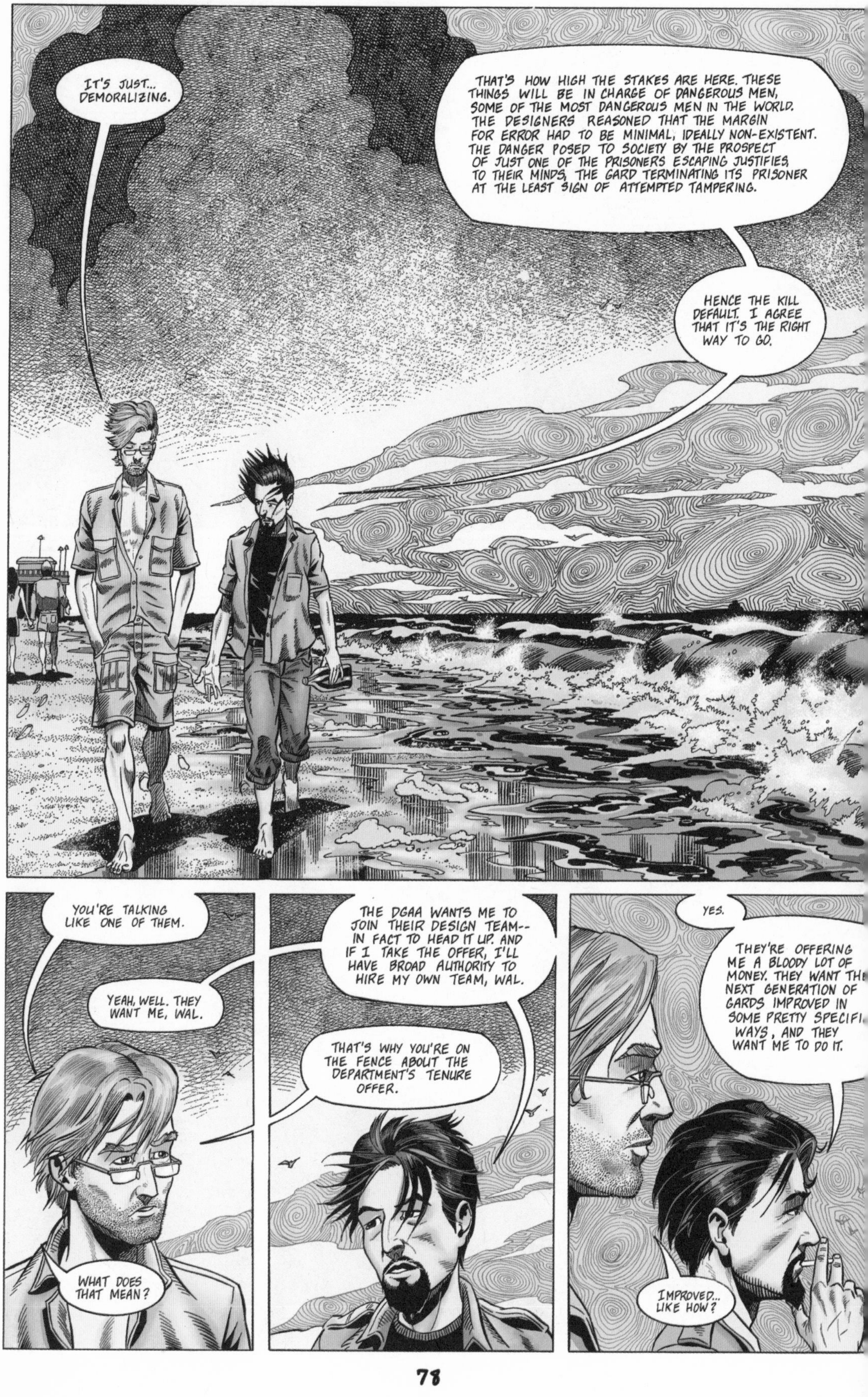

IT'S JUST... DEMORALIZING.
THAT'S HOW HIGH THE STAKES ARE HERE. THESE THINGS WILL BE IN CHARGE OF DANGEROUS MEN, SOME OF THE MOST DANGEROUS MEN IN THE WORLD. THE DESIGNERS REASONED THAT THE MARGIN FOR ERROR HAD TO BE MINIMAL, IDEALLY NON-EXISTENT. THE DANGER POSED TO SOCIETY BY THE PROSPECT OF JUST ONE OF THE PRISONERS ESCAPING JUSTIFIES, TO THEIR MINDS, THE GARD TERMINATING ITS PRISONER AT THE LEAST SIGN OF ATTEMPTED TAMPERING.
HENCE THE KILL DEFAULT. I AGREE THAT IT'S THE RIGHT WAY TO GO.
YOU'RE TALKING LIKE ONE OF THEM.
YEAH, WELL. THEY WANT ME, WAL.
WHAT DOES THAT MEAN?
THE DGAA WANTS ME TO JOIN THEIR DESIGN TEAM-- IN FACT TO HEAD IT UP. AND IF I TAKE THE OFFER, I'LL HAVE BROAD AUTHORITY TO HIRE MY OWN TEAM, WAL.
THAT'S WHY YOU'RE ON THE FENCE ABOUT THE DEPARTMENT'S TENURE OFFER.
YES.
THEY'RE OFFERING ME A BLOODY LOT OF MONEY. THEY WANT TH NEXT GENERATION OF GARDS IMPROVED IN SOME PRETTY SPECIFI WAYS, AND THEY WANT ME TO DO IT.
IMPROVED... LIKE HOW?

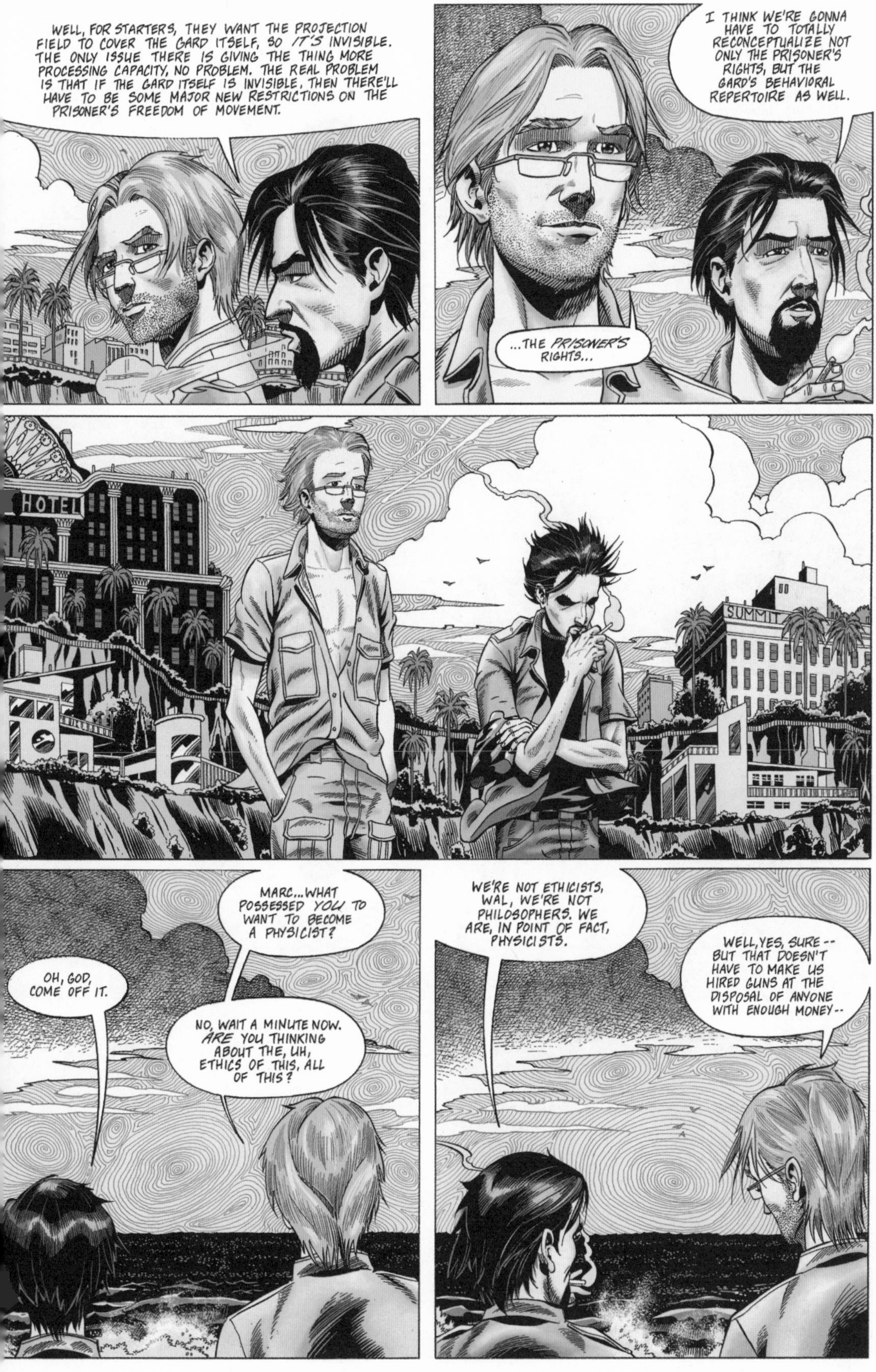
WELL, FOR STARTERS, THEY WANT THE PROJECTION FIELD TO COVER THE GARD ITSELF, SO IT'S INVISIBLE. THE ONLY ISSUE THERE IS GIVING THE THING MORE PROCESSING CAPACITY, NO PROBLEM. THE REAL PROBLEM IS THAT IF THE GARD ITSELF IS INVISIBLE, THEN THERE'LL HAVE TO BE SOME MAJOR NEW RESTRICTIONS ON THE PRISONER'S FREEDOM OF MOVEMENT.
I THINK WE'RE GONNA HAVE TO TOTALLY RECONCEPTUALIZE NOT ONLY THE PRISONER'S RIGHTS, BUT THE GARD'S BEHAVIORAL REPERTOIRE AS WELL.
...THE PRISONER'S RIGHTS...
HOTEL
SUMMIT
OH, GOD, COME OFF IT.
MARC...WHAT POSSESSED YOU TO WANT TO BECOME A PHYSICIST?
NO, WAIT A MINUTE NOW. ARE YOU THINKING ABOUT THE, UH, ETHICS OF THIS, ALL OF THIS?
WE'RE NOT ETHICISTS, WAL, WE'RE NOT PHILOSOPHERS. WE ARE, IN POINT OF FACT, PHYSICISTS.
WELL, YES, SURE -- BUT THAT DOESN'T HAVE TO MAKE US HIRED GUNS AT THE DISPOSAL OF ANYONE WITH ENOUGH MONEY --

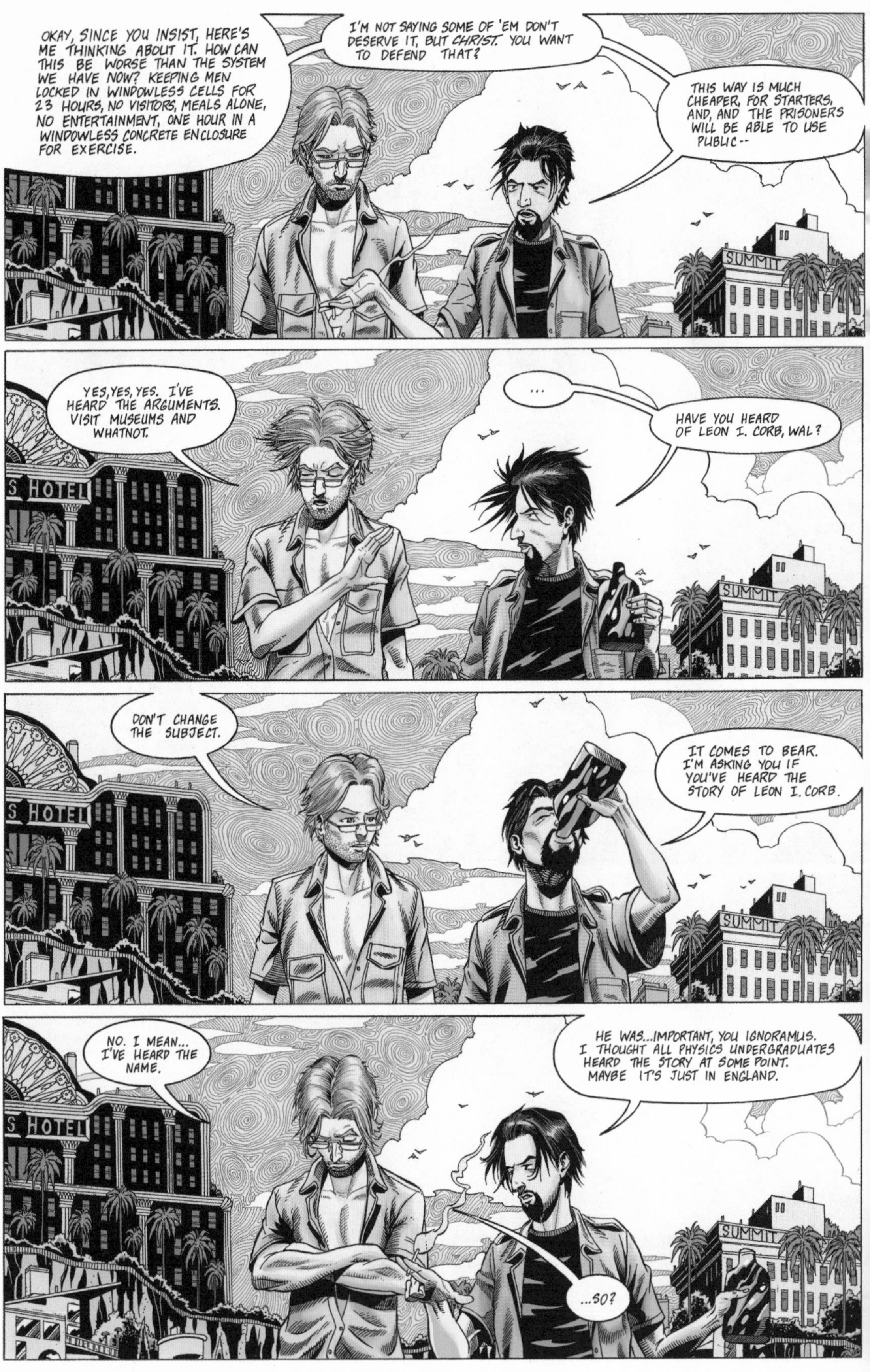
OKAY, SINCE YOU INSIST, HERE'S ME THINKING ABOUT IT. HOW CAN THIS BE WORSE THAN THE SYSTEM WE HAVE NOW? KEEPING MEN LOCKED IN WINDOWLESS CELLS FOR 23 HOURS, NO VISITORS, MEALS ALONE, NO ENTERTAINMENT, ONE HOUR IN A WINDOWLESS CONCRETE ENCLOSURE FOR EXERCISE.
I'M NOT SAYING SOME OF 'EM DON'T DESERVE IT, BUT *CHRIST.* YOU WANT TO DEFEND THAT?
THIS WAY IS MUCH CHEAPER, FOR STARTERS, AND, AND THE PRISONERS WILL BE ABLE TO USE PUBLIC--
SUMMIT
YES, YES, YES. I'VE HEARD THE ARGUMENTS. VISIT MUSEUMS AND WHATNOT.
...
HAVE YOU HEARD OF LEON I. CORB, WAL?
S HOTEL
SUMMIT
DON'T CHANGE THE SUBJECT.
IT COMES TO BEAR. I'M ASKING YOU IF YOU'VE HEARD THE STORY OF LEON I. CORB.
S HOTEL
SUMMIT
NO. I MEAN... I'VE HEARD THE NAME.
HE WAS...IMPORTANT, YOU IGNORAMUS. I THOUGHT ALL PHYSICS UNDERGRADUATES HEARD THE STORY AT SOME POINT. MAYBE IT'S JUST IN ENGLAND.
S HOTEL
SUMMIT
...SO?

HE WAS BORN IN 1901 IN AUSTRIA.

"THE SON OF NOBLES."

'VERY WEALTHY, VERY PRIVILEGED.'

"STUDIED WITH HEISENBERG IN WÜRZBURG AS A KID."

"GOT HIS DOCTORATE IN 1927. FOR HIS THESIS HE BOMBARDED NICKEL SAMPLES WITH ELECTRONS, SAW THAT THEY BOUNCED OFF THE NICKEL IN A WAY SIMILAR TO THE WAY X-RAYS BOUNCE OFF, AND CONCLUDED THAT ELECTRONS HAVE WAVE-LIKE PROPERTIES."

"MAX BORN IN GÖTTINGEN GOT WIND OF CORB'S RESULTS AND SAW THAT THEY CONFIRMED DeBROGLIE'S UP-TO-THAT-POINT IGNORED WAVE THEORY OF PARTICLES."

$$\psi_0(Q) = \left(\frac{m\omega}{\pi \hbar}\right)^{1/4} e^{-x^2/2L^2} \quad \psi_0(Q) = \left(\frac{}{}\right)^{1/4}$$

$$L = \sqrt{\frac{\hbar}{m\omega}}$$

$$\mathcal{E}_0 = \frac{\hbar\omega}{2}$$

$$\mathcal{E}_n = \left(n + \frac{1}{2}\right)\hbar$$

$$Q = x/L$$

$$\left(-\frac{d^2}{dQ^2} + Q^2\right)\psi = \frac{\mathcal{E}}{\mathcal{E}_0}\psi = \hbar\omega$$

$$a^+ = \frac{1}{\sqrt{2}}\left(-\frac{d}{dQ} + Q\right)$$

$$a_- = \frac{1}{\sqrt{2}}\left(\frac{d}{dQ}\right)$$

$$(Q) = 2QH_{n-1}(Q) - 2($$

$$\psi_n(Q) = A_n H_n($$

"THAT WAVE THEORY BECAME THE CORNERSTONE OF QUANTUM MECHANICS."

SO LEON CORB HAD WON HIMSELF A PLACE IN THE HISTORY OF PHYSICS AT THE TENDER AGE OF 26.

REMARKABLE KID, RIGHT?

YEAH, SURE.

81

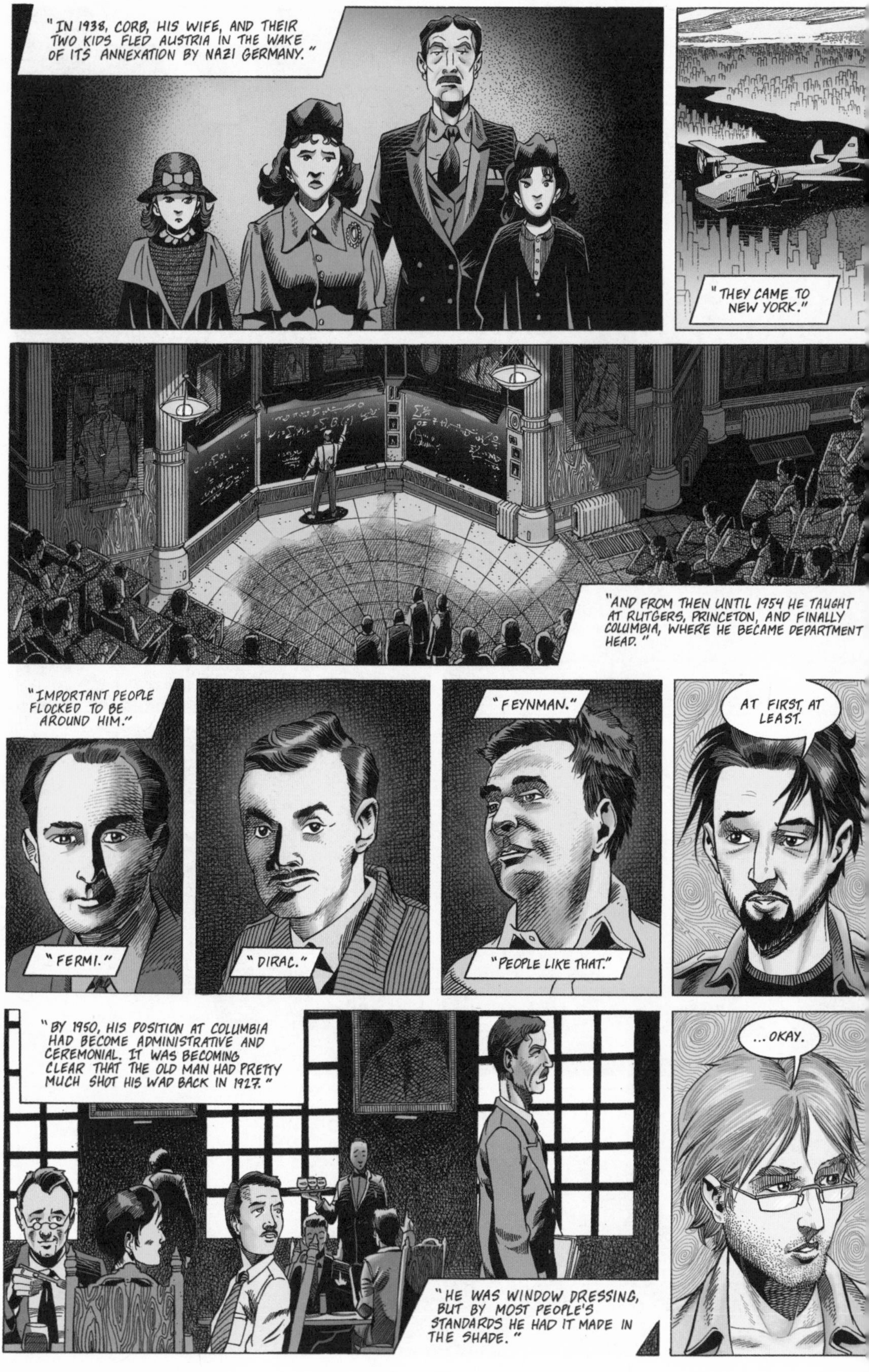
"IN 1938, CORB, HIS WIFE, AND THEIR TWO KIDS FLED AUSTRIA IN THE WAKE OF ITS ANNEXATION BY NAZI GERMANY."
"THEY CAME TO NEW YORK."
"AND FROM THEN UNTIL 1954 HE TAUGHT AT RUTGERS, PRINCETON, AND FINALLY COLUMBIA, WHERE HE BECAME DEPARTMENT HEAD."
"IMPORTANT PEOPLE FLOCKED TO BE AROUND HIM."
"FERMI."
"DIRAC."
"FEYNMAN."
"PEOPLE LIKE THAT."
AT FIRST, AT LEAST.
"BY 1950, HIS POSITION AT COLUMBIA HAD BECOME ADMINISTRATIVE AND CEREMONIAL. IT WAS BECOMING CLEAR THAT THE OLD MAN HAD PRETTY MUCH SHOT HIS WAD BACK IN 1927."
"HE WAS WINDOW DRESSING, BUT BY MOST PEOPLE'S STANDARDS HE HAD IT MADE IN THE SHADE."
...OKAY.

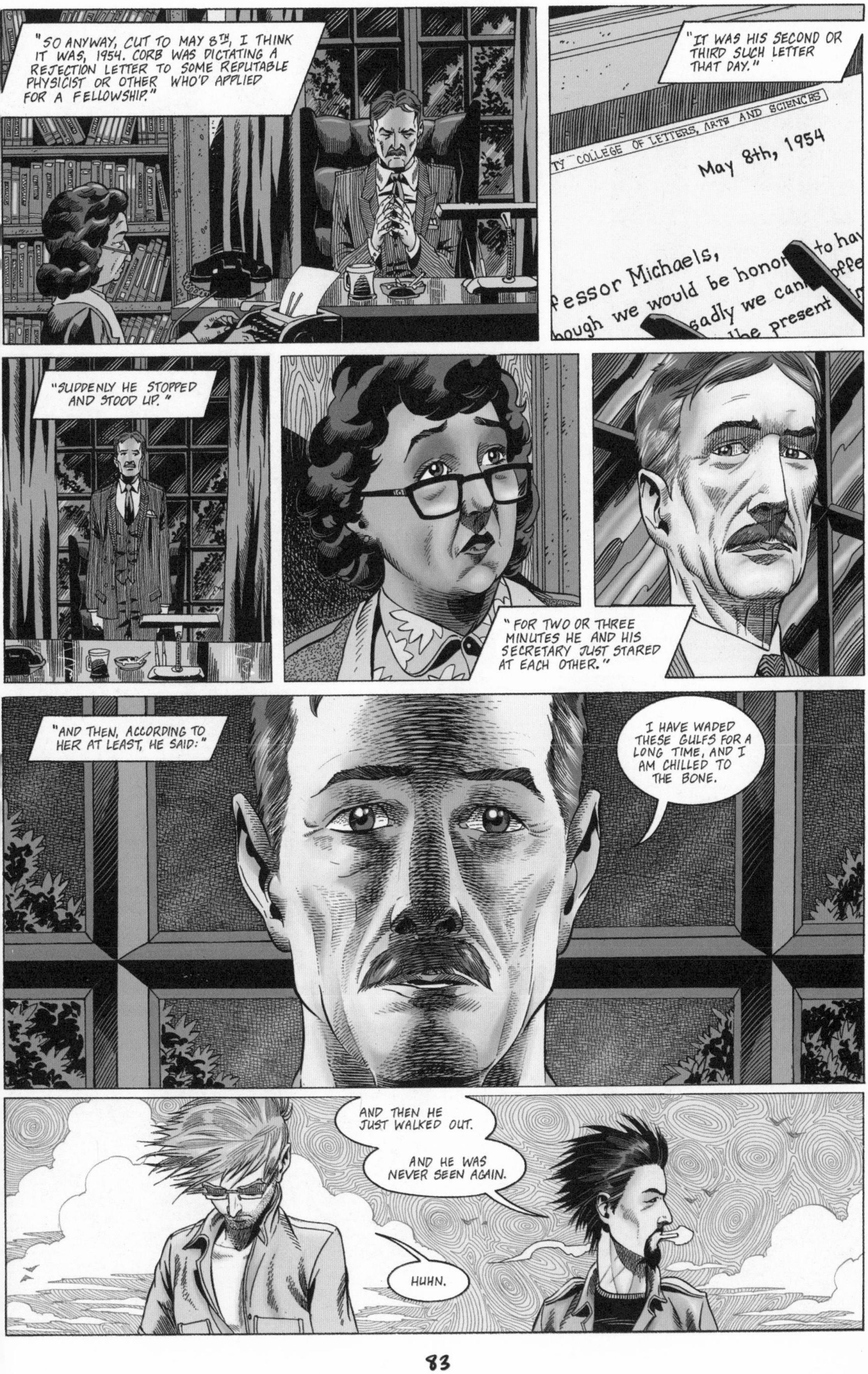
"SO ANYWAY, CUT TO MAY 8TH, I THINK IT WAS, 1954. CORB WAS DICTATING A REJECTION LETTER TO SOME REPUTABLE PHYSICIST OR OTHER WHO'D APPLIED FOR A FELLOWSHIP."
"IT WAS HIS SECOND OR THIRD SUCH LETTER THAT DAY."
TY COLLEGE OF LETTERS, ARTS AND SCIENCES
May 8th, 1954
fessor Michaels,
we would be honor
ough
sadly we can
the present
"SUDDENLY HE STOPPED AND STOOD UP."
"FOR TWO OR THREE MINUTES HE AND HIS SECRETARY JUST STARED AT EACH OTHER."
"AND THEN, ACCORDING TO HER AT LEAST, HE SAID:"
I HAVE WADED THESE GULFS FOR A LONG TIME, AND I AM CHILLED TO THE BONE.
AND THEN HE JUST WALKED OUT.
AND HE WAS NEVER SEEN AGAIN.
HUHN.

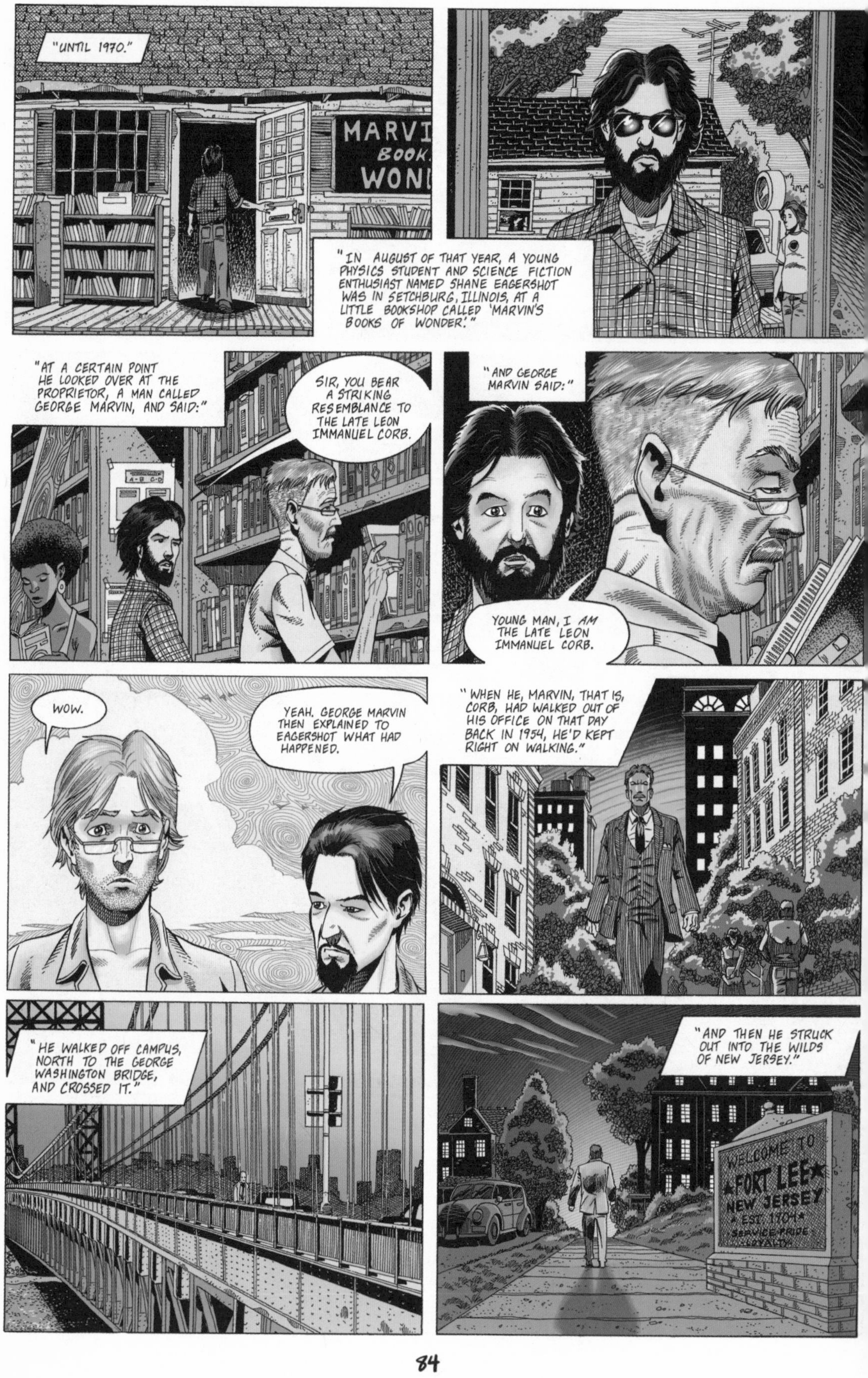
"UNTIL 1970."
MARVI
BOOK
WON
"IN AUGUST OF THAT YEAR, A YOUNG PHYSICS STUDENT AND SCIENCE FICTION ENTHUSIAST NAMED SHANE EAGERSHOT WAS IN SETCHBURG, ILLINOIS, AT A LITTLE BOOKSHOP CALLED 'MARVIN'S BOOKS OF WONDER.'"
"AT A CERTAIN POINT HE LOOKED OVER AT THE PROPRIETOR, A MAN CALLED GEORGE MARVIN, AND SAID:"
SIR, YOU BEAR A STRIKING RESEMBLANCE TO THE LATE LEON IMMANUEL CORB.
"AND GEORGE MARVIN SAID:"
YOUNG MAN, I *AM* THE LATE LEON IMMANUEL CORB.
WOW.
YEAH. GEORGE MARVIN THEN EXPLAINED TO EAGERSHOT WHAT HAD HAPPENED.
"WHEN HE, MARVIN, THAT IS, CORB, HAD WALKED OUT OF HIS OFFICE ON THAT DAY BACK IN 1954, HE'D KEPT RIGHT ON WALKING."
"HE WALKED OFF CAMPUS, NORTH TO THE GEORGE WASHINGTON BRIDGE, AND CROSSED IT."
"AND THEN HE STRUCK OUT INTO THE WILDS OF NEW JERSEY."
WELCOME TO
FORT LEE
NEW JERSEY
EST. 1904
SERVICE PRIDE
LOYALTY

"HE WALKED FOR THREE DAYS WITH NO FOOD AND NO SLEEP."

"HE COLLAPSED SOMEWHERE OUTSIDE OF PHILADELPHIA AND WAS HOSPITALIZED."

"UPON RELEASE, HE STARTED WALKING AGAIN."

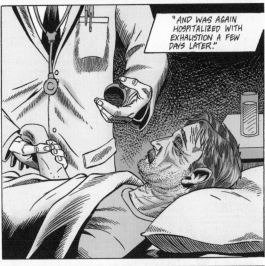

"AND WAS AGAIN HOSPITALIZED WITH EXHAUSTION A FEW DAYS LATER."

"HE REPEATED THIS CYCLE OF MARCHING, COLLAPSING, AND HOSPITALIZATION FIVE OR SIX MORE TIMES, UNTIL HE FINALLY FOUND HIMSELF IN SETCHBURG, ILLINOIS. AND THERE HE STOPPED."

WELCOME TO ★ SETCHBURG ★ ILLINOIS INC. 1893 POP. 702

85

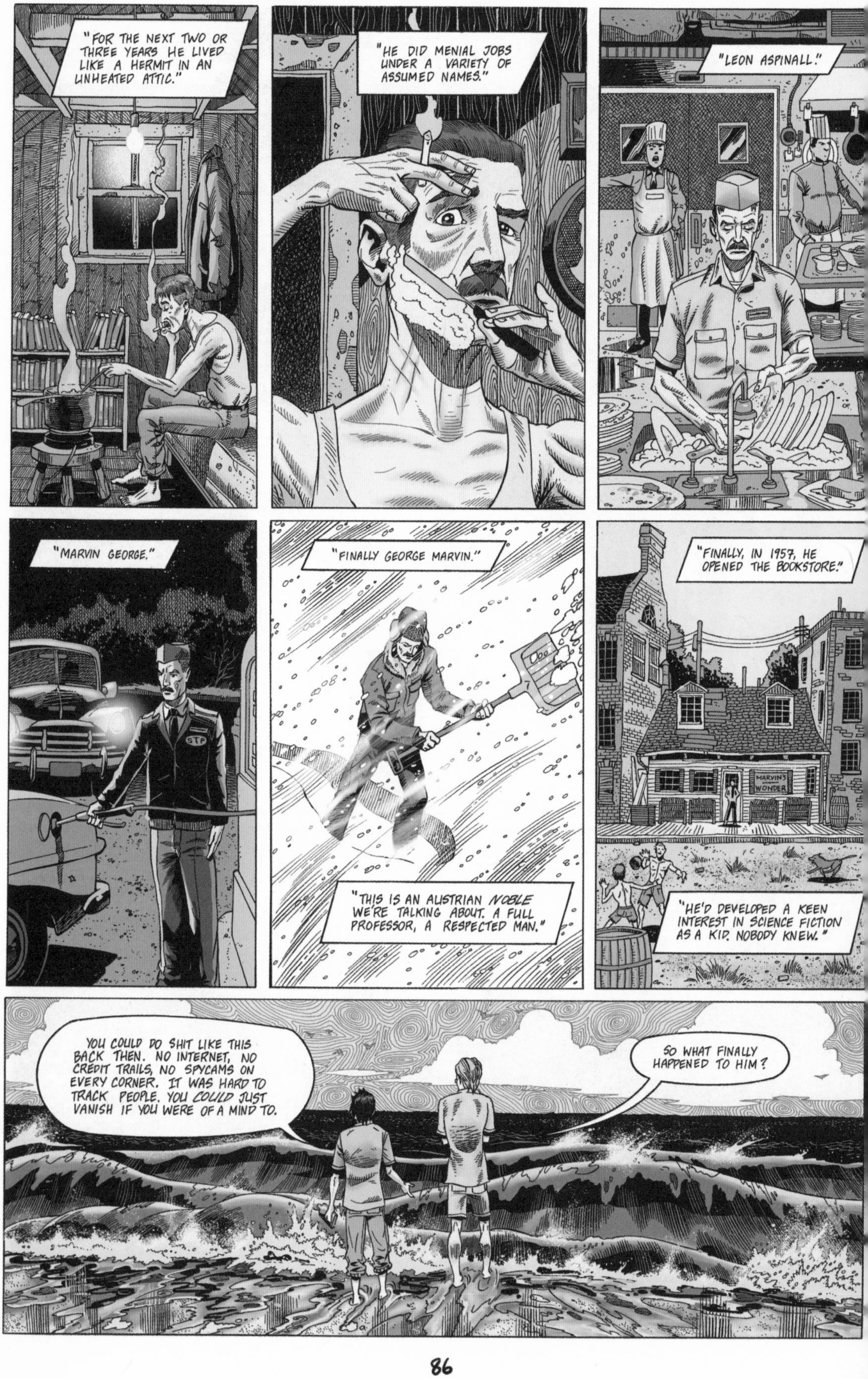
"FOR THE NEXT TWO OR THREE YEARS HE LIVED LIKE A HERMIT IN AN UNHEATED ATTIC."
"HE DID MENIAL JOBS UNDER A VARIETY OF ASSUMED NAMES."
"LEON ASPINALL."
"MARVIN GEORGE."
STP
"FINALLY GEORGE MARVIN."
"THIS IS AN AUSTRIAN NOBLE WE'RE TALKING ABOUT. A FULL PROFESSOR, A RESPECTED MAN."
"FINALLY, IN 1957, HE OPENED THE BOOKSTORE."
MARVIN'S WONDER
"HE'D DEVELOPED A KEEN INTEREST IN SCIENCE FICTION AS A KID. NOBODY KNEW."
YOU COULD DO SHIT LIKE THIS BACK THEN. NO INTERNET, NO CREDIT TRAILS, NO SPYCAMS ON EVERY CORNER. IT WAS HARD TO TRACK PEOPLE. YOU COULD JUST VANISH IF YOU WERE OF A MIND TO.
SO WHAT FINALLY HAPPENED TO HIM?

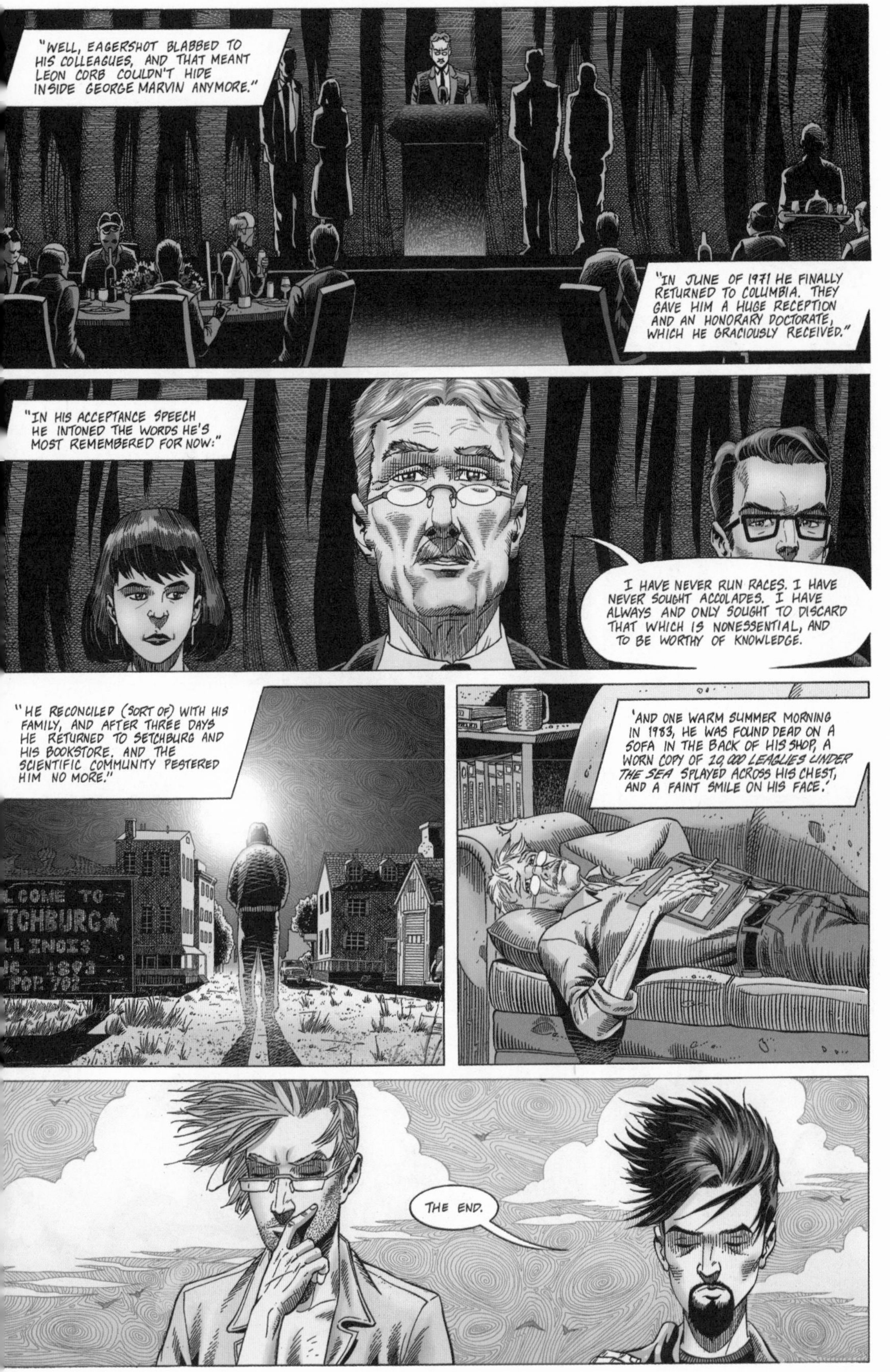
"WELL, EAGERSHOT BLABBED TO HIS COLLEAGUES, AND THAT MEANT LEON CORB COULDN'T HIDE INSIDE GEORGE MARVIN ANYMORE."
"IN JUNE OF 1971 HE FINALLY RETURNED TO COLUMBIA. THEY GAVE HIM A HUGE RECEPTION AND AN HONORARY DOCTORATE, WHICH HE GRACIOUSLY RECEIVED."
"IN HIS ACCEPTANCE SPEECH HE INTONED THE WORDS HE'S MOST REMEMBERED FOR NOW:"
I HAVE NEVER RUN RACES. I HAVE NEVER SOUGHT ACCOLADES. I HAVE ALWAYS AND ONLY SOUGHT TO DISCARD THAT WHICH IS NONESSENTIAL, AND TO BE WORTHY OF KNOWLEDGE.
"HE RECONCILED (SORT OF) WITH HIS FAMILY, AND AFTER THREE DAYS HE RETURNED TO SETCHBURG AND HIS BOOKSTORE. AND THE SCIENTIFIC COMMUNITY PESTERED HIM NO MORE."
TCHBURG
LLINOIS
POP. 702
'AND ONE WARM SUMMER MORNING IN 1983, HE WAS FOUND DEAD ON A SOFA IN THE BACK OF HIS SHOP, A WORN COPY OF 20,000 LEAGUES UNDER THE SEA SPLAYED ACROSS HIS CHEST, AND A FAINT SMILE ON HIS FACE.'
THE END.

IS THAT A TRUE STORY?

YOU TELL ME. WHAT *IS* TRUTH?

GIMME A BREAK.

WELL...ACCORDING TO GEORGE MARVIN IT WAS THE TRUTH. BUT THERE WAS NO SHORTAGE OF PEOPLE WHO THOUGHT GEORGE MARVIN WAS JUST AN OLD CRACKPOT WHO SAW THE CHANCE TO FOB HIMSELF OFF AS SOMEONE IMPORTANT AND WENT FOR IT.

SO WHAT'S THE POINT?

WHY DON'T YOU TELL ME THE P--

MARC!

THE POINT IS THIS. ASSUME THE STORY IS TRUE. THEN WHAT YOU HAD WAS A GREAT MAN WHO WAS MISERABLE IN HIS GREATNESS, SO HE TURNED HIMSELF INTO A NOBODY.

NOW ASSUME IT'S FALSE, THAT GEORGE MARVIN WAS LYING. THEN WHAT YOU HAD WAS A NOBODY WHO WAS MISERABLE IN HIS NOBODINESS, AND SO HE TURNED HIMSELF INTO A GREAT MAN.

MAYBE NONE OF IT MATTERS IN THE LONG RUN, GREAT MAN OR NOBODY, SIX OF ONE, HALF A DOZEN OF THE OTHER. BUT MOST PEOPLE NEVER HAVE A CHOICE LIKE THIS TO MAKE. MOST PEOPLE ARE NOBODIES WHETHER THEY LIKE IT OR NOT. BUT I THINK YOU'RE DIFFERENT, WAL.

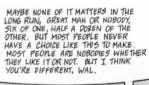

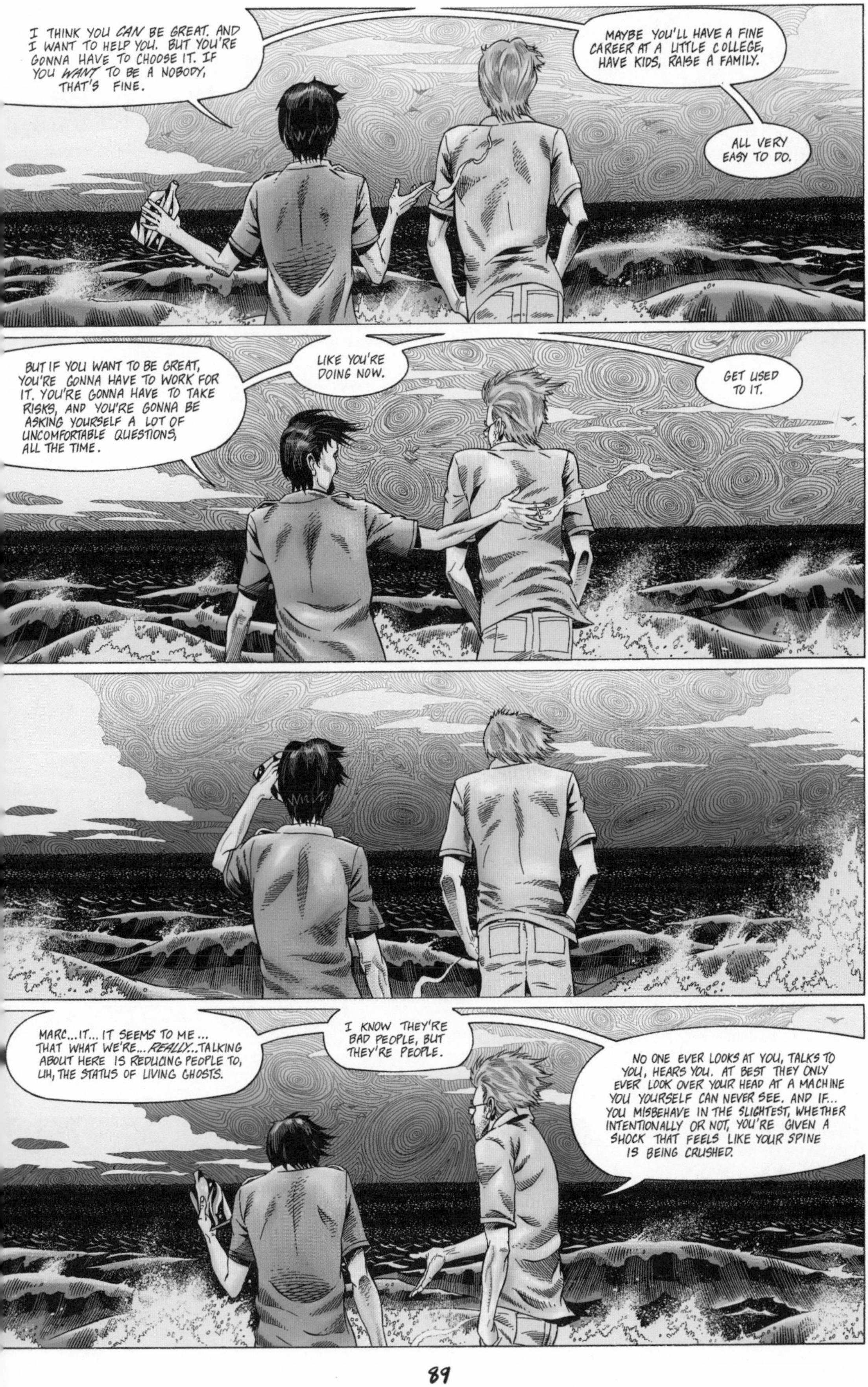
I THINK YOU CAN BE GREAT. AND I WANT TO HELP YOU. BUT YOU'RE GONNA HAVE TO CHOOSE IT. IF YOU WANT TO BE A NOBODY, THAT'S FINE.
MAYBE YOU'LL HAVE A FINE CAREER AT A LITTLE COLLEGE, HAVE KIDS, RAISE A FAMILY.
ALL VERY EASY TO DO.
BUT IF YOU WANT TO BE GREAT, YOU'RE GONNA HAVE TO WORK FOR IT. YOU'RE GONNA HAVE TO TAKE RISKS, AND YOU'RE GONNA BE ASKING YOURSELF A LOT OF UNCOMFORTABLE QUESTIONS, ALL THE TIME.
LIKE YOU'RE DOING NOW.
GET USED TO IT.
MARC... IT... IT SEEMS TO ME... THAT WHAT WE'RE... REALLY... TALKING ABOUT HERE IS REDUCING PEOPLE TO, UH, THE STATUS OF LIVING GHOSTS.
I KNOW THEY'RE BAD PEOPLE, BUT THEY'RE PEOPLE.
NO ONE EVER LOOKS AT YOU, TALKS TO YOU, HEARS YOU. AT BEST THEY ONLY EVER LOOK OVER YOUR HEAD AT A MACHINE YOU YOURSELF CAN NEVER SEE. AND IF... YOU MISBEHAVE IN THE SLIGHTEST, WHETHER INTENTIONALLY OR NOT, YOU'RE GIVEN A SHOCK THAT FEELS LIKE YOUR SPINE IS BEING CRUSHED.

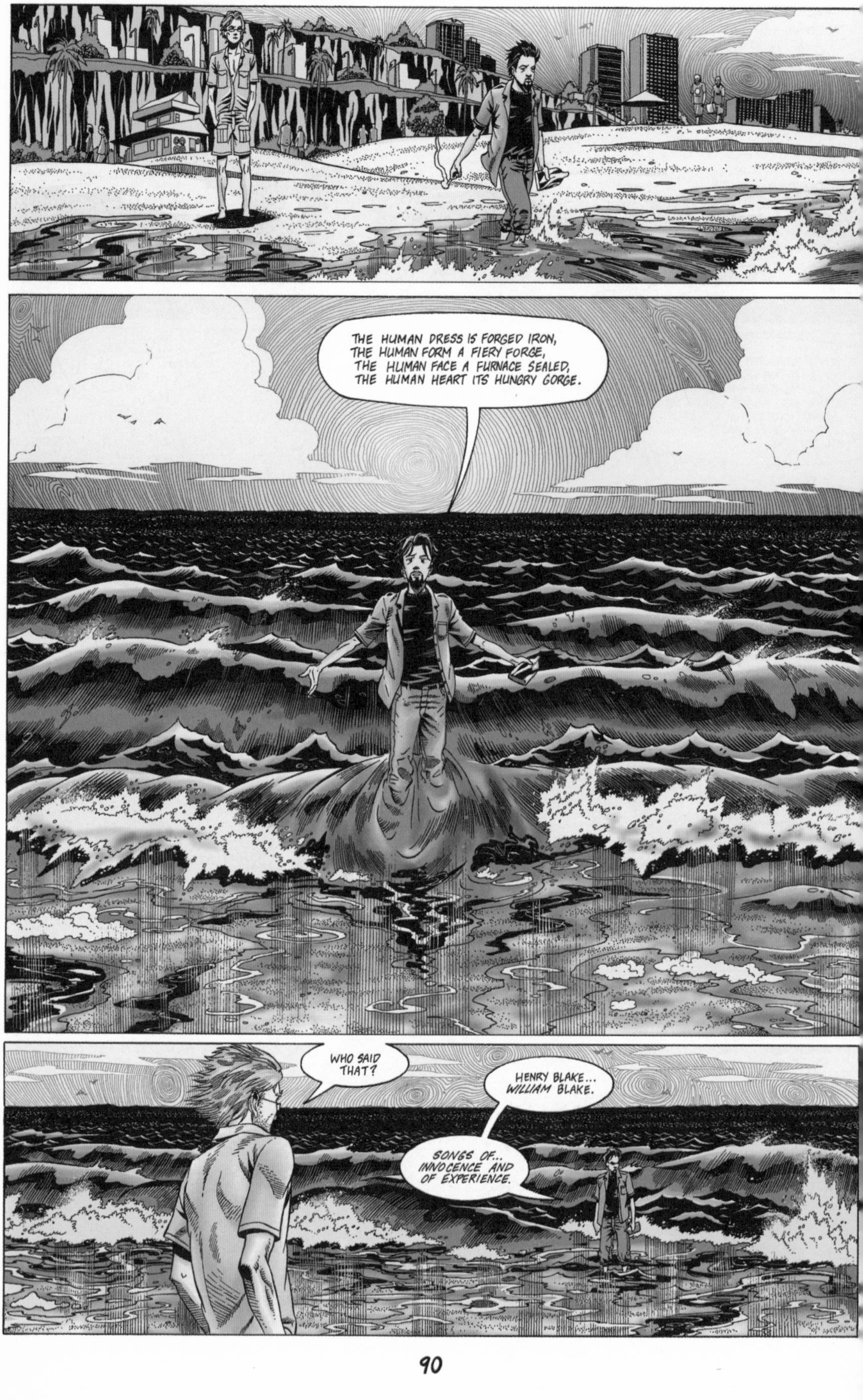
THE HUMAN DRESS IS FORGED IRON,
THE HUMAN FORM A FIERY FORGE,
THE HUMAN FACE A FURNACE SEALED,
THE HUMAN HEART ITS HUNGRY GORGE.
WHO SAID THAT?
HENRY BLAKE... WILLIAM BLAKE.
SONGS OF... INNOCENCE AND OF EXPERIENCE.

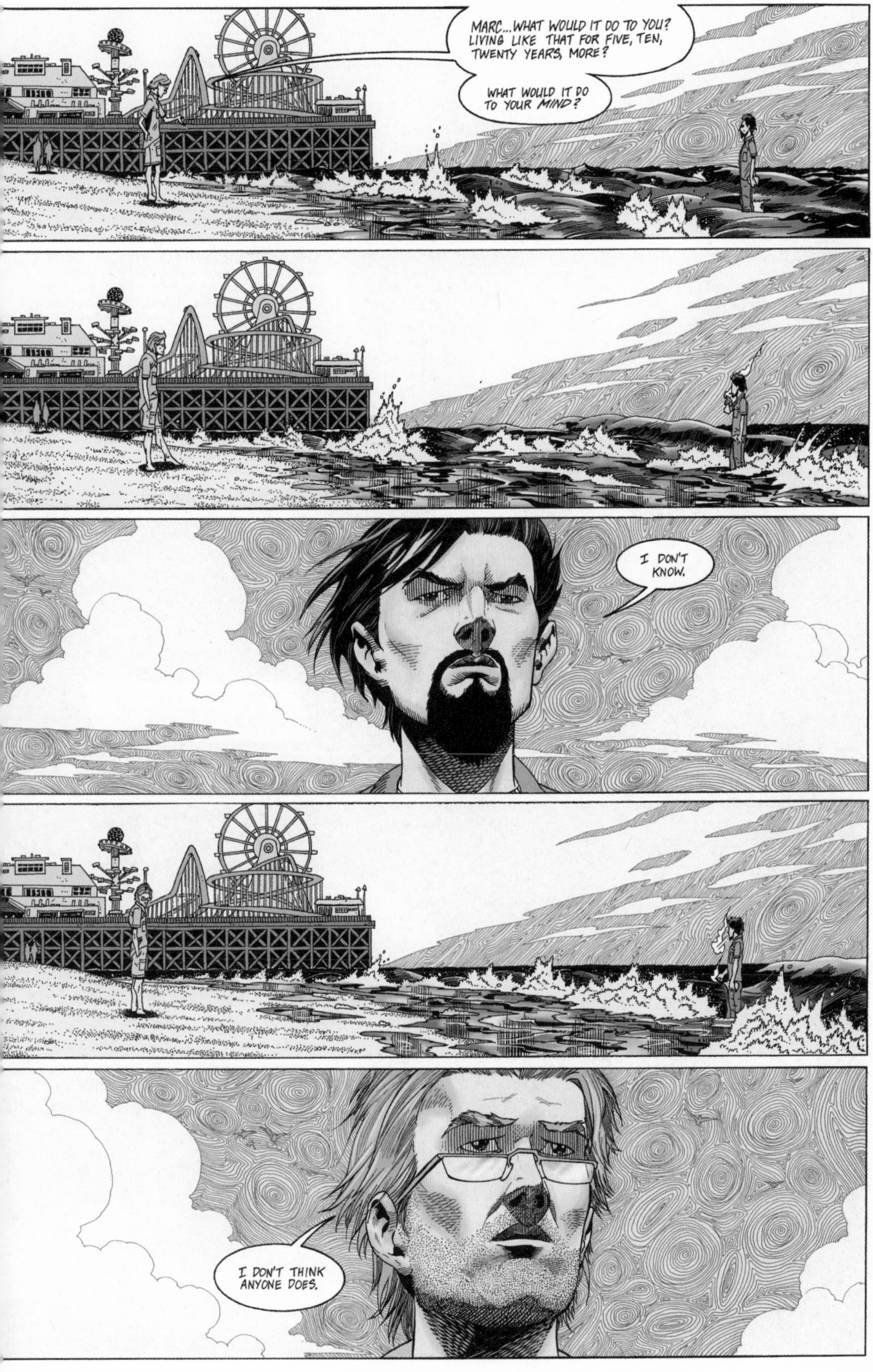
MARC...WHAT WOULD IT DO TO YOU? LIVING LIKE THAT FOR FIVE, TEN, TWENTY YEARS, MORE?
WHAT WOULD IT DO TO YOUR MIND?
I DON'T KNOW.
I DON'T THINK ANYONE DOES.

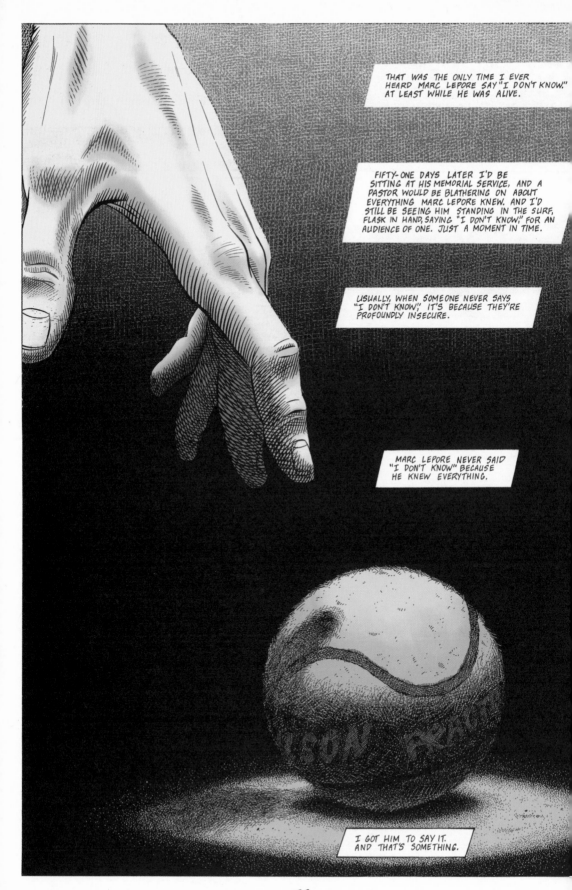

THAT WAS THE ONLY TIME I EVER HEARD MARC LEPORE SAY "I DON'T KNOW." AT LEAST WHILE HE WAS ALIVE.

FIFTY-ONE DAYS LATER I'D BE SITTING AT HIS MEMORIAL SERVICE, AND A PASTOR WOULD BE BLATHERING ON ABOUT EVERYTHING MARC LEPORE KNEW. AND I'D STILL BE SEEING HIM STANDING IN THE SURF, FLASK IN HAND, SAYING "I DON'T KNOW," FOR AN AUDIENCE OF ONE. JUST A MOMENT IN TIME.

USUALLY, WHEN SOMEONE NEVER SAYS "I DON'T KNOW," IT'S BECAUSE THEY'RE PROFOUNDLY INSECURE.

MARC LEPORE NEVER SAID "I DON'T KNOW" BECAUSE HE KNEW EVERYTHING.

I GOT HIM TO SAY IT. AND THAT'S SOMETHING.

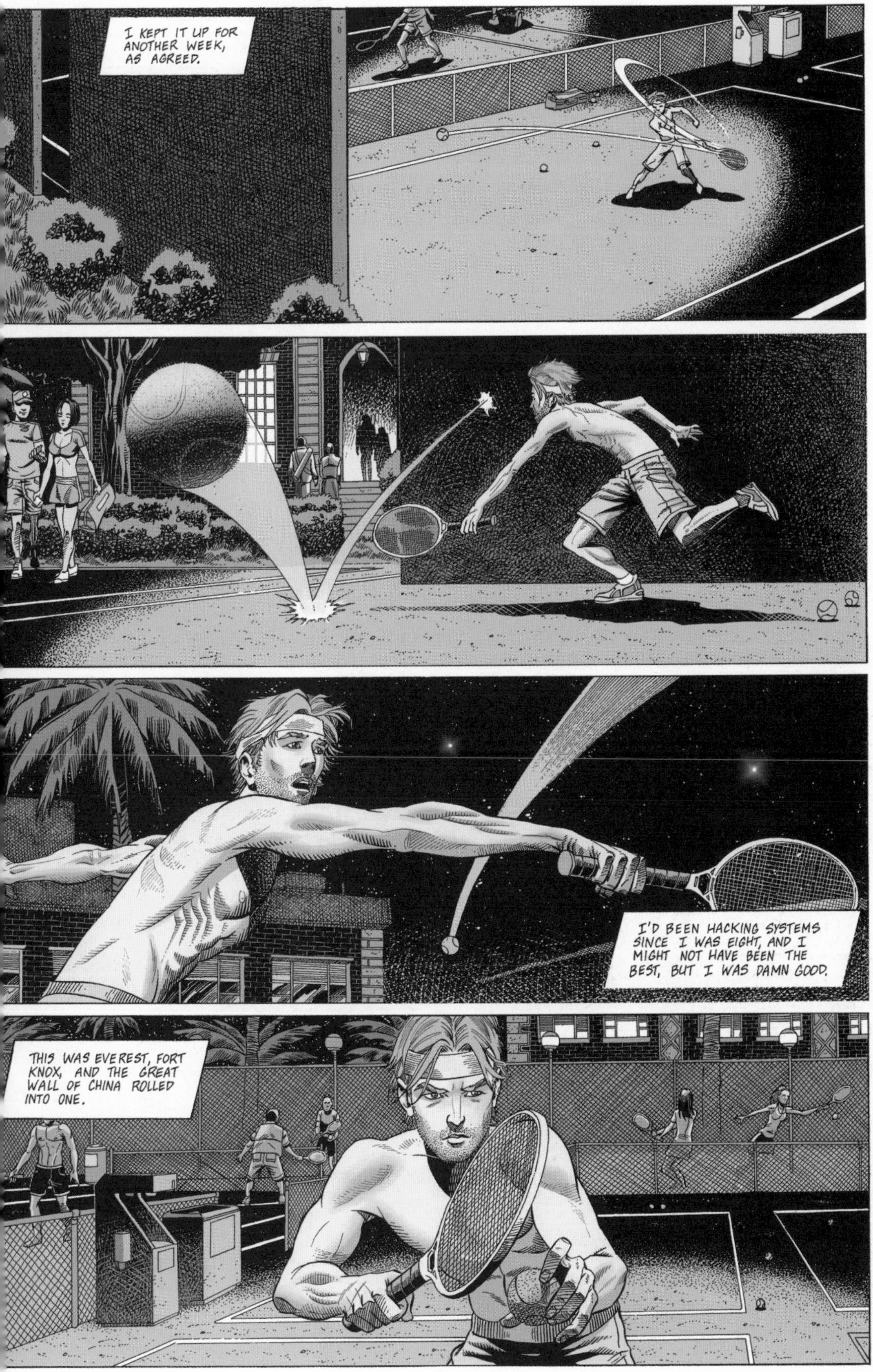
I KEPT IT UP FOR ANOTHER WEEK, AS AGREED.
I'D BEEN HACKING SYSTEMS SINCE I WAS EIGHT, AND I MIGHT NOT HAVE BEEN THE BEST, BUT I WAS DAMN GOOD.
THIS WAS EVEREST, FORT KNOX, AND THE GREAT WALL OF CHINA ROLLED INTO ONE.

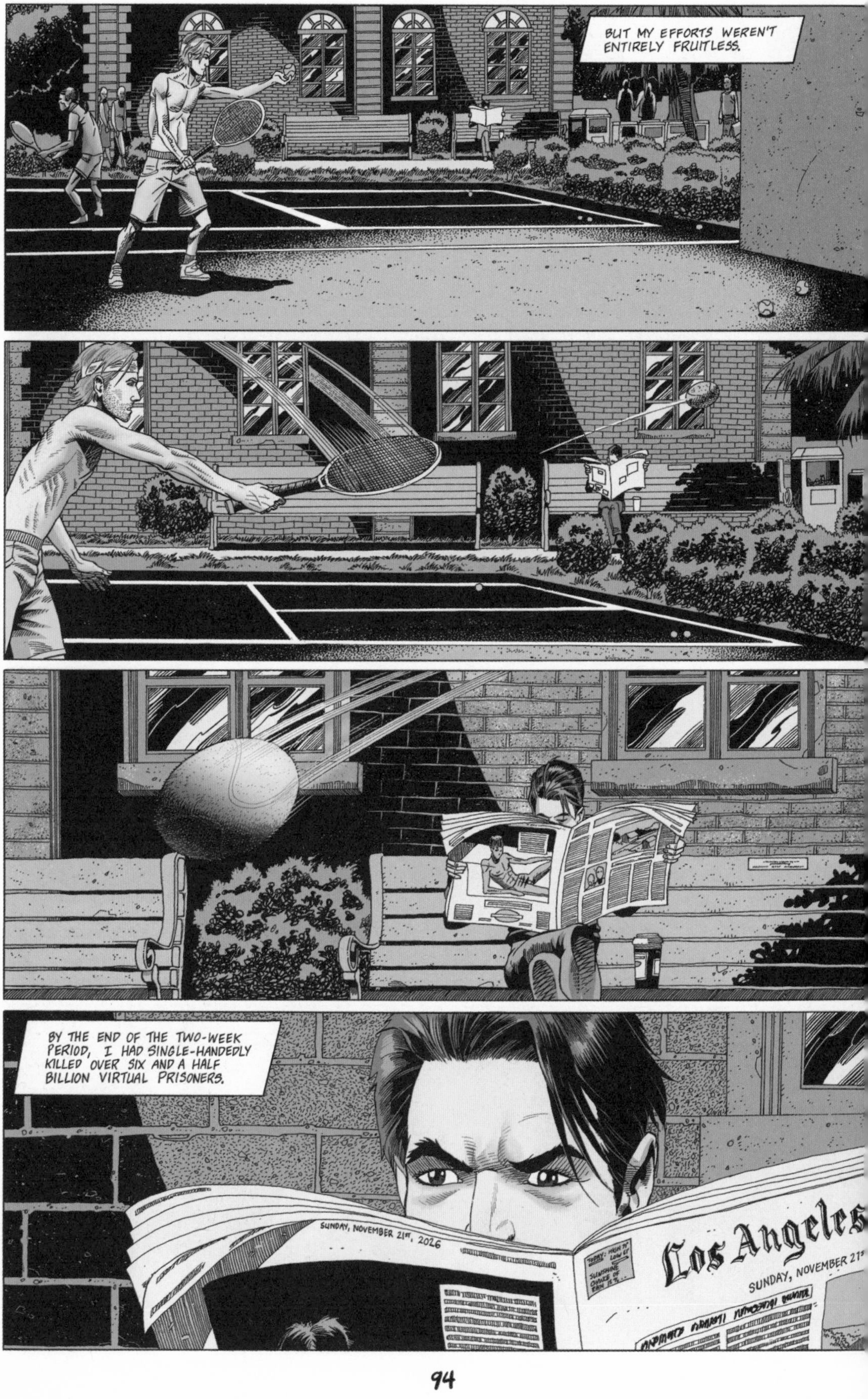
BUT MY EFFORTS WEREN'T ENTIRELY FRUITLESS.
BY THE END OF THE TWO-WEEK PERIOD, I HAD SINGLE-HANDEDLY KILLED OVER SIX AND A HALF BILLION VIRTUAL PRISONERS.
SUNDAY, NOVEMBER 21ST, 2026
Los Angeles
SUNDAY, NOVEMBER 21ST

JANUARY 20TH, 2011. 4:35 P.M.

95

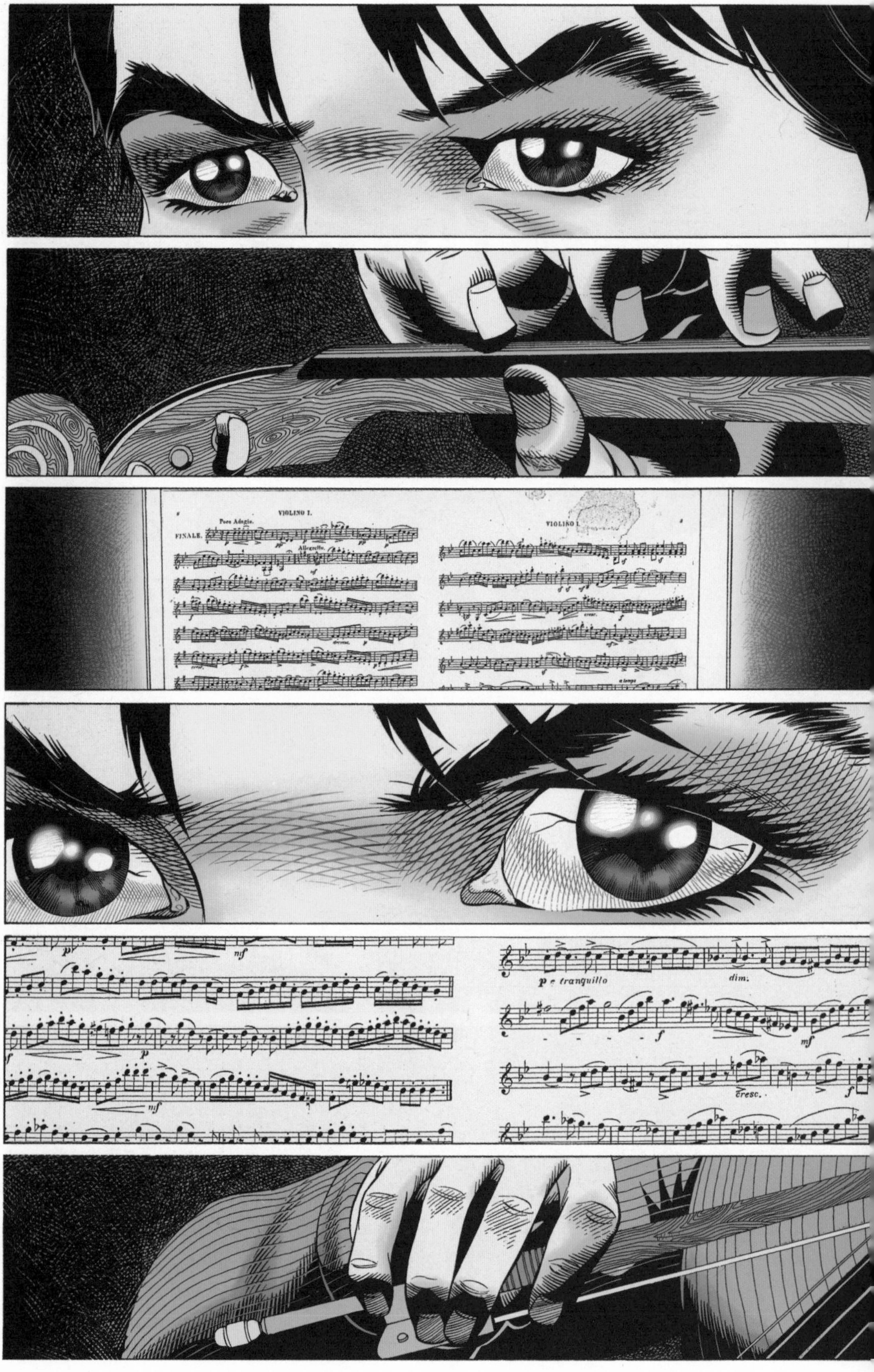
VIOLINO I.
Poco Adagio.
FINALE.
Allegretto.
VIOLINO I.
p tranquillo
dim.
cresc.

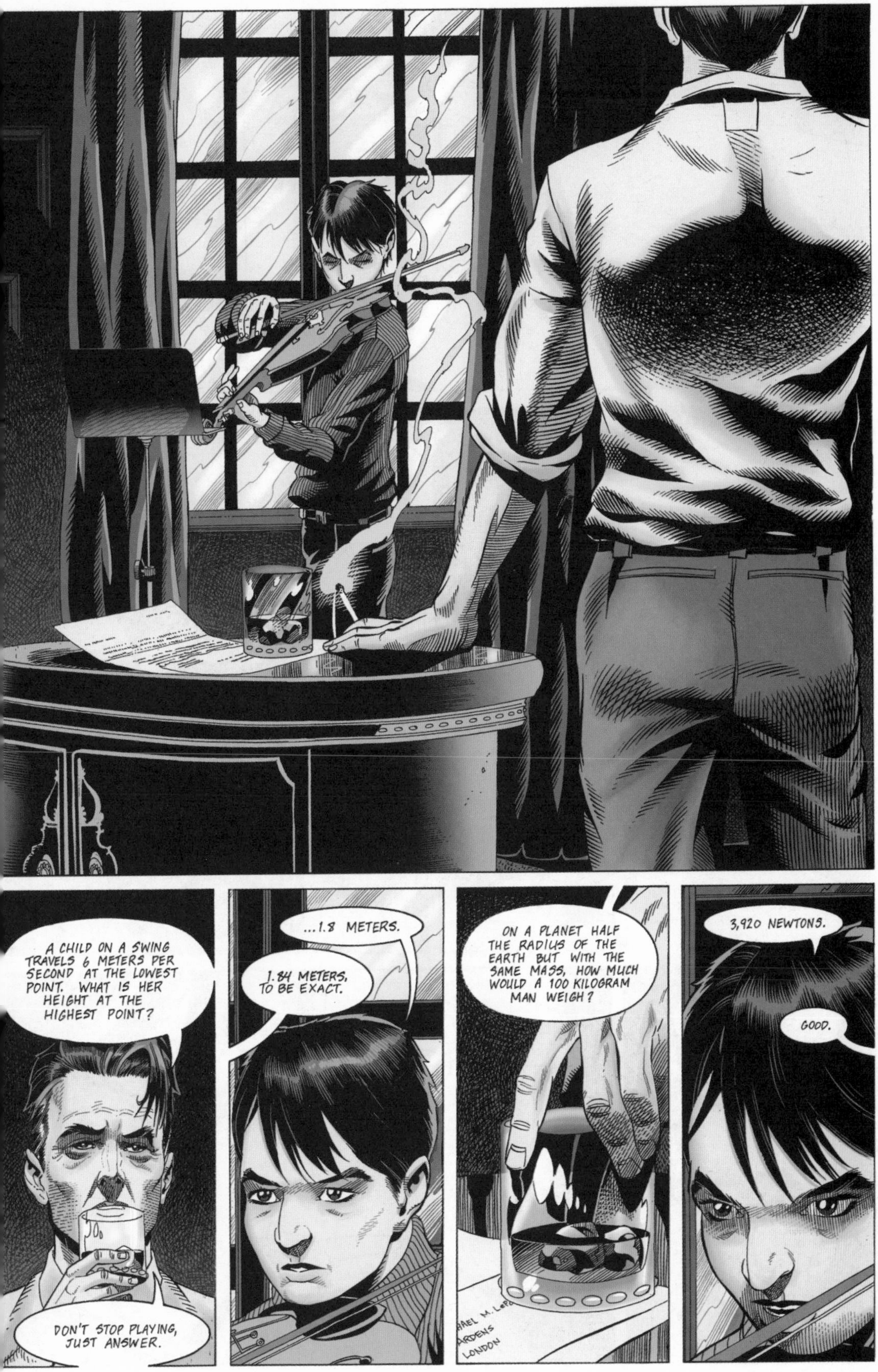

A CHILD ON A SWING TRAVELS 6 METERS PER SECOND AT THE LOWEST POINT. WHAT IS HER HEIGHT AT THE HIGHEST POINT?
DON'T STOP PLAYING, JUST ANSWER.
...1.8 METERS.
1.84 METERS, TO BE EXACT.
ON A PLANET HALF THE RADIUS OF THE EARTH BUT WITH THE SAME MASS, HOW MUCH WOULD A 100 KILOGRAM MAN WEIGH?
3,920 NEWTONS.
GOOD.

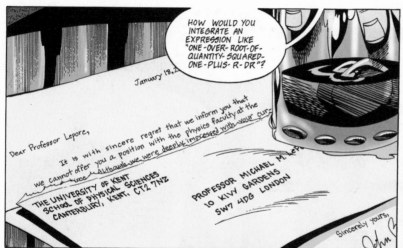

HOW WOULD YOU INTEGRATE AN EXPRESSION LIKE "ONE-OVER-ROOT-OF-QUANTITY-SQUARED-ONE-PLUS-R-DR"?

January 18, 2

Dear Professor Lepore,

It is with sincere regret that we inform you that we cannot offer you a position with the physics faculty at the ~~although~~ we were deeply impressed with ~~your cur~~

THE UNIVERSITY OF KENT
SCHOOL OF PHYSICAL SCIENCES
CANTERBURY, KENT, CT2 7NZ

PROFESSOR MICHAEL M. LE
10 KIVY GARDENS
SW7 4DG LONDON

Sincerely yours,
John

INTEGRATION BY PARTS.

NO! TRIGONOMETRIC SUBSTITUTION. SLOW DOWN HERE, ADAGIO! I'M GETTING DIZZY.

INSIDE THE STAR, THE GRAVITATIONAL POTENTIAL INCREASES LINEARLY WITH DISTANCE. ONCE OUTSIDE, IT DROPS OFF AS ONE OVER R.

GOOD.

HOW DOES THE GRAVITATIONAL POTENTIAL VARY WITH DISTANCE FROM THE CENTER OF A STAR WITH UNIFORM DENSITY?

WHAT IS THE LIMIT OF SINE-X-OVER-X AS X APPROACHES ZERO?

...

...ZERO?

ONE!

WAKE UP!

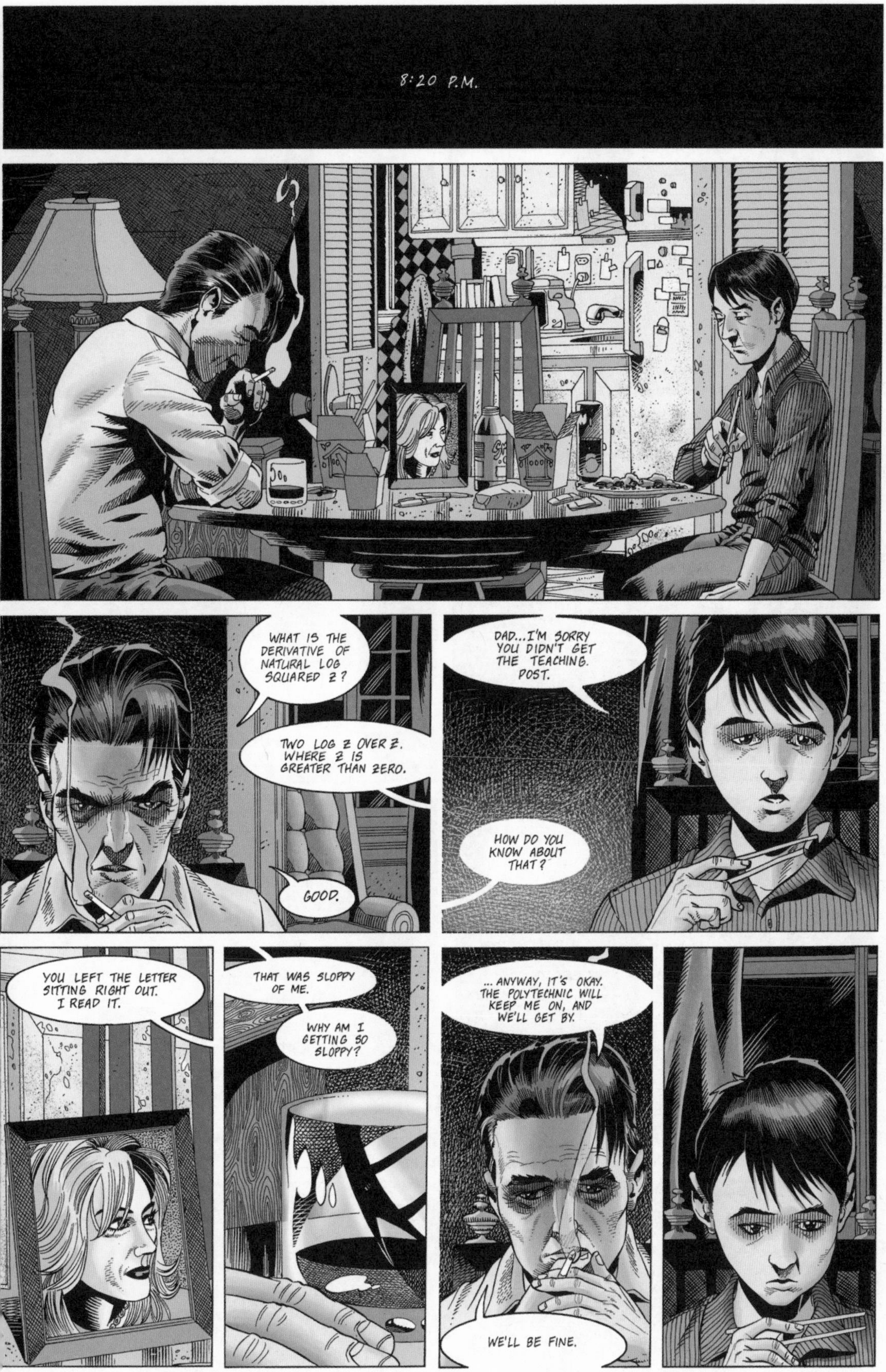
8:20 P.M.
WHAT IS THE DERIVATIVE OF NATURAL LOG SQUARED Z?
TWO LOG Z OVER Z. WHERE Z IS GREATER THAN ZERO.
GOOD.
DAD...I'M SORRY YOU DIDN'T GET THE TEACHING POST.
HOW DO YOU KNOW ABOUT THAT?
YOU LEFT THE LETTER SITTING RIGHT OUT. I READ IT.
THAT WAS SLOPPY OF ME.
WHY AM I GETTING SO SLOPPY?
... ANYWAY, IT'S OKAY. THE POLYTECHNIC WILL KEEP ME ON, AND WE'LL GET BY.
WE'LL BE FINE.

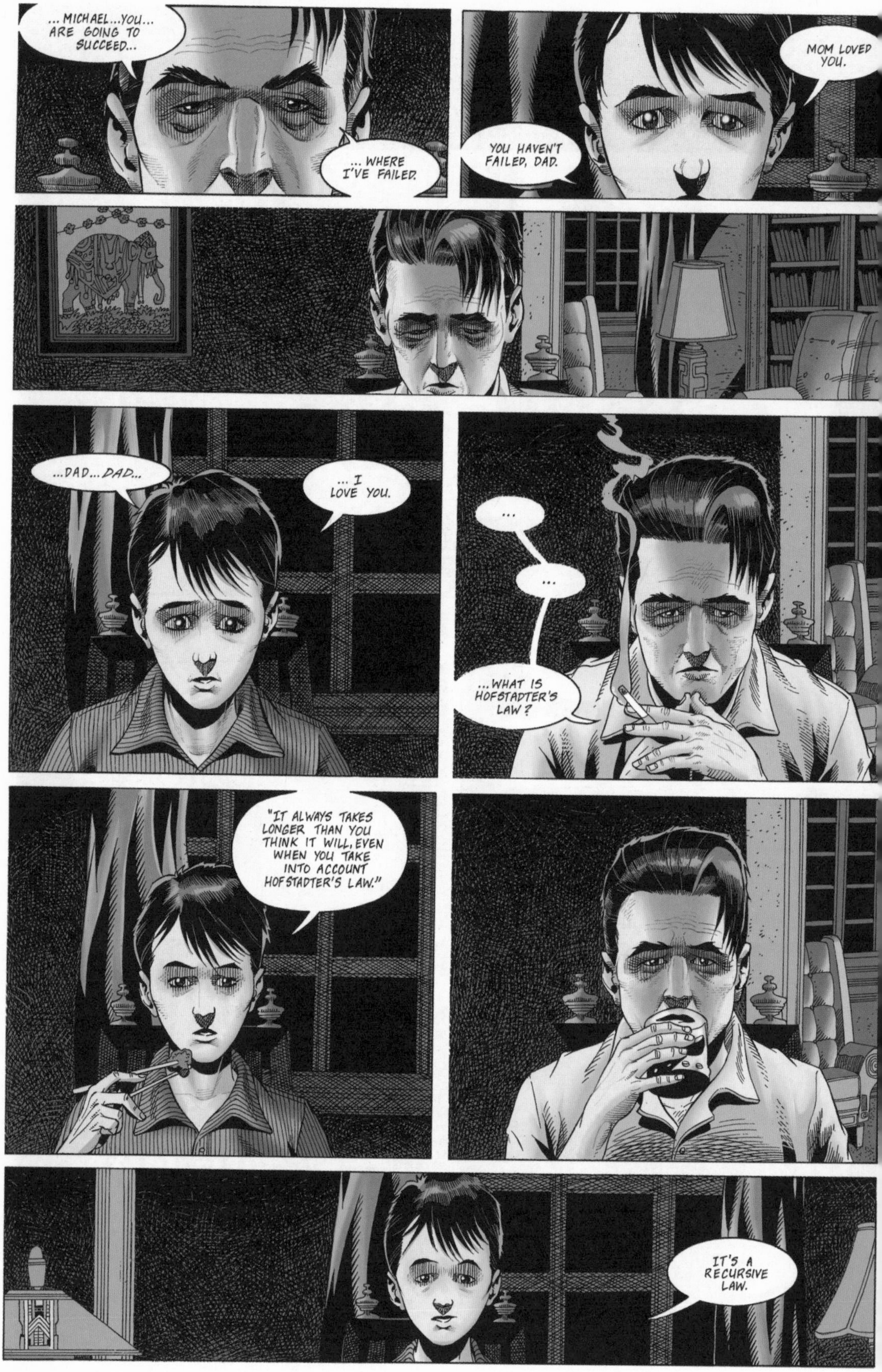
... MICHAEL...YOU... ARE GOING TO SUCCEED...
... WHERE I'VE FAILED.
MOM LOVED YOU.
YOU HAVEN'T FAILED, DAD.
...DAD...DAD...
... I LOVE YOU.
...
...
...WHAT IS HOFSTADTER'S LAW?
"IT ALWAYS TAKES LONGER THAN YOU THINK IT WILL, EVEN WHEN YOU TAKE INTO ACCOUNT HOFSTADTER'S LAW."
IT'S A RECURSIVE LAW.

11:05 P.M.

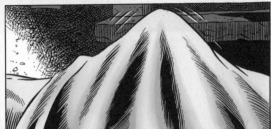

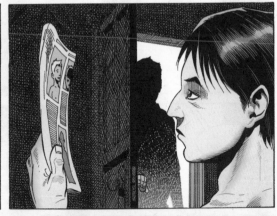

G'NIGHT, DAD.

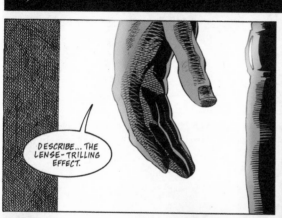

DESCRIBE... THE LENSE-TRILLING EFFECT.

IT'S A GENERAL RELATIVISTIC PRECESSION IN THE ROTATION OF A BODY NEAR A SECOND, MASSIVE ROTATING BODY CAUSED BY GRAVITOMAGNETIC FRAME DRAGGING.

WHA' YOU GOT THERE?

DAD, IT'S NOTHING. PLEASE, I WANT TO SLEEP--

DUN' LOOK T'ME LIKE YOU WAN' SLEEP. WUZ' THIS THEN?

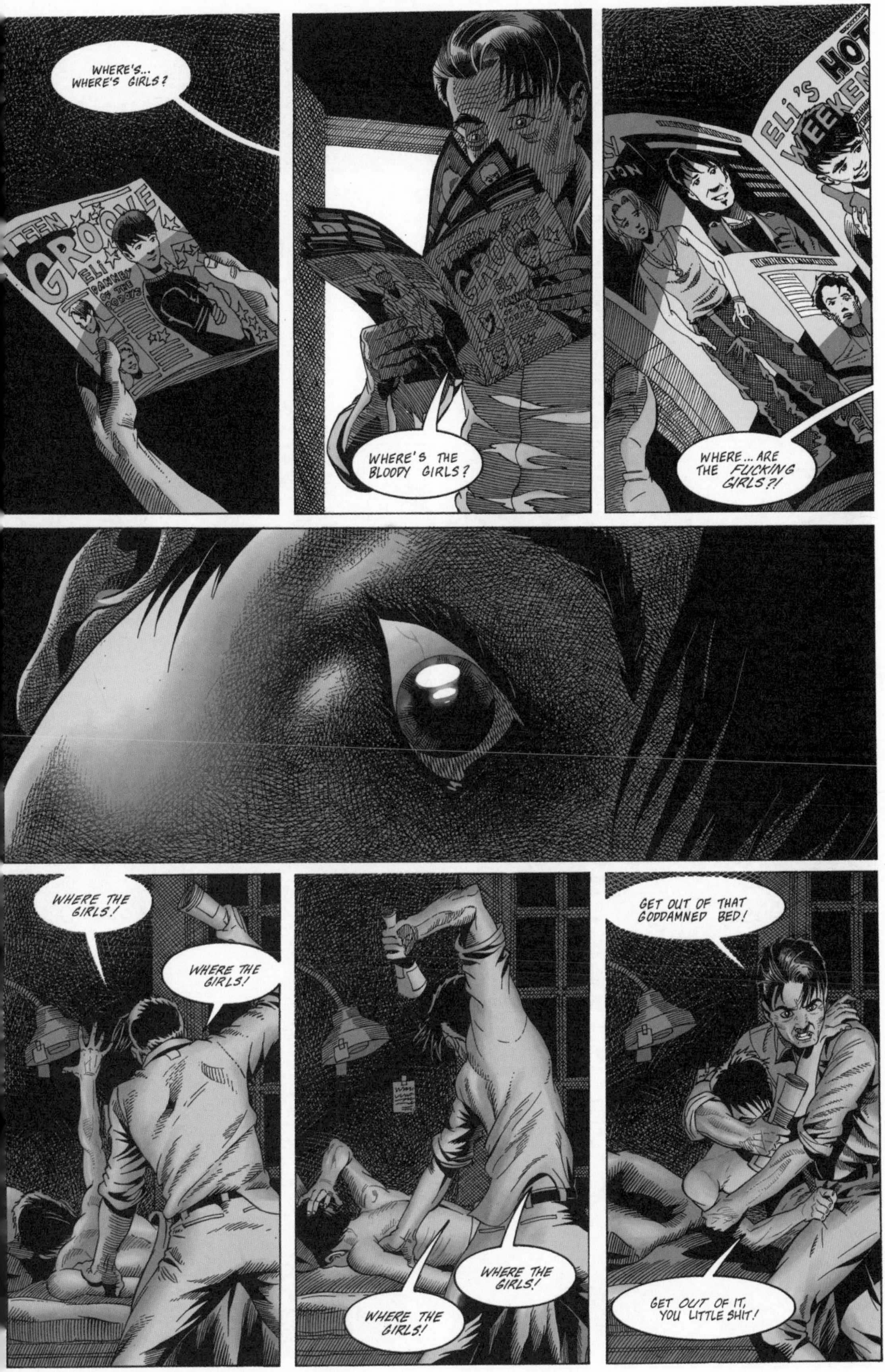
WHERE'S... WHERE'S GIRLS?
TEEN GROOVE
ELI
DANNY OF THE FOBOYS
WHERE'S THE BLOODY GIRLS?
ELI'S HOT WEEKEND
WHERE... ARE THE FUCKING GIRLS?!
WHERE THE GIRLS!
WHERE THE GIRLS!
WHERE THE GIRLS!
WHERE THE GIRLS!
GET OUT OF THAT GODDAMNED BED!
GET OUT OF IT, YOU LITTLE SHIT!

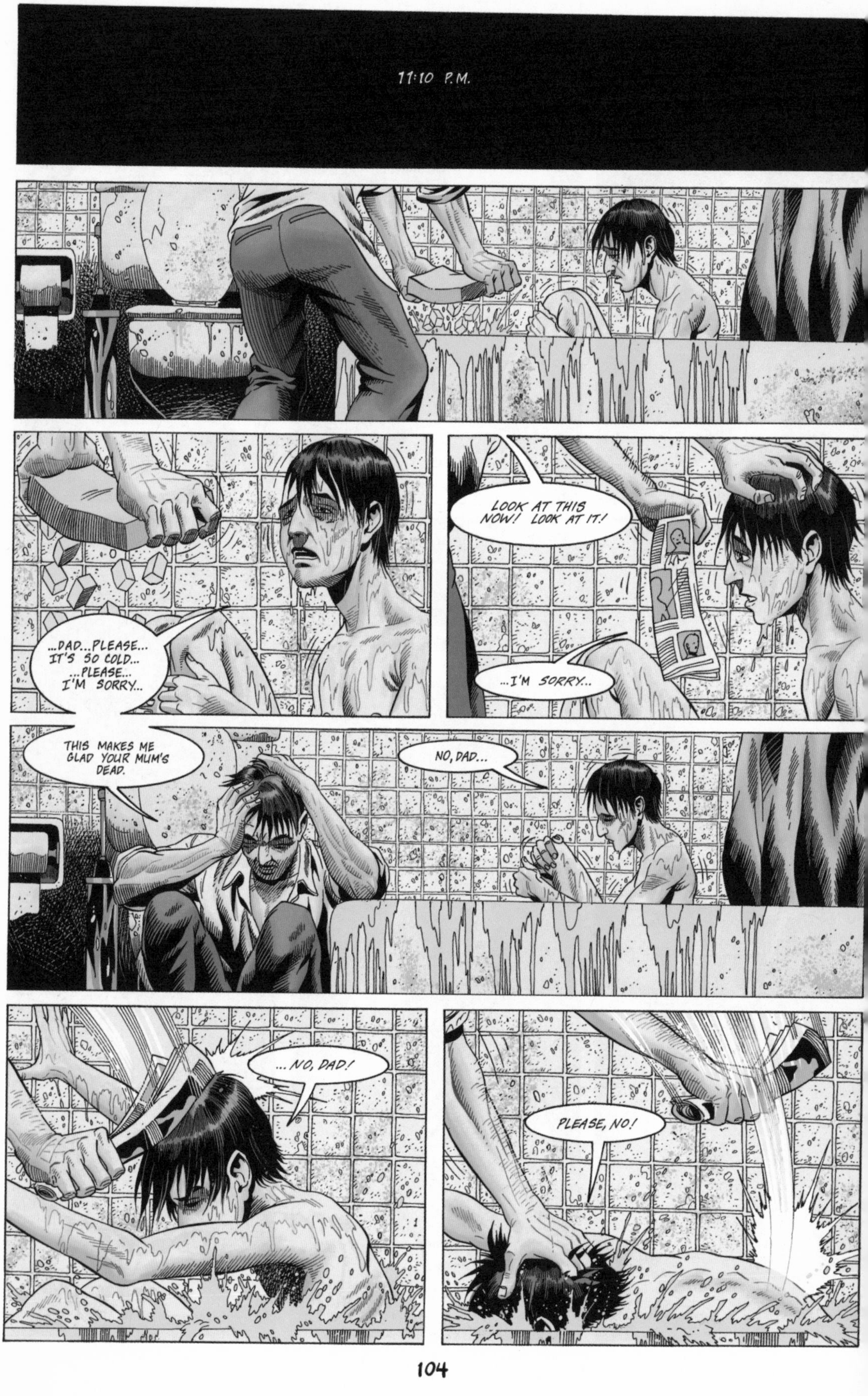
11:10 P.M.
...DAD...PLEASE... IT'S SO COLD... ...PLEASE... I'M SORRY...
LOOK AT THIS NOW! LOOK AT IT!
...I'M SORRY...
THIS MAKES ME GLAD YOUR MUM'S DEAD.
NO, DAD...
...NO, DAD!
PLEASE, NO!

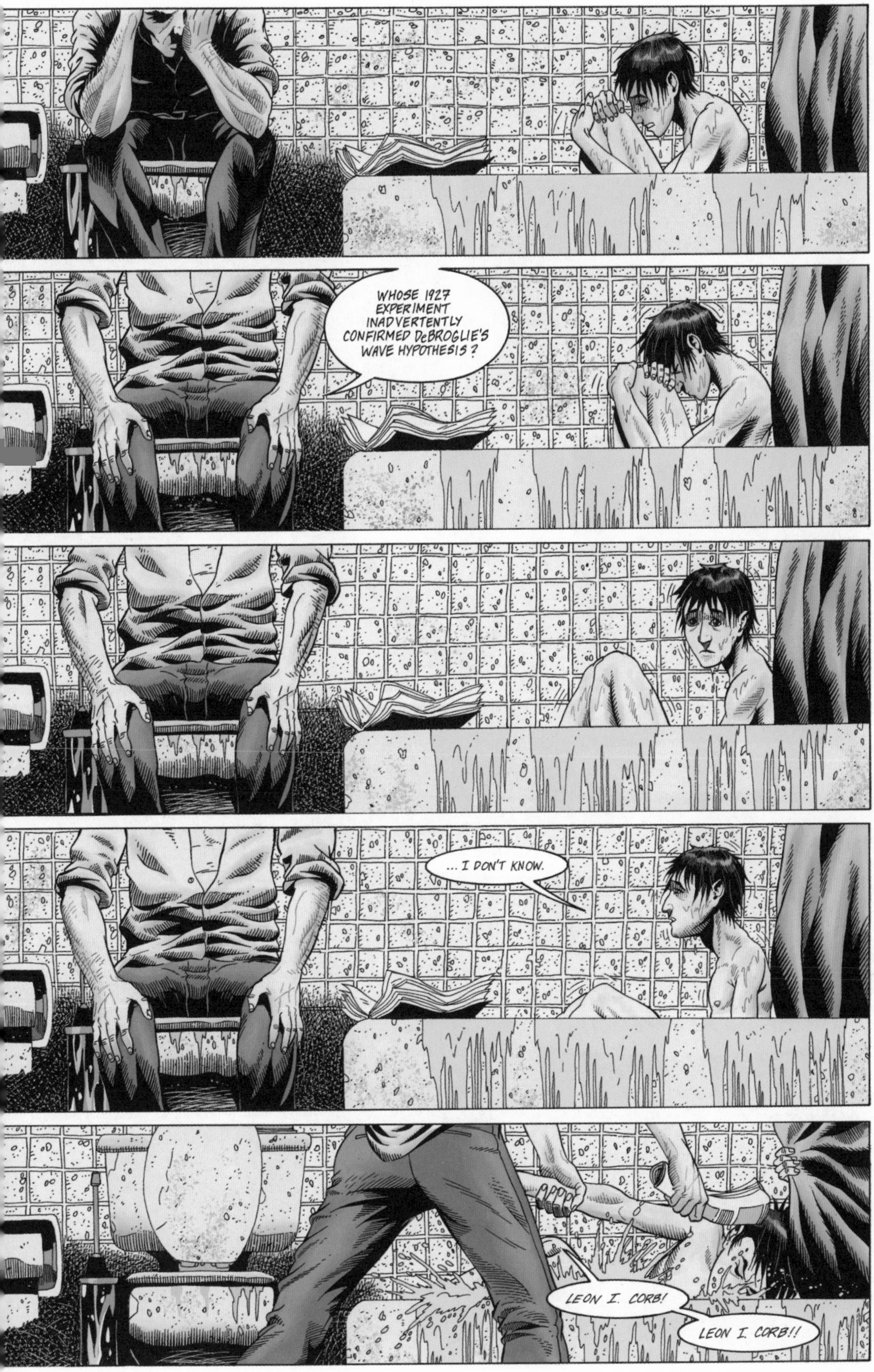
WHOSE 1927 EXPERIMENT INADVERTENTLY CONFIRMED DeBROGLIE'S WAVE HYPOTHESIS?
... I DON'T KNOW.
LEON I. CORB!
LEON I. CORB!!

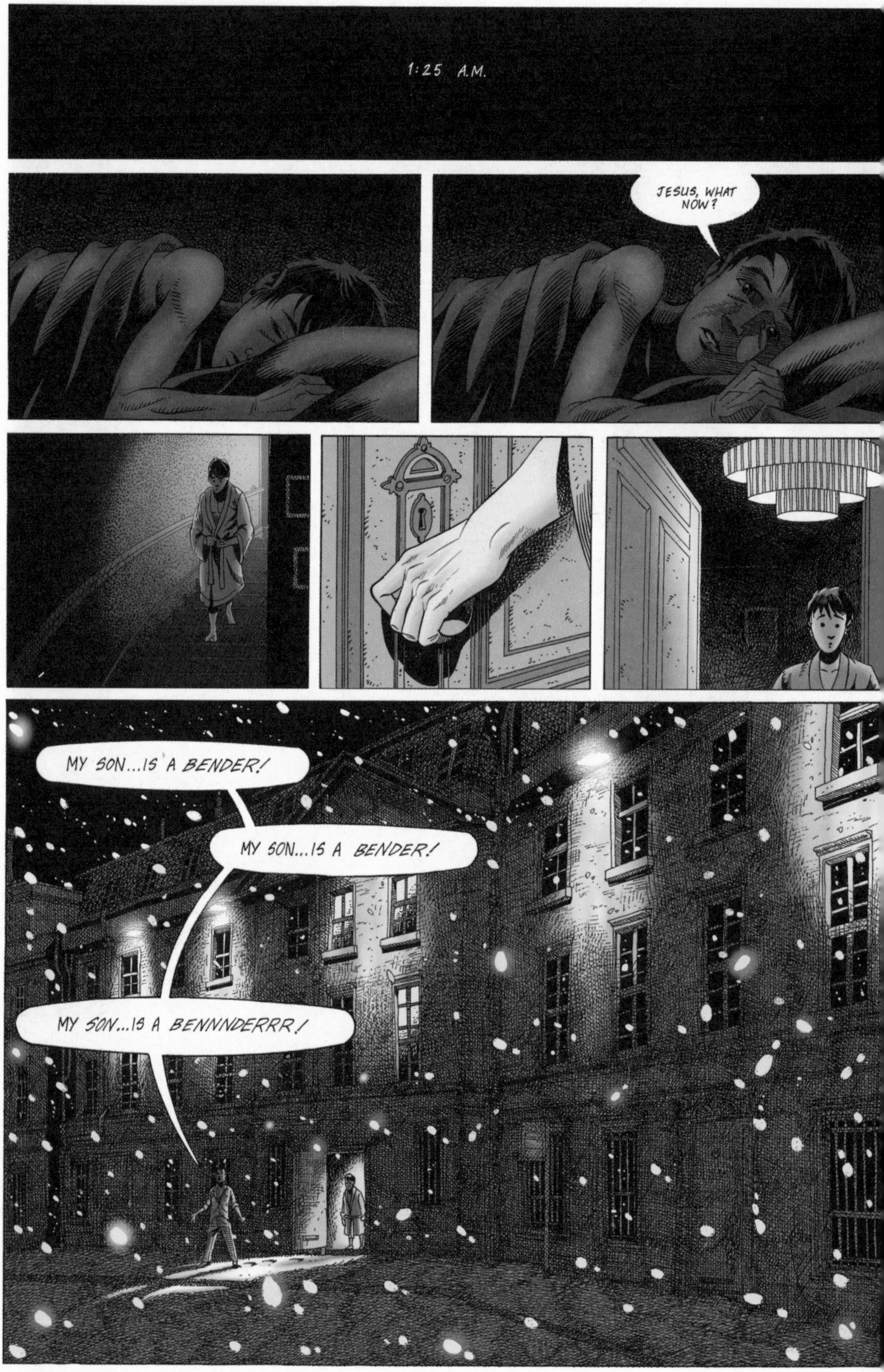
1:25 A.M.
JESUS, WHAT NOW?
MY SON...IS A BENDER!
MY SON...IS A BENDER!
MY SON...IS A BENNNDERRR!

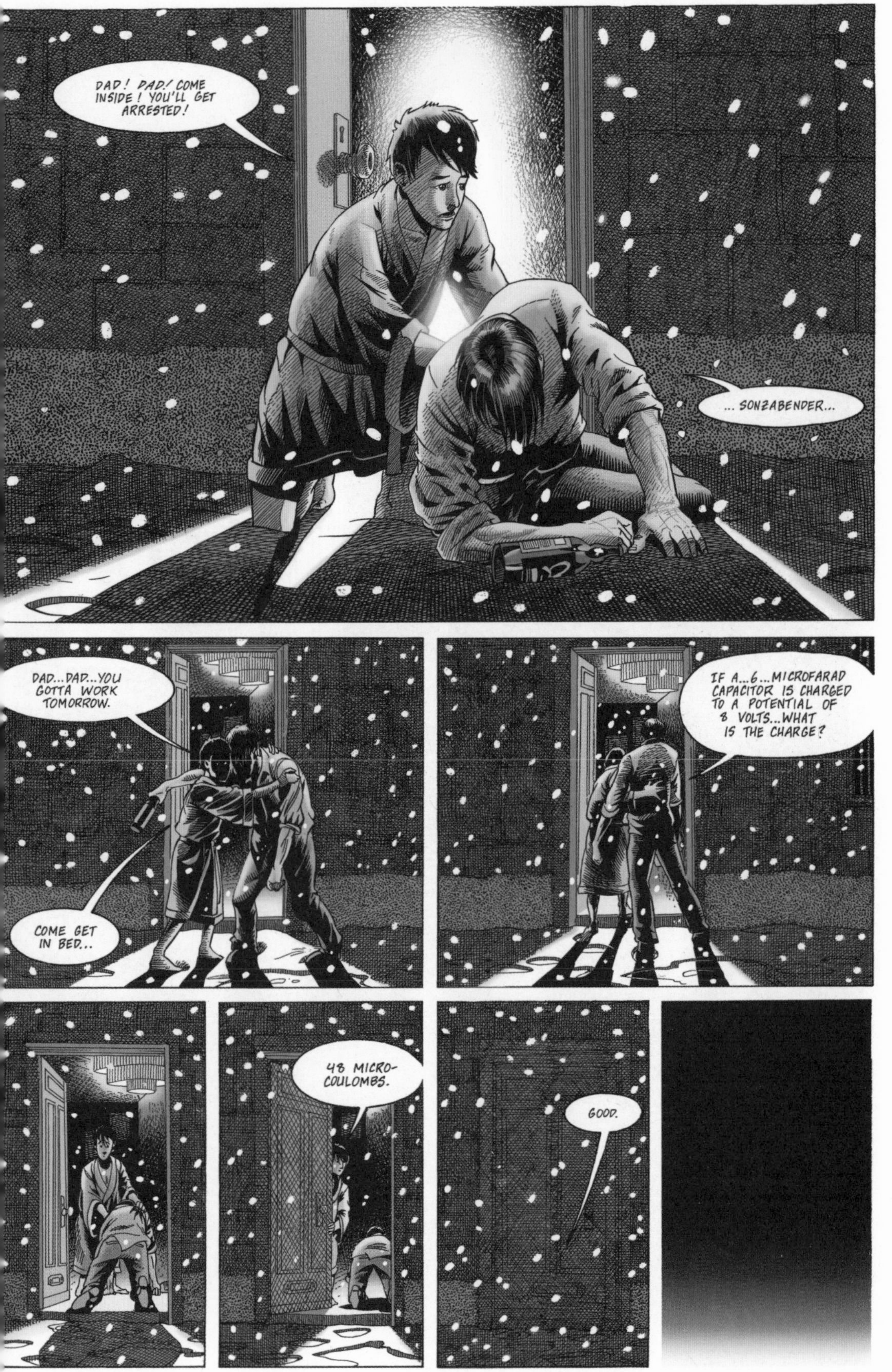
DAD! DAD! COME INSIDE! YOU'LL GET ARRESTED!
... SONZABENDER...
DAD...DAD...YOU GOTTA WORK TOMORROW.
COME GET IN BED...
IF A...6...MICROFARAD CAPACITOR IS CHARGED TO A POTENTIAL OF 8 VOLTS...WHAT IS THE CHARGE?
48 MICRO-COULOMBS.
GOOD.

4

ADVANTAGE: LEPORE

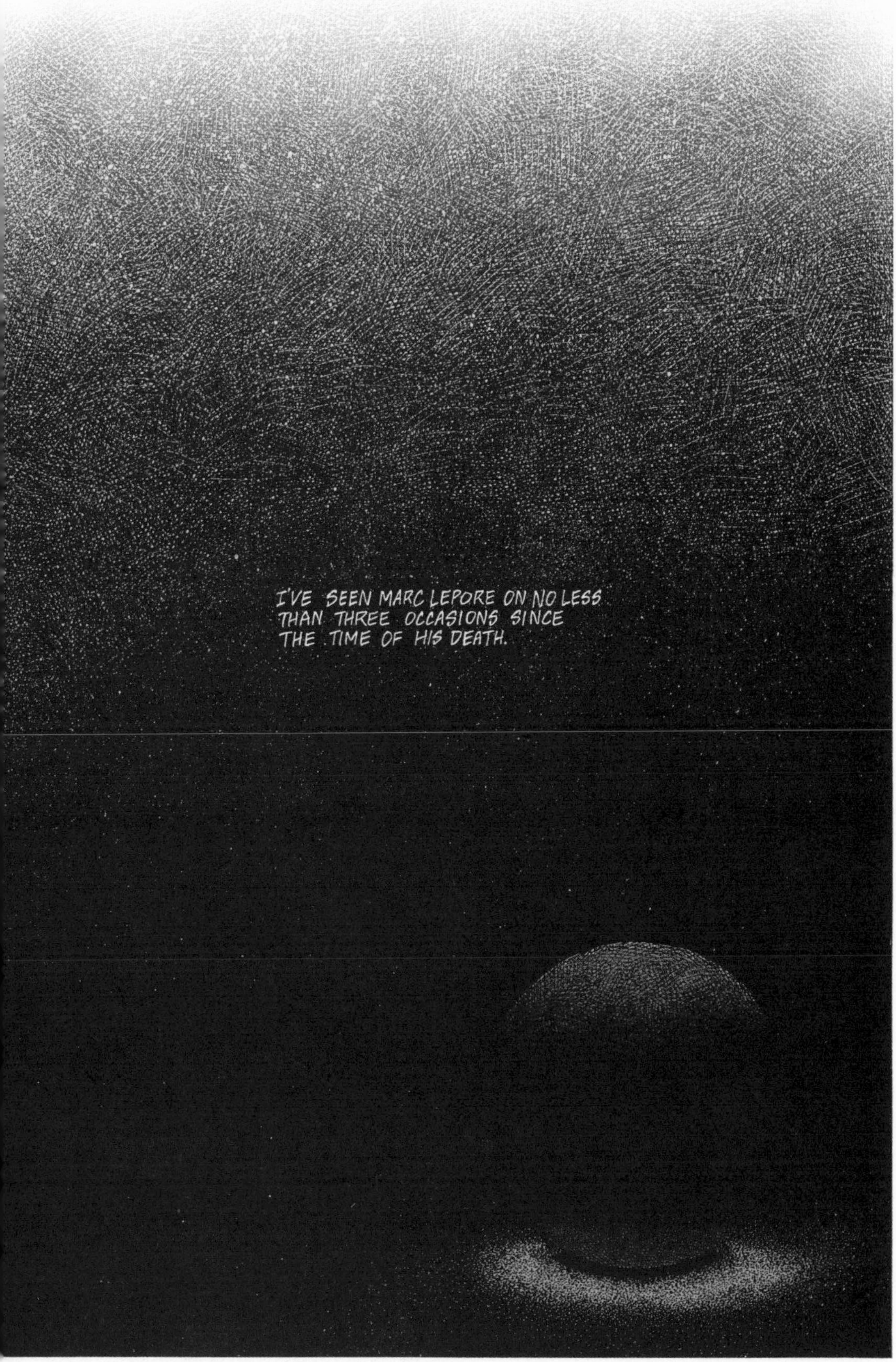
I'VE SEEN MARC LEPORE ON NO LESS THAN THREE OCCASIONS SINCE THE TIME OF HIS DEATH.

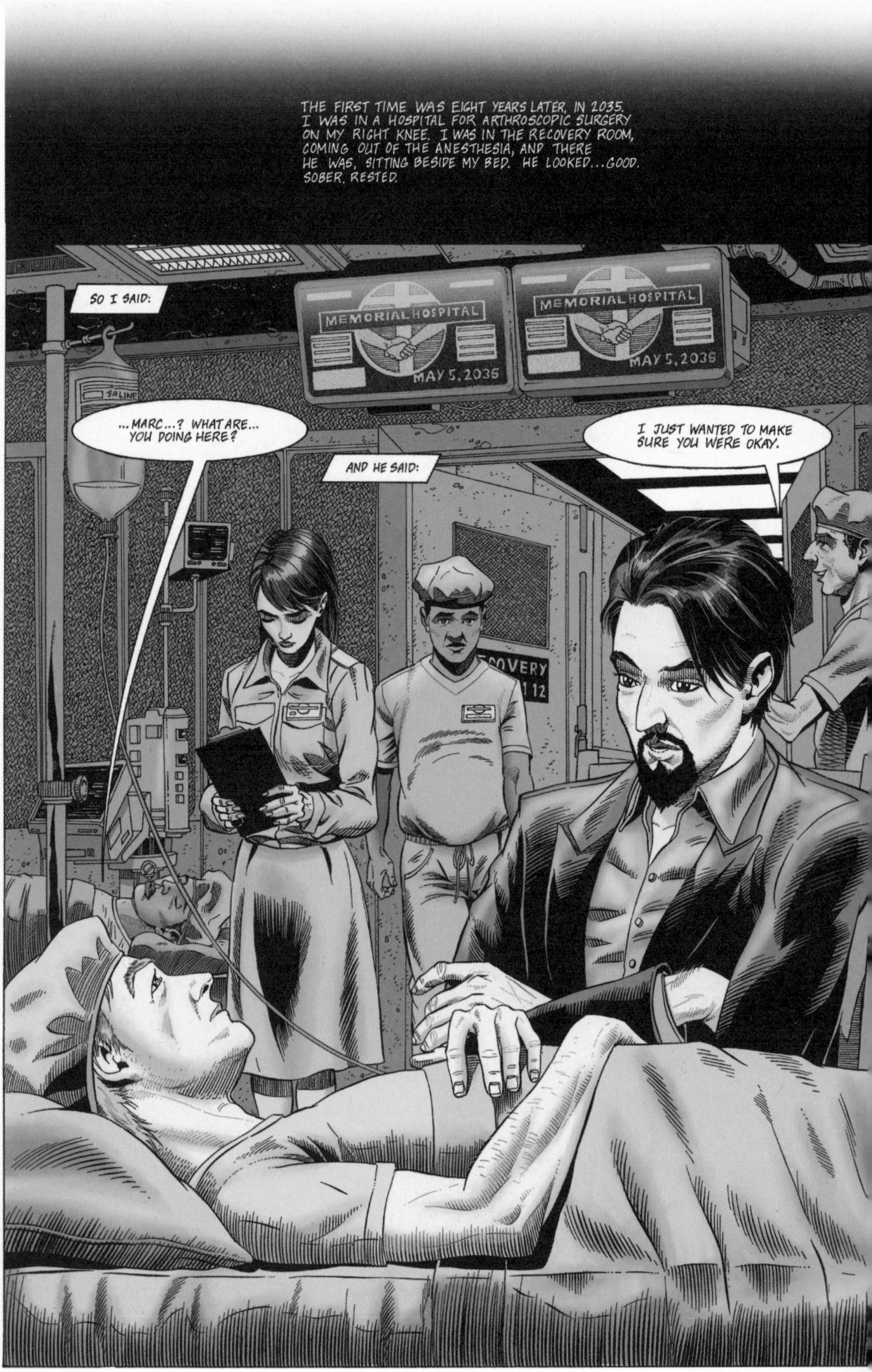
THE FIRST TIME WAS EIGHT YEARS LATER, IN 2035. I WAS IN A HOSPITAL FOR ARTHROSCOPIC SURGERY ON MY RIGHT KNEE. I WAS IN THE RECOVERY ROOM, COMING OUT OF THE ANESTHESIA, AND THERE HE WAS, SITTING BESIDE MY BED. HE LOOKED... GOOD. SOBER. RESTED.
SO I SAID:
MEMORIAL HOSPITAL
MAY 5, 2035
MEMORIAL HOSPITAL
MAY 5, 2035
SALINE
...MARC...? WHAT ARE... YOU DOING HERE?
AND HE SAID:
I JUST WANTED TO MAKE SURE YOU WERE OKAY.

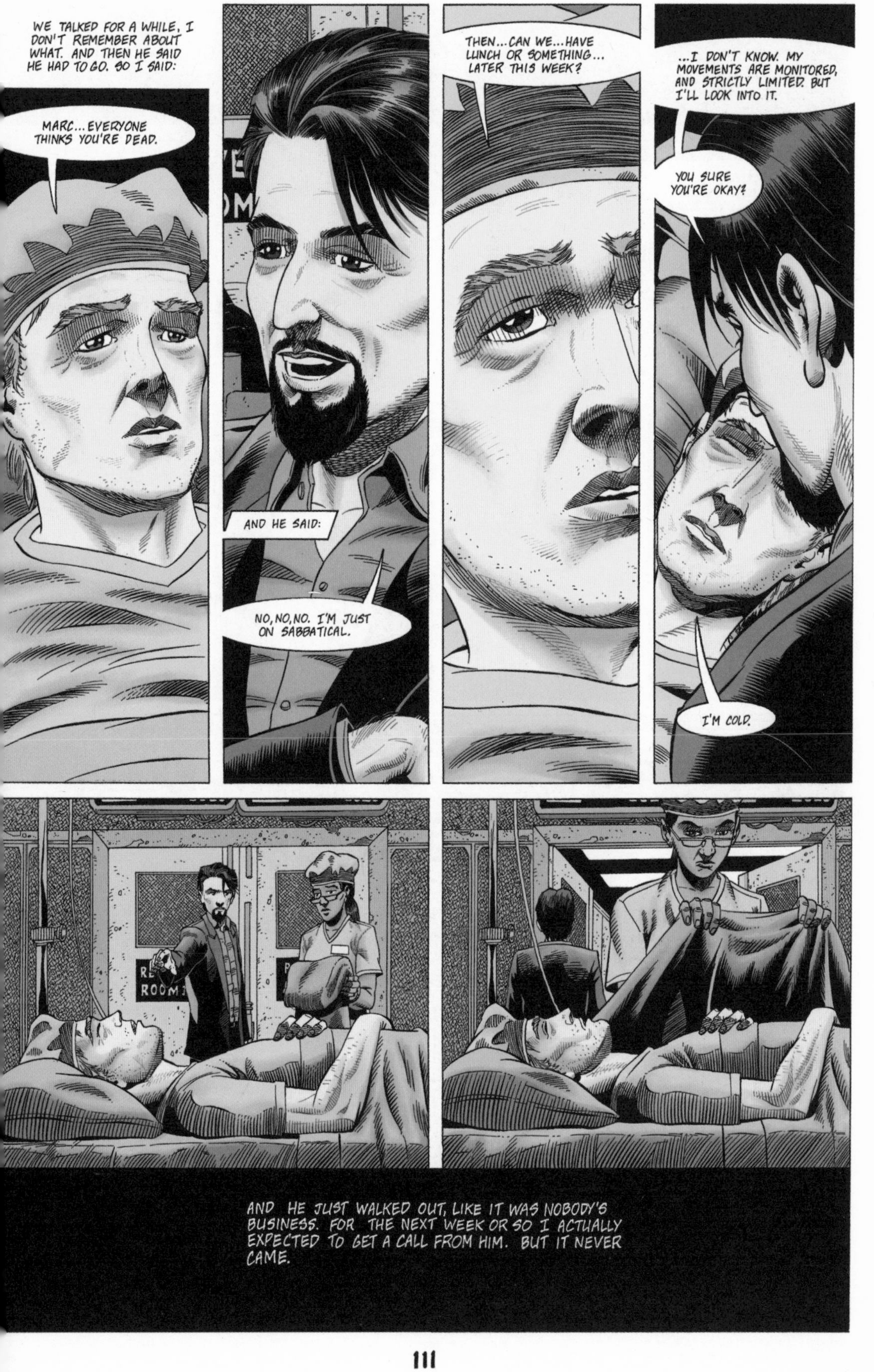
WE TALKED FOR A WHILE, I DON'T REMEMBER ABOUT WHAT. AND THEN HE SAID HE HAD TO GO. SO I SAID:
MARC... EVERYONE THINKS YOU'RE DEAD.
AND HE SAID:
NO, NO, NO. I'M JUST ON SABBATICAL.
THEN... CAN WE... HAVE LUNCH OR SOMETHING... LATER THIS WEEK?
...I DON'T KNOW. MY MOVEMENTS ARE MONITORED, AND STRICTLY LIMITED. BUT I'LL LOOK INTO IT.
YOU SURE YOU'RE OKAY?
I'M COLD.
AND HE JUST WALKED OUT, LIKE IT WAS NOBODY'S BUSINESS. FOR THE NEXT WEEK OR SO I ACTUALLY EXPECTED TO GET A CALL FROM HIM. BUT IT NEVER CAME.

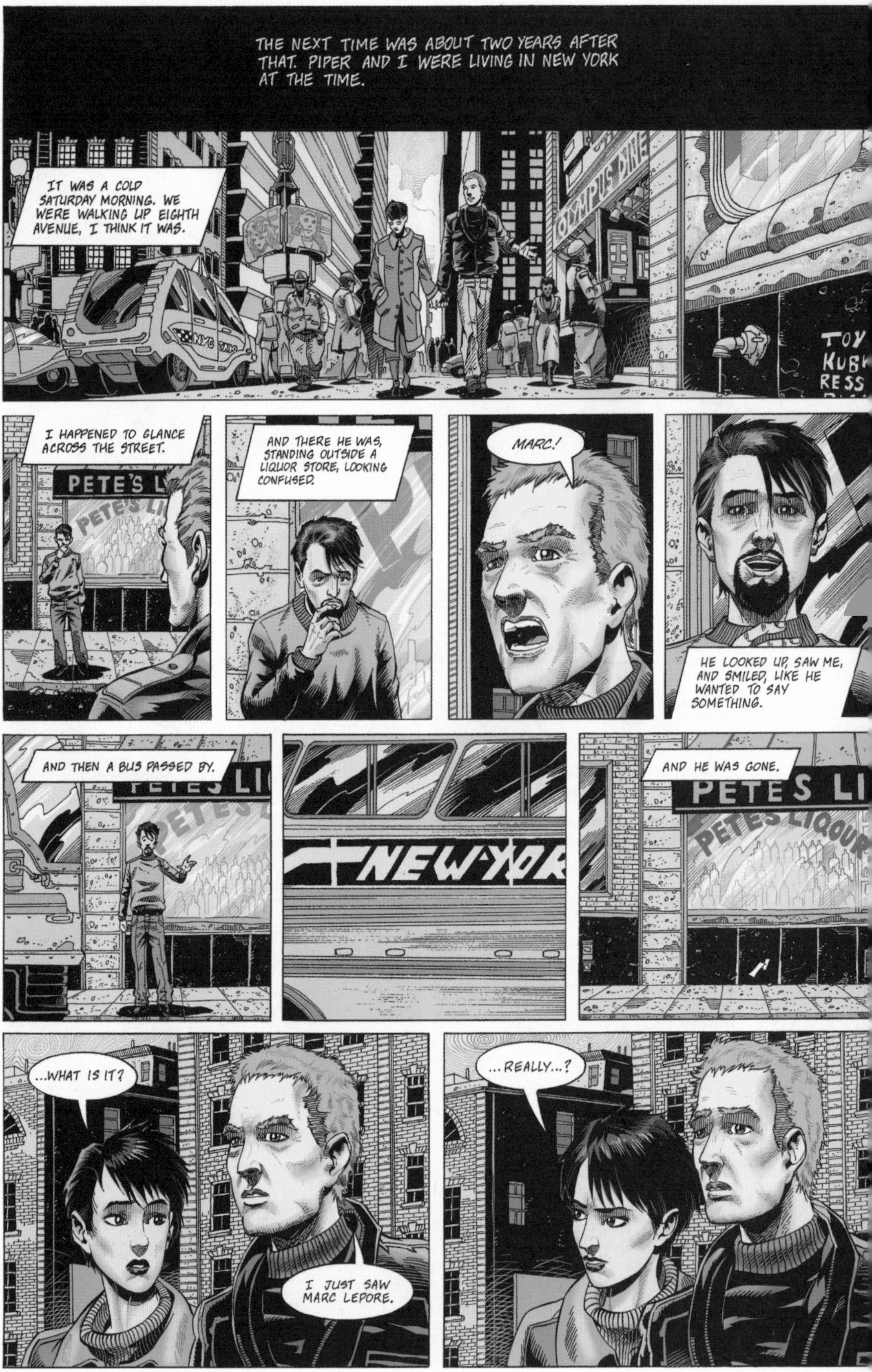
THE NEXT TIME WAS ABOUT TWO YEARS AFTER THAT. PIPER AND I WERE LIVING IN NEW YORK AT THE TIME.
IT WAS A COLD SATURDAY MORNING. WE WERE WALKING UP EIGHTH AVENUE, I THINK IT WAS.
OLYMPUS DINE
NYC TAXI
I HAPPENED TO GLANCE ACROSS THE STREET.
PETE'S LI
AND THERE HE WAS, STANDING OUTSIDE A LIQUOR STORE, LOOKING CONFUSED.
MARC!
HE LOOKED UP, SAW ME, AND SMILED, LIKE HE WANTED TO SAY SOMETHING.
AND THEN A BUS PASSED BY.
NEW-YOR
AND HE WAS GONE.
PETES LI
PETES LIQUOR
...WHAT IS IT?
I JUST SAW MARC LEPORE.
...REALLY...?

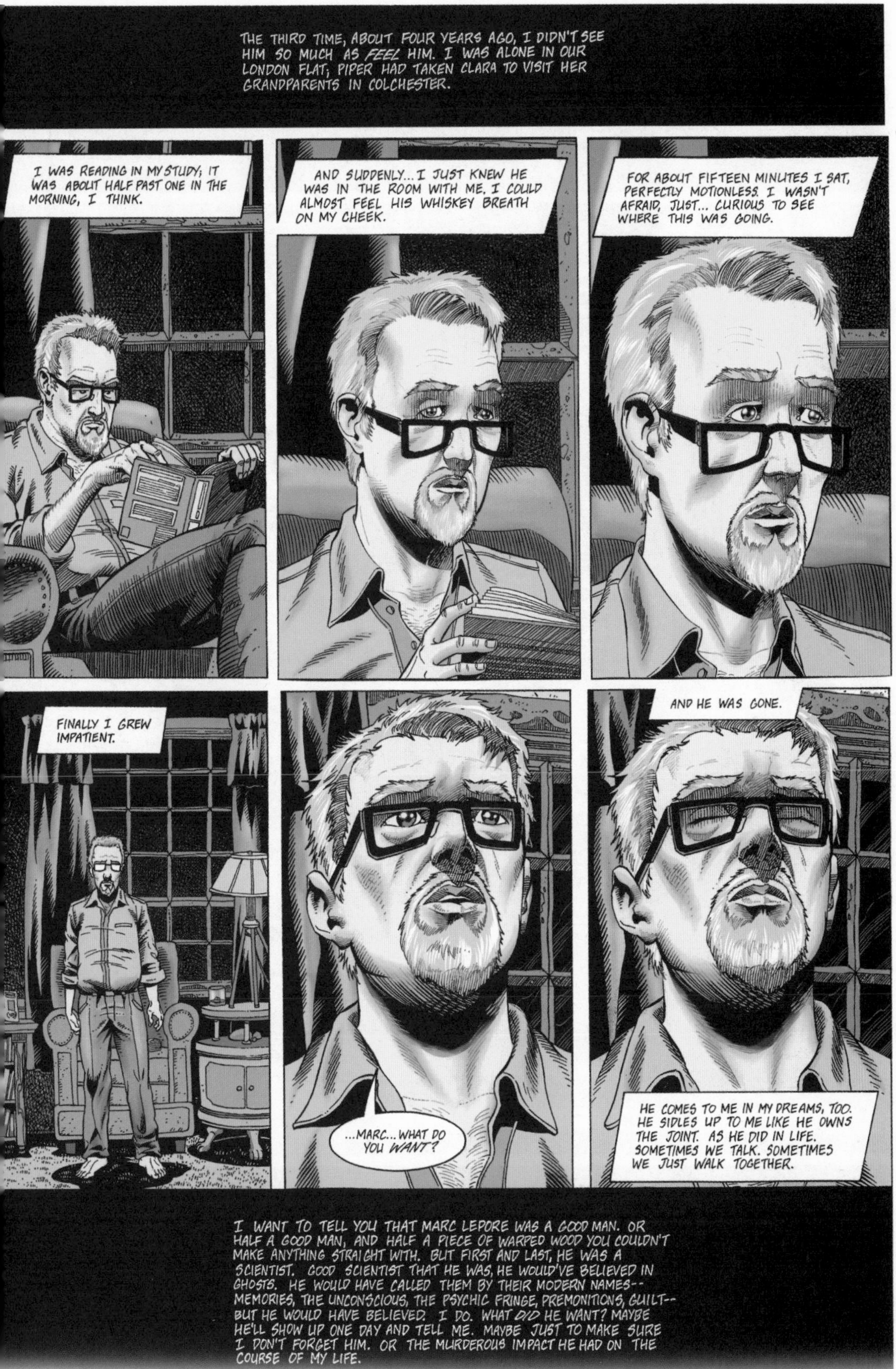

THE THIRD TIME, ABOUT FOUR YEARS AGO, I DIDN'T SEE HIM SO MUCH AS *FEEL* HIM. I WAS ALONE IN OUR LONDON FLAT; PIPER HAD TAKEN CLARA TO VISIT HER GRANDPARENTS IN COLCHESTER.
I WAS READING IN MY STUDY; IT WAS ABOUT HALF PAST ONE IN THE MORNING, I THINK.
AND SUDDENLY... I JUST KNEW HE WAS IN THE ROOM WITH ME. I COULD ALMOST FEEL HIS WHISKEY BREATH ON MY CHEEK.
FOR ABOUT FIFTEEN MINUTES I SAT, PERFECTLY MOTIONLESS. I WASN'T AFRAID, JUST... CURIOUS TO SEE WHERE THIS WAS GOING.
FINALLY I GREW IMPATIENT.
...MARC... WHAT DO YOU *WANT*?
AND HE WAS GONE.
HE COMES TO ME IN MY DREAMS, TOO. HE SIDLES UP TO ME LIKE HE OWNS THE JOINT. AS HE DID IN LIFE. SOMETIMES WE TALK. SOMETIMES WE JUST WALK TOGETHER.
I WANT TO TELL YOU THAT MARC LEPORE WAS A GOOD MAN. OR HALF A GOOD MAN, AND HALF A PIECE OF WARPED WOOD YOU COULDN'T MAKE ANYTHING STRAIGHT WITH. BUT FIRST AND LAST, HE WAS A SCIENTIST. GOOD SCIENTIST THAT HE WAS, HE WOULD'VE BELIEVED IN GHOSTS. HE WOULD HAVE CALLED THEM BY THEIR MODERN NAMES-- MEMORIES, THE UNCONSCIOUS, THE PSYCHIC FRINGE, PREMONITIONS, GUILT-- BUT HE WOULD HAVE BELIEVED. I DO. WHAT *DID* HE WANT? MAYBE HE'LL SHOW UP ONE DAY AND TELL ME. MAYBE JUST TO MAKE SURE I DON'T FORGET HIM. OR THE MURDEROUS IMPACT HE HAD ON THE COURSE OF MY LIFE.

BY JANUARY OF 2028, PHASE THREE OF THE GARD PROGRAM WAS BEING IMPLEMENTED. OVER 4,000 GARD PRISONERS WERE NOW LIVING IN PLAIN SIGHT, SO TO SPEAK, IN LOS ANGELES, CHICAGO, NEW YORK CITY, BALTIMORE, AND HOUSTON. THERE WAS THE OCCASIONAL PERFUNCTORY PROTEST, THE OCCASIONAL ANGRY EDITORIAL.

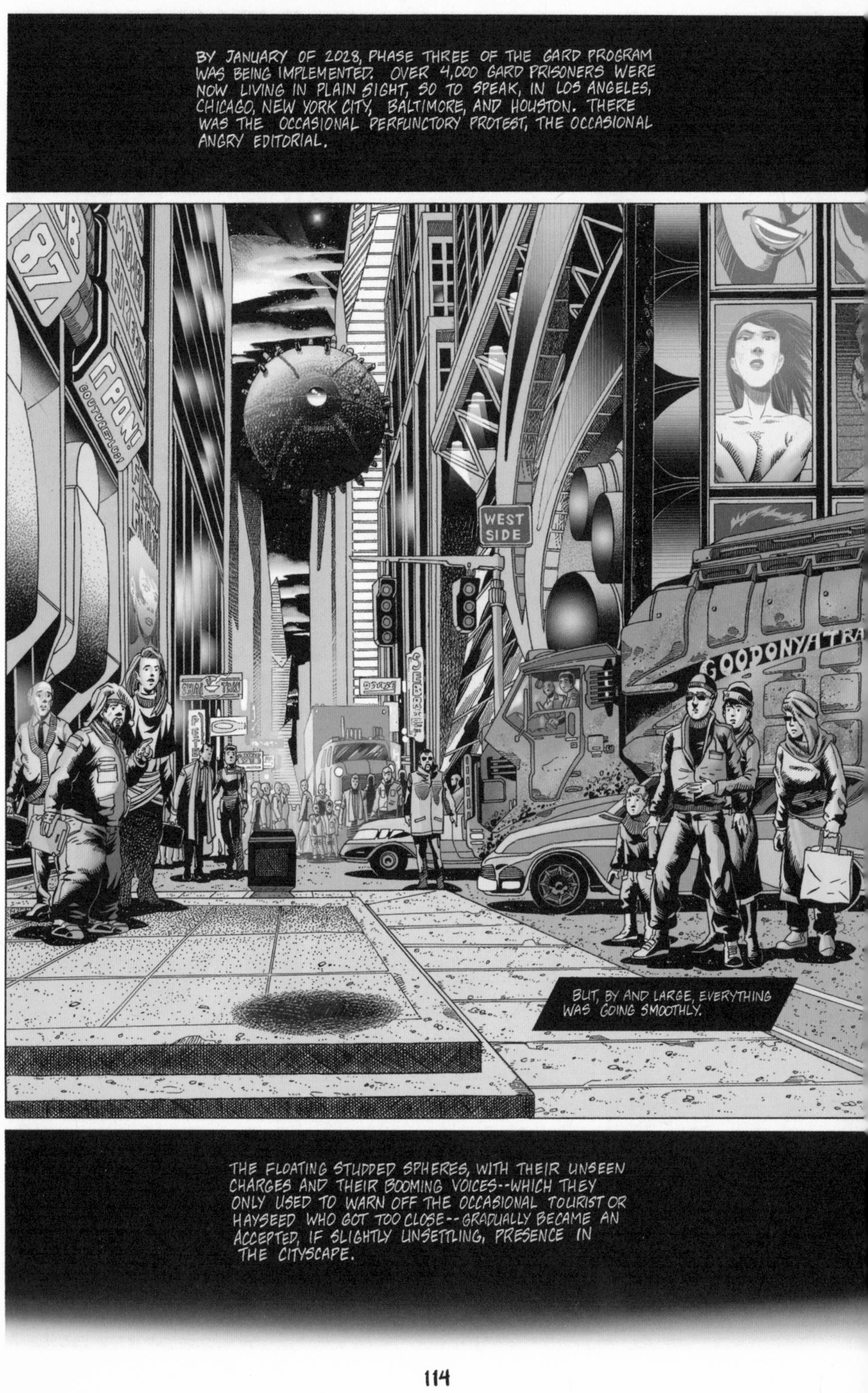

WEST SIDE
BUT, BY AND LARGE, EVERYTHING WAS GOING SMOOTHLY.

THE FLOATING STUDDED SPHERES, WITH THEIR UNSEEN CHARGES AND THEIR BOOMING VOICES--WHICH THEY ONLY USED TO WARN OFF THE OCCASIONAL TOURIST OR HAYSEED WHO GOT TOO CLOSE--GRADUALLY BECAME AN ACCEPTED, IF SLIGHTLY UNSETTLING, PRESENCE IN THE CITYSCAPE.

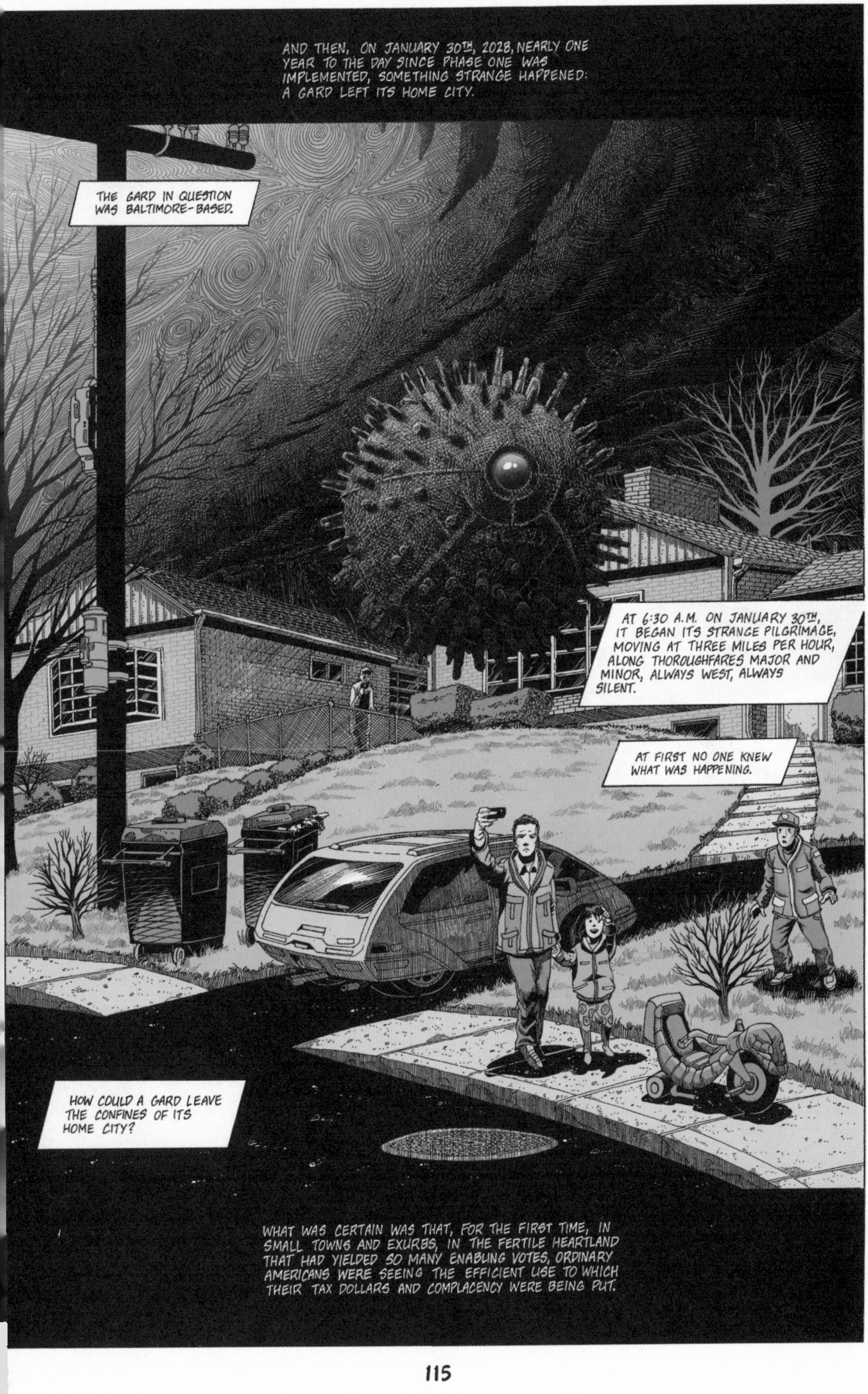
AND THEN, ON JANUARY 30TH, 2028, NEARLY ONE YEAR TO THE DAY SINCE PHASE ONE WAS IMPLEMENTED, SOMETHING STRANGE HAPPENED: A GARD LEFT ITS HOME CITY.
THE GARD IN QUESTION WAS BALTIMORE-BASED.
AT 6:30 A.M. ON JANUARY 30TH, IT BEGAN ITS STRANGE PILGRIMAGE, MOVING AT THREE MILES PER HOUR, ALONG THOROUGHFARES MAJOR AND MINOR, ALWAYS WEST, ALWAYS SILENT.
AT FIRST NO ONE KNEW WHAT WAS HAPPENING.
HOW COULD A GARD LEAVE THE CONFINES OF ITS HOME CITY?
WHAT WAS CERTAIN WAS THAT, FOR THE FIRST TIME, IN SMALL TOWNS AND EXURBS, IN THE FERTILE HEARTLAND THAT HAD YIELDED SO MANY ENABLING VOTES, ORDINARY AMERICANS WERE SEEING THE EFFICIENT USE TO WHICH THEIR TAX DOLLARS AND COMPLACENCY WERE BEING PUT.

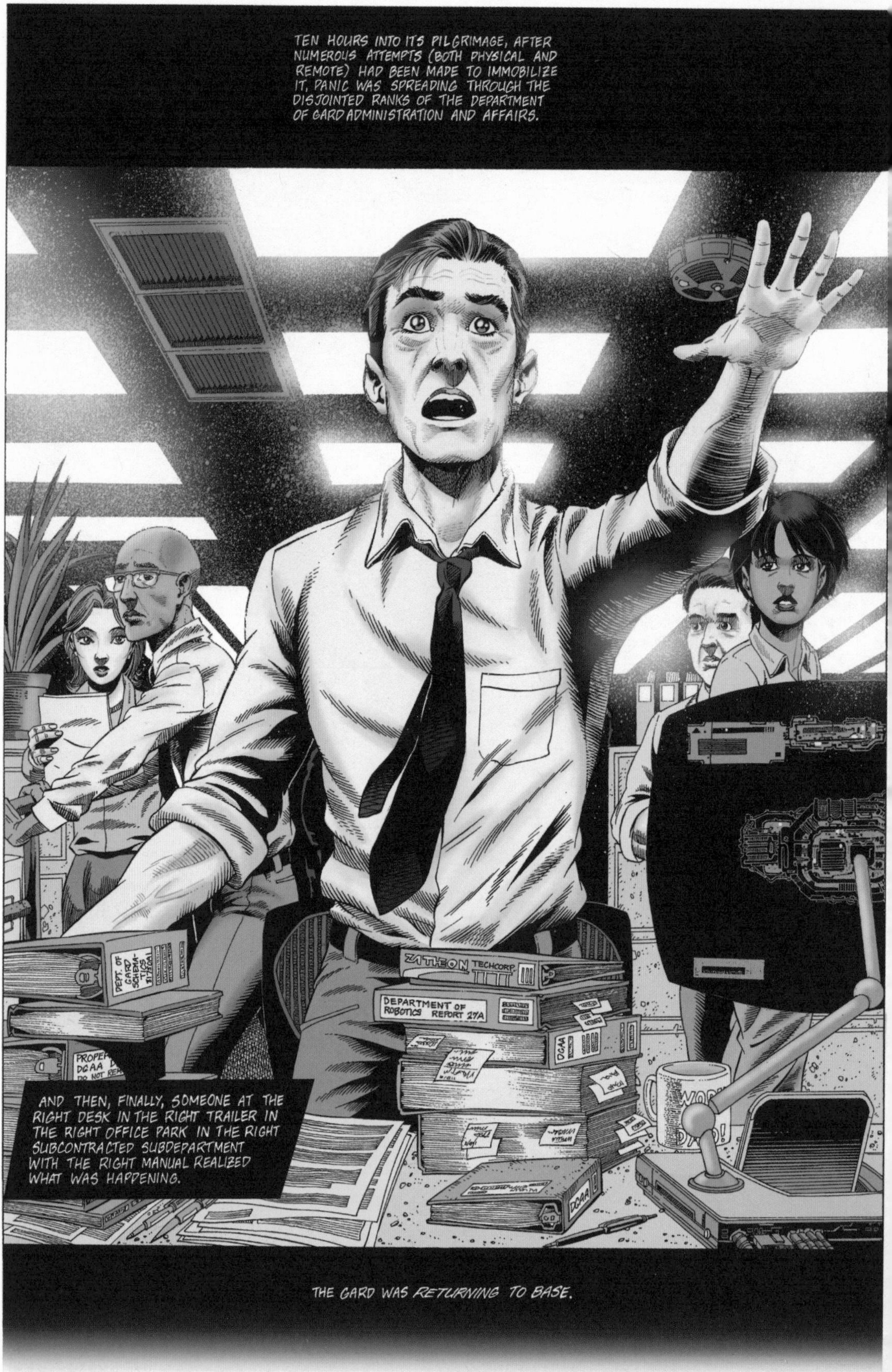
TEN HOURS INTO ITS PILGRIMAGE, AFTER NUMEROUS ATTEMPTS (BOTH PHYSICAL AND REMOTE) HAD BEEN MADE TO IMMOBILIZE IT, PANIC WAS SPREADING THROUGH THE DISJOINTED RANKS OF THE DEPARTMENT OF CARD ADMINISTRATION AND AFFAIRS.
ZATHEON TECHCORP
DEPARTMENT OF ROBOTICS REPORT 27A
DGAA
DGAA
AND THEN, FINALLY, SOMEONE AT THE RIGHT DESK IN THE RIGHT TRAILER IN THE RIGHT OFFICE PARK IN THE RIGHT SUBCONTRACTED SUBDEPARTMENT WITH THE RIGHT MANUAL REALIZED WHAT WAS HAPPENING.
THE CARD WAS *RETURNING* TO BASE.

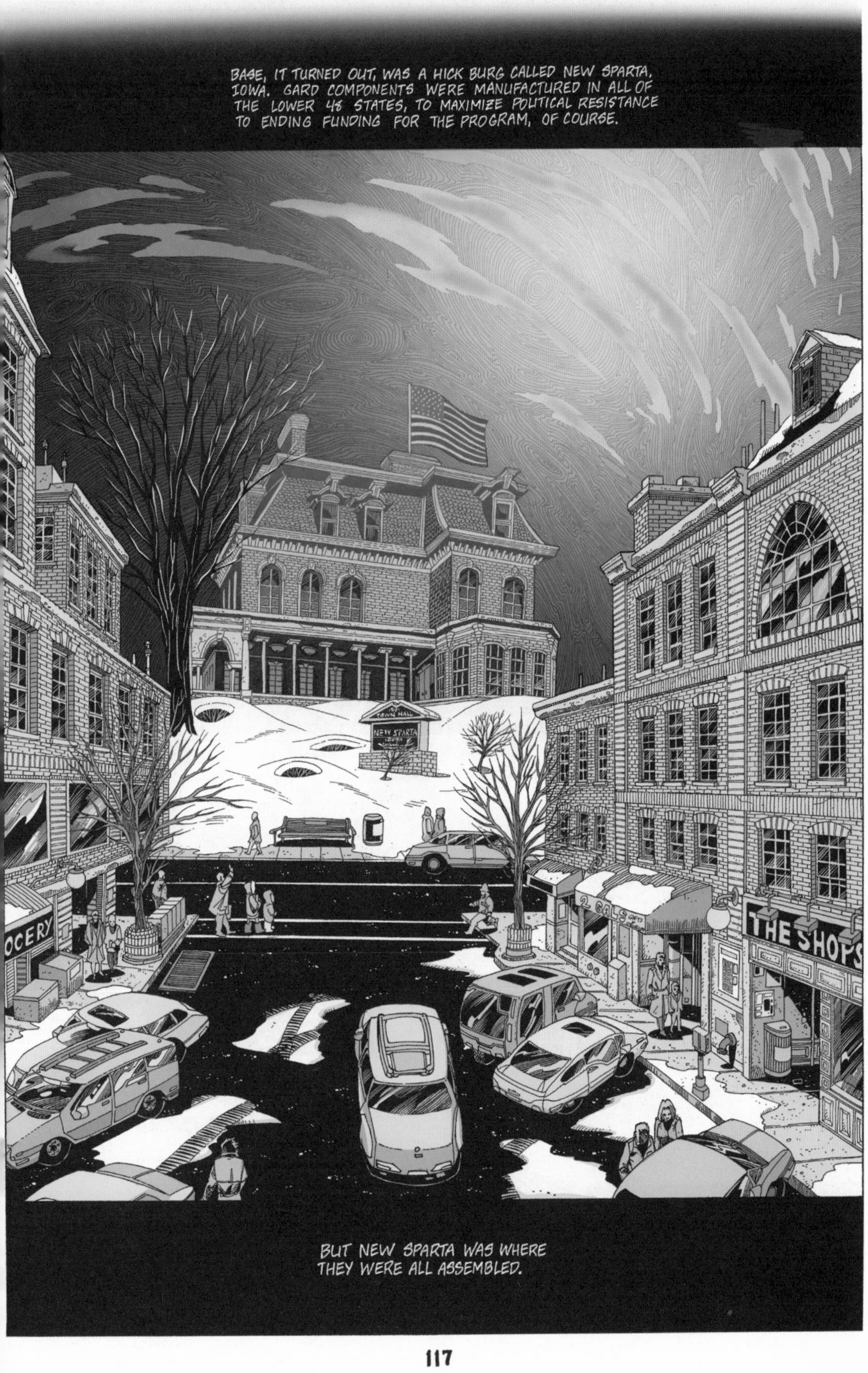
BASE, IT TURNED OUT, WAS A HICK BURG CALLED NEW SPARTA, IOWA. GARD COMPONENTS WERE MANUFACTURED IN ALL OF THE LOWER 48 STATES, TO MAXIMIZE POLITICAL RESISTANCE TO ENDING FUNDING FOR THE PROGRAM, OF COURSE.
TOWN HALL
NEW SPARTA
OCERY
2 GALS
THE SHOPS
BUT NEW SPARTA WAS WHERE THEY WERE ALL ASSEMBLED.

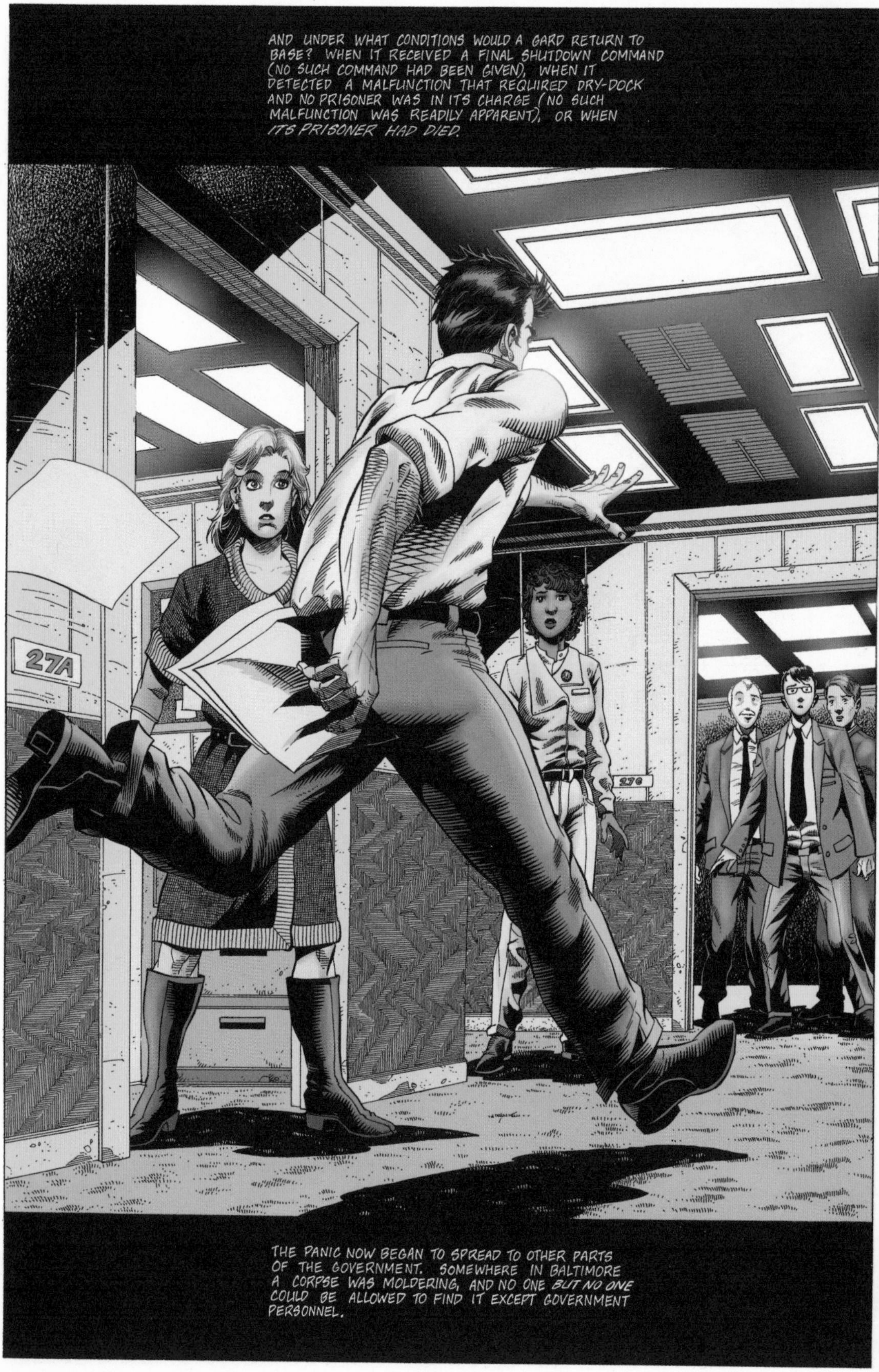
AND UNDER WHAT CONDITIONS WOULD A GARD RETURN TO BASE? WHEN IT RECEIVED A FINAL SHUTDOWN COMMAND (NO SUCH COMMAND HAD BEEN GIVEN), WHEN IT DETECTED A MALFUNCTION THAT REQUIRED DRY-DOCK AND NO PRISONER WAS IN ITS CHARGE (NO SUCH MALFUNCTION WAS READILY APPARENT), OR WHEN *ITS PRISONER HAD DIED.*
27A
THE PANIC NOW BEGAN TO SPREAD TO OTHER PARTS OF THE GOVERNMENT. SOMEWHERE IN BALTIMORE A CORPSE WAS MOLDERING, AND NO ONE *BUT NO ONE* COULD BE ALLOWED TO FIND IT EXCEPT GOVERNMENT PERSONNEL.

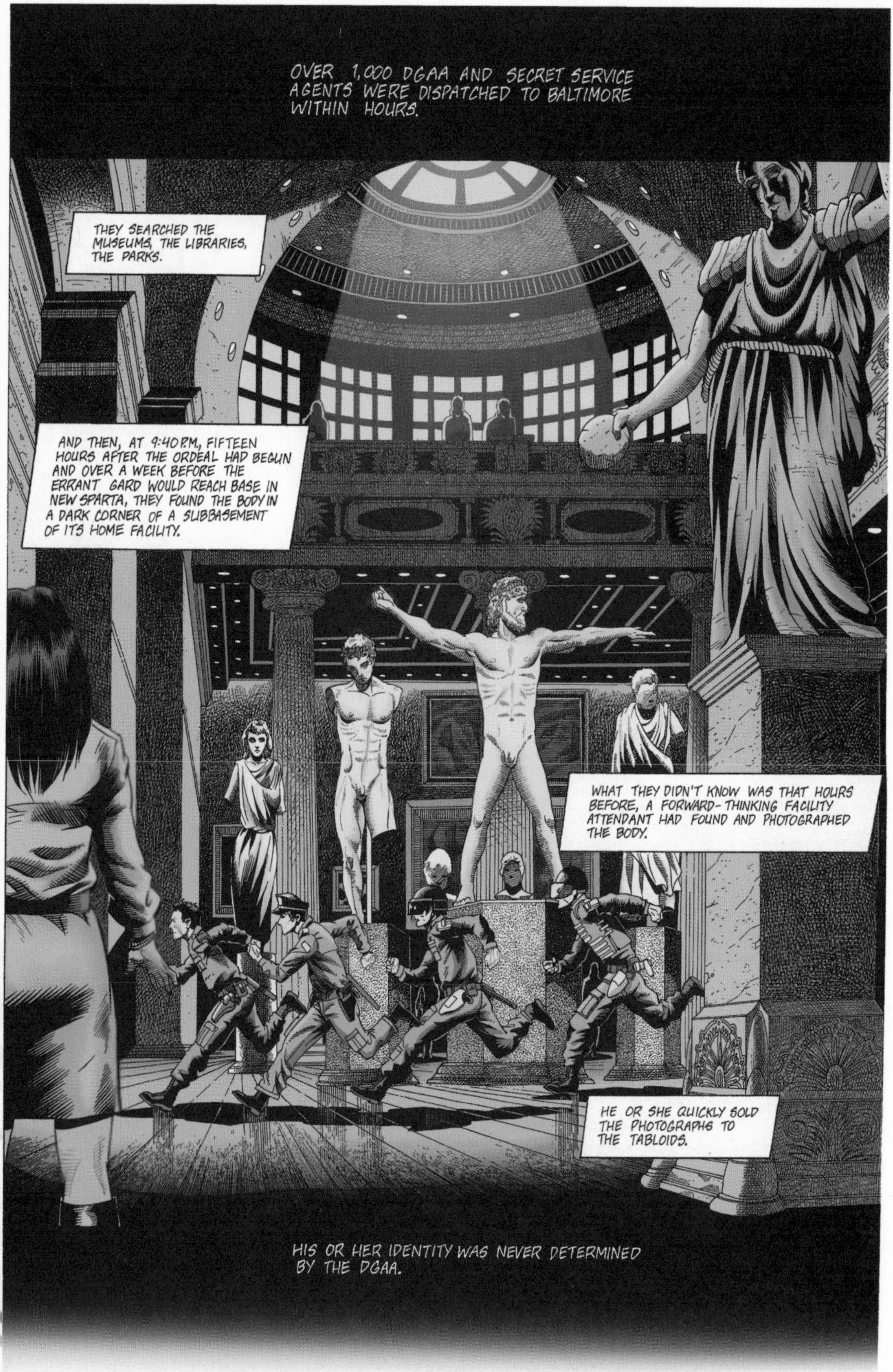
OVER 1,000 DGAA AND SECRET SERVICE AGENTS WERE DISPATCHED TO BALTIMORE WITHIN HOURS.
THEY SEARCHED THE MUSEUMS, THE LIBRARIES, THE PARKS.
AND THEN, AT 9:40 P.M., FIFTEEN HOURS AFTER THE ORDEAL HAD BEGUN AND OVER A WEEK BEFORE THE ERRANT GARD WOULD REACH BASE IN NEW SPARTA, THEY FOUND THE BODY IN A DARK CORNER OF A SUBBASEMENT OF ITS HOME FACILITY.
WHAT THEY DIDN'T KNOW WAS THAT HOURS BEFORE, A FORWARD-THINKING FACILITY ATTENDANT HAD FOUND AND PHOTOGRAPHED THE BODY.
HE OR SHE QUICKLY SOLD THE PHOTOGRAPHS TO THE TABLOIDS.
HIS OR HER IDENTITY WAS NEVER DETERMINED BY THE DGAA.

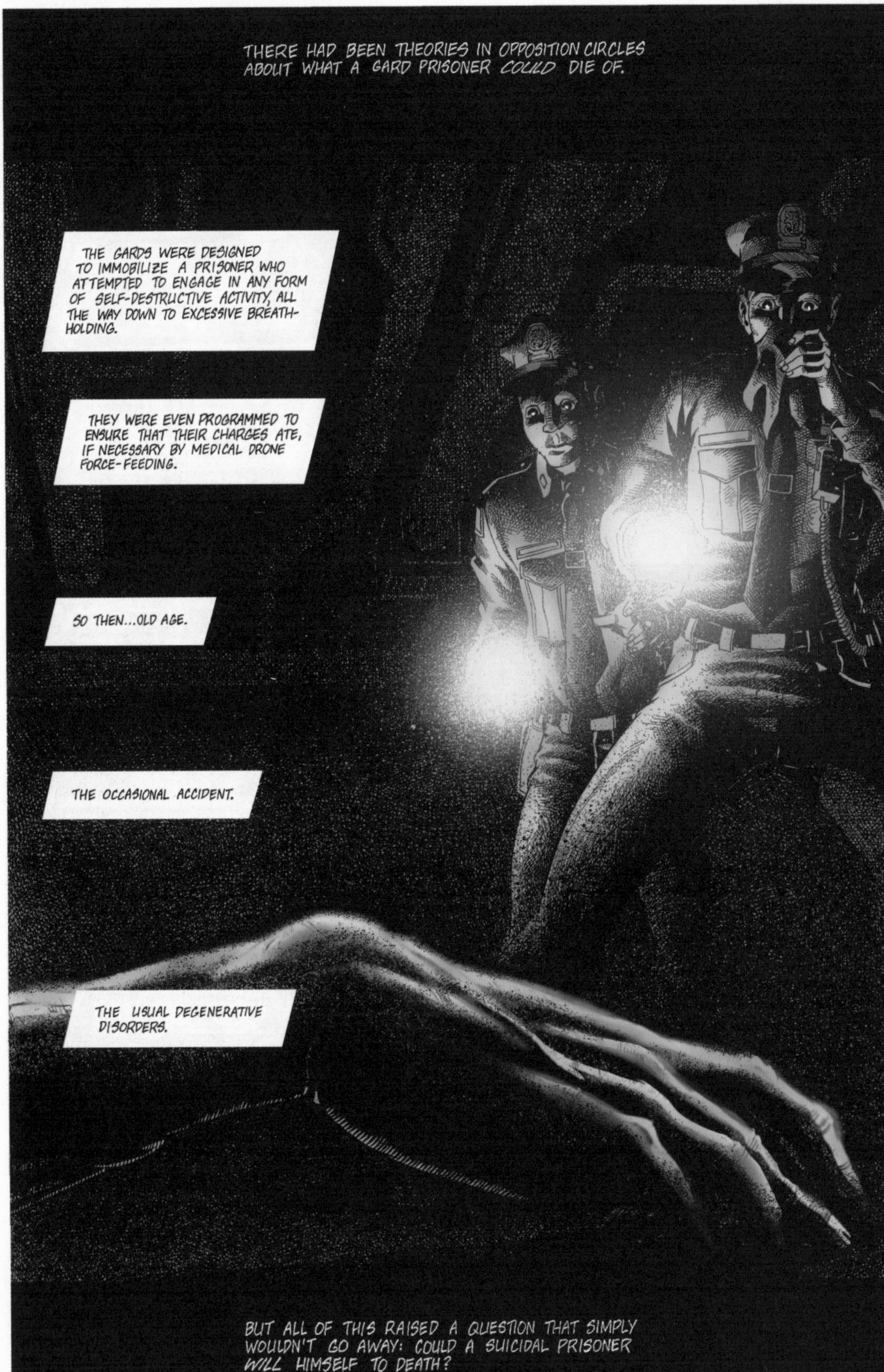

THERE HAD BEEN THEORIES IN OPPOSITION CIRCLES ABOUT WHAT A GARD PRISONER *COULD* DIE OF.
THE GARDS WERE DESIGNED TO IMMOBILIZE A PRISONER WHO ATTEMPTED TO ENGAGE IN ANY FORM OF SELF-DESTRUCTIVE ACTIVITY, ALL THE WAY DOWN TO EXCESSIVE BREATH-HOLDING.
THEY WERE EVEN PROGRAMMED TO ENSURE THAT THEIR CHARGES ATE, IF NECESSARY BY MEDICAL DRONE FORCE-FEEDING.
SO THEN...OLD AGE.
THE OCCASIONAL ACCIDENT.
THE USUAL DEGENERATIVE DISORDERS.
BUT ALL OF THIS RAISED A QUESTION THAT SIMPLY WOULDN'T GO AWAY: COULD A SUICIDAL PRISONER *WILL* HIMSELF TO DEATH?

THE GOVERNMENT, IT WAS WHISPERED, HAD
SECRETLY EXECUTED ALL THOSE SUPERMAX
LIFERS, AND THE GARDS WERE ACTUALLY
JUST CHEAP FLOATING TOYS, PROGRAMMED
TO WANDER THE STREETS IN A WAY THAT WAS
ONLY APPARENTLY PURPOSEFUL.

High today: 74°
Low today: 62°

Tonight:
High: 58°
Low: 52°

Los An

Tuesday, January 31st, 2028

Gruesome Discovery at
Baltimore GARD Facility

Ma

of I

Derek Tauch, A.P.

N UNIDENTIFIED worker at the Department
GARD Administration and Affairs home facil-
in the Waltherson section of Baltimore
photos of a body he or she discover-
sub basement late Mond-
at the office of t-

Mayor
greeted

GOD HELP ME, HALF THE TIME I WISHED THAT WAS
THE TRUTH.

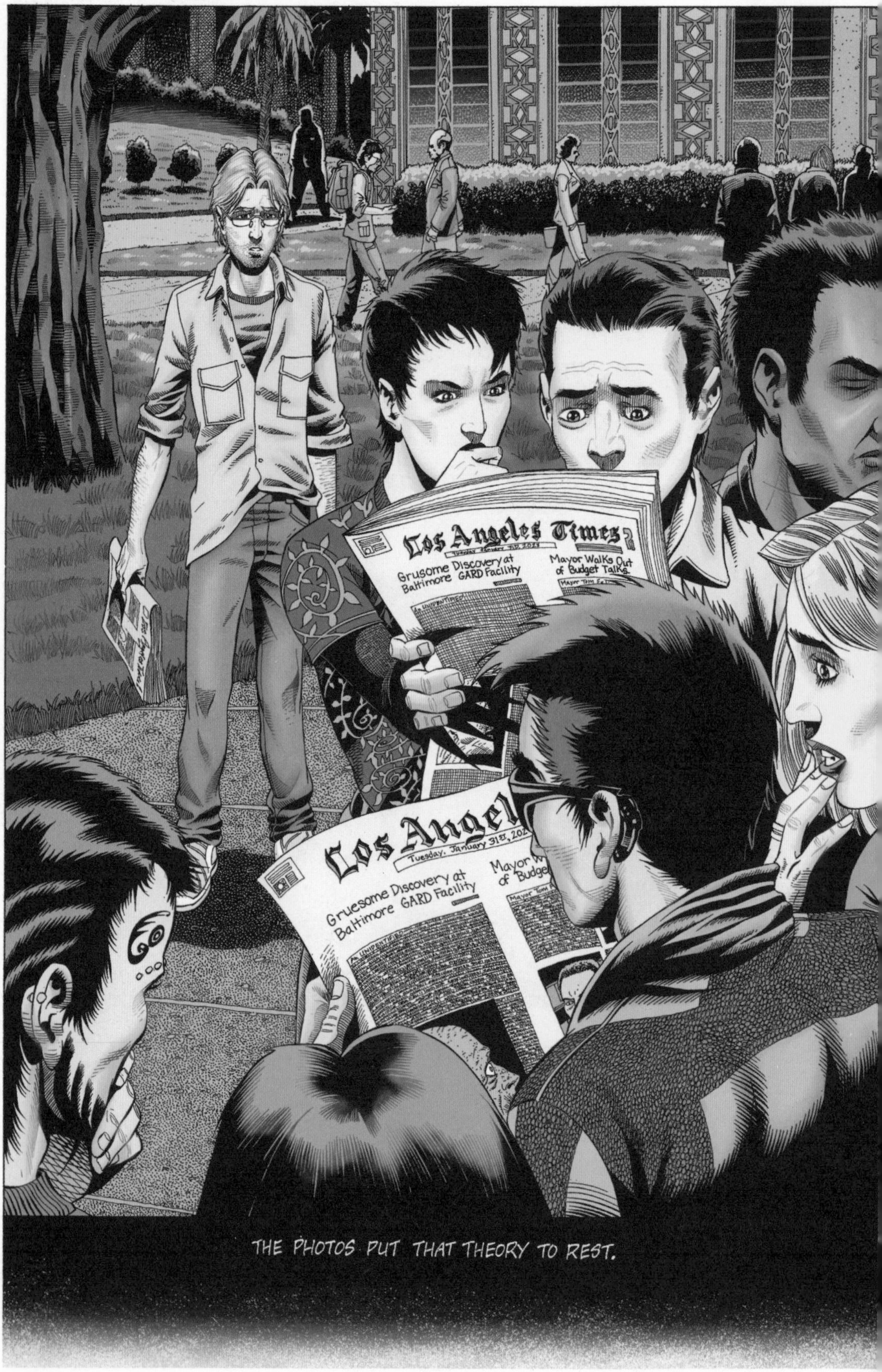
Los Angeles Times
Grusome Discovery at Baltimore GARD Facility
Mayor Walks Out of Budget Talks
Gruesome Discovery at Baltimore GARD Facility
THE PHOTOS PUT THAT THEORY TO REST.

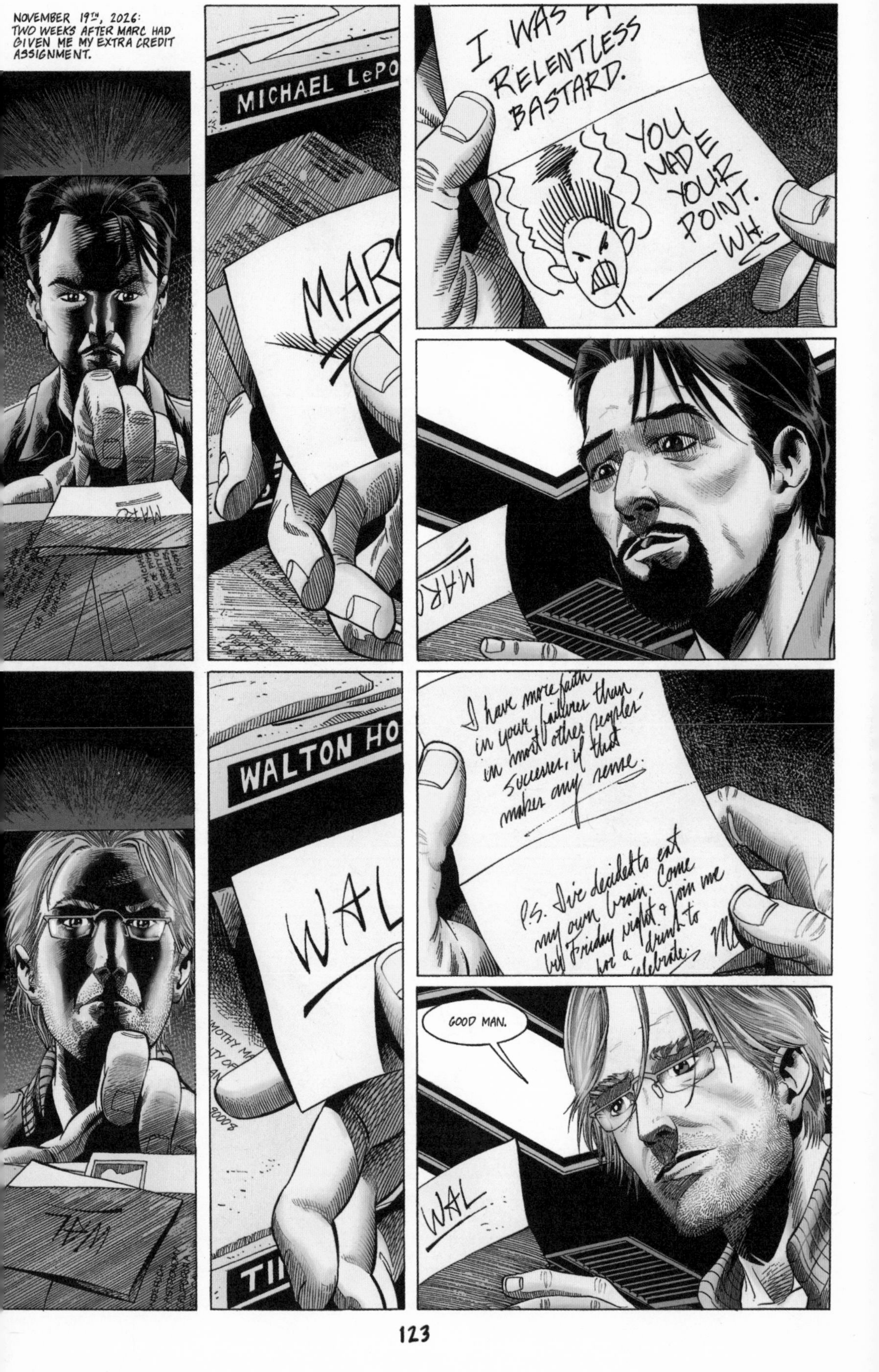
NOVEMBER 19TH, 2026: TWO WEEKS AFTER MARC HAD GIVEN ME MY EXTRA CREDIT ASSIGNMENT.
MICHAEL LePO
MARC
I WAS A RELENTLESS BASTARD.
YOU MADE YOUR POINT. —WH.
WALTON HO
WAL
I have more faith in your failures than in most other peoples' successes, if that makes any sense.
P.S. I've decided to eat my own brain. Come by Friday night & join me for a drink to celebrate.
GOOD MAN.

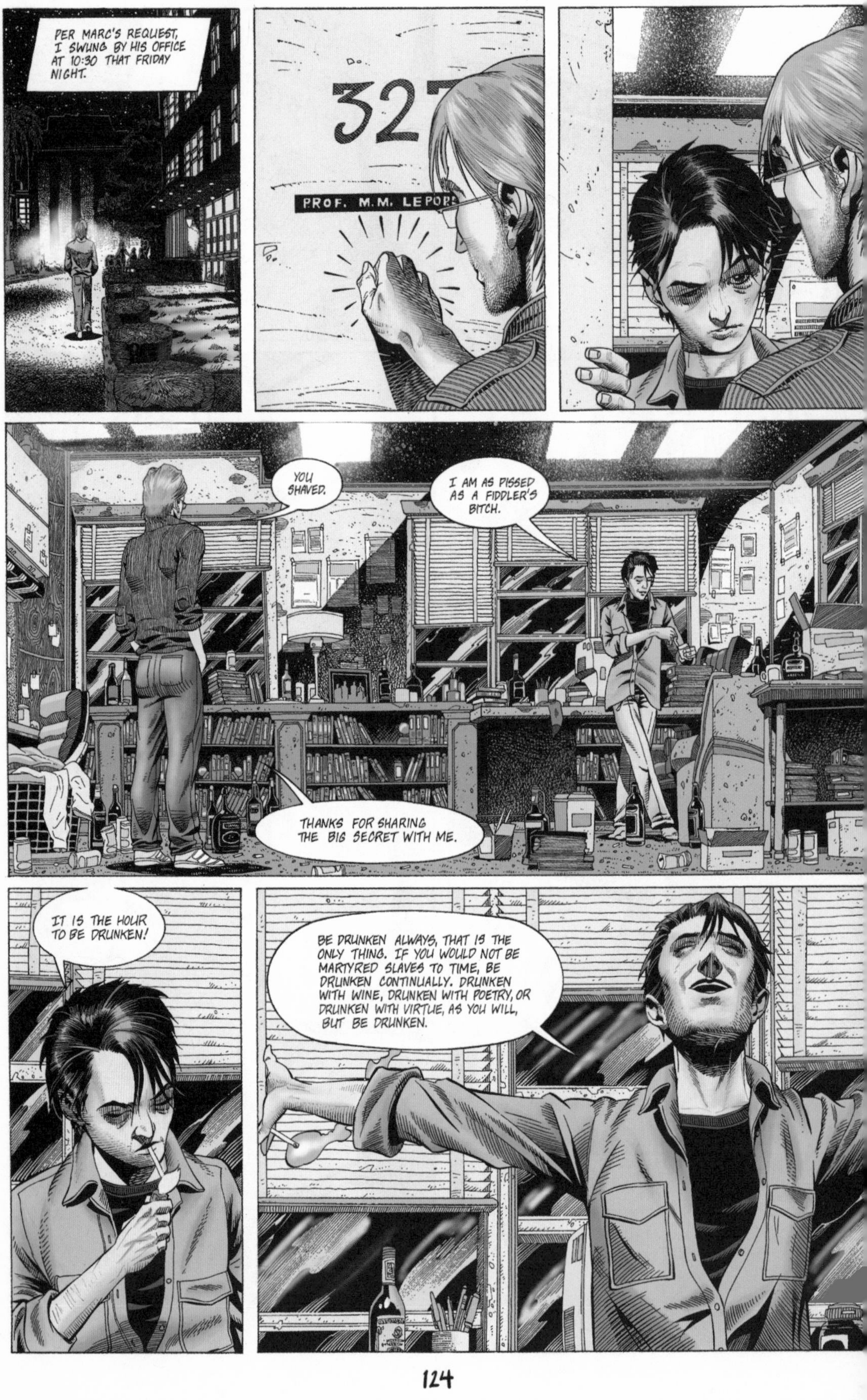
PER MARC'S REQUEST, I SWUNG BY HIS OFFICE AT 10:30 THAT FRIDAY NIGHT.
327
PROF. M.M. LEPORE
YOU SHAVED.
I AM AS PISSED AS A FIDDLER'S BITCH.
THANKS FOR SHARING THE BIG SECRET WITH ME.
IT IS THE HOUR TO BE DRUNKEN!
BE DRUNKEN ALWAYS, THAT IS THE ONLY THING. IF YOU WOULD NOT BE MARTYRED SLAVES TO TIME, BE DRUNKEN CONTINUALLY. DRUNKEN WITH WINE, DRUNKEN WITH POETRY, OR DRUNKEN WITH VIRTUE, AS YOU WILL, BUT BE DRUNKEN.

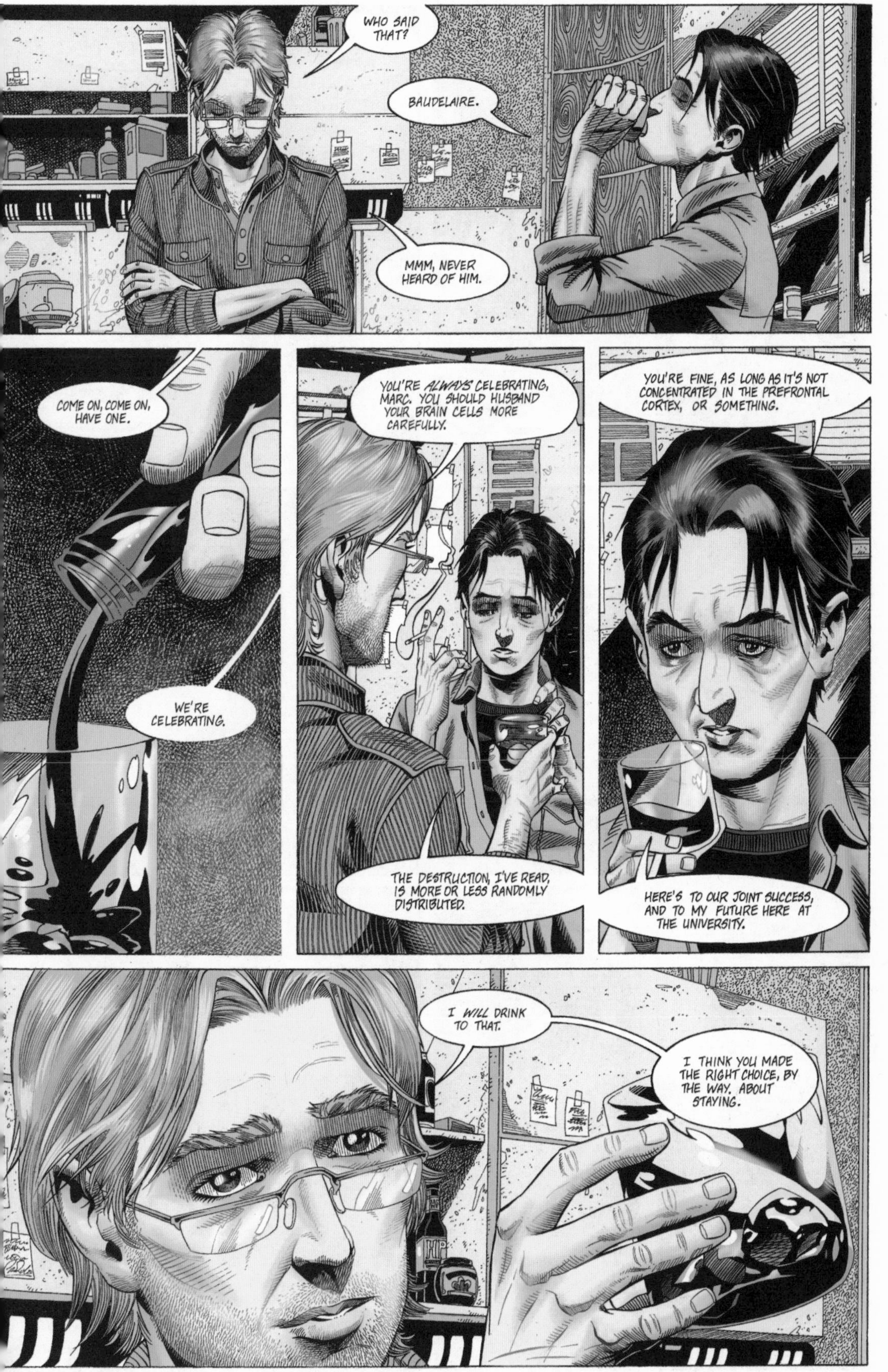
WHO SAID THAT?
BAUDELAIRE.
MMM, NEVER HEARD OF HIM.
COME ON, COME ON, HAVE ONE.
WE'RE CELEBRATING.
YOU'RE *ALWAYS* CELEBRATING, MARC. YOU SHOULD HUSBAND YOUR BRAIN CELLS MORE CAREFULLY.
THE DESTRUCTION, I'VE READ, IS MORE OR LESS RANDOMLY DISTRIBUTED.
YOU'RE FINE, AS LONG AS IT'S NOT CONCENTRATED IN THE PREFRONTAL CORTEX, OR SOMETHING.
HERE'S TO OUR JOINT SUCCESS, AND TO MY FUTURE HERE AT THE UNIVERSITY.
I *WILL* DRINK TO THAT.
I THINK YOU MADE THE RIGHT CHOICE, BY THE WAY. ABOUT STAYING.

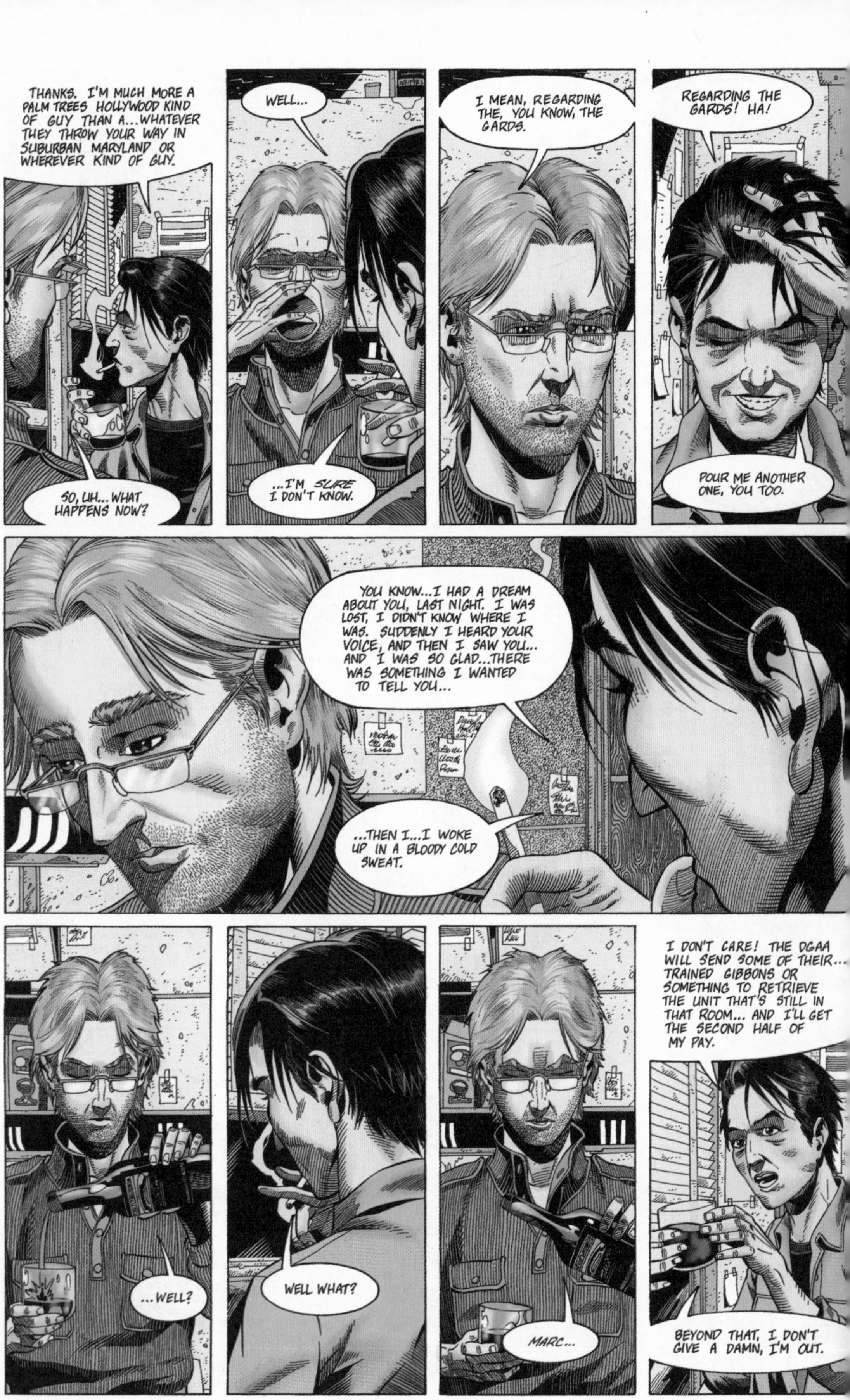
THANKS. I'M MUCH MORE A PALM TREES HOLLYWOOD KIND OF GUY THAN A...WHATEVER THEY THROW YOUR WAY IN SUBURBAN MARYLAND OR WHEREVER KIND OF GUY.
SO, UH...WHAT HAPPENS NOW?
WELL...
...I'M SURE I DON'T KNOW.
I MEAN, REGARDING THE, YOU KNOW, THE CARDS.
REGARDING THE CARDS! HA!
POUR ME ANOTHER ONE, YOU TOO.
YOU KNOW...I HAD A DREAM ABOUT YOU, LAST NIGHT. I WAS LOST, I DIDN'T KNOW WHERE I WAS. SUDDENLY I HEARD YOUR VOICE, AND THEN I SAW YOU... AND I WAS SO GLAD...THERE WAS SOMETHING I WANTED TO TELL YOU...
...THEN I...I WOKE UP IN A BLOODY COLD SWEAT.
...WELL?
WELL WHAT?
MARC...
I DON'T CARE! THE DGAA WILL SEND SOME OF THEIR... TRAINED GIBBONS OR SOMETHING TO RETRIEVE THE UNIT THAT'S STILL IN THAT ROOM... AND I'LL GET THE SECOND HALF OF MY PAY.
BEYOND THAT, I DON'T GIVE A DAMN, I'M OUT.

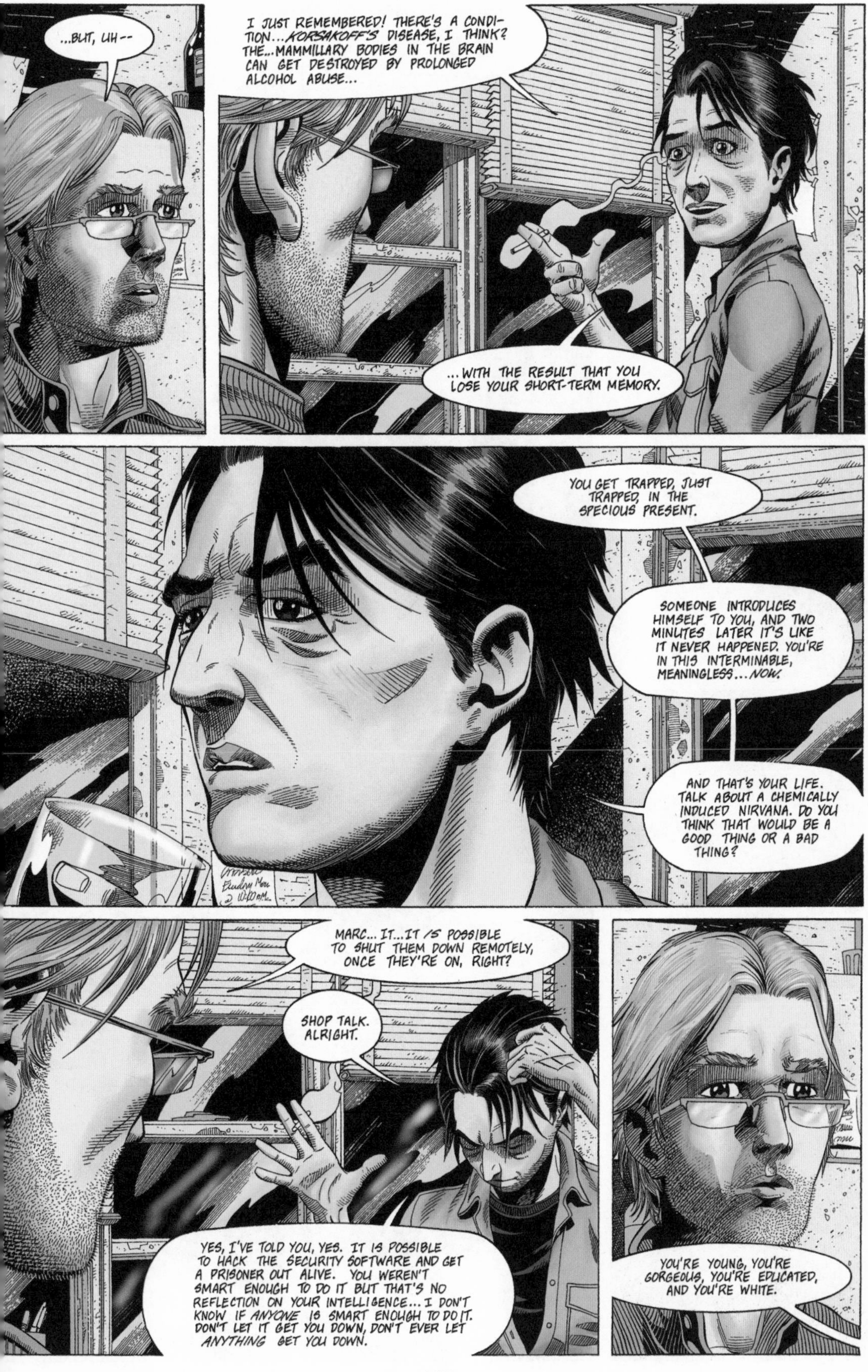

...BUT, UH--
I JUST REMEMBERED! THERE'S A CONDITION... KORSAKOFF'S DISEASE, I THINK? THE...MAMMILLARY BODIES IN THE BRAIN CAN GET DESTROYED BY PROLONGED ALCOHOL ABUSE...
...WITH THE RESULT THAT YOU LOSE YOUR SHORT-TERM MEMORY.
YOU GET TRAPPED, JUST TRAPPED, IN THE SPECIOUS PRESENT.
SOMEONE INTRODUCES HIMSELF TO YOU, AND TWO MINUTES LATER IT'S LIKE IT NEVER HAPPENED. YOU'RE IN THIS INTERMINABLE, MEANINGLESS... NOW.
AND THAT'S YOUR LIFE. TALK ABOUT A CHEMICALLY INDUCED NIRVANA. DO YOU THINK THAT WOULD BE A GOOD THING OR A BAD THING?
MARC... IT...IT IS POSSIBLE TO SHUT THEM DOWN REMOTELY, ONCE THEY'RE ON, RIGHT?
SHOP TALK. ALRIGHT.
YES, I'VE TOLD YOU, YES. IT IS POSSIBLE TO HACK THE SECURITY SOFTWARE AND GET A PRISONER OUT ALIVE. YOU WEREN'T SMART ENOUGH TO DO IT BUT THAT'S NO REFLECTION ON YOUR INTELLIGENCE... I DON'T KNOW IF ANYONE IS SMART ENOUGH TO DO IT. DON'T LET IT GET YOU DOWN, DON'T EVER LET ANYTHING GET YOU DOWN.
YOU'RE YOUNG, YOU'RE GORGEOUS, YOU'RE EDUCATED, AND YOU'RE WHITE.

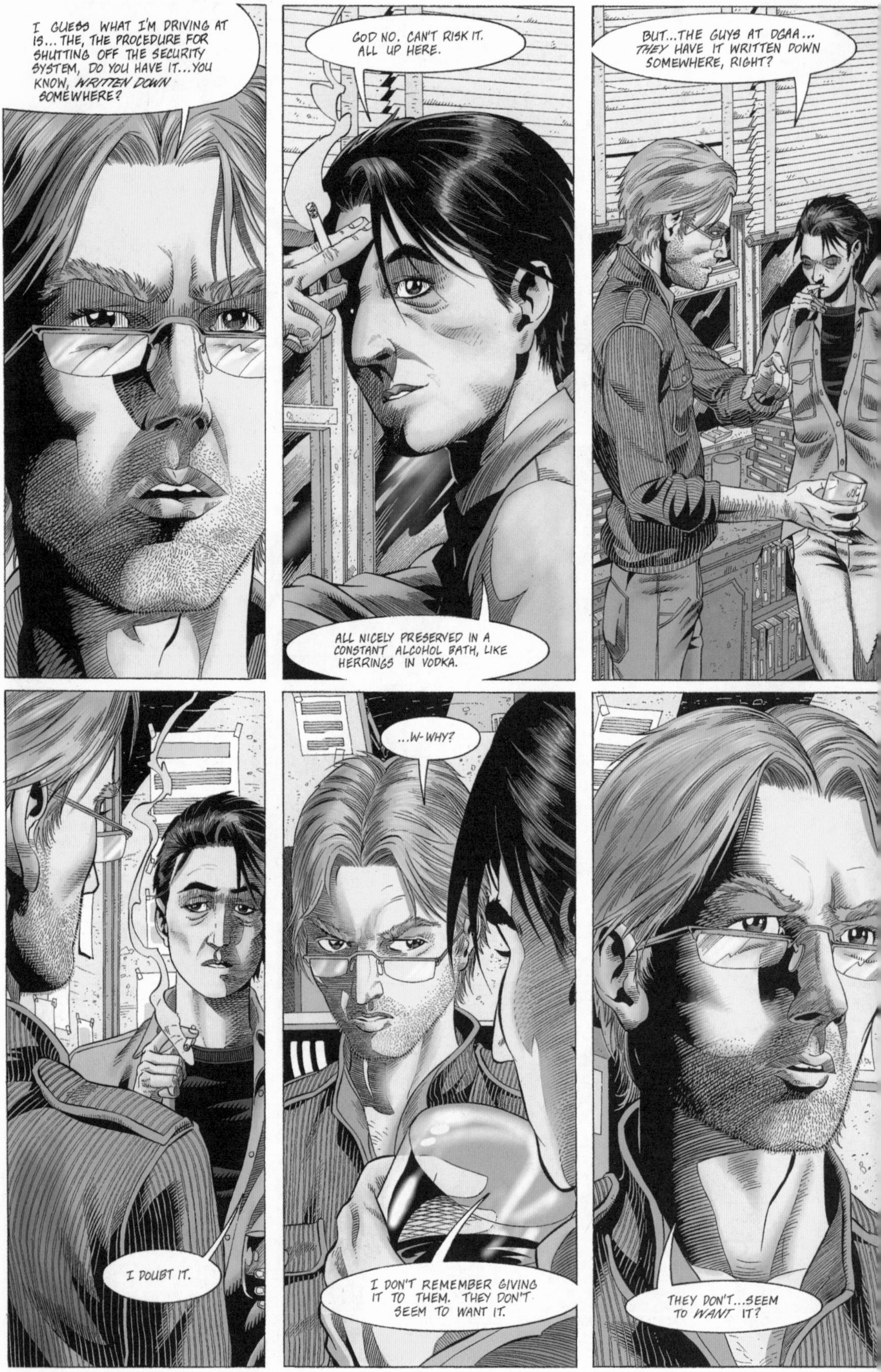
I GUESS WHAT I'M DRIVING AT IS... THE, THE PROCEDURE FOR SHUTTING OFF THE SECURITY SYSTEM, DO YOU HAVE IT...YOU KNOW, *WRITTEN DOWN* SOMEWHERE?
GOD NO. CAN'T RISK IT. ALL UP HERE.
ALL NICELY PRESERVED IN A CONSTANT ALCOHOL BATH, LIKE HERRINGS IN VODKA.
BUT...THE GUYS AT DGAA... *THEY* HAVE IT WRITTEN DOWN SOMEWHERE, RIGHT?
I DOUBT IT.
...W-WHY?
I DON'T REMEMBER GIVING IT TO THEM. THEY DON'T SEEM TO WANT IT.
THEY DON'T...SEEM TO *WANT* IT?

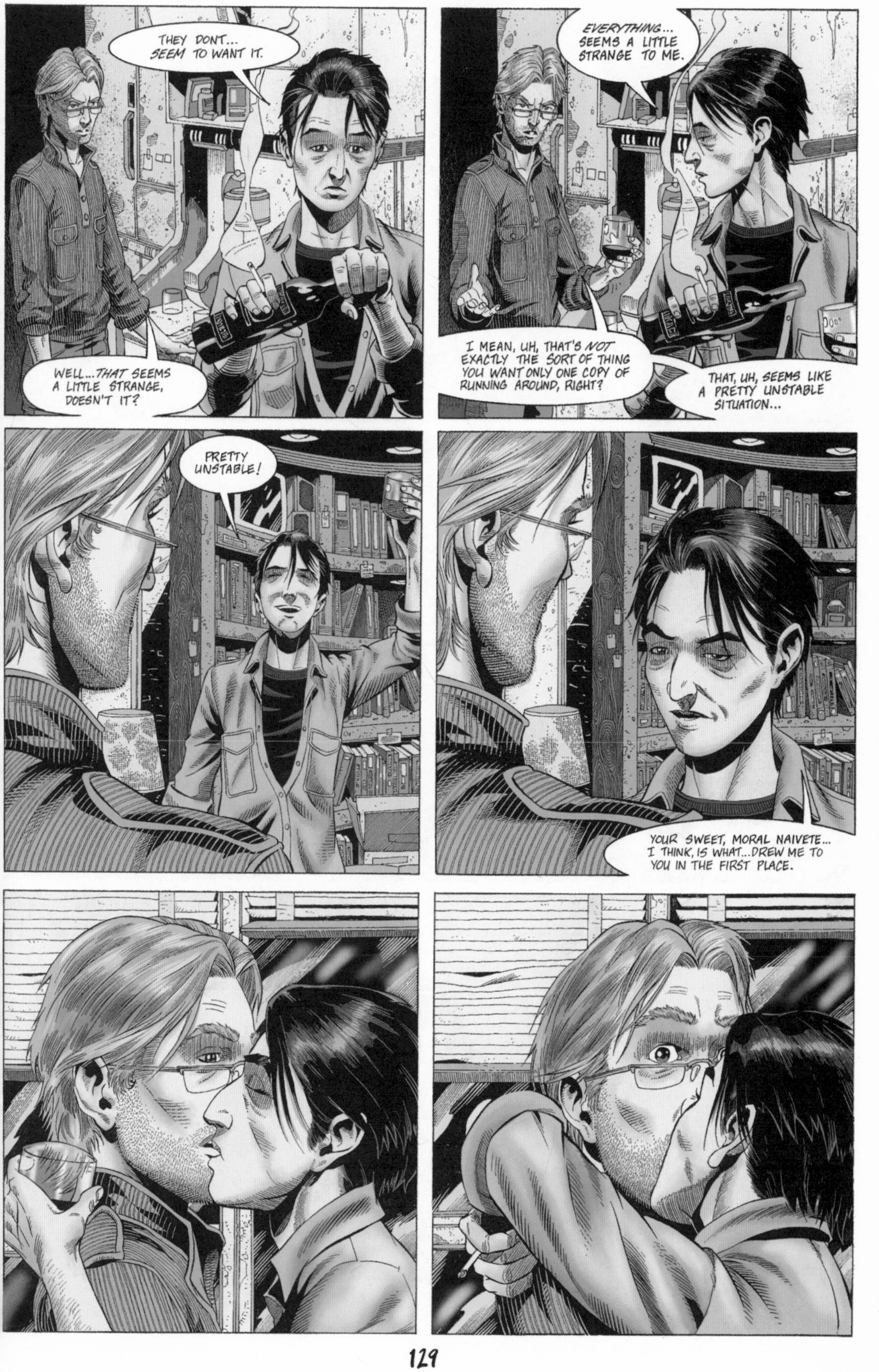
THEY DONT...
SEEM TO WANT IT.
WELL...THAT SEEMS
A LITTLE STRANGE,
DOESN'T IT?
EVERYTHING...
SEEMS A LITTLE
STRANGE TO ME.
I MEAN, UH, THAT'S NOT
EXACTLY THE SORT OF THING
YOU WANT ONLY ONE COPY OF
RUNNING AROUND, RIGHT?
THAT, UH, SEEMS LIKE
A PRETTY UNSTABLE
SITUATION...
PRETTY
UNSTABLE!
YOUR SWEET, MORAL NAIVETE...
I THINK, IS WHAT...DREW ME TO
YOU IN THE FIRST PLACE.

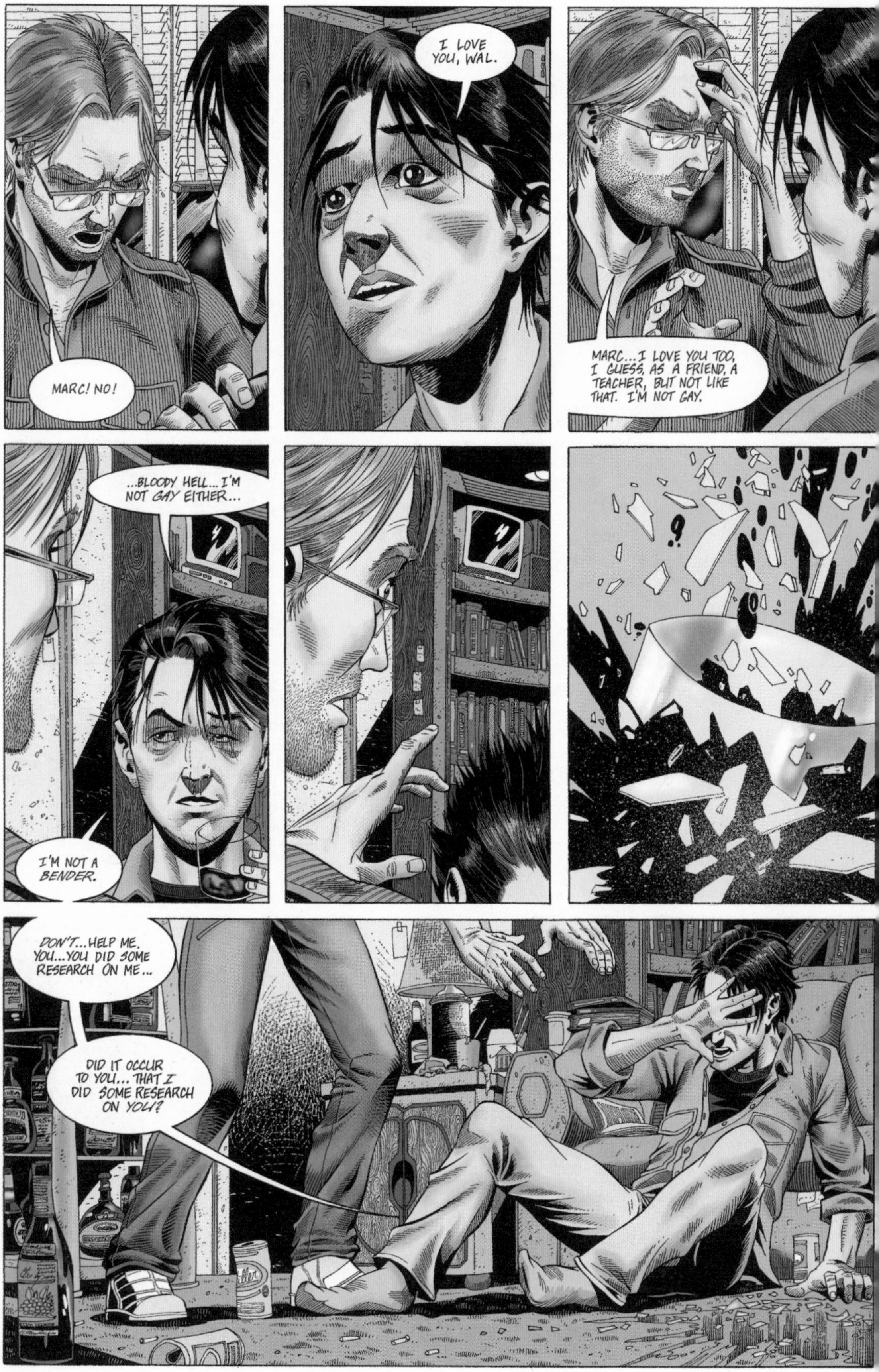
MARC! NO!
I LOVE YOU, WAL.
MARC... I LOVE YOU TOO, I GUESS, AS A FRIEND, A TEACHER, BUT NOT LIKE THAT. I'M NOT GAY.
...BLOODY HELL... I'M NOT GAY EITHER...
I'M NOT A BENDER.
DON'T... HELP ME. YOU... YOU DID SOME RESEARCH ON ME...
DID IT OCCUR TO YOU... THAT I DID SOME RESEARCH ON YOU!?

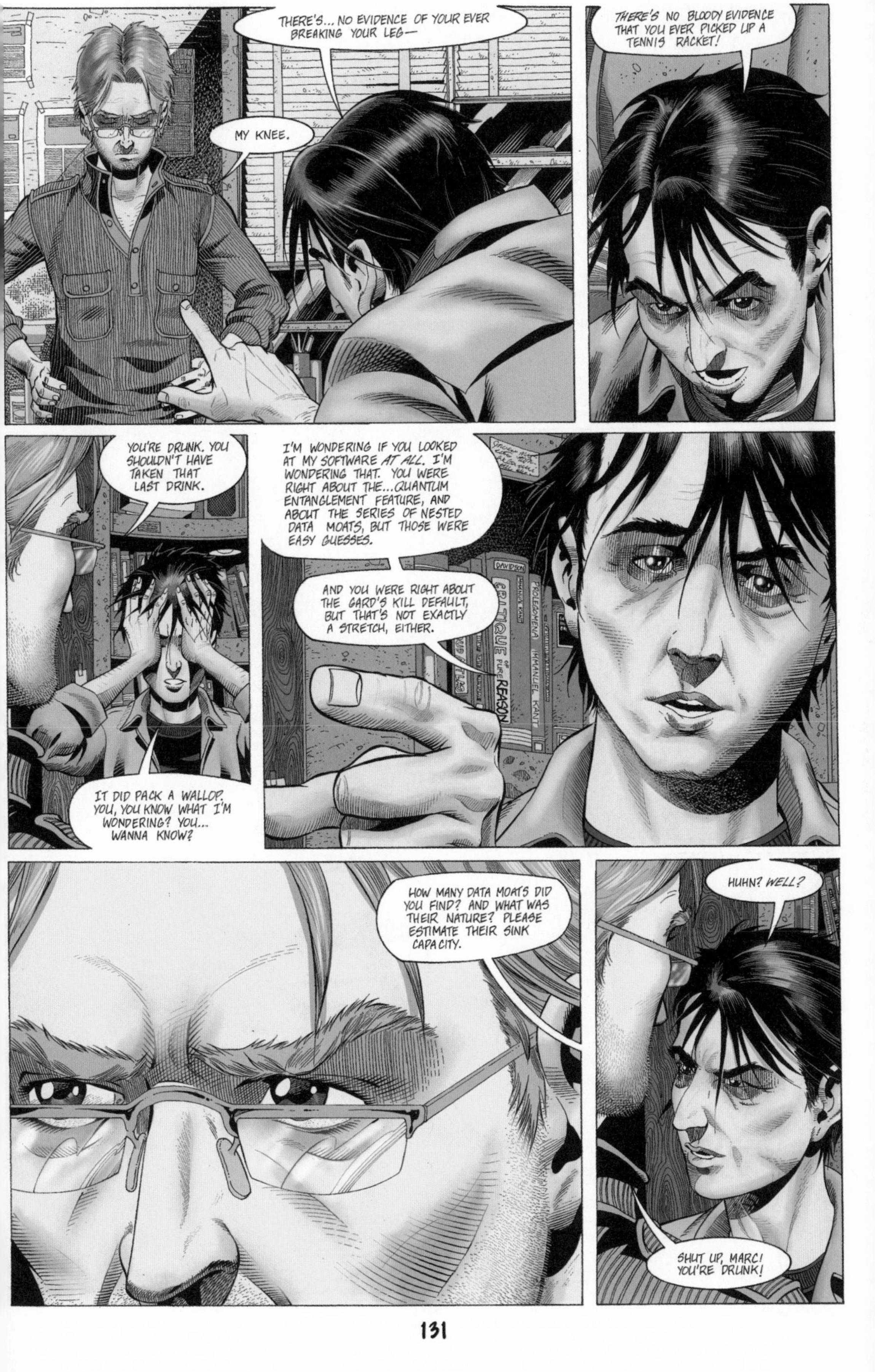
THERE'S... NO EVIDENCE OF YOUR EVER BREAKING YOUR LEG—
MY KNEE.
THERE'S NO BLOODY EVIDENCE THAT YOU EVER PICKED UP A TENNIS RACKET!
YOU'RE DRUNK. YOU SHOULDN'T HAVE TAKEN THAT LAST DRINK.
IT DID PACK A WALLOP. YOU, YOU KNOW WHAT I'M WONDERING? YOU... WANNA KNOW?
I'M WONDERING IF YOU LOOKED AT MY SOFTWARE AT ALL. I'M WONDERING THAT. YOU WERE RIGHT ABOUT THE... QUANTUM ENTANGLEMENT FEATURE, AND ABOUT THE SERIES OF NESTED DATA MOATS, BUT THOSE WERE EASY GUESSES.
AND YOU WERE RIGHT ABOUT THE GARD'S KILL DEFAULT, BUT THAT'S NOT EXACTLY A STRETCH, EITHER.
DAVIDSON
PROLEGOMENA IMMANUEL KANT
CRITIQUE OF PURE REASON
IMMANUEL KANT
HOW MANY DATA MOATS DID YOU FIND? AND WHAT WAS THEIR NATURE? PLEASE ESTIMATE THEIR SINK CAPACITY.
HUHN? WELL?
SHUT UP, MARC! YOU'RE DRUNK!

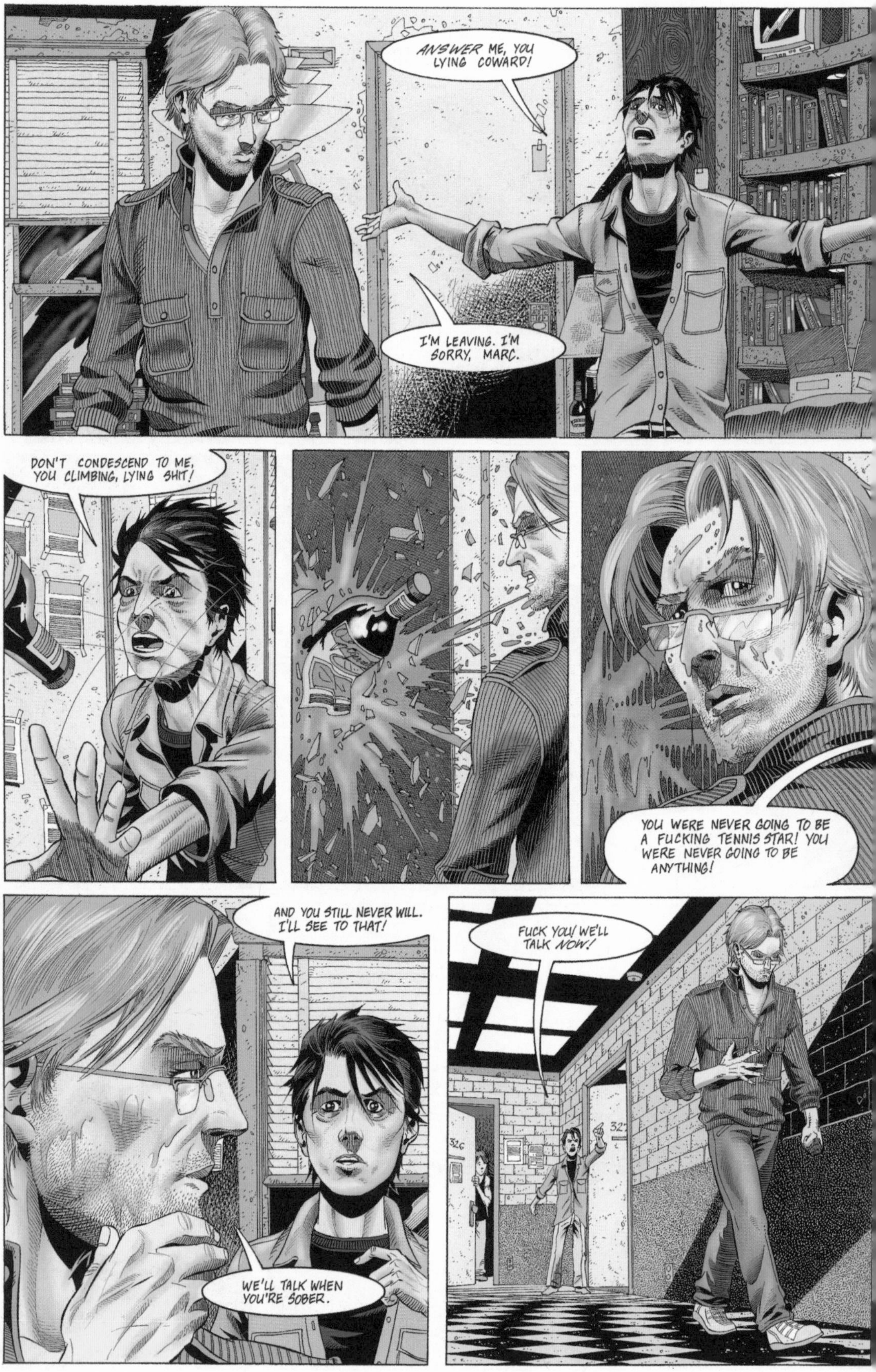
ANSWER ME, YOU LYING COWARD!
I'M LEAVING. I'M SORRY, MARC.
DON'T CONDESCEND TO ME, YOU CLIMBING, LYING SHIT!
YOU WERE NEVER GOING TO BE A FUCKING TENNIS STAR! YOU WERE NEVER GOING TO BE ANYTHING!
AND YOU STILL NEVER WILL. I'LL SEE TO THAT!
WE'LL TALK WHEN YOU'RE SOBER.
FUCK YOU! WE'LL TALK NOW!
326
327

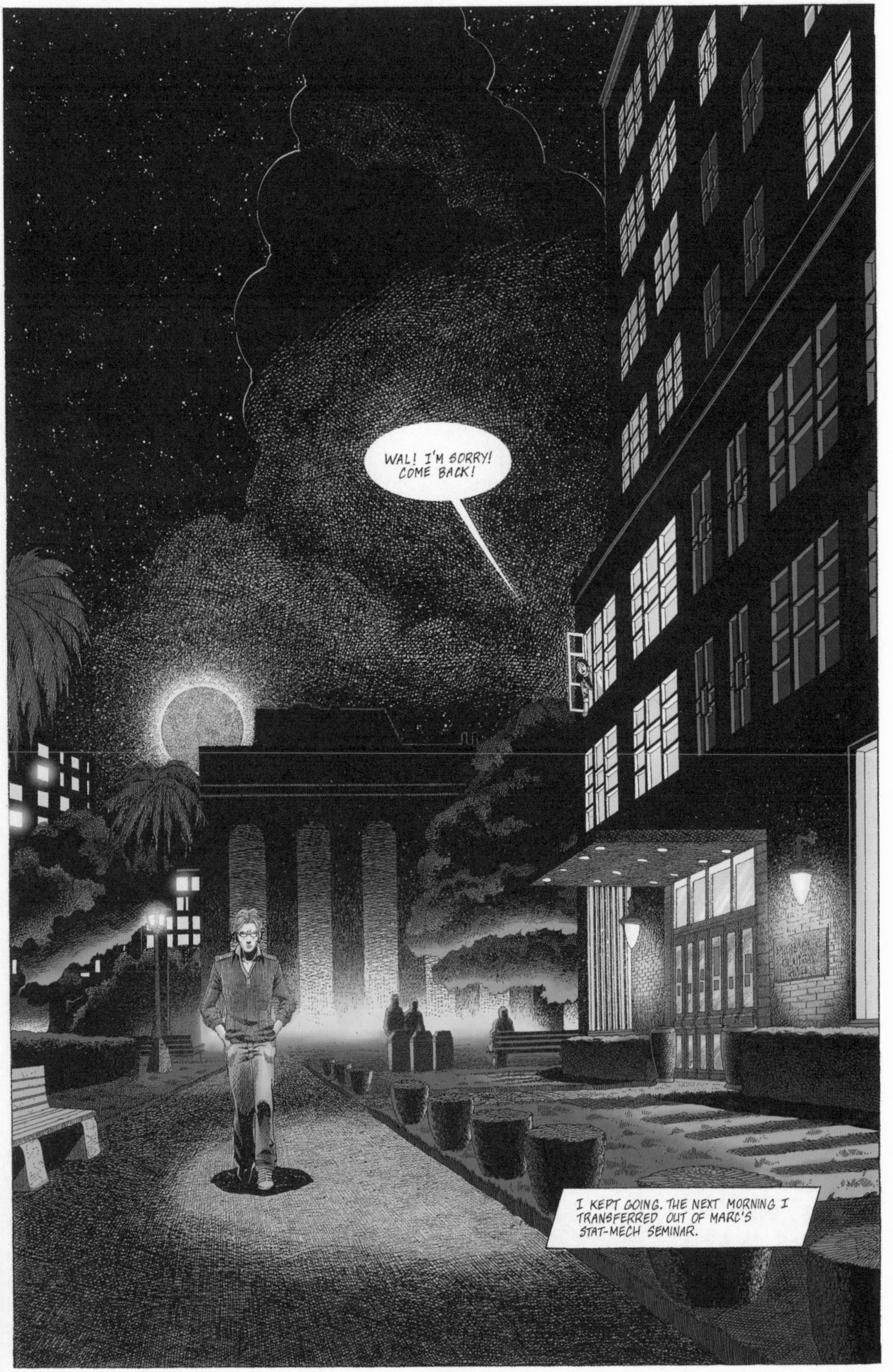
WAL! I'M SORRY! COME BACK!
I KEPT GOING. THE NEXT MORNING I TRANSFERRED OUT OF MARC'S STAT-MECH SEMINAR.

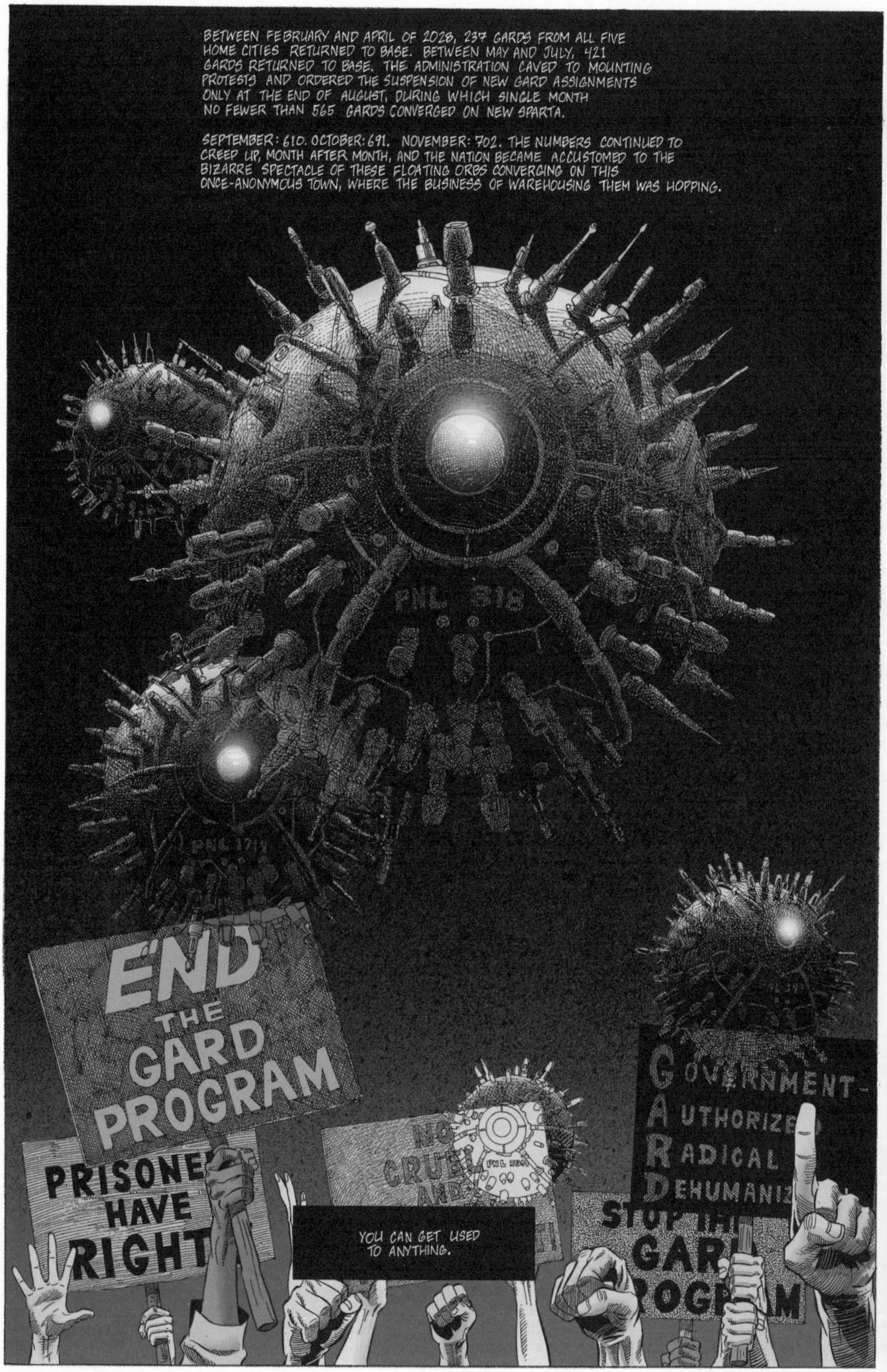
BETWEEN FEBRUARY AND APRIL OF 2028, 237 GARDS FROM ALL FIVE HOME CITIES RETURNED TO BASE. BETWEEN MAY AND JULY, 421 GARDS RETURNED TO BASE. THE ADMINISTRATION CAVED TO MOUNTING PROTESTS AND ORDERED THE SUSPENSION OF NEW GARD ASSIGNMENTS ONLY AT THE END OF AUGUST, DURING WHICH SINGLE MONTH NO FEWER THAN 565 GARDS CONVERGED ON NEW SPARTA.
SEPTEMBER: 610. OCTOBER: 691. NOVEMBER: 702. THE NUMBERS CONTINUED TO CREEP UP, MONTH AFTER MONTH, AND THE NATION BECAME ACCUSTOMED TO THE BIZARRE SPECTACLE OF THESE FLOATING ORBS CONVERGING ON THIS ONCE-ANONYMOUS TOWN, WHERE THE BUSINESS OF WAREHOUSING THEM WAS HOPPING.
PNL 518
END THE GARD PROGRAM
PRISONE HAVE RIGHT
GOVERNMENT- AUTHORIZE RADICAL DEHUMANIZ
STOP TH GAR OGRAM
YOU CAN GET USED TO ANYTHING.

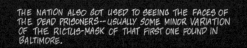

THE NATION ALSO GOT USED TO SEEING THE FACES OF THE DEAD PRISONERS--USUALLY SOME MINOR VARIATION OF THE RICTUS-MASK OF THAT FIRST ONE FOUND IN BALTIMORE.

THE PHOTOS WERE SHOT BY ANYONE WHO HAPPENED UPON THE BODY, AND USUALLY SOLD IMMEDIATELY TO THE MEDIA.

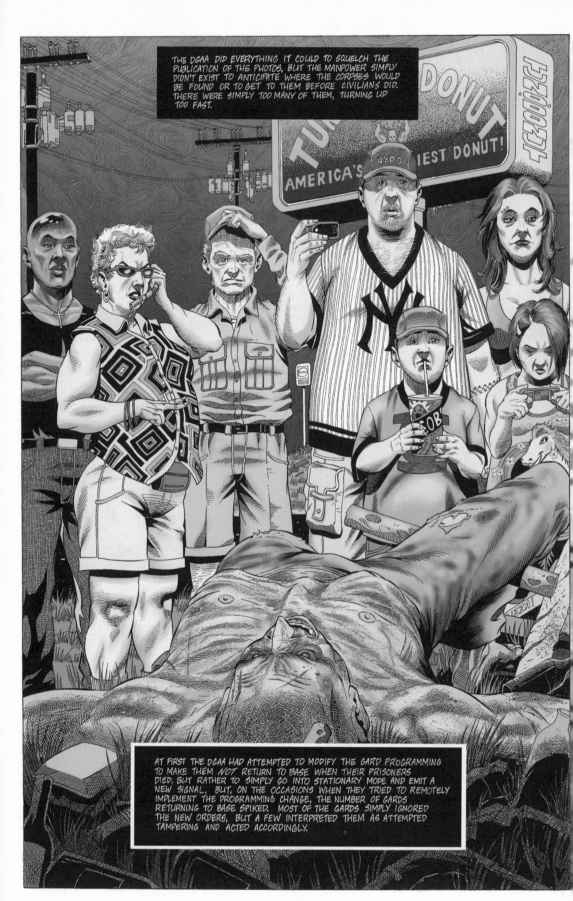

THE DGAA DID EVERYTHING IT COULD TO SQUELCH THE PUBLICATION OF THE PHOTOS, BUT THE MANPOWER SIMPLY DIDN'T EXIST TO ANTICIPATE WHERE THE CORPSES WOULD BE FOUND OR TO GET TO THEM BEFORE CIVILIANS DID. THERE WERE SIMPLY TOO MANY OF THEM, TURNING UP TOO FAST.

AT FIRST THE DGAA HAD ATTEMPTED TO MODIFY THE GARD PROGRAMMING TO MAKE THEM *NOT* RETURN TO BASE WHEN THEIR PRISONERS DIED, BUT RATHER TO SIMPLY GO INTO STATIONARY MODE AND EMIT A NEW SIGNAL. BUT, ON THE OCCASIONS WHEN THEY TRIED TO REMOTELY IMPLEMENT THE PROGRAMMING CHANGE, THE NUMBER OF GARDS RETURNING TO BASE SPIKED. MOST OF THE GARDS SIMPLY IGNORED THE NEW ORDERS, BUT A FEW INTERPRETED THEM AS ATTEMPTED TAMPERING AND ACTED ACCORDINGLY.

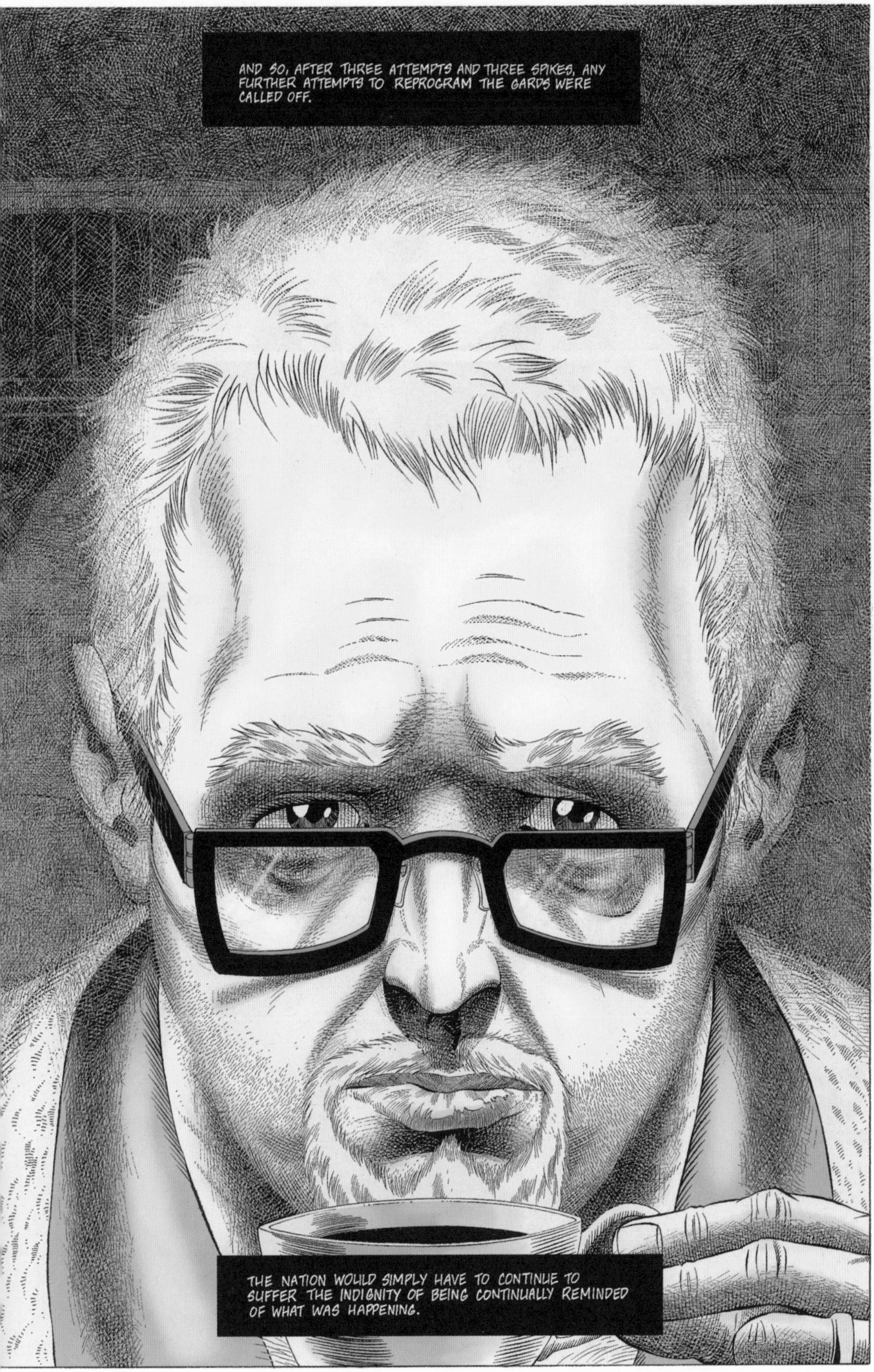
AND SO, AFTER THREE ATTEMPTS AND THREE SPIKES, ANY FURTHER ATTEMPTS TO REPROGRAM THE GARDS WERE CALLED OFF.
THE NATION WOULD SIMPLY HAVE TO CONTINUE TO SUFFER THE INDIGNITY OF BEING CONTINUALLY REMINDED OF WHAT WAS HAPPENING.

...SO YOU MADE SURE THE LOCK WORKED RIGHT?

YES, SWEETIE. ME AND MY FRIEND BOTH MADE DARN SURE OF THAT. AND THEN WE SORT OF HAD A FIGHT, ABOUT SOMETHING ELSE, AND THEN WE WEREN'T REALLY FRIENDS ANYMORE.

THAT SOUNDS SILLY, WALTON.

OH, IT WAS VERY SILLY.

AND YOU KNOW WHAT THE WORST PART WAS?

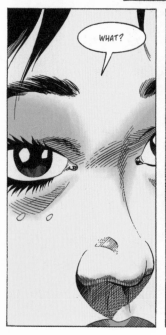

WHAT?

WE WERE SO MAD AT EACH OTHER, WE FORGOT ABOUT ALL THOSE PEOPLE.

THOUSANDS OF THEM, LOCKED INSIDE THE BALLOONS, AND THE BALLOONS ALL HAD THE EXACT SAME LOCK, BUT MY FRIEND HAD ONLY MADE ONE KEY.

WHY'S THAT BAD?

WELL...YOU KNOW HOW YOU'RE ALWAYS LOSING THINGS?

YEAH, LIKE I LOST CRAZY BILLY.

...RIGHT. WELL, GROWN-UPS LOSE THINGS, TOO.

I MEAN, UH, YOU'VE GOT THE OCTOPUS EYEBALL COOKIES IN THE OVEN, AND YOU'VE GOT THAT OVEN LOCKED UP GOOD AND TIGHT. BUT THEN YOU REMEMBER THAT THEY'RE *NOT* OCTOPUS EYEBALL COOKIES AT ALL.

THEY'RE ACTUALLY SUGAR COOKIES WITH PINK SPRINKLES.

YAY!

RIGHT. SO NOW YOU WANT THOSE COOKIES *OUT.* AND THEN YOU FIND OUT THAT YOU'VE LOST THE KEY TO THE LOCK. NOW IF YOU'VE GOT A COPY OF THAT KEY, YOU'RE OKAY.

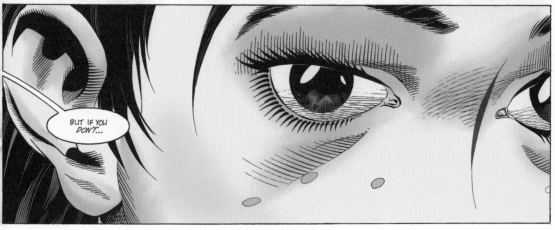

BUT IF YOU DON'T...

5

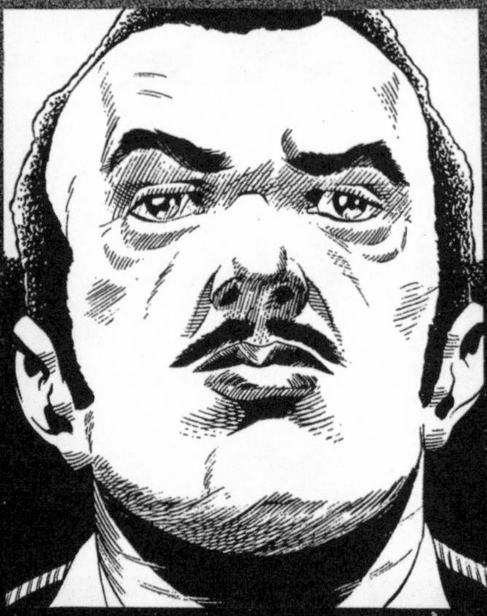

GAME, SET, MATCH

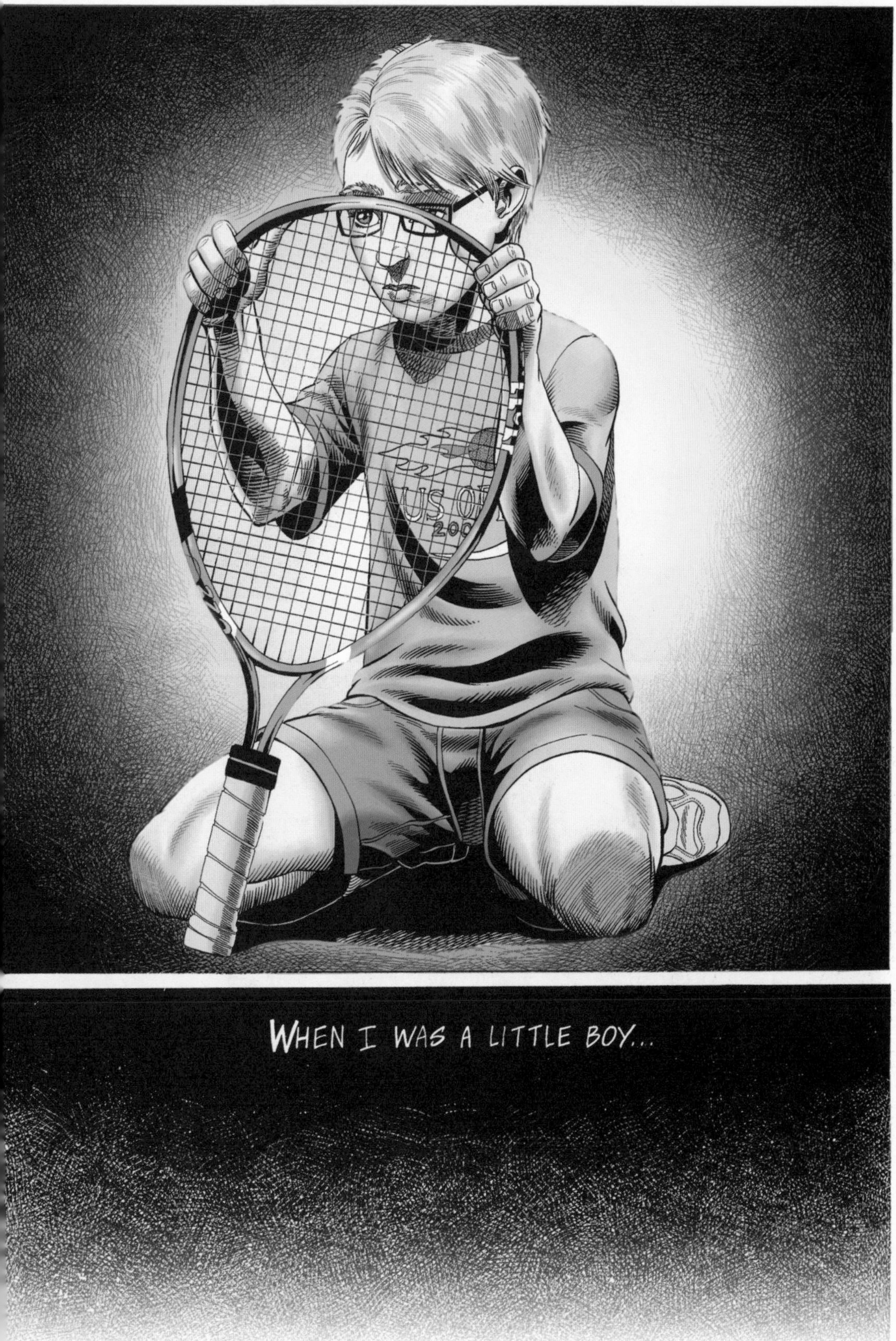
WHEN I WAS A LITTLE BOY...

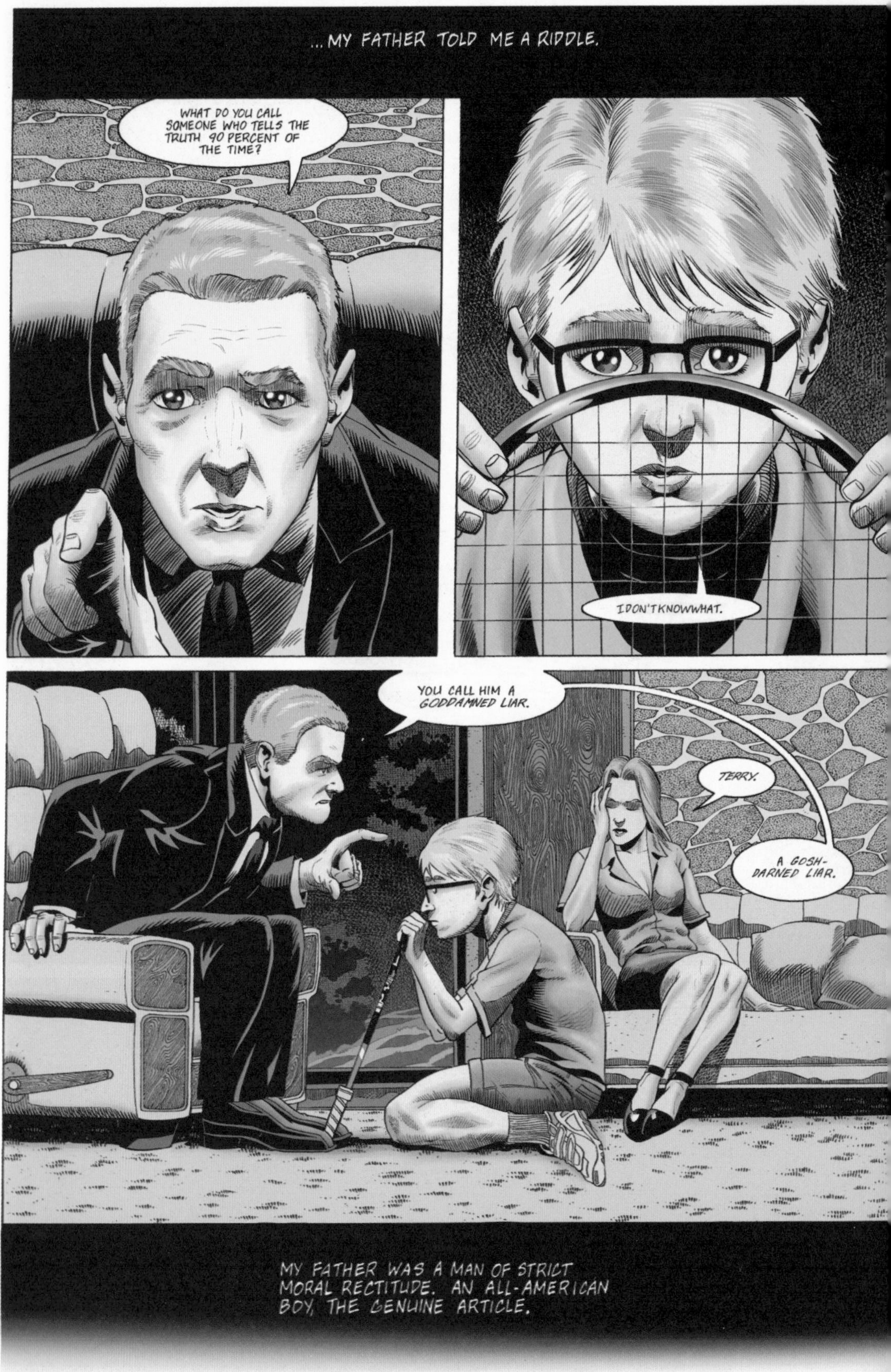
...MY FATHER TOLD ME A RIDDLE.
WHAT DO YOU CALL SOMEONE WHO TELLS THE TRUTH 90 PERCENT OF THE TIME?
IDON'TKNOWWHAT.
YOU CALL HIM A GODDAMNED LIAR.
TERRY.
A GOSH-DARNED LIAR.
MY FATHER WAS A MAN OF STRICT MORAL RECTITUDE. AN ALL-AMERICAN BOY, THE GENUINE ARTICLE.

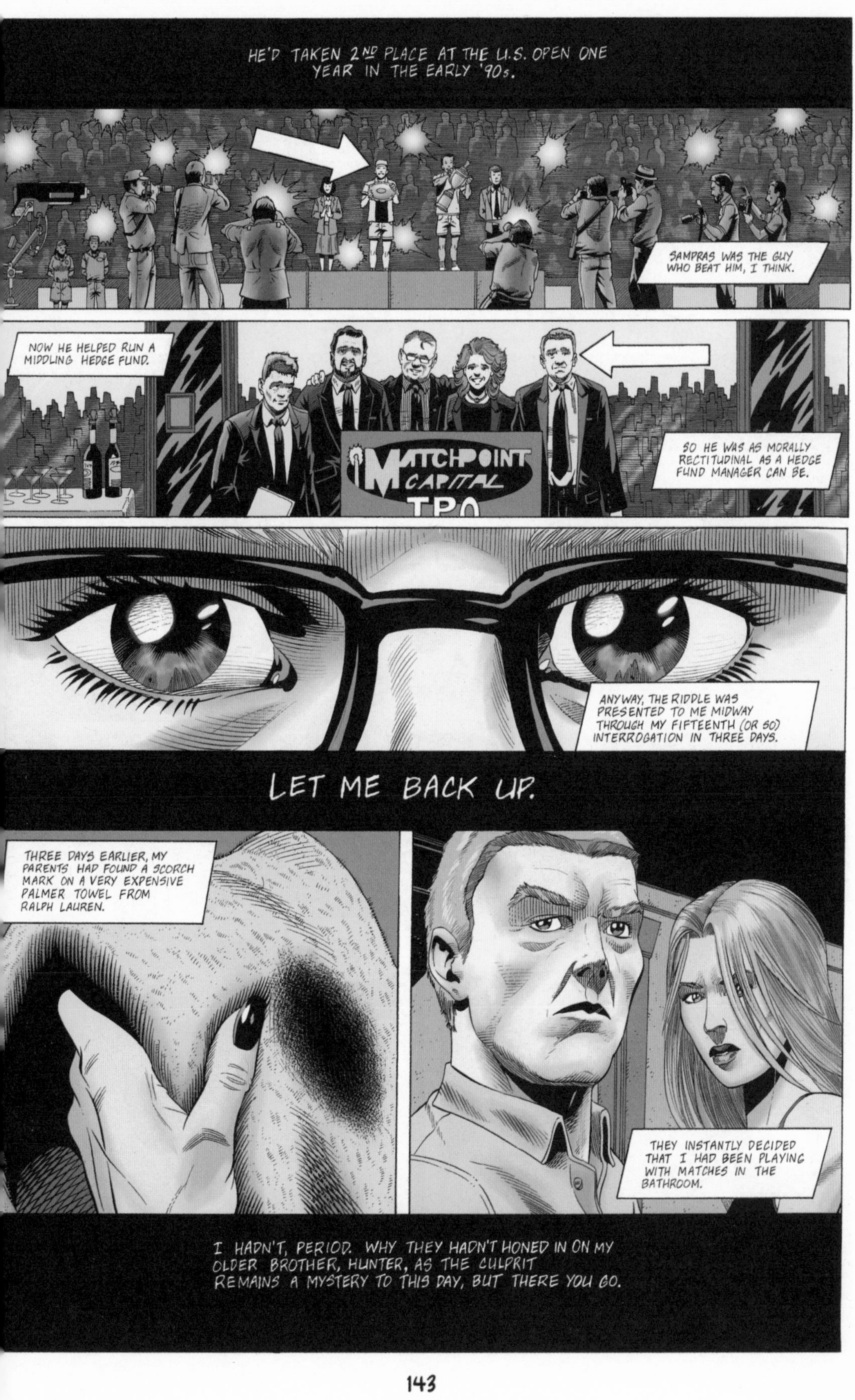
HE'D TAKEN 2ND PLACE AT THE U.S. OPEN ONE YEAR IN THE EARLY '90s.
SAMPRAS WAS THE GUY WHO BEAT HIM, I THINK.
NOW HE HELPED RUN A MIDDLING HEDGE FUND.
MATCHPOINT CAPITAL
SO HE WAS AS MORALLY RECTITUDINAL AS A HEDGE FUND MANAGER CAN BE.
ANYWAY, THE RIDDLE WAS PRESENTED TO ME MIDWAY THROUGH MY FIFTEENTH (OR SO) INTERROGATION IN THREE DAYS.
LET ME BACK UP.
THREE DAYS EARLIER, MY PARENTS HAD FOUND A SCORCH MARK ON A VERY EXPENSIVE PALMER TOWEL FROM RALPH LAUREN.
THEY INSTANTLY DECIDED THAT I HAD BEEN PLAYING WITH MATCHES IN THE BATHROOM.
I HADN'T, PERIOD. WHY THEY HADN'T HONED IN ON MY OLDER BROTHER, HUNTER, AS THE CULPRIT REMAINS A MYSTERY TO THIS DAY, BUT THERE YOU GO.

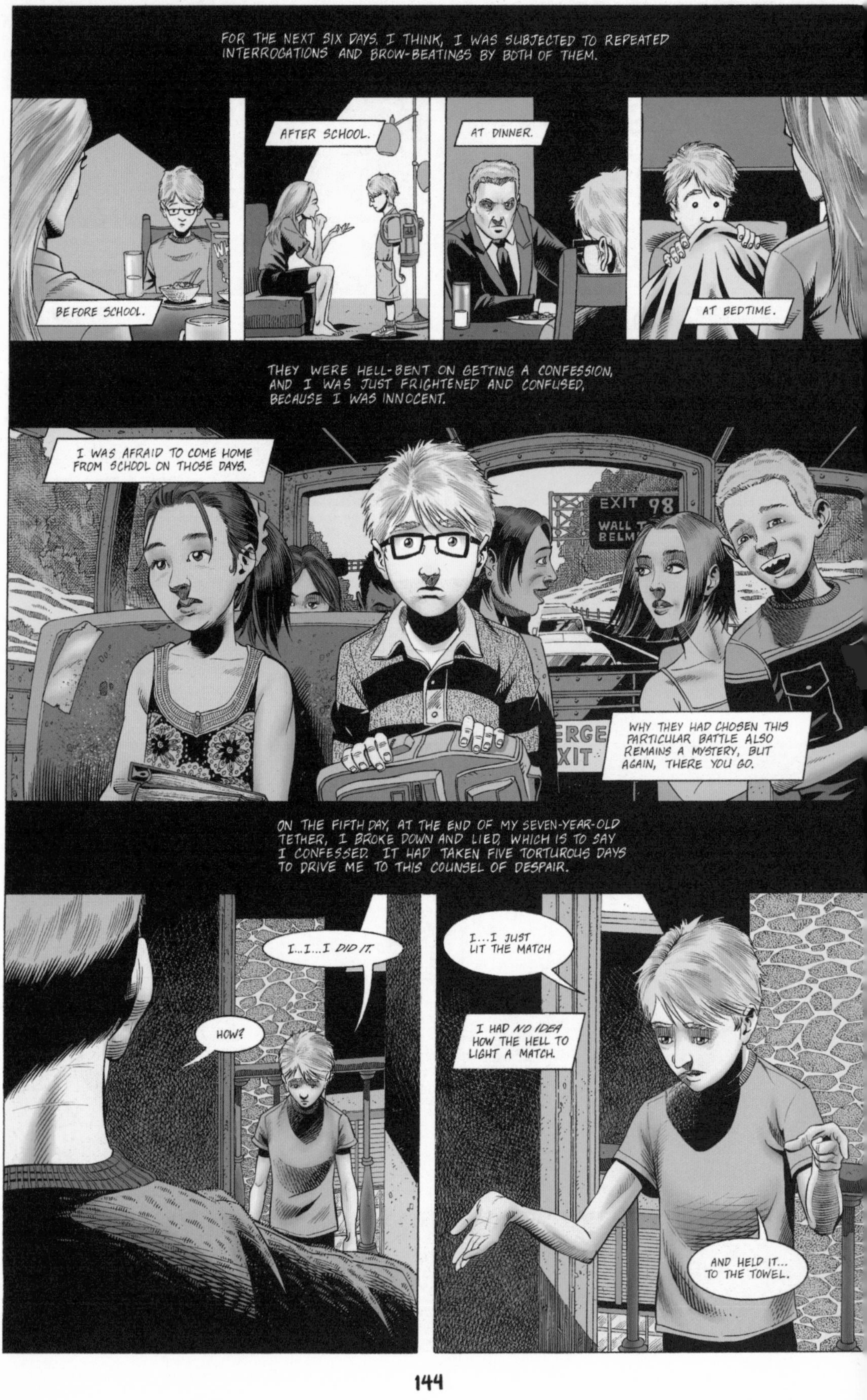

FOR THE NEXT SIX DAYS, I THINK, I WAS SUBJECTED TO REPEATED INTERROGATIONS AND BROW-BEATINGS BY BOTH OF THEM.
BEFORE SCHOOL.
AFTER SCHOOL.
AT DINNER.
AT BEDTIME.
THEY WERE HELL-BENT ON GETTING A CONFESSION, AND I WAS JUST FRIGHTENED AND CONFUSED, BECAUSE I WAS INNOCENT.
I WAS AFRAID TO COME HOME FROM SCHOOL ON THOSE DAYS.
EXIT 98
WHY THEY HAD CHOSEN THIS PARTICULAR BATTLE ALSO REMAINS A MYSTERY, BUT AGAIN, THERE YOU GO.
ON THE FIFTH DAY, AT THE END OF MY SEVEN-YEAR-OLD TETHER, I BROKE DOWN AND LIED, WHICH IS TO SAY I CONFESSED. IT HAD TAKEN FIVE TORTUROUS DAYS TO DRIVE ME TO THIS COUNSEL OF DESPAIR.
I...I...I *DID IT.*
HOW?
I...I JUST LIT THE MATCH
I HAD *NO IDEA* HOW THE HELL TO LIGHT A MATCH.
AND HELD IT... TO THE TOWEL.

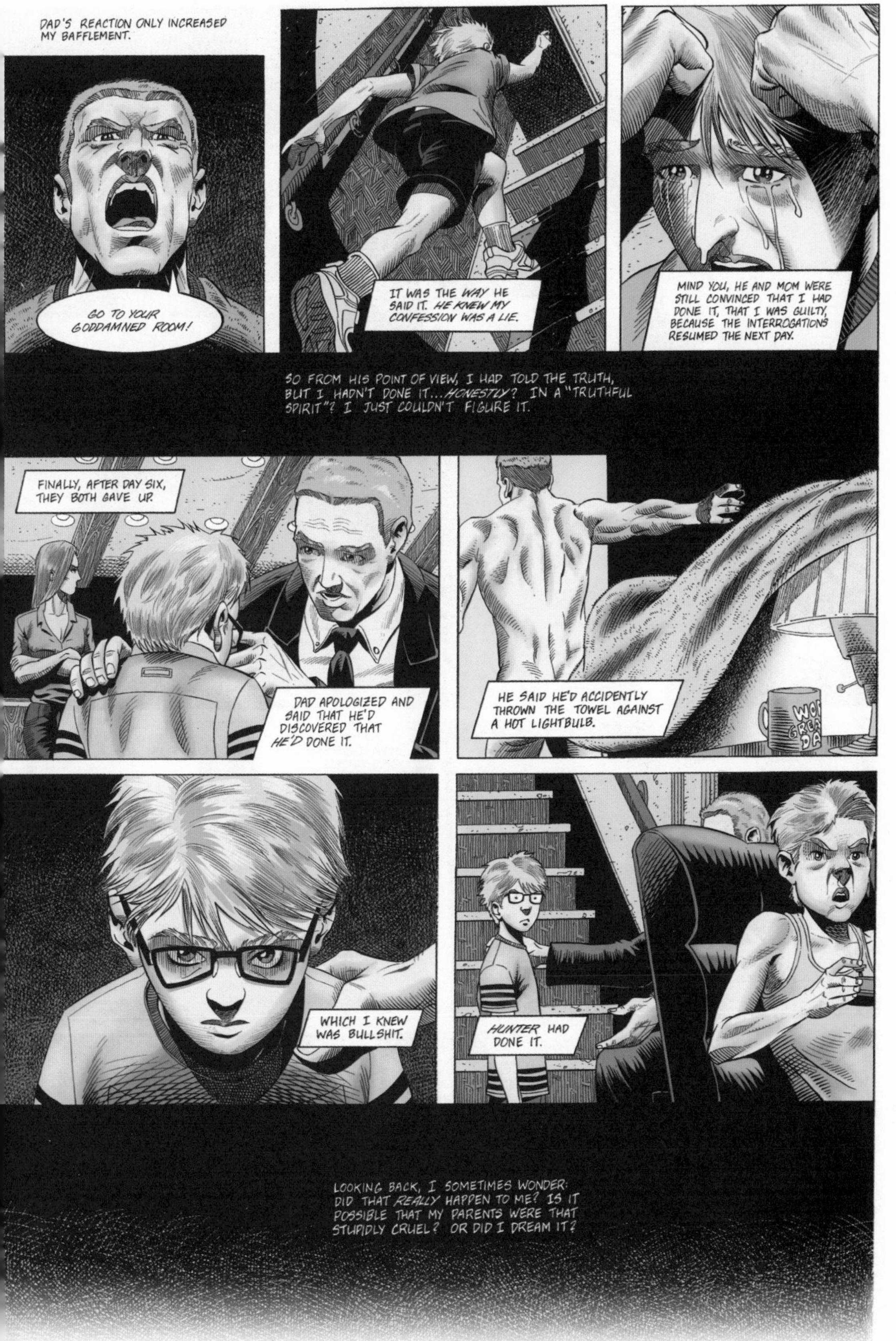
DAD'S REACTION ONLY INCREASED MY BAFFLEMENT.
GO TO YOUR GODDAMNED ROOM!
IT WAS THE *WAY* HE SAID IT. *HE KNEW MY CONFESSION WAS A LIE.*
MIND YOU, HE AND MOM WERE STILL CONVINCED THAT I HAD DONE IT, THAT I WAS GUILTY, BECAUSE THE INTERROGATIONS RESUMED THE NEXT DAY.
SO FROM HIS POINT OF VIEW, I HAD TOLD THE TRUTH, BUT I HADN'T DONE IT... *HONESTLY*? IN A "TRUTHFUL SPIRIT"? I JUST COULDN'T FIGURE IT.
FINALLY, AFTER DAY SIX, THEY BOTH GAVE UP.
DAD APOLOGIZED AND SAID THAT HE'D DISCOVERED THAT *HE'D* DONE IT.
HE SAID HE'D ACCIDENTLY THROWN THE TOWEL AGAINST A HOT LIGHTBULB.
WHICH I KNEW WAS BULLSHIT.
HUNTER HAD DONE IT.
LOOKING BACK, I SOMETIMES WONDER: DID THAT *REALLY* HAPPEN TO ME? IS IT POSSIBLE THAT MY PARENTS WERE THAT STUPIDLY CRUEL? OR DID I DREAM IT?

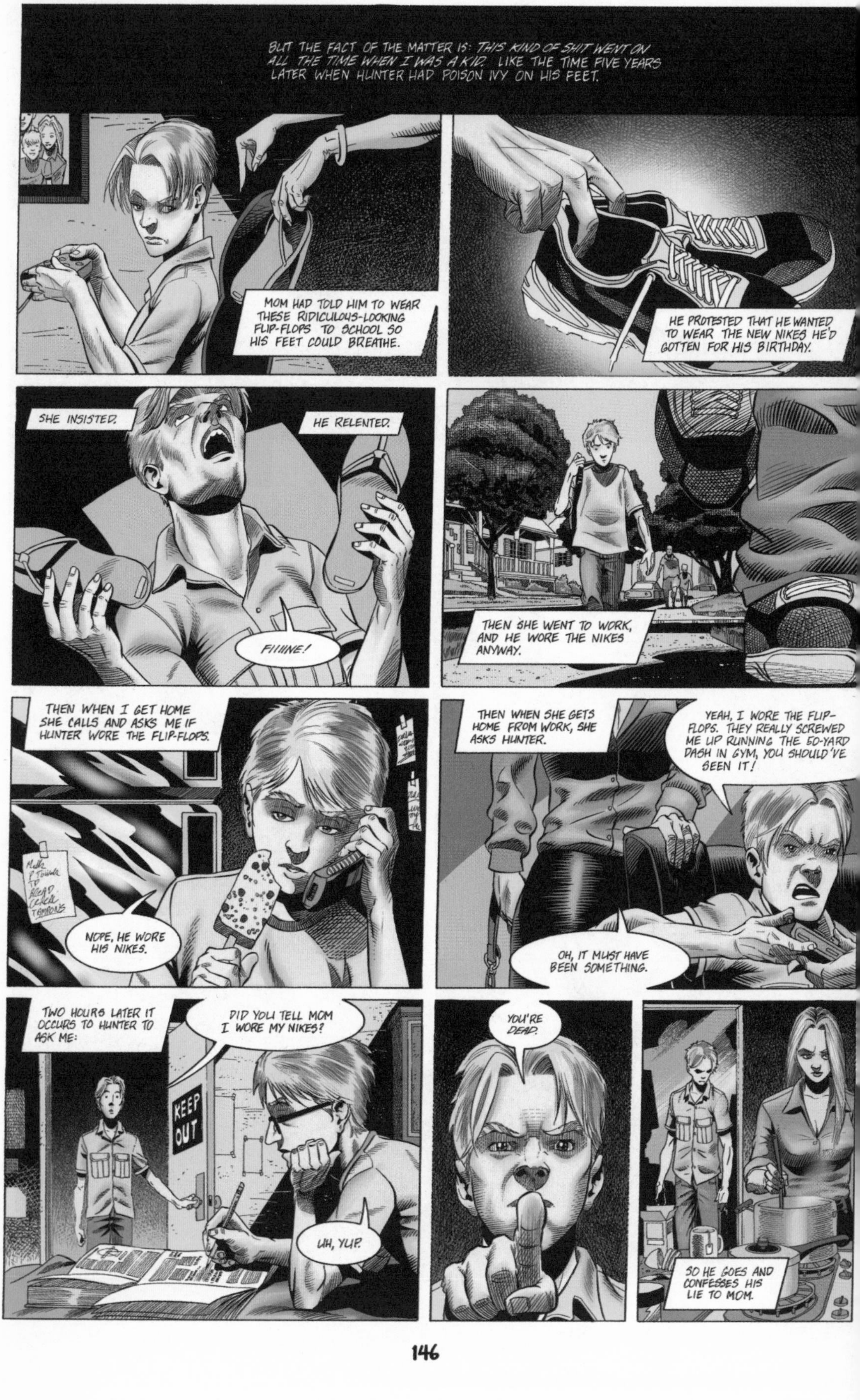
BUT THE FACT OF THE MATTER IS: THIS KIND OF SHIT WENT ON ALL THE TIME WHEN I WAS A KID. LIKE THE TIME FIVE YEARS LATER WHEN HUNTER HAD POISON IVY ON HIS FEET.
MOM HAD TOLD HIM TO WEAR THESE RIDICULOUS-LOOKING FLIP-FLOPS TO SCHOOL SO HIS FEET COULD BREATHE.
HE PROTESTED THAT HE WANTED TO WEAR THE NEW NIKES HE'D GOTTEN FOR HIS BIRTHDAY.
SHE INSISTED.
HE RELENTED.
FIIIINE!
THEN SHE WENT TO WORK, AND HE WORE THE NIKES ANYWAY.
THEN WHEN I GET HOME SHE CALLS AND ASKS ME IF HUNTER WORE THE FLIP-FLOPS.
NOPE, HE WORE HIS NIKES.
THEN WHEN SHE GETS HOME FROM WORK, SHE ASKS HUNTER.
YEAH, I WORE THE FLIP-FLOPS. THEY REALLY SCREWED ME UP RUNNING THE 50-YARD DASH IN GYM, YOU SHOULD'VE SEEN IT!
OH, IT MUST HAVE BEEN SOMETHING.
TWO HOURS LATER IT OCCURS TO HUNTER TO ASK ME:
DID YOU TELL MOM I WORE MY NIKES?
KEEP OUT
UH, YUP.
YOU'RE DEAD.
SO HE GOES AND CONFESSES HIS LIE TO MOM.

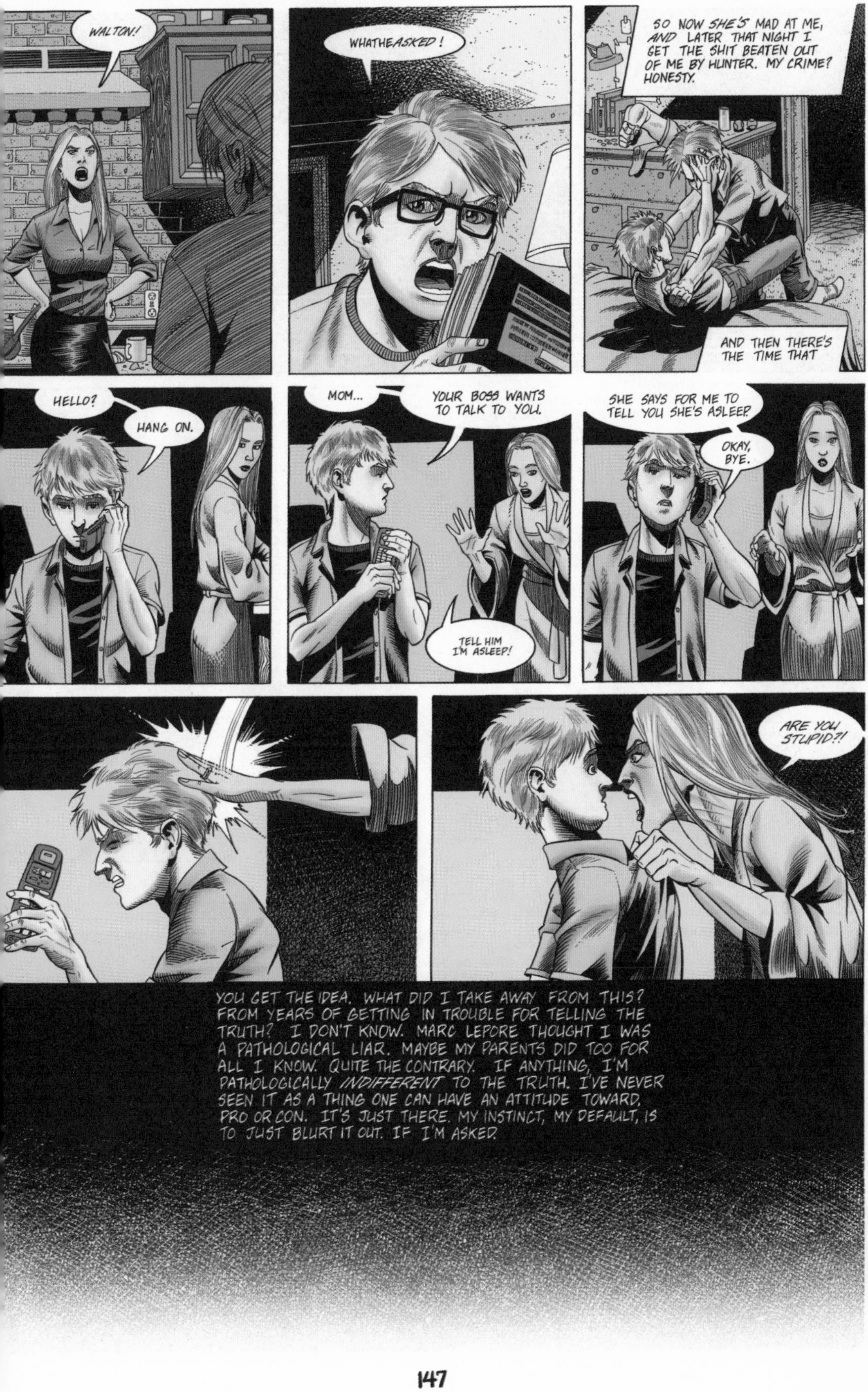

WALTON!
WHATHEASKED!
SO NOW SHE'S MAD AT ME, AND LATER THAT NIGHT I GET THE SHIT BEATEN OUT OF ME BY HUNTER. MY CRIME? HONESTY.
AND THEN THERE'S THE TIME THAT
HELLO?
HANG ON.
MOM...
YOUR BOSS WANTS TO TALK TO YOU.
TELL HIM I'M ASLEEP!
SHE SAYS FOR ME TO TELL YOU SHE'S ASLEEP.
OKAY, BYE.
ARE YOU STUPID?!
YOU GET THE IDEA. WHAT DID I TAKE AWAY FROM THIS? FROM YEARS OF GETTING IN TROUBLE FOR TELLING THE TRUTH? I DON'T KNOW. MARC LEPORE THOUGHT I WAS A PATHOLOGICAL LIAR. MAYBE MY PARENTS DID TOO FOR ALL I KNOW. QUITE THE CONTRARY. IF ANYTHING, I'M PATHOLOGICALLY INDIFFERENT TO THE TRUTH. I'VE NEVER SEEN IT AS A THING ONE CAN HAVE AN ATTITUDE TOWARD, PRO OR CON. IT'S JUST THERE. MY INSTINCT, MY DEFAULT, IS TO JUST BLURT IT OUT. IF I'M ASKED.

ANYWAY, CUT TO MAY OF 2021.

HERE'S OUR NOW SEVENTEEN-YEAR-OLD HERO PLAYING FOR SEA GIRT HIGH AT THE REGIONAL QUARTER FINALS.

THE KID I WAS UP AGAINST WAS TREVOR MAYHUGH FROM NEPTUNE HIGH.

THIS GUY WAS A *HYDRA*.

HE WAS TOYING WITH ME, RUNNING ME RAGGED, BEATING MY ASS INTO THE ASPHALT.

HE KNEW IT AND I KNEW IT.

MY PAIN WASN'T DECREASED BY THE FACT THAT DAD WAS WATCHING.

THE MAN WHO'D HAD ME OUT ON THE COURTS PRACTICALLY EVERY SATURDAY SINCE I WAS FOUR.

DON'T SWING TILL I ACTUALLY *SERVE* THE THING, WALTON. BE PATIENT.

LOOK AT THE BALL, NOT YOUR RACKET.

TENNIS AT THE ATLANTIC CLUB

THE MAN WHO PROUDLY DISPLAYED HIS U.S. OPEN 2ND PLACE TROPHY IN THE FAMILY ROOM, AND WHO DIDN'T SIGN TENNIS BALLS DURING HIS TWO-HOUR TRAIN COMMUTE INTO MANHATTAN, BECAUSE NO ONE EVER ASKED HIM TO.

148

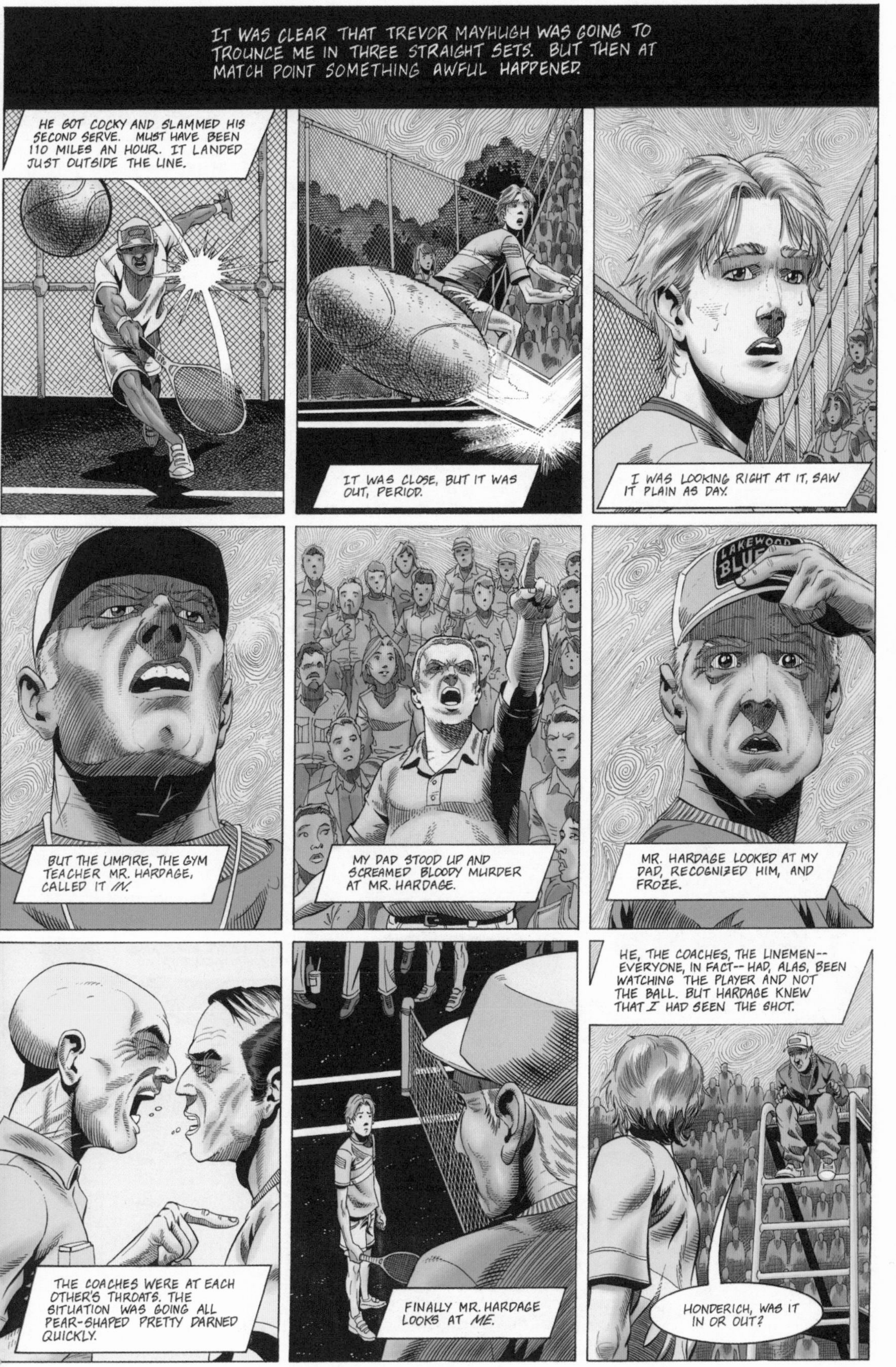
IT WAS CLEAR THAT TREVOR MAYHUGH WAS GOING TO TROUNCE ME IN THREE STRAIGHT SETS. BUT THEN AT MATCH POINT SOMETHING AWFUL HAPPENED.
HE GOT COCKY AND SLAMMED HIS SECOND SERVE. MUST HAVE BEEN 110 MILES AN HOUR. IT LANDED JUST OUTSIDE THE LINE.
IT WAS CLOSE, BUT IT WAS OUT, PERIOD.
I WAS LOOKING RIGHT AT IT, SAW IT PLAIN AS DAY.
BUT THE UMPIRE, THE GYM TEACHER MR. HARDAGE, CALLED IT *IN*.
MY DAD STOOD UP AND SCREAMED BLOODY MURDER AT MR. HARDAGE.
LAKEWOOD BLUE
MR. HARDAGE LOOKED AT MY DAD, RECOGNIZED HIM, AND FROZE.
THE COACHES WERE AT EACH OTHER'S THROATS. THE SITUATION WAS GOING ALL PEAR-SHAPED PRETTY DARNED QUICKLY.
FINALLY MR. HARDAGE LOOKS AT *ME*.
HE, THE COACHES, THE LINEMEN-- EVERYONE, IN FACT-- HAD, ALAS, BEEN WATCHING THE PLAYER AND NOT THE BALL. BUT HARDAGE KNEW THAT *I* HAD SEEN THE SHOT.
HONDERICH, WAS IT IN OR OUT?

I'D LIKE TO SAY THAT FOR THE BRIEFEST OF MOMENTS, I CONSIDERED LYING, SAYING THAT IT WAS IN, JUST TO GET OUT OF THERE AND END MY ORDEAL. BUT NAH, THAT DIDN'T HAPPEN.

IT WAS OUT.

JUST COULDN'T STOP MYSELF.

LIAR!

LIAR!

LIAR!

LIAR!

LIAR!

MORE CHAOS, LOUDER SCREAMING.

FINALLY I SEE TREVOR MAYHUGH SAYING SOMETHING TO HIS COACH.

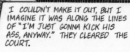
I COULDN'T MAKE IT OUT, BUT I IMAGINE IT WAS ALONG THE LINES OF "I'M JUST GONNA KICK HIS ASS, ANYWAY." THEY CLEARED THE COURT.

THE GAME WENT ON.

I KNOW IT'S HARD, CHAMP, BUT SOMETIMES YOU GOTTA KNOW WHEN TO SAVE YOUR STRENGTH AND LET A SHOT GO.

LOSING IS NOT ALWAYS THE WORST THING, TAKE IT FROM A GUY WHO KNOWS.

TENNIS IS ABOUT FINESSE—PICKING YOUR BATTLES, BEING PATIENT, STRATEGIZING.

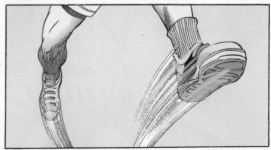

WALTON...

151

I'M SORRY, DAD.
I COULDN'T HELP IT...

JUST LAY STILL,
WALTON. LAY STILL.

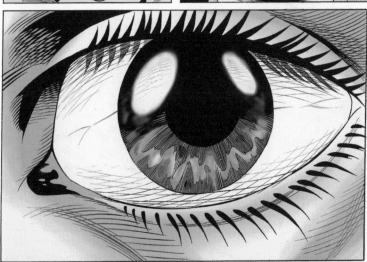

GO TO YOUR
GODDAMNED ROOM!

AND THAT SUMMER, IN MY ROOM, I
DISCOVERED THAT I WAS REALLY GOOD
AT CALCULUS.

AND MY ORDEAL BEGAN.

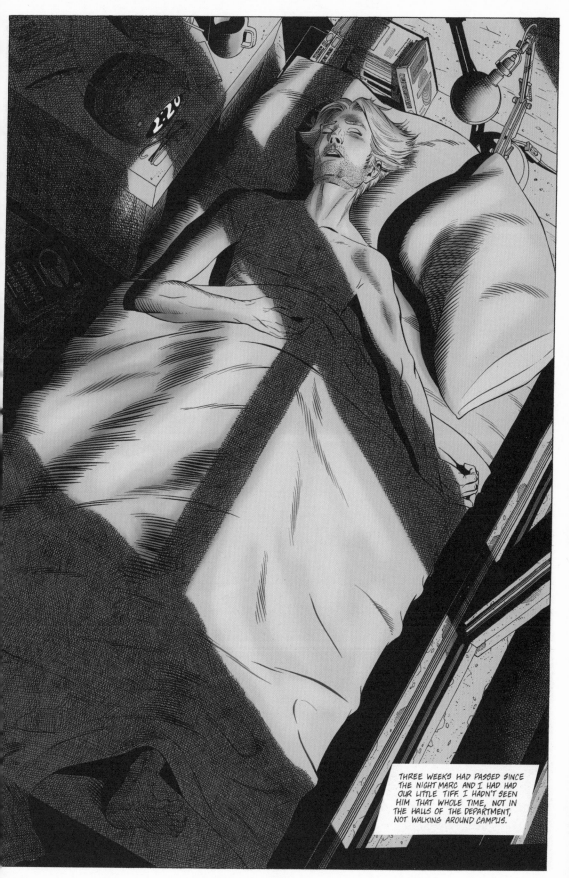

THREE WEEKS HAD PASSED SINCE THE NIGHT MARC AND I HAD HAD OUR LITTLE TIFF. I HADN'T SEEN HIM THAT WHOLE TIME, NOT IN THE HALLS OF THE DEPARTMENT, NOT WALKING AROUND CAMPUS.

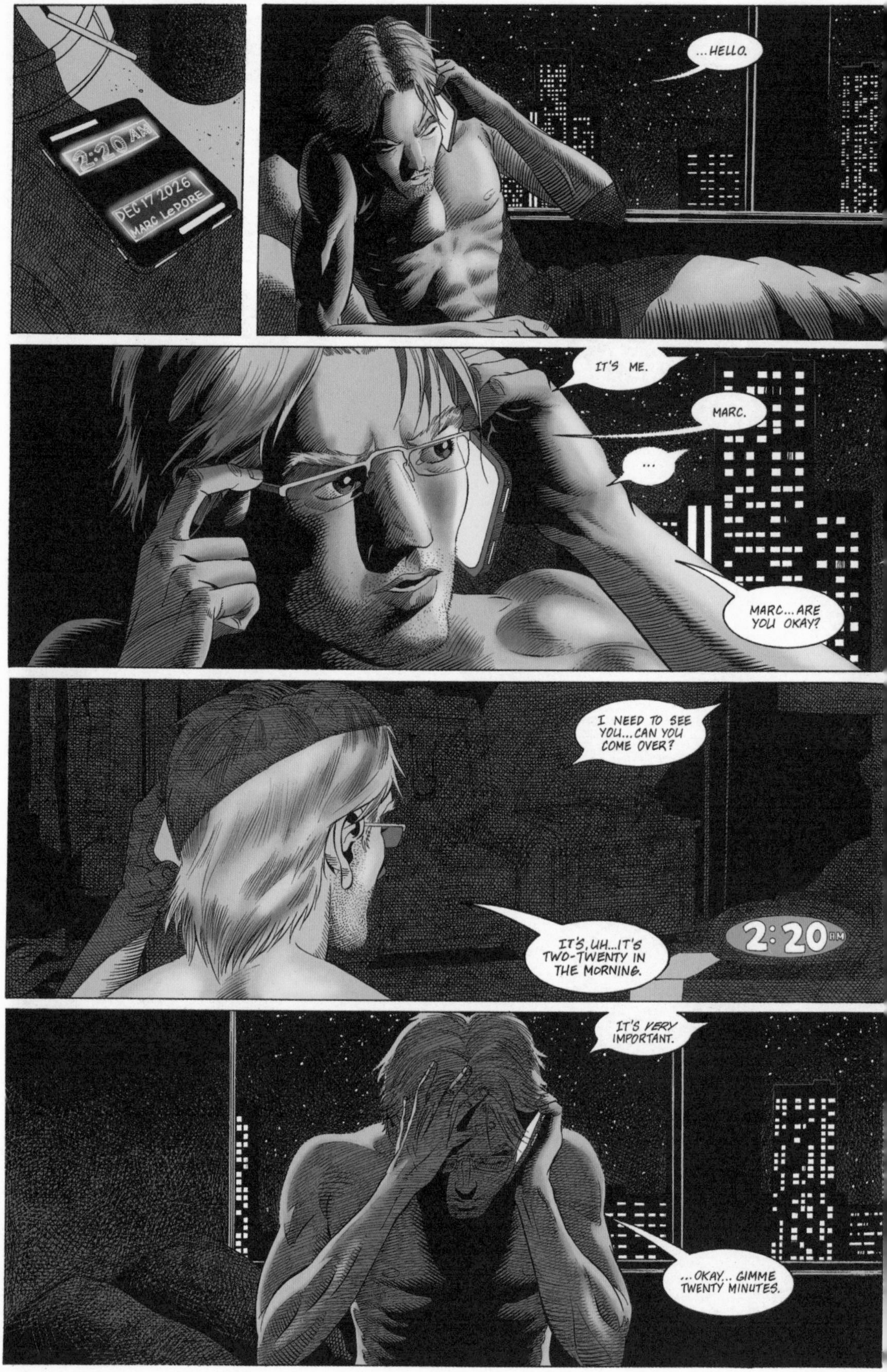
2:20 AM
DEC 17 2026
MARC LePORE
...HELLO.
IT'S ME.
MARC.
...
MARC...ARE YOU OKAY?
I NEED TO SEE YOU...CAN YOU COME OVER?
IT'S, UH...IT'S TWO-TWENTY IN THE MORNING.
2:20 AM
IT'S VERY IMPORTANT.
...OKAY... GIMME TWENTY MINUTES.

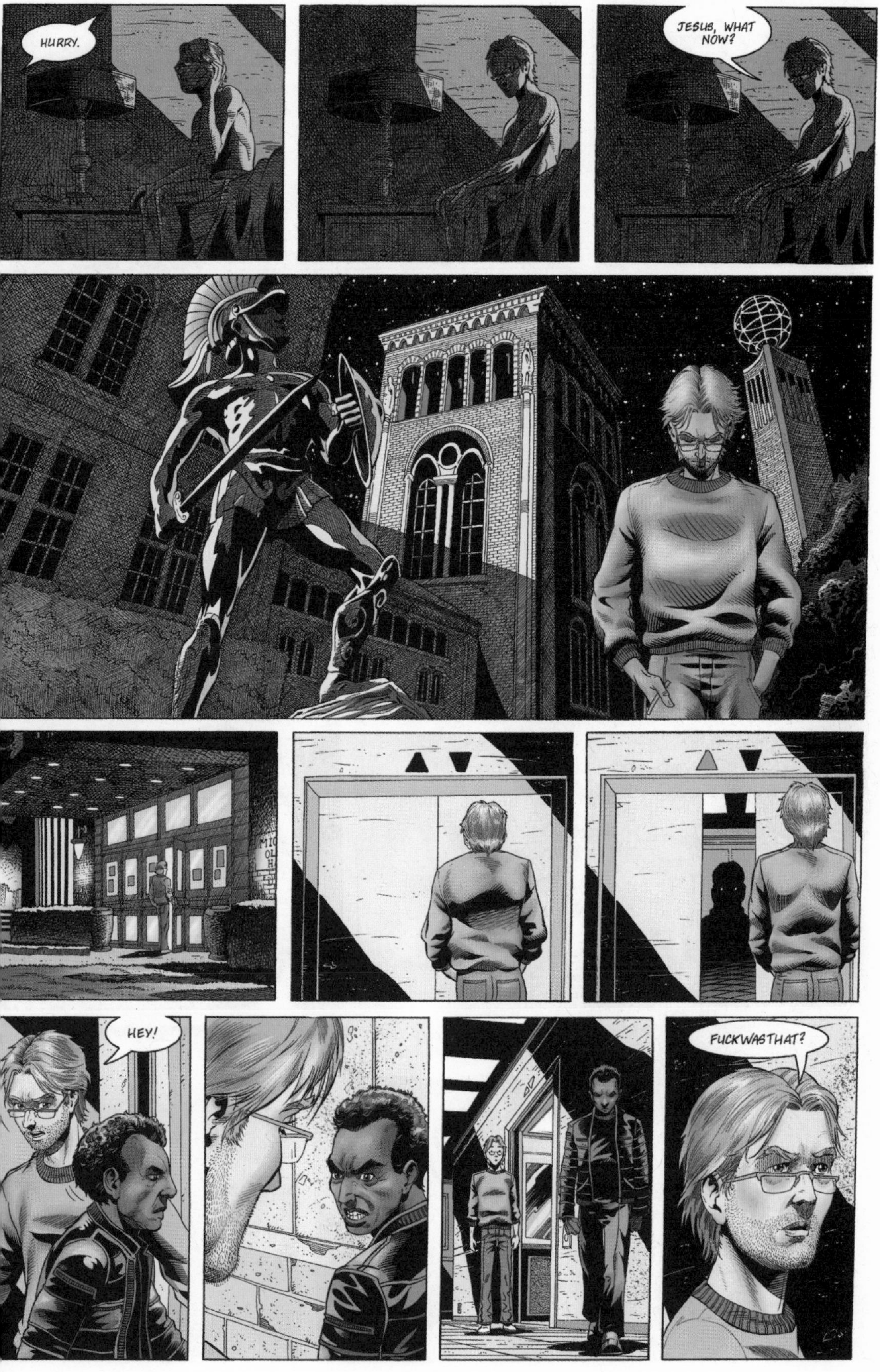
HURRY.
JESUS, WHAT NOW?
HEY!
FUCKWASTHAT?

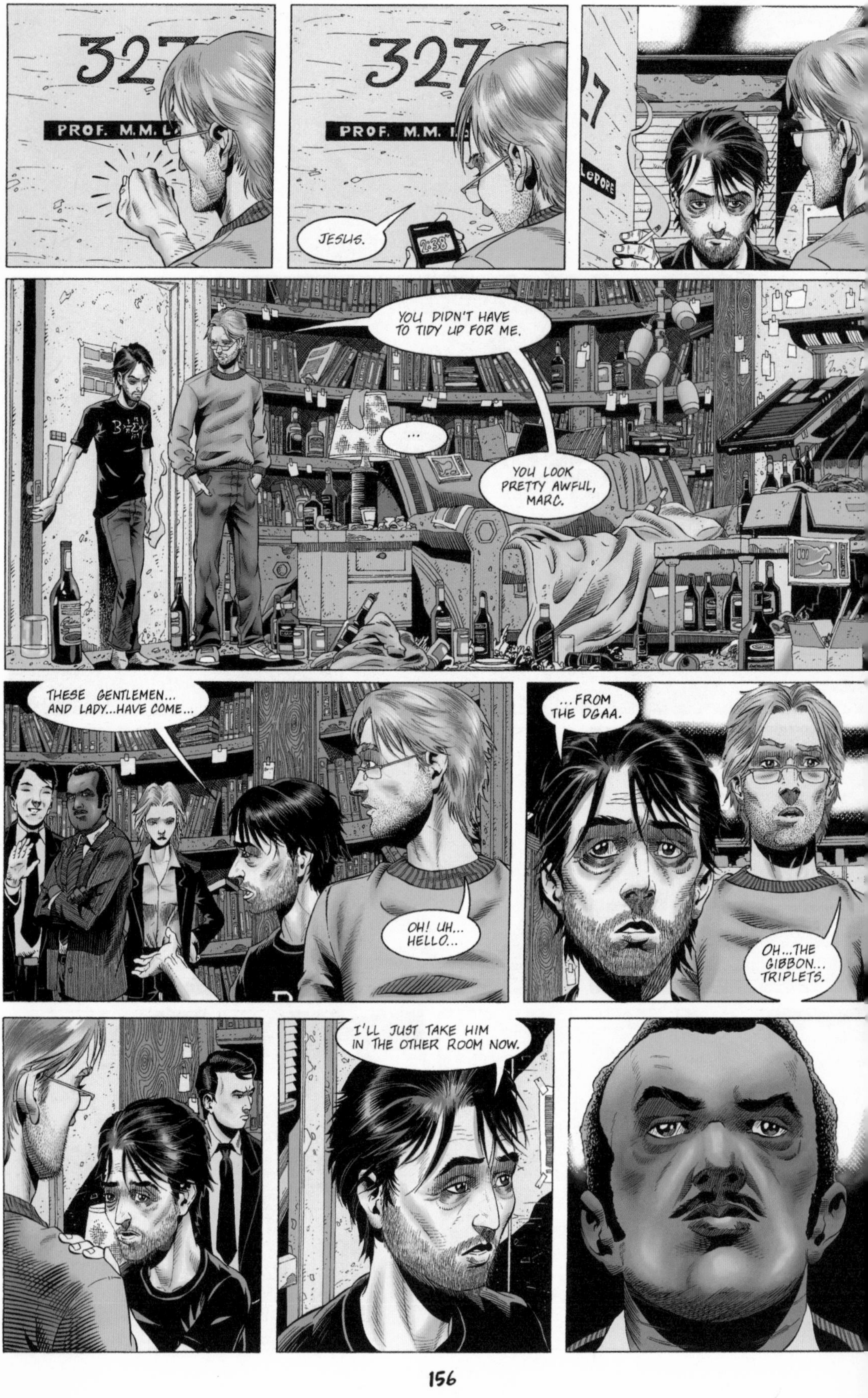
327
PROF. M.M. L
327
PROF. M.M. L
JESUS.
2:38
LEPORE
YOU DIDN'T HAVE TO TIDY UP FOR ME.
...
YOU LOOK PRETTY AWFUL, MARC.
THESE GENTLEMEN... AND LADY...HAVE COME...
OH! UH... HELLO...
...FROM THE DGAA.
OH...THE GIBBON... TRIPLETS.
I'LL JUST TAKE HIM IN THE OTHER ROOM NOW.

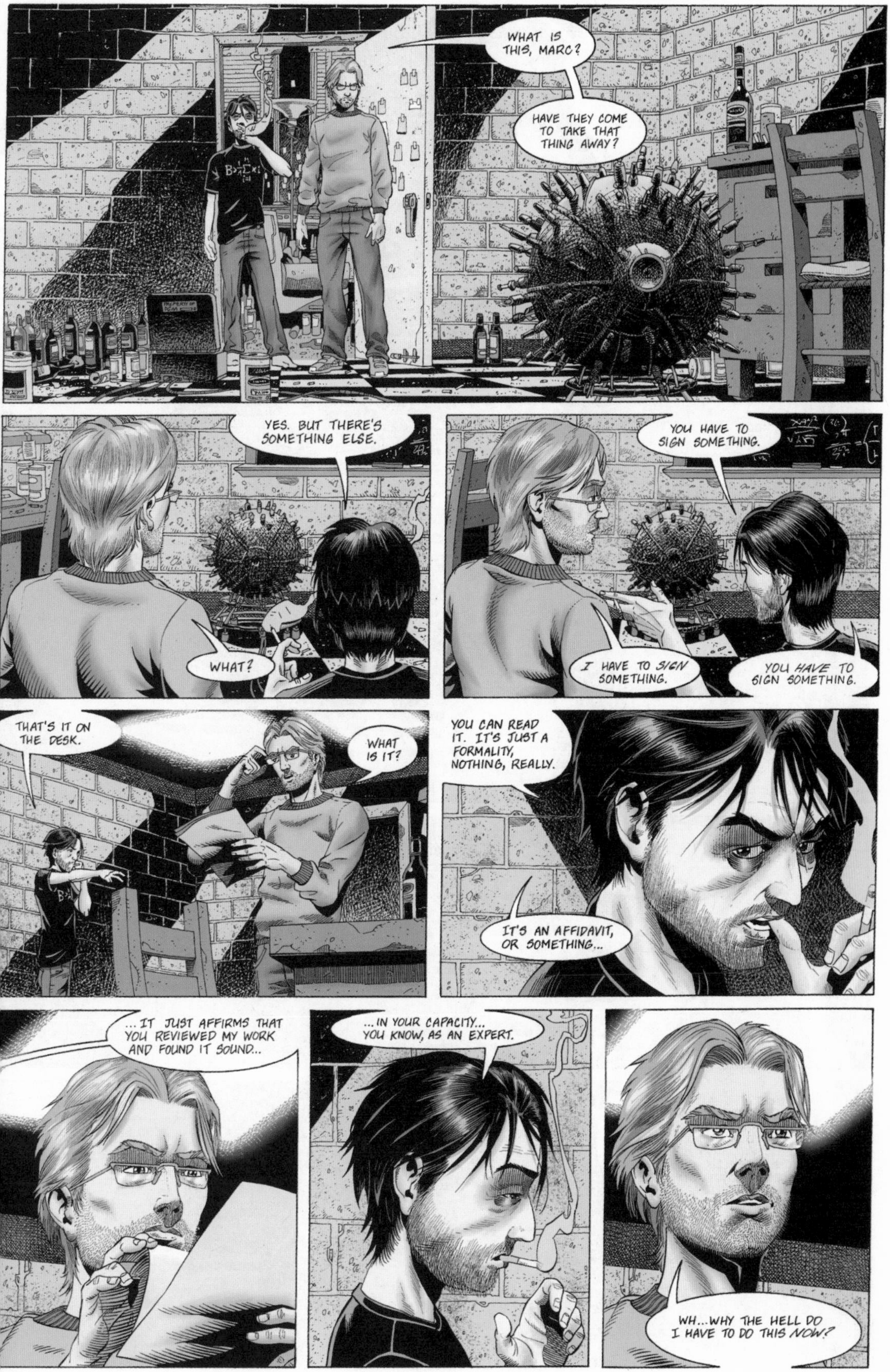
WHAT IS THIS, MARC?
HAVE THEY COME TO TAKE THAT THING AWAY?
YES. BUT THERE'S SOMETHING ELSE.
WHAT?
YOU HAVE TO SIGN SOMETHING.
I HAVE TO SIGN SOMETHING.
YOU HAVE TO SIGN SOMETHING.
THAT'S IT ON THE DESK.
WHAT IS IT?
YOU CAN READ IT. IT'S JUST A FORMALITY, NOTHING, REALLY.
IT'S AN AFFIDAVIT, OR SOMETHING...
...IT JUST AFFIRMS THAT YOU REVIEWED MY WORK AND FOUND IT SOUND...
...IN YOUR CAPACITY... YOU KNOW, AS AN EXPERT.
WH...WHY THE HELL DO I HAVE TO DO THIS NOW?

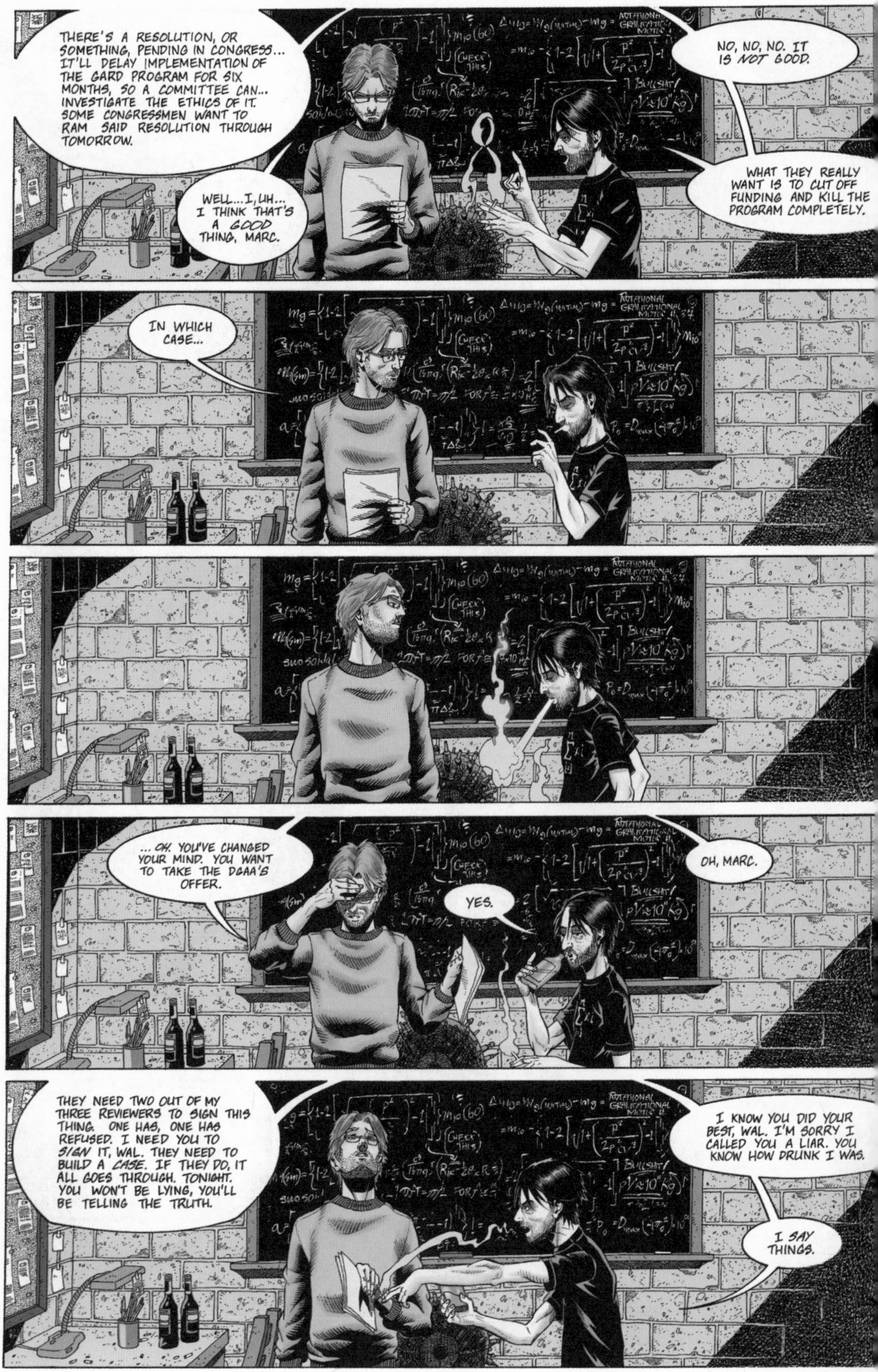
THERE'S A RESOLUTION, OR SOMETHING, PENDING IN CONGRESS... IT'LL DELAY IMPLEMENTATION OF THE GARD PROGRAM FOR SIX MONTHS, SO A COMMITTEE CAN... INVESTIGATE THE ETHICS OF IT. SOME CONGRESSMEN WANT TO RAM SAID RESOLUTION THROUGH TOMORROW.
WELL... I, UH... I THINK THAT'S A GOOD THING, MARC.
NO, NO, NO. IT IS NOT GOOD.
WHAT THEY REALLY WANT IS TO CUT OFF FUNDING AND KILL THE PROGRAM COMPLETELY.
IN WHICH CASE...
... OH. YOU'VE CHANGED YOUR MIND. YOU WANT TO TAKE THE DGAA'S OFFER.
YES.
OH, MARC.
THEY NEED TWO OUT OF MY THREE REVIEWERS TO SIGN THIS THING. ONE HAS, ONE HAS REFUSED. I NEED YOU TO SIGN IT, WAL. THEY NEED TO BUILD A CASE. IF THEY DO, IT ALL GOES THROUGH. TONIGHT. YOU WON'T BE LYING, YOU'LL BE TELLING THE TRUTH.
I KNOW YOU DID YOUR BEST, WAL. I'M SORRY I CALLED YOU A LIAR. YOU KNOW HOW DRUNK I WAS.
I SAY THINGS.

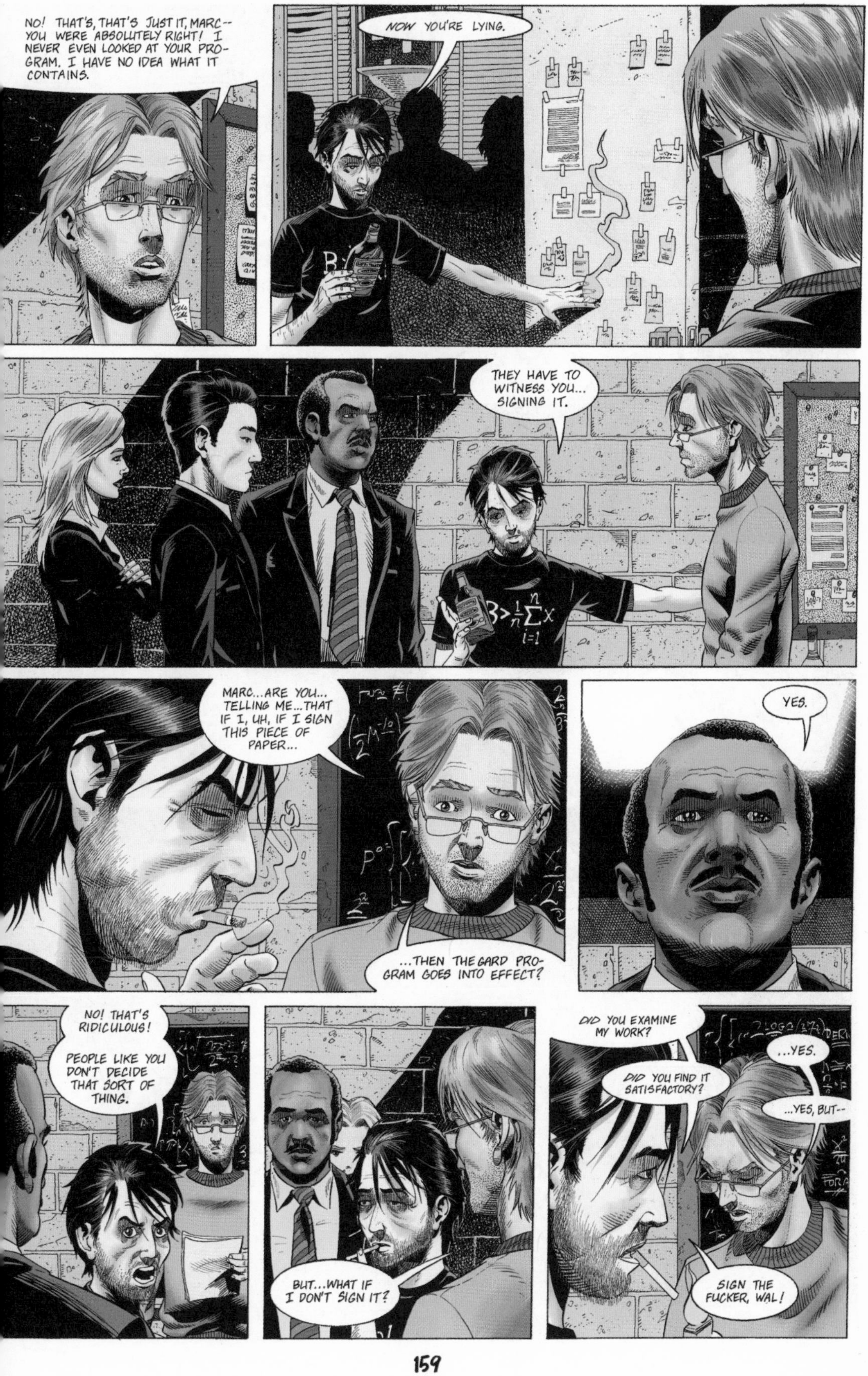
NO! THAT'S, THAT'S JUST IT, MARC-- YOU WERE ABSOLUTELY RIGHT! I NEVER EVEN LOOKED AT YOUR PROGRAM. I HAVE NO IDEA WHAT IT CONTAINS.
NOW YOU'RE LYING.
THEY HAVE TO WITNESS YOU... SIGNING IT.
MARC...ARE YOU... TELLING ME...THAT IF I, UH, IF I SIGN THIS PIECE OF PAPER...
...THEN THE GARD PROGRAM GOES INTO EFFECT?
YES.
NO! THAT'S RIDICULOUS!
PEOPLE LIKE YOU DON'T DECIDE THAT SORT OF THING.
BUT...WHAT IF I DON'T SIGN IT?
DID YOU EXAMINE MY WORK?
...YES.
DID YOU FIND IT SATISFACTORY?
...YES, BUT--
SIGN THE FUCKER, WAL!

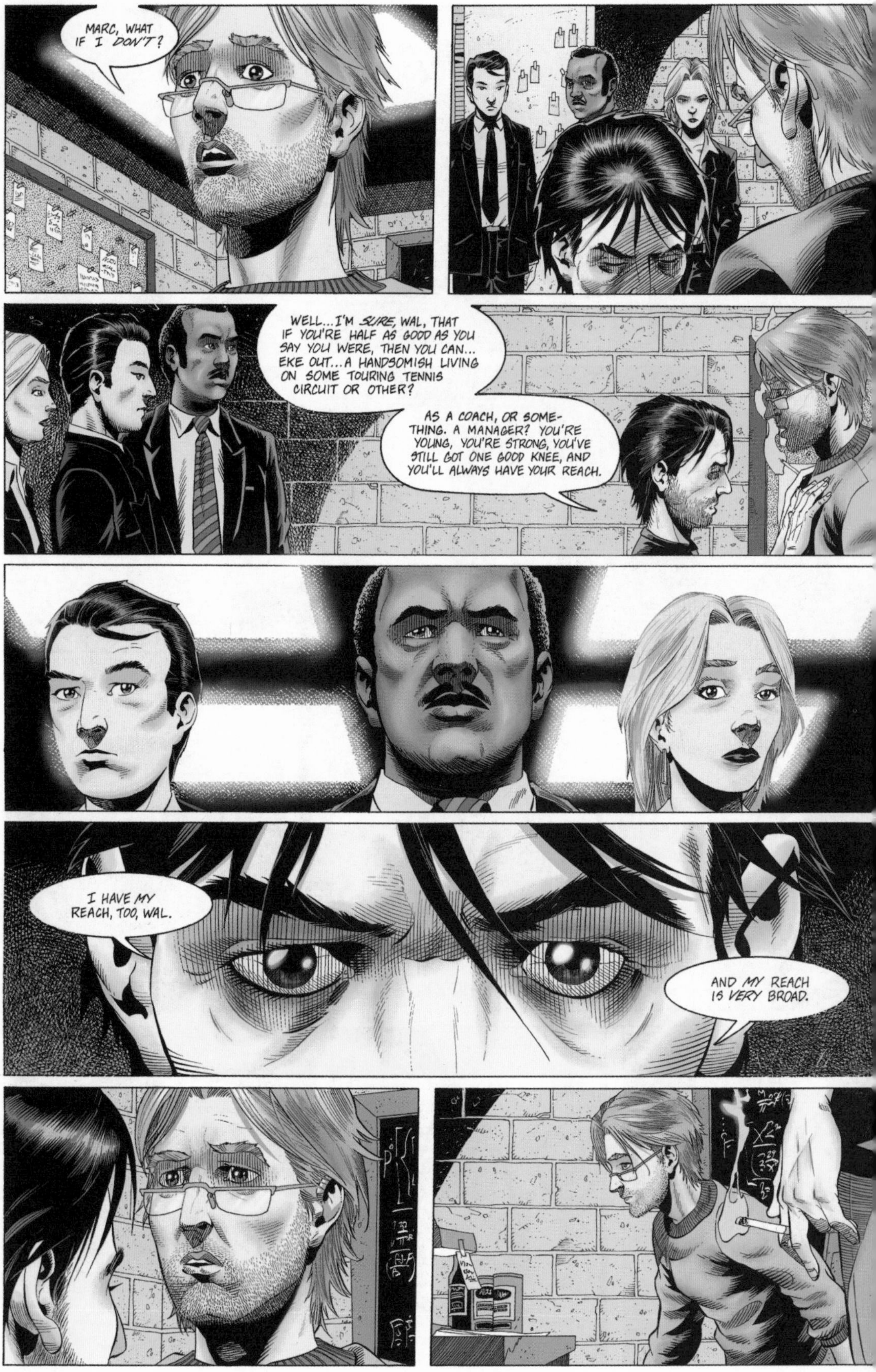

MARC, WHAT IF I DON'T?
WELL... I'M SURE, WAL, THAT IF YOU'RE HALF AS GOOD AS YOU SAY YOU WERE, THEN YOU CAN... EKE OUT... A HANDSOMISH LIVING ON SOME TOURING TENNIS CIRCUIT OR OTHER?
AS A COACH, OR SOMETHING. A MANAGER? YOU'RE YOUNG, YOU'RE STRONG, YOU'VE STILL GOT ONE GOOD KNEE, AND YOU'LL ALWAYS HAVE YOUR REACH.
I HAVE MY REACH, TOO, WAL.
AND MY REACH IS VERY BROAD.

THIS PAGE INTENTIONALLY LEFT BLANK
THIS MAN INTENTIONAL LEFT BLANK
THIS PAGE INTENTIONALLY LEFT BLANK
THIS PAGE INTENTIONALLY LEFT BLANK
FUNNILY ENOUGH, I CAN'T ACTUALLY REMEMBER SIGNING IT.
I DO REMEMBER LOOKING DOWN AT MY SIGNATURE ON THE PAGE. BUT NOT SIGNING IT.
WALTON H
I REMEMBER THE DGAA PEOPLE TOOK THE FORM AND LEFT IN AN AWFUL HURRY.
AND I REMEMBER MARC OFFERED ME A DRINK, WHICH I ACCEPTED.
AND THEN I WENT BACK TO MY ROOM AND GOT BACK INTO BED.

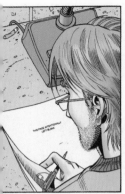

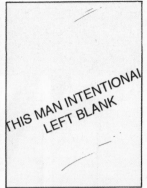

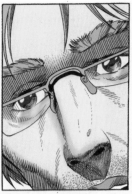

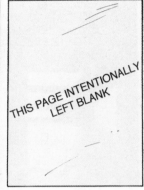

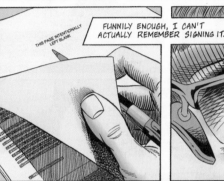

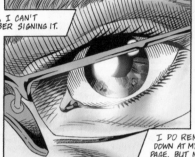

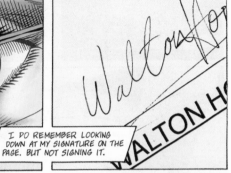

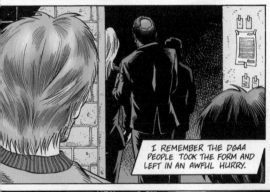

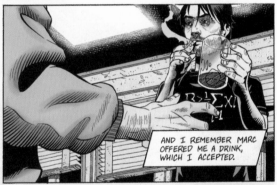

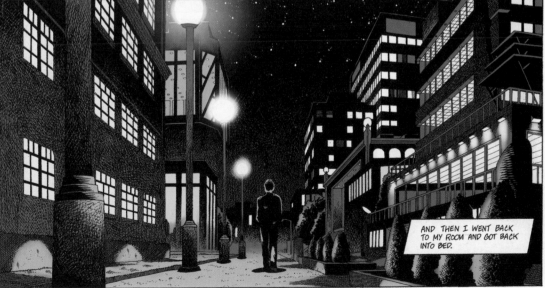

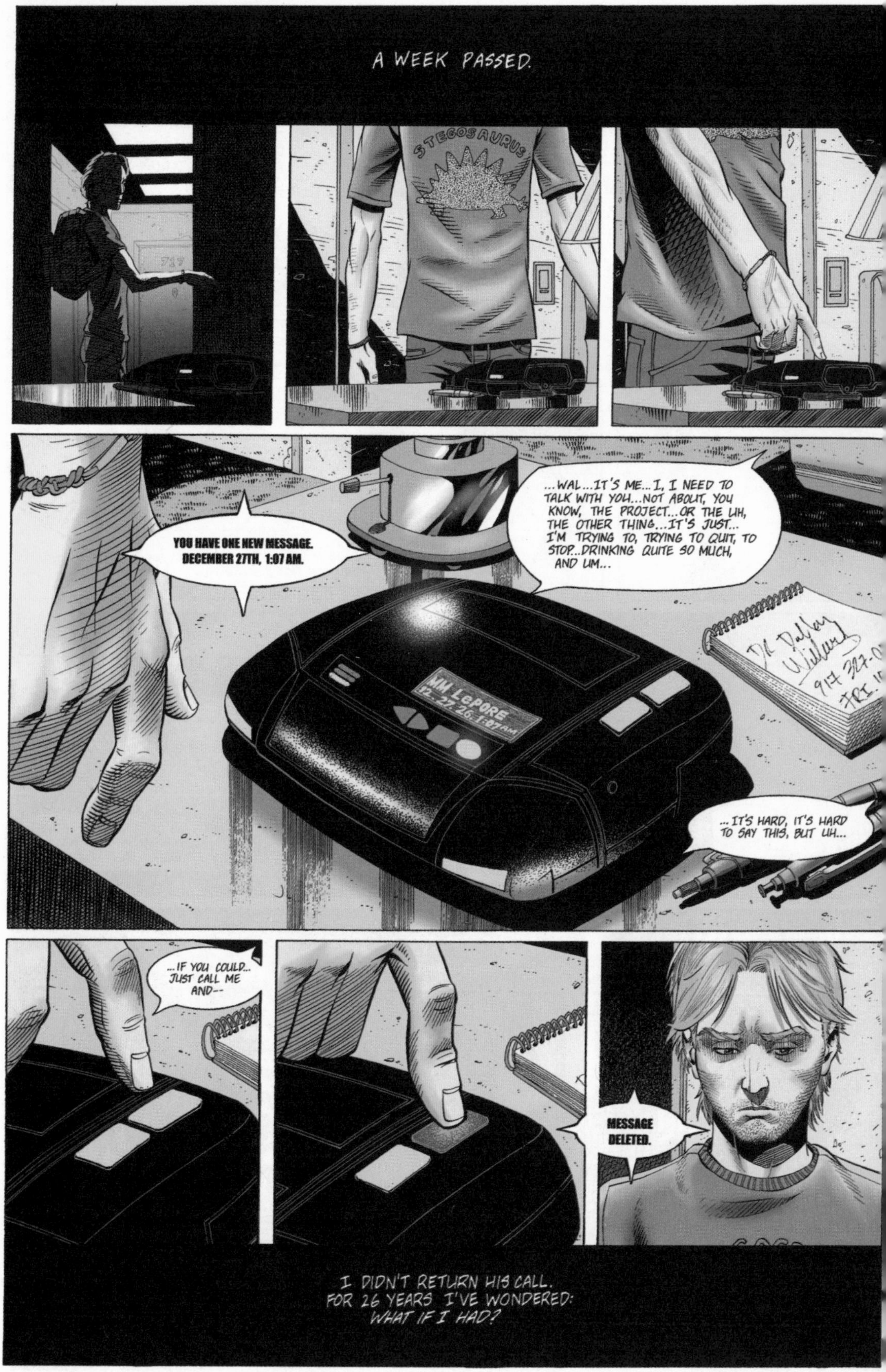
A WEEK PASSED.
STEGOSAURUS
YOU HAVE ONE NEW MESSAGE. DECEMBER 27TH, 1:07 AM.
...WAL...IT'S ME...I, I NEED TO TALK WITH YOU...NOT ABOUT, YOU KNOW, THE PROJECT...OR THE UH, THE OTHER THING...IT'S JUST... I'M TRYING TO, TRYING TO QUIT, TO STOP...DRINKING QUITE SO MUCH, AND UM...
MM LePORE
12.27.26 1:07AM
...IT'S HARD, IT'S HARD TO SAY THIS, BUT UH...
...IF YOU COULD... JUST CALL ME AND--
MESSAGE DELETED.
I DIDN'T RETURN HIS CALL.
FOR 26 YEARS I'VE WONDERED:
WHAT IF I HAD?

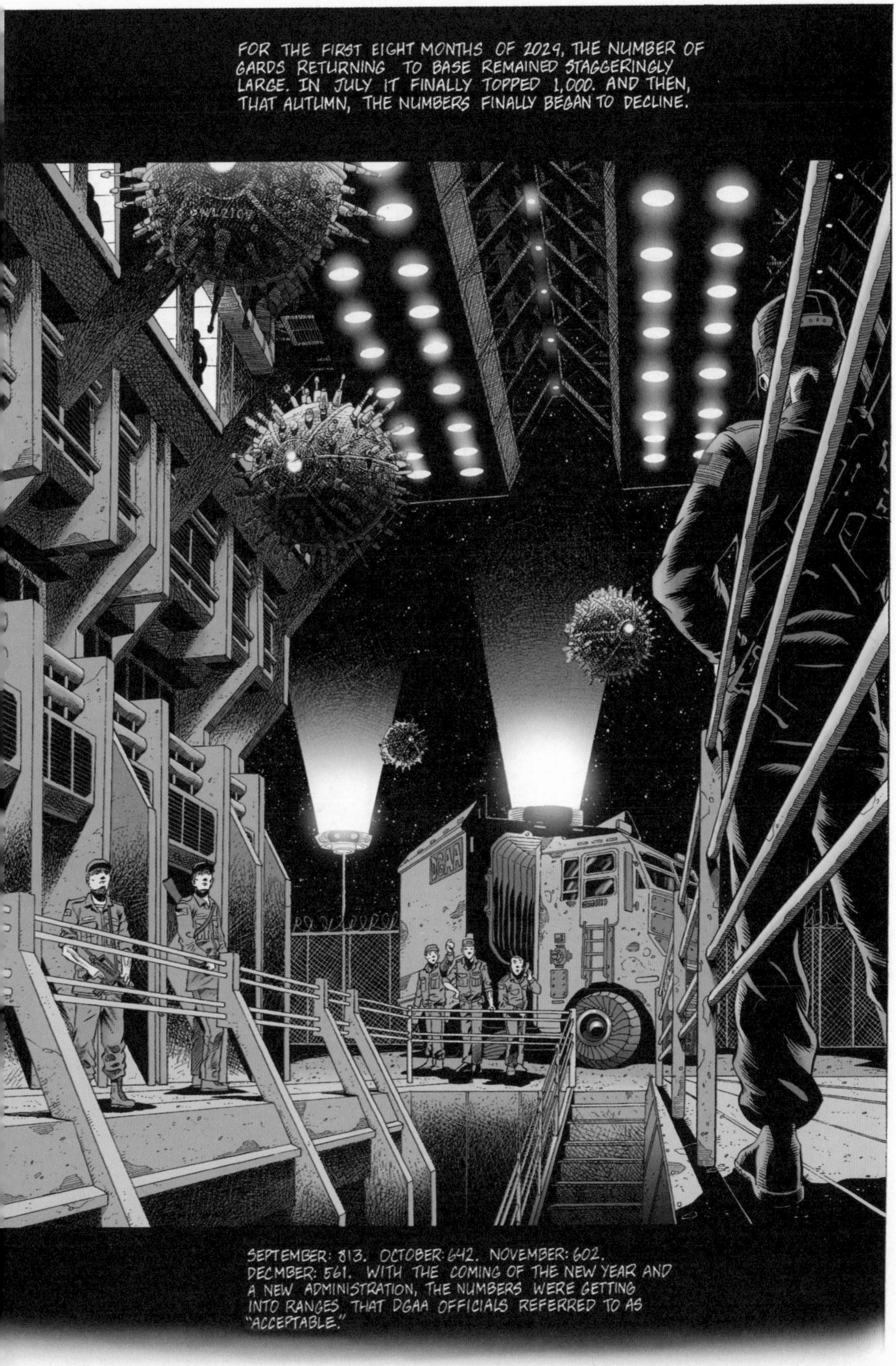
FOR THE FIRST EIGHT MONTHS OF 2029, THE NUMBER OF GARDS RETURNING TO BASE REMAINED STAGGERINGLY LARGE. IN JULY IT FINALLY TOPPED 1,000. AND THEN, THAT AUTUMN, THE NUMBERS FINALLY BEGAN TO DECLINE.
DGAA
SEPTEMBER: 813. OCTOBER: 642. NOVEMBER: 602. DECMBER: 561. WITH THE COMING OF THE NEW YEAR AND A NEW ADMINISTRATION, THE NUMBERS WERE GETTING INTO RANGES THAT DGAA OFFICIALS REFERRED TO AS "ACCEPTABLE."

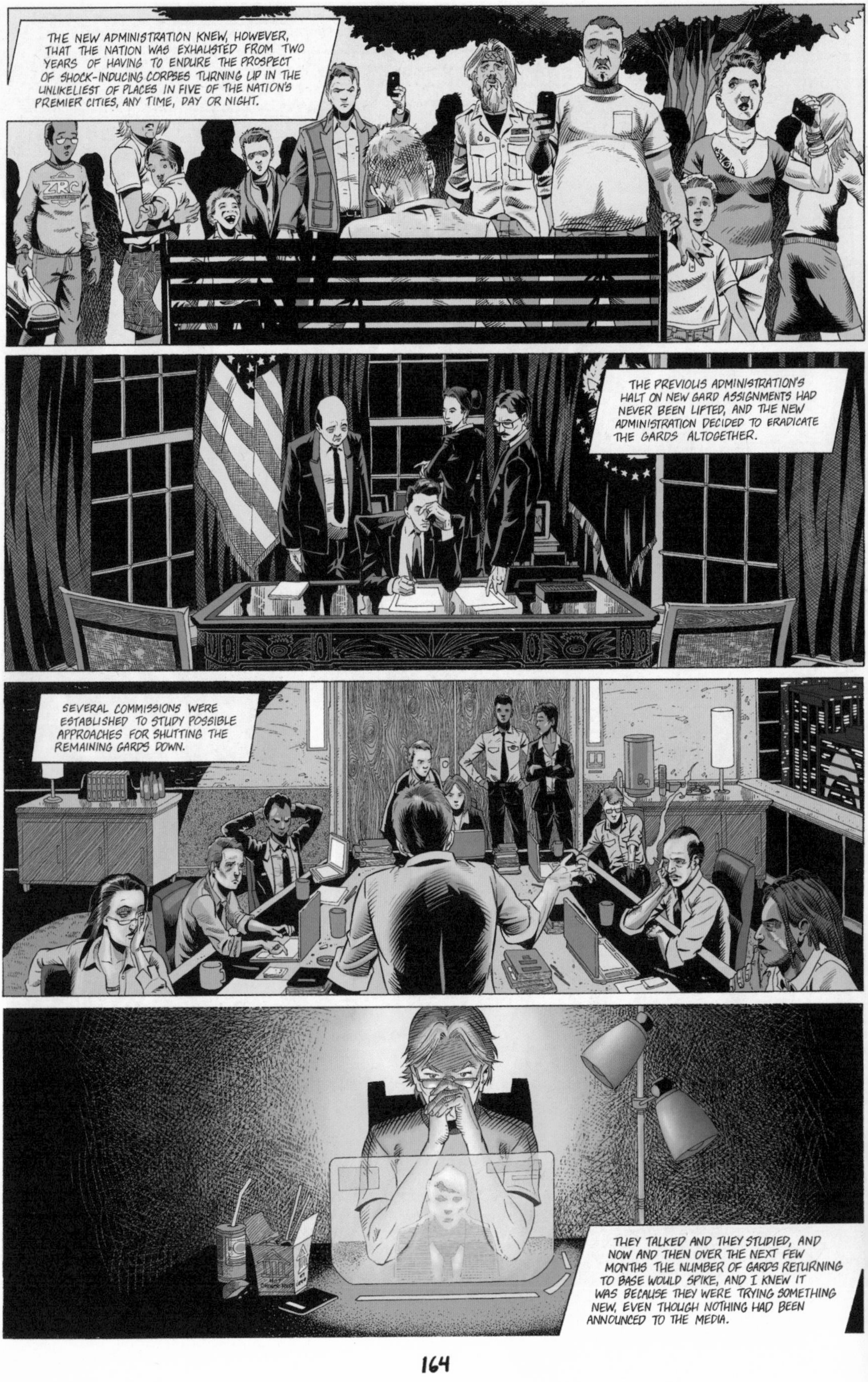
THE NEW ADMINISTRATION KNEW, HOWEVER, THAT THE NATION WAS EXHAUSTED FROM TWO YEARS OF HAVING TO ENDURE THE PROSPECT OF SHOCK-INDUCING CORPSES TURNING UP IN THE UNLIKELIEST OF PLACES IN FIVE OF THE NATION'S PREMIER CITIES, ANY TIME, DAY OR NIGHT.
ZRC
THE PREVIOUS ADMINISTRATION'S HALT ON NEW GARD ASSIGNMENTS HAD NEVER BEEN LIFTED, AND THE NEW ADMINISTRATION DECIDED TO ERADICATE THE GARDS ALTOGETHER.
SEVERAL COMMISSIONS WERE ESTABLISHED TO STUDY POSSIBLE APPROACHES FOR SHUTTING THE REMAINING GARDS DOWN.
THEY TALKED AND THEY STUDIED, AND NOW AND THEN OVER THE NEXT FEW MONTHS THE NUMBER OF GARDS RETURNING TO BASE WOULD SPIKE, AND I KNEW IT WAS BECAUSE THEY WERE TRYING SOMETHING NEW, EVEN THOUGH NOTHING HAD BEEN ANNOUNCED TO THE MEDIA.

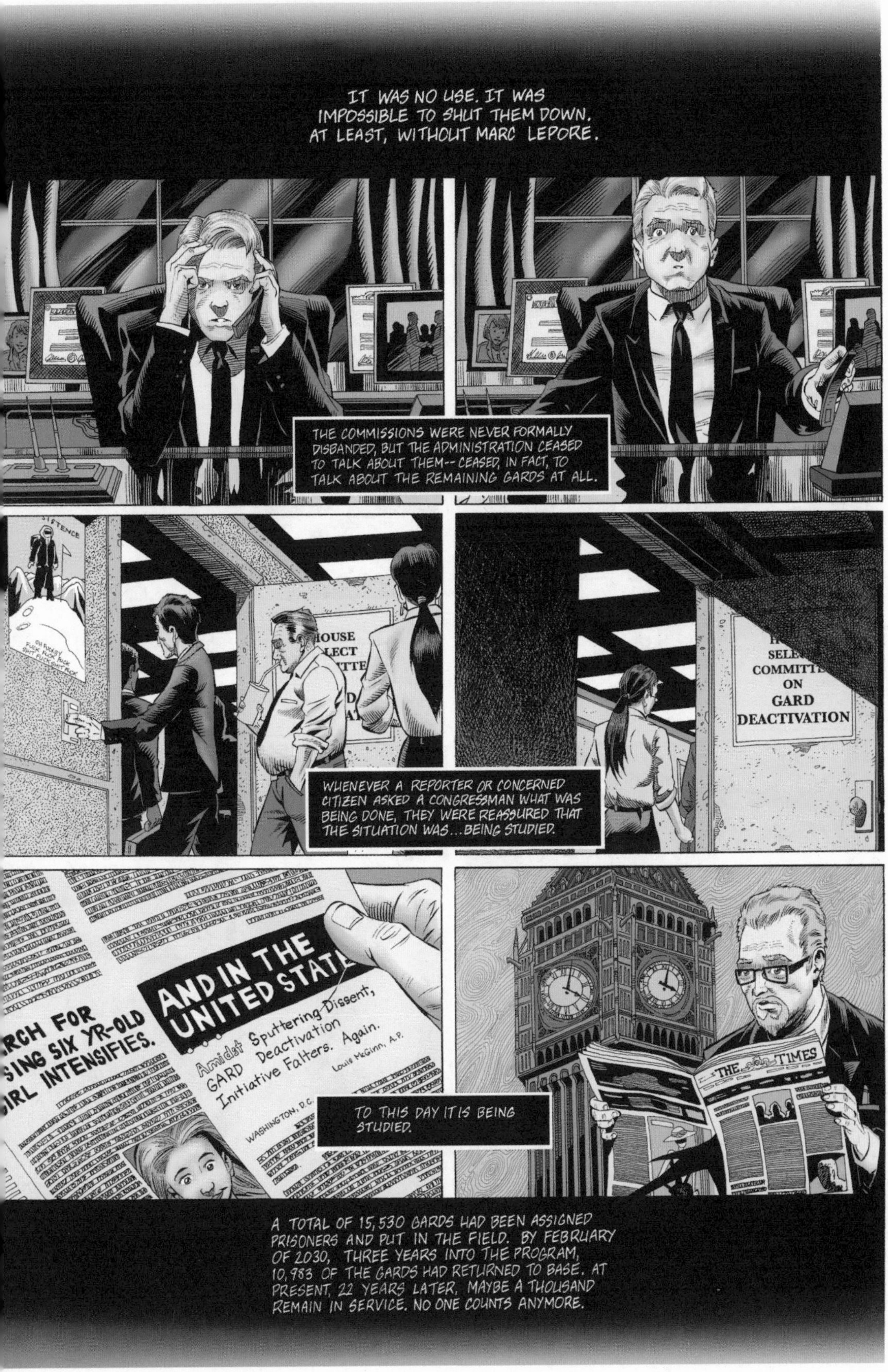
IT WAS NO USE. IT WAS IMPOSSIBLE TO SHUT THEM DOWN. AT LEAST, WITHOUT MARC LEPORE.
THE COMMISSIONS WERE NEVER FORMALLY DISBANDED, BUT THE ADMINISTRATION CEASED TO TALK ABOUT THEM-- CEASED, IN FACT, TO TALK ABOUT THE REMAINING GARDS AT ALL.
HOUSE SELECT COMMITTEE ON GARD DEACTIVATION
WHENEVER A REPORTER OR CONCERNED CITIZEN ASKED A CONGRESSMAN WHAT WAS BEING DONE, THEY WERE REASSURED THAT THE SITUATION WAS...BEING STUDIED.
AND IN THE UNITED STATE
Amidst Sputtering Dissent, GARD Deactivation Initiative Falters. Again.
Louis McGinn, A.P.
WASHINGTON, D.C.
RCH FOR SING SIX YR-OLD GIRL INTENSIFIES.
TO THIS DAY IT IS BEING STUDIED.
THE TIMES
A TOTAL OF 15,530 GARDS HAD BEEN ASSIGNED PRISONERS AND PUT IN THE FIELD. BY FEBRUARY OF 2030, THREE YEARS INTO THE PROGRAM, 10,983 OF THE GARDS HAD RETURNED TO BASE. AT PRESENT, 22 YEARS LATER, MAYBE A THOUSAND REMAIN IN SERVICE. NO ONE COUNTS ANYMORE.

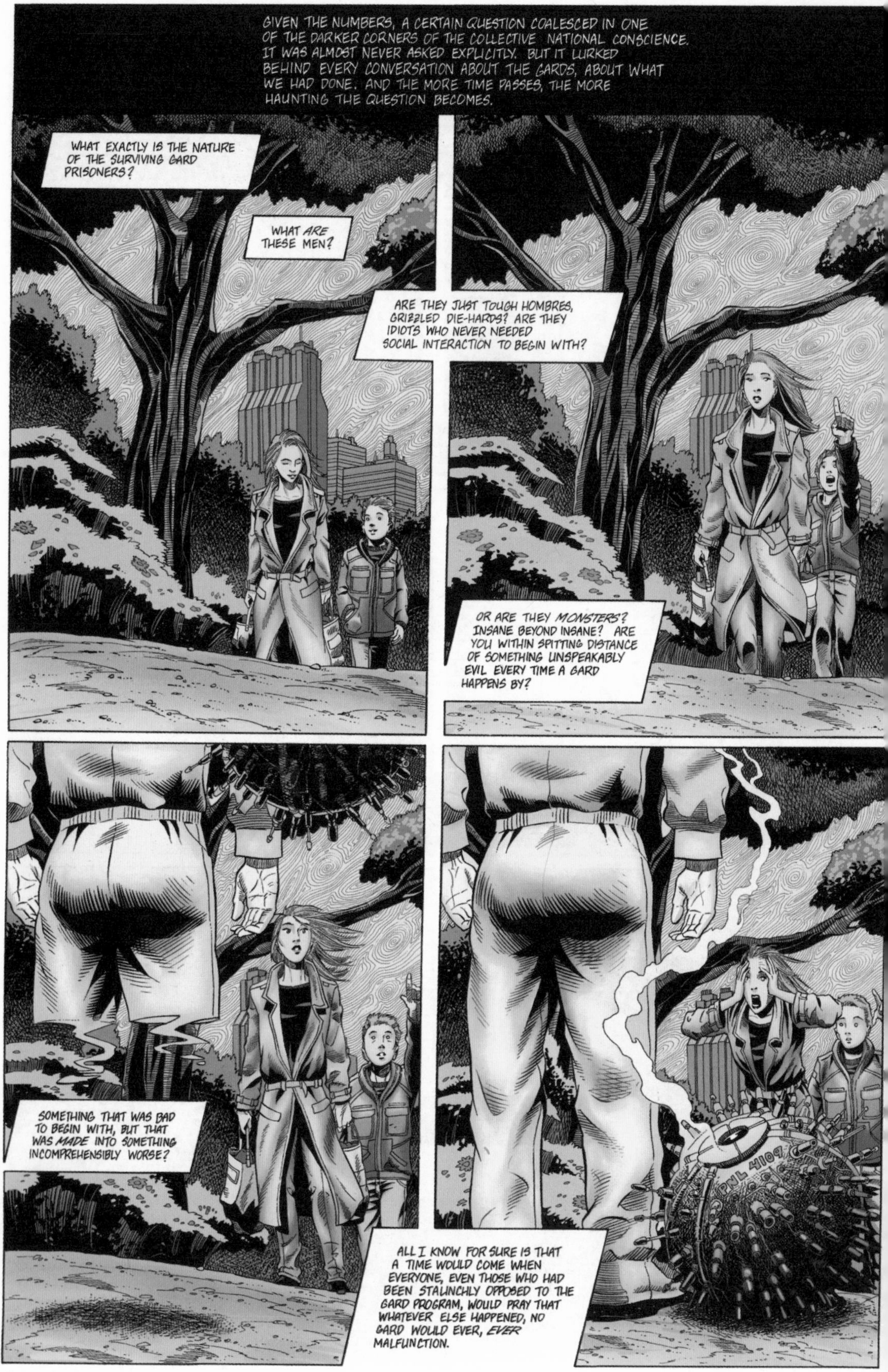
GIVEN THE NUMBERS, A CERTAIN QUESTION COALESCED IN ONE OF THE DARKER CORNERS OF THE COLLECTIVE NATIONAL CONSCIENCE. IT WAS ALMOST NEVER ASKED EXPLICITLY. BUT IT LURKED BEHIND EVERY CONVERSATION ABOUT THE GARDS, ABOUT WHAT WE HAD DONE. AND THE MORE TIME PASSES, THE MORE HAUNTING THE QUESTION BECOMES.
WHAT EXACTLY IS THE NATURE OF THE SURVIVING GARD PRISONERS?
WHAT *ARE* THESE MEN?
ARE THEY JUST TOUGH HOMBRES, GRIZZLED DIE-HARDS? ARE THEY IDIOTS WHO NEVER NEEDED SOCIAL INTERACTION TO BEGIN WITH?
OR ARE THEY *MONSTERS*? INSANE BEYOND INSANE? ARE YOU WITHIN SPITTING DISTANCE OF SOMETHING UNSPEAKABLY EVIL EVERY TIME A GARD HAPPENS BY?
SOMETHING THAT WAS BAD TO BEGIN WITH, BUT THAT WAS *MADE* INTO SOMETHING INCOMPREHENSIBLY WORSE?
PNL 4109
ALL I KNOW FOR SURE IS THAT A TIME WOULD COME WHEN EVERYONE, EVEN THOSE WHO HAD BEEN STAUNCHLY OPPOSED TO THE GARD PROGRAM, WOULD PRAY THAT WHATEVER ELSE HAPPENED, NO GARD WOULD EVER, *EVER* MALFUNCTION.

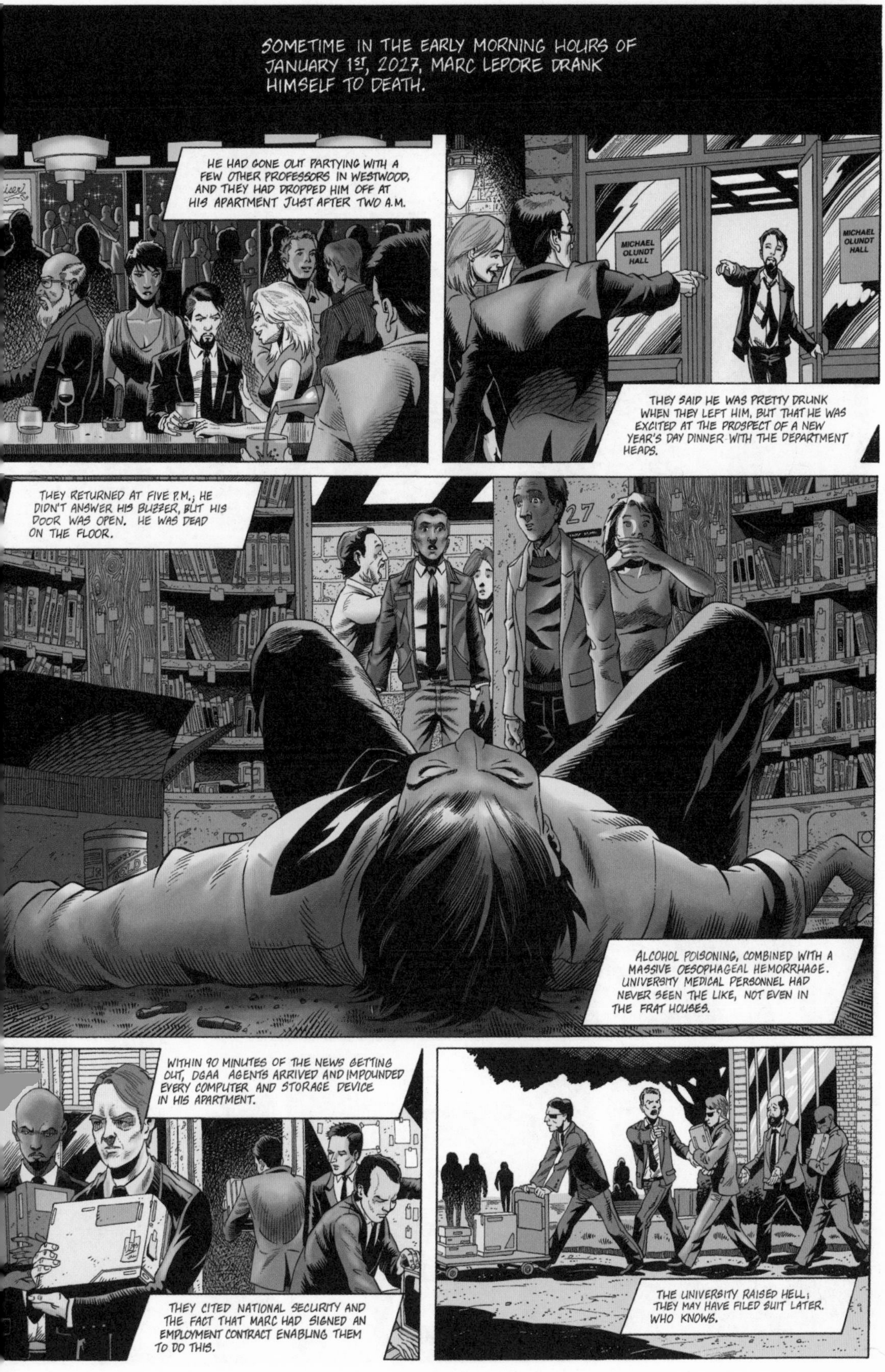
SOMETIME IN THE EARLY MORNING HOURS OF JANUARY 1ST, 2027, MARC LEPORE DRANK HIMSELF TO DEATH.
HE HAD GONE OUT PARTYING WITH A FEW OTHER PROFESSORS IN WESTWOOD, AND THEY HAD DROPPED HIM OFF AT HIS APARTMENT JUST AFTER TWO A.M.
MICHAEL OLUNDT HALL
MICHAEL OLUNDT HALL
THEY SAID HE WAS PRETTY DRUNK WHEN THEY LEFT HIM, BUT THAT HE WAS EXCITED AT THE PROSPECT OF A NEW YEAR'S DAY DINNER WITH THE DEPARTMENT HEADS.
THEY RETURNED AT FIVE P.M.; HE DIDN'T ANSWER HIS BUZZER, BUT HIS DOOR WAS OPEN. HE WAS DEAD ON THE FLOOR.
27
ALCOHOL POISONING, COMBINED WITH A MASSIVE OESOPHAGEAL HEMORRHAGE. UNIVERSITY MEDICAL PERSONNEL HAD NEVER SEEN THE LIKE, NOT EVEN IN THE FRAT HOUSES.
WITHIN 90 MINUTES OF THE NEWS GETTING OUT, DGAA AGENTS ARRIVED AND IMPOUNDED EVERY COMPUTER AND STORAGE DEVICE IN HIS APARTMENT.
THEY CITED NATIONAL SECURITY AND THE FACT THAT MARC HAD SIGNED AN EMPLOYMENT CONTRACT ENABLING THEM TO DO THIS.
THE UNIVERSITY RAISED HELL; THEY MAY HAVE FILED SUIT LATER. WHO KNOWS.

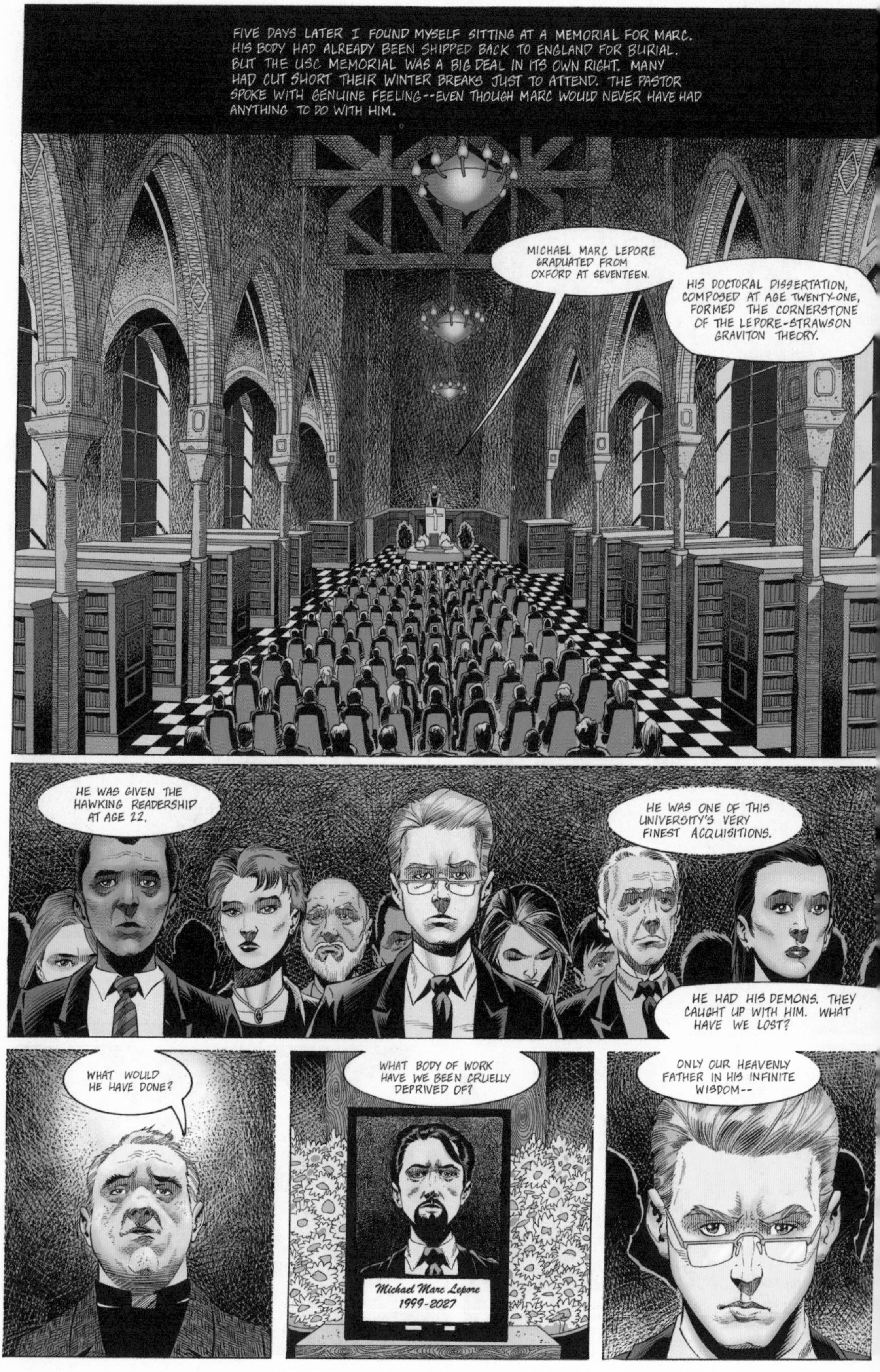
FIVE DAYS LATER I FOUND MYSELF SITTING AT A MEMORIAL FOR MARC. HIS BODY HAD ALREADY BEEN SHIPPED BACK TO ENGLAND FOR BURIAL. BUT THE USC MEMORIAL WAS A BIG DEAL IN ITS OWN RIGHT. MANY HAD CUT SHORT THEIR WINTER BREAKS JUST TO ATTEND. THE PASTOR SPOKE WITH GENUINE FEELING--EVEN THOUGH MARC WOULD NEVER HAVE HAD ANYTHING TO DO WITH HIM.
MICHAEL MARC LEPORE GRADUATED FROM OXFORD AT SEVENTEEN.
HIS DOCTORAL DISSERTATION, COMPOSED AT AGE TWENTY-ONE, FORMED THE CORNERSTONE OF THE LEPORE-STRAWSON GRAVITON THEORY.
HE WAS GIVEN THE HAWKING READERSHIP AT AGE 22.
HE WAS ONE OF THIS UNIVERSITY'S VERY FINEST ACQUISITIONS.
HE HAD HIS DEMONS. THEY CAUGHT UP WITH HIM. WHAT HAVE WE LOST?
WHAT WOULD HE HAVE DONE?
WHAT BODY OF WORK HAVE WE BEEN CRUELLY DEPRIVED OF?
Michael Marc Lepore
1999-2027
ONLY OUR HEAVENLY FATHER IN HIS INFINITE WISDOM--

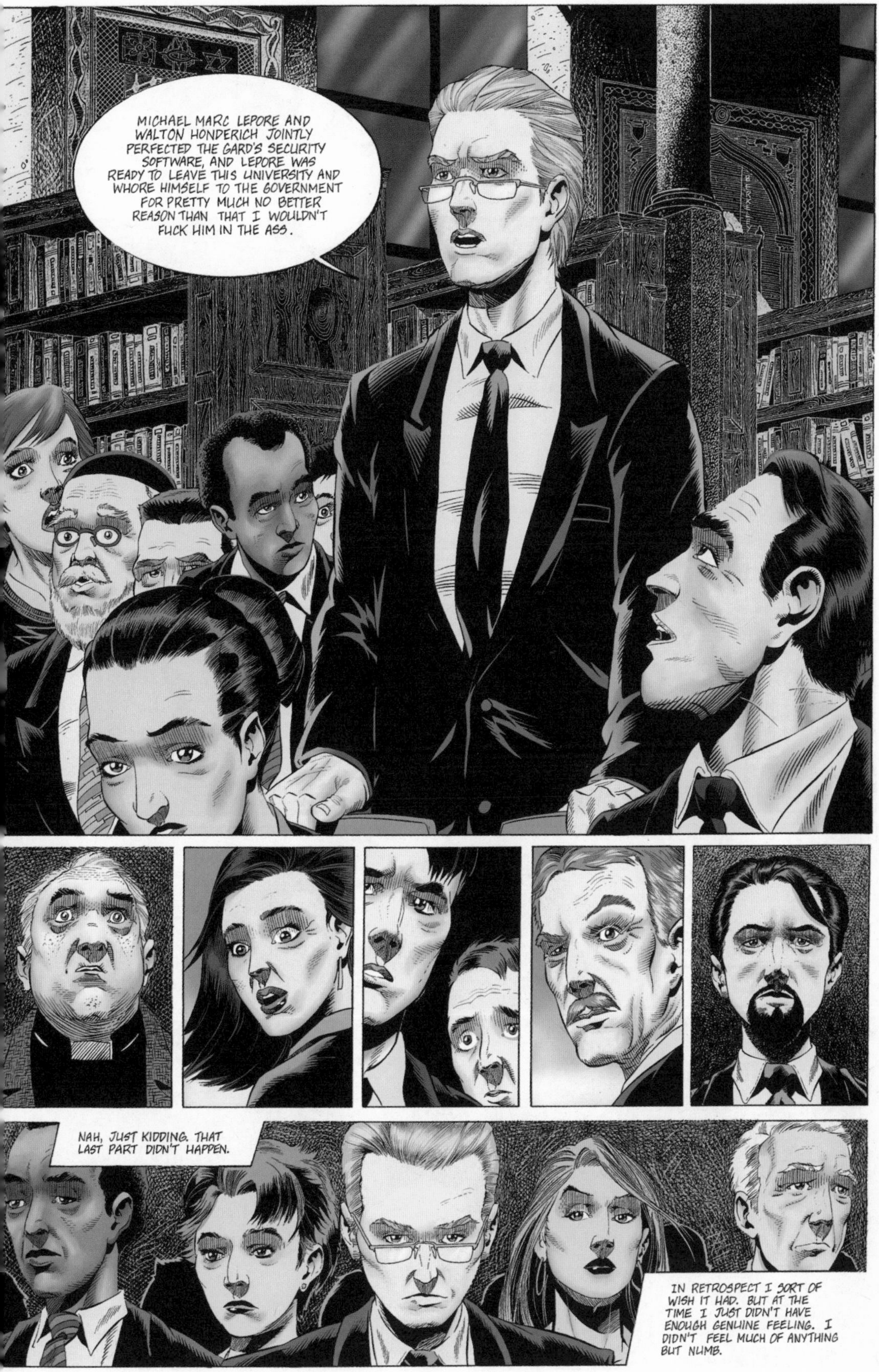
MICHAEL MARC LEPORE AND WALTON HONDERICH JOINTLY PERFECTED THE GARD'S SECURITY SOFTWARE, AND LEPORE WAS READY TO LEAVE THIS UNIVERSITY AND WHORE HIMSELF TO THE GOVERNMENT FOR PRETTY MUCH NO BETTER REASON THAN THAT I WOULDN'T FUCK HIM IN THE ASS.
NAH, JUST KIDDING. THAT LAST PART DIDN'T HAPPEN.
IN RETROSPECT I SORT OF WISH IT HAD. BUT AT THE TIME I JUST DIDN'T HAVE ENOUGH GENUINE FEELING. I DIDN'T FEEL MUCH OF ANYTHING BUT NUMB.

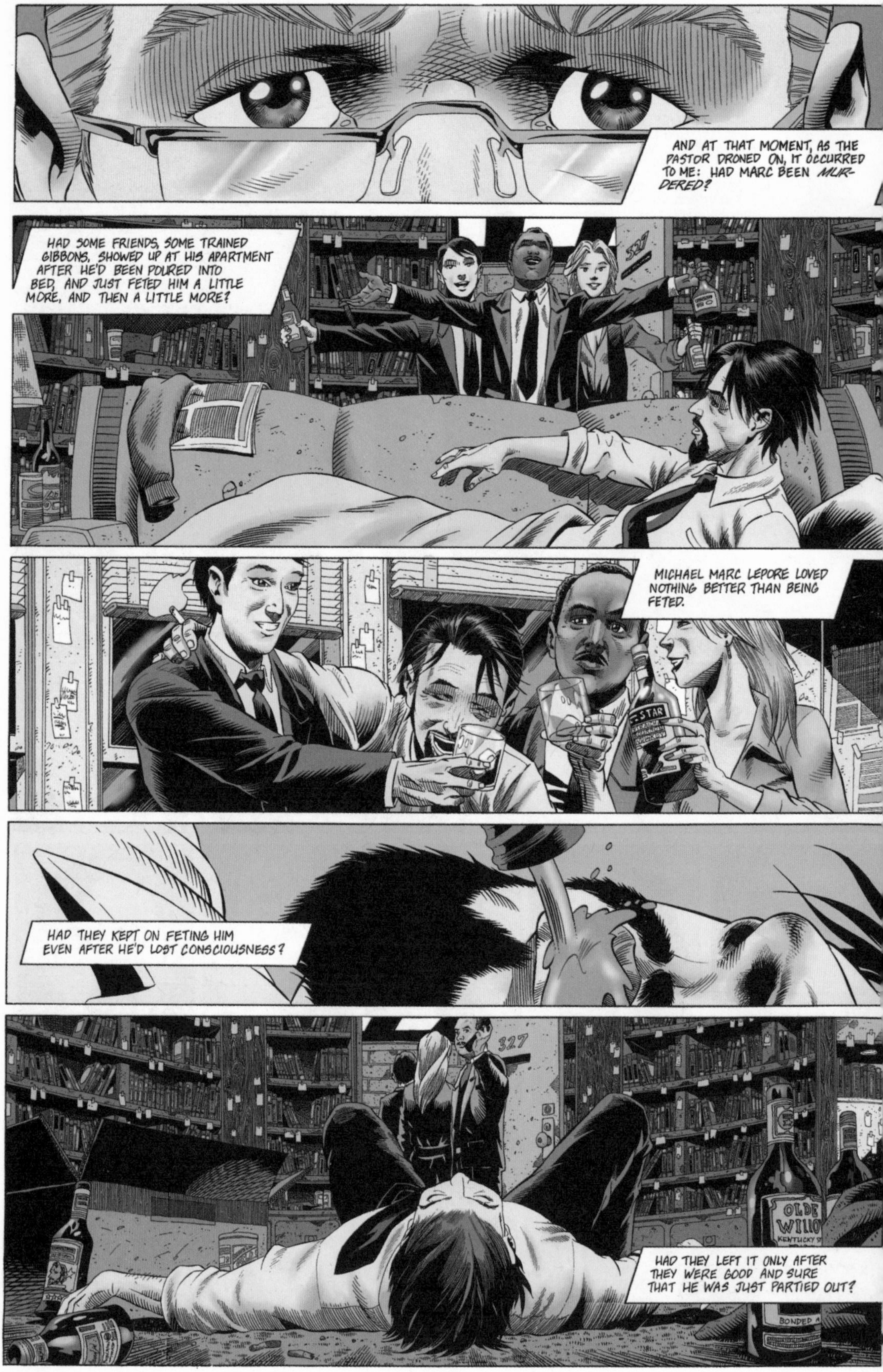
AND AT THAT MOMENT, AS THE PASTOR DRONED ON, IT OCCURRED TO ME: HAD MARC BEEN MURDERED?
HAD SOME FRIENDS, SOME TRAINED GIBBONS, SHOWED UP AT HIS APARTMENT AFTER HE'D BEEN POURED INTO BED, AND JUST FETED HIM A LITTLE MORE, AND THEN A LITTLE MORE?
MICHAEL MARC LEPORE LOVED NOTHING BETTER THAN BEING FETED.
HAD THEY KEPT ON FETING HIM EVEN AFTER HE'D LOST CONSCIOUSNESS?
HAD THEY LEFT IT ONLY AFTER THEY WERE GOOD AND SURE THAT HE WAS JUST PARTIED OUT?

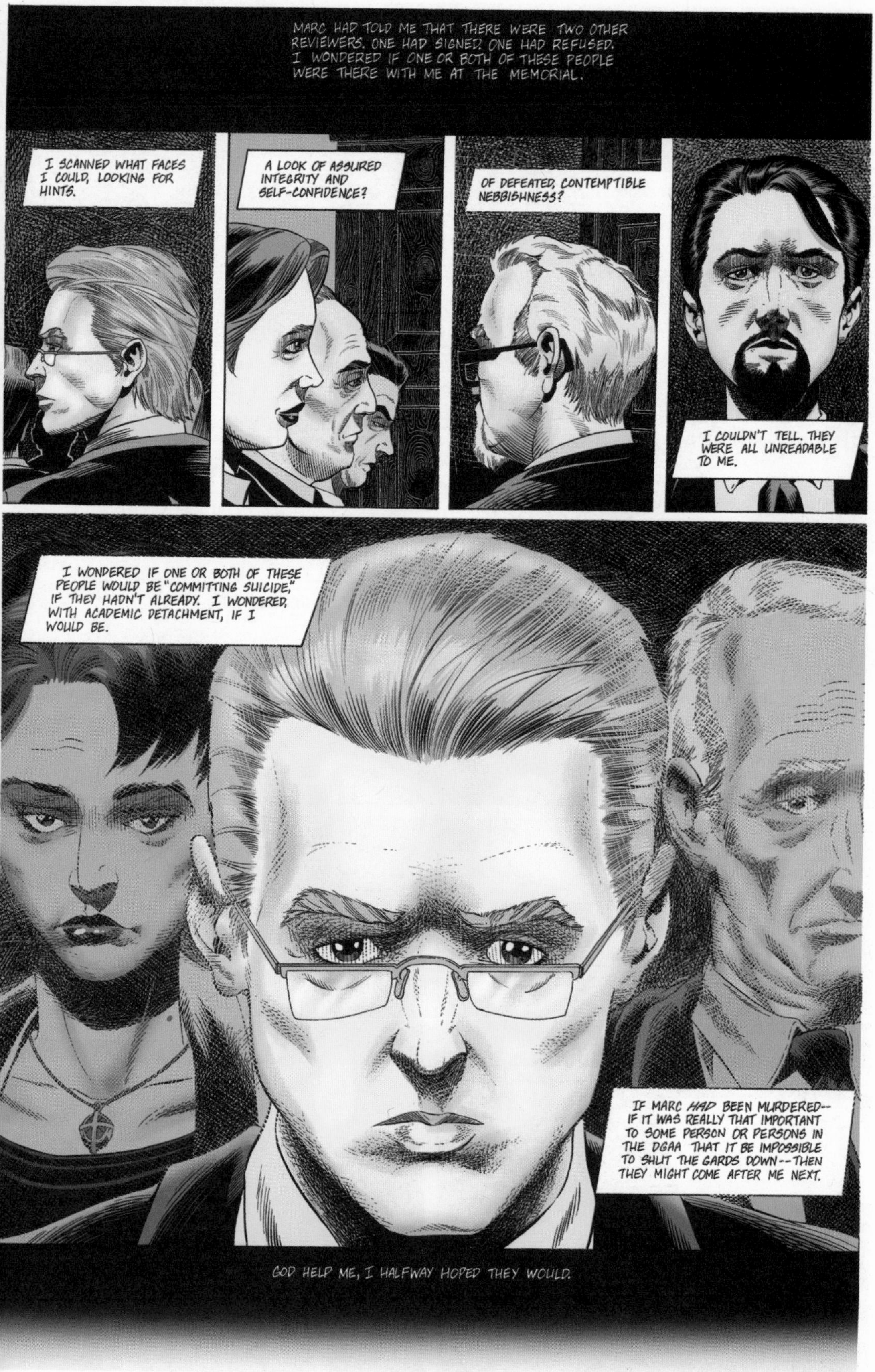

MARC HAD TOLD ME THAT THERE WERE TWO OTHER REVIEWERS. ONE HAD SIGNED. ONE HAD REFUSED. I WONDERED IF ONE OR BOTH OF THESE PEOPLE WERE THERE WITH ME AT THE MEMORIAL.
I SCANNED WHAT FACES I COULD, LOOKING FOR HINTS.
A LOOK OF ASSURED INTEGRITY AND SELF-CONFIDENCE?
OF DEFEATED, CONTEMPTIBLE NEBBISHNESS?
I COULDN'T TELL. THEY WERE ALL UNREADABLE TO ME.
I WONDERED IF ONE OR BOTH OF THESE PEOPLE WOULD BE "COMMITTING SUICIDE," IF THEY HADN'T ALREADY. I WONDERED, WITH ACADEMIC DETACHMENT, IF I WOULD BE.
IF MARC *HAD* BEEN MURDERED-- IF IT WAS REALLY THAT IMPORTANT TO SOME PERSON OR PERSONS IN THE DGAA THAT IT BE IMPOSSIBLE TO SHUT THE GARDS DOWN--THEN THEY MIGHT COME AFTER ME NEXT.
GOD HELP ME, I HALFWAY HOPED THEY WOULD.

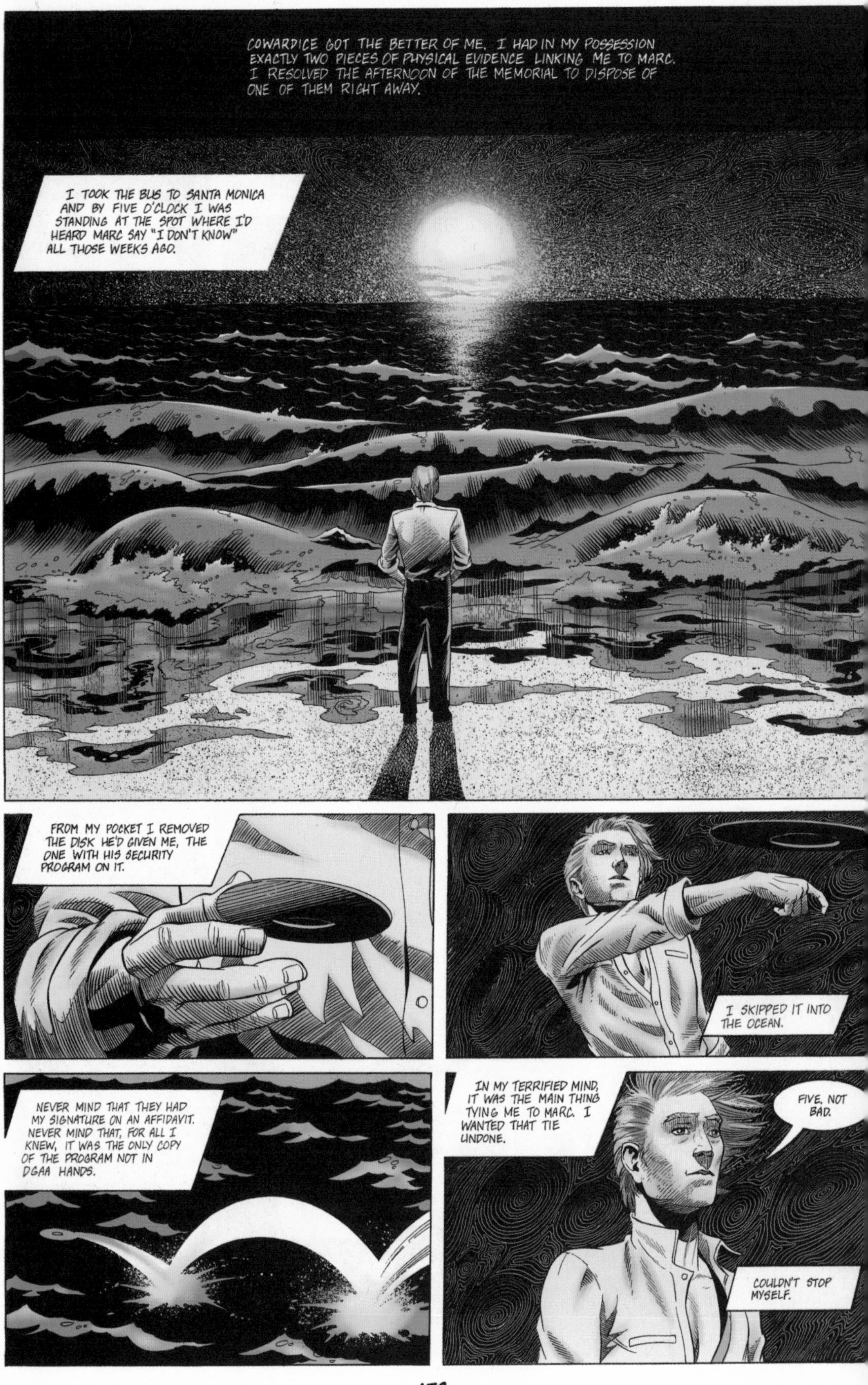
COWARDICE GOT THE BETTER OF ME. I HAD IN MY POSSESSION EXACTLY TWO PIECES OF PHYSICAL EVIDENCE LINKING ME TO MARC. I RESOLVED THE AFTERNOON OF THE MEMORIAL TO DISPOSE OF ONE OF THEM RIGHT AWAY.
I TOOK THE BUS TO SANTA MONICA AND BY FIVE O'CLOCK I WAS STANDING AT THE SPOT WHERE I'D HEARD MARC SAY "I DON'T KNOW" ALL THOSE WEEKS AGO.
FROM MY POCKET I REMOVED THE DISK HE'D GIVEN ME, THE ONE WITH HIS SECURITY PROGRAM ON IT.
I SKIPPED IT INTO THE OCEAN.
NEVER MIND THAT THEY HAD MY SIGNATURE ON AN AFFIDAVIT. NEVER MIND THAT, FOR ALL I KNEW, IT WAS THE ONLY COPY OF THE PROGRAM NOT IN DGAA HANDS.
IN MY TERRIFIED MIND, IT WAS THE MAIN THING TYING ME TO MARC. I WANTED THAT TIE UNDONE.
FIVE, NOT BAD.
COULDN'T STOP MYSELF.

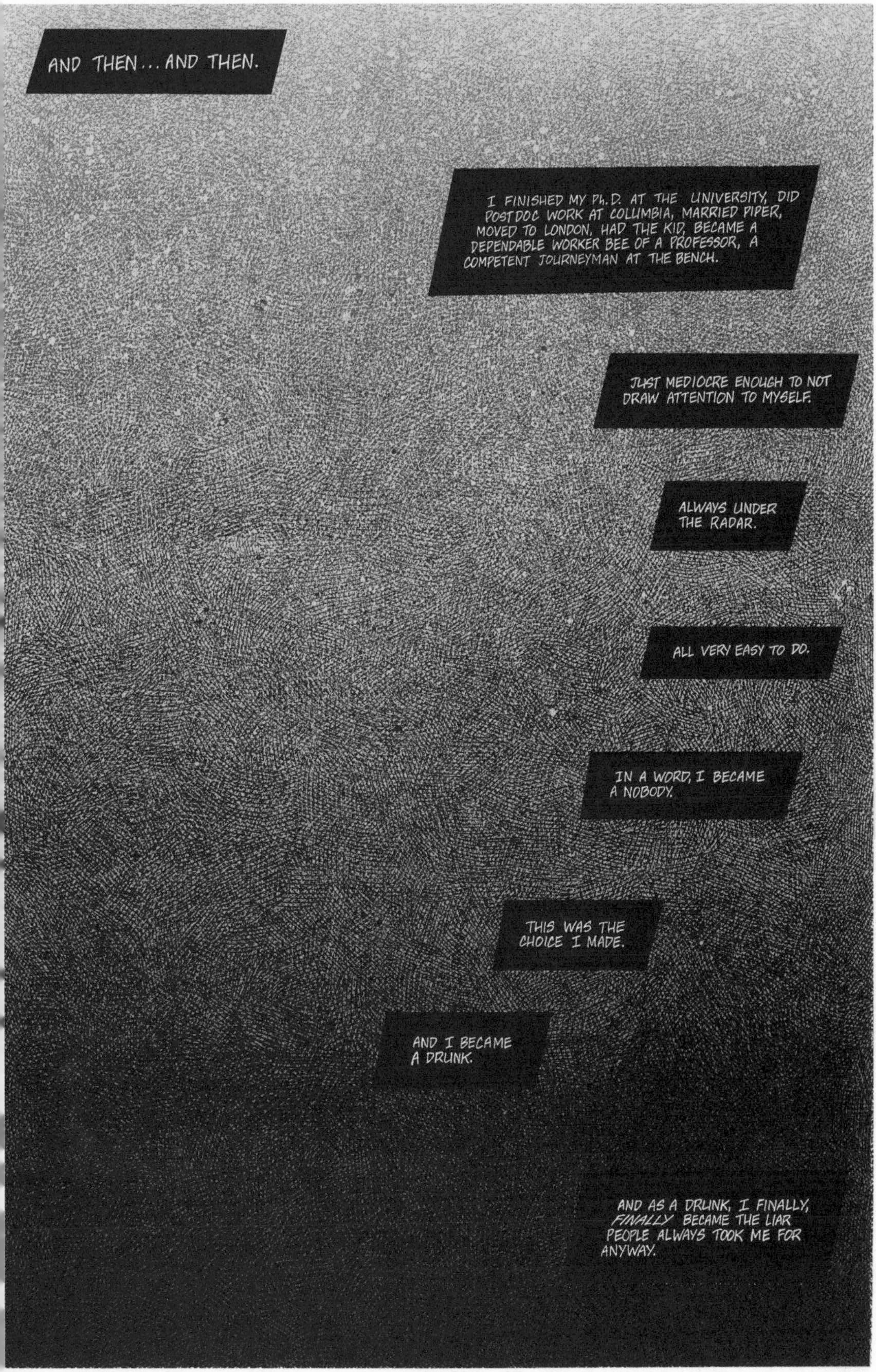
AND THEN... AND THEN.
I FINISHED MY Ph.D. AT THE UNIVERSITY, DID POSTDOC WORK AT COLUMBIA, MARRIED PIPER, MOVED TO LONDON, HAD THE KID, BECAME A DEPENDABLE WORKER BEE OF A PROFESSOR, A COMPETENT JOURNEYMAN AT THE BENCH.
JUST MEDIOCRE ENOUGH TO NOT DRAW ATTENTION TO MYSELF.
ALWAYS UNDER THE RADAR.
ALL VERY EASY TO DO.
IN A WORD, I BECAME A NOBODY.
THIS WAS THE CHOICE I MADE.
AND I BECAME A DRUNK.
AND AS A DRUNK, I FINALLY, *FINALLY* BECAME THE LIAR PEOPLE ALWAYS TOOK ME FOR ANYWAY.

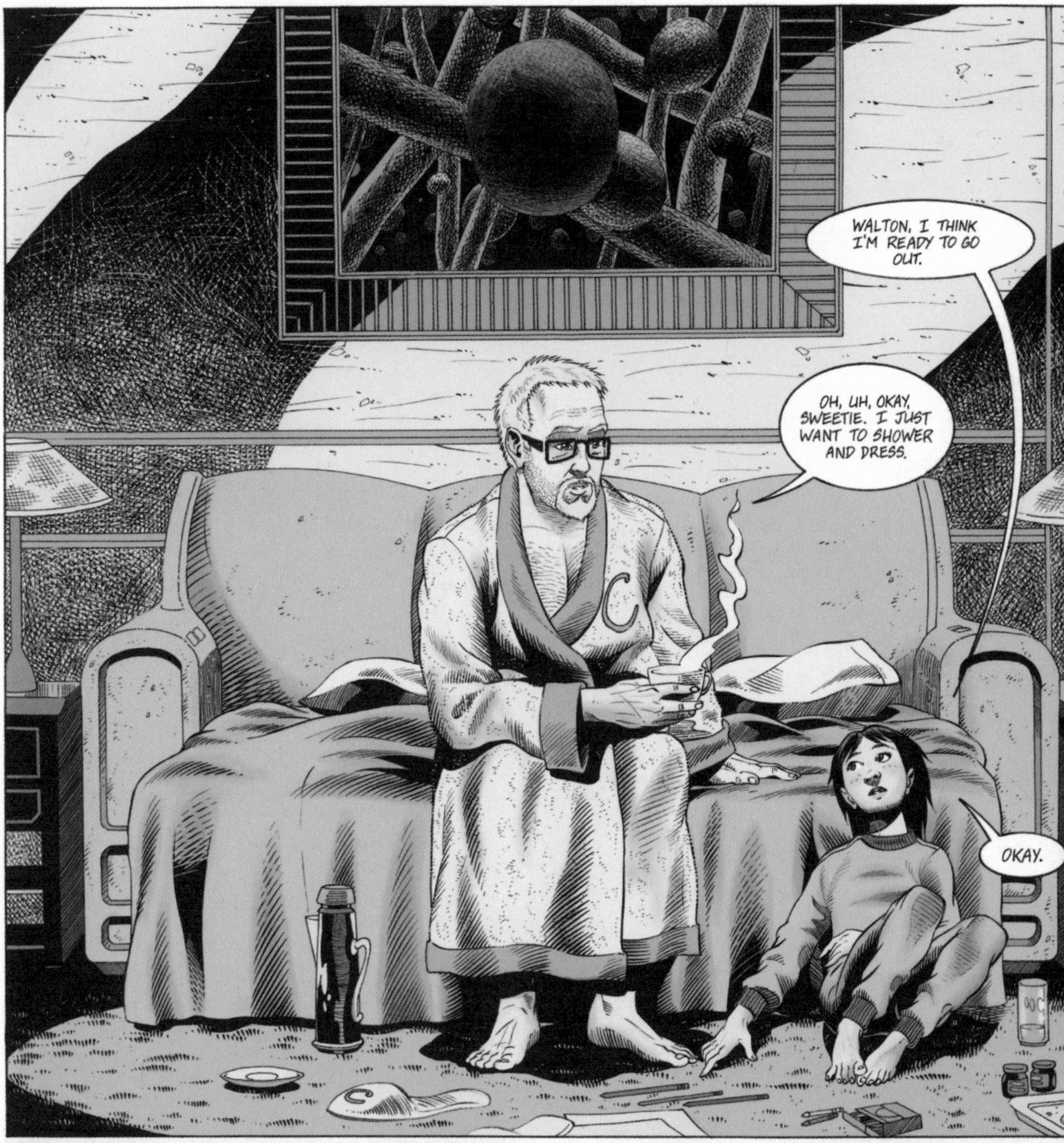
WALTON, I THINK I'M READY TO GO OUT.
OH, UH, OKAY, SWEETIE. I JUST WANT TO SHOWER AND DRESS.
OKAY.

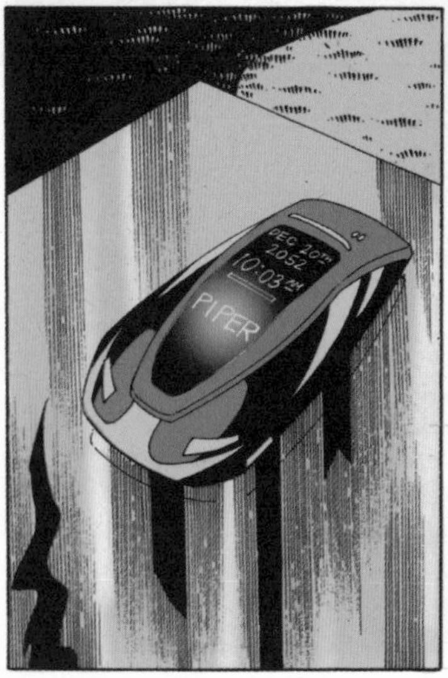
DEC 10th 2052
10:03 AM
PIPER

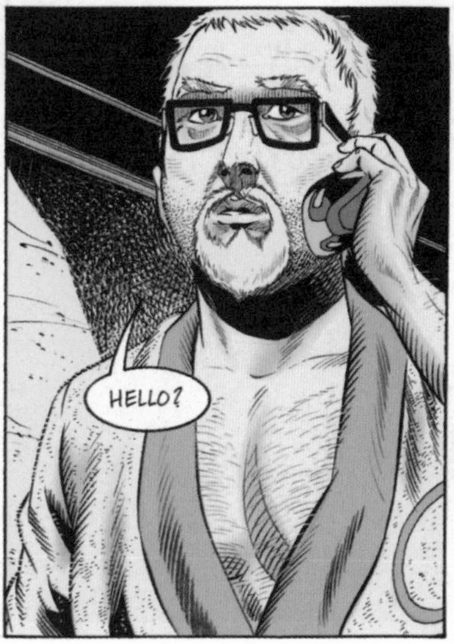
HELLO?

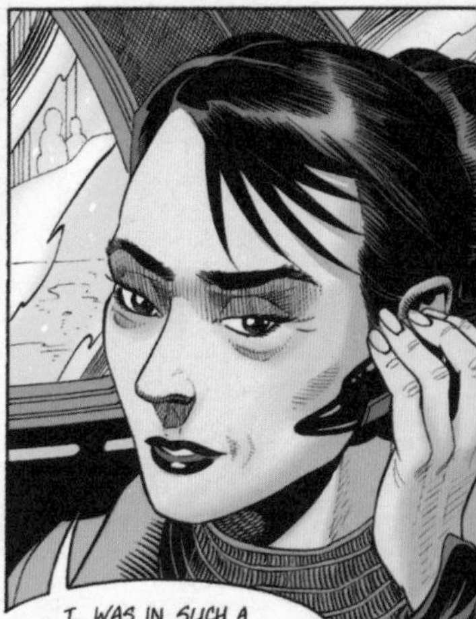
I WAS IN SUCH A HURRY I FORGOT TO ASK WHAT THE PLAN IS.

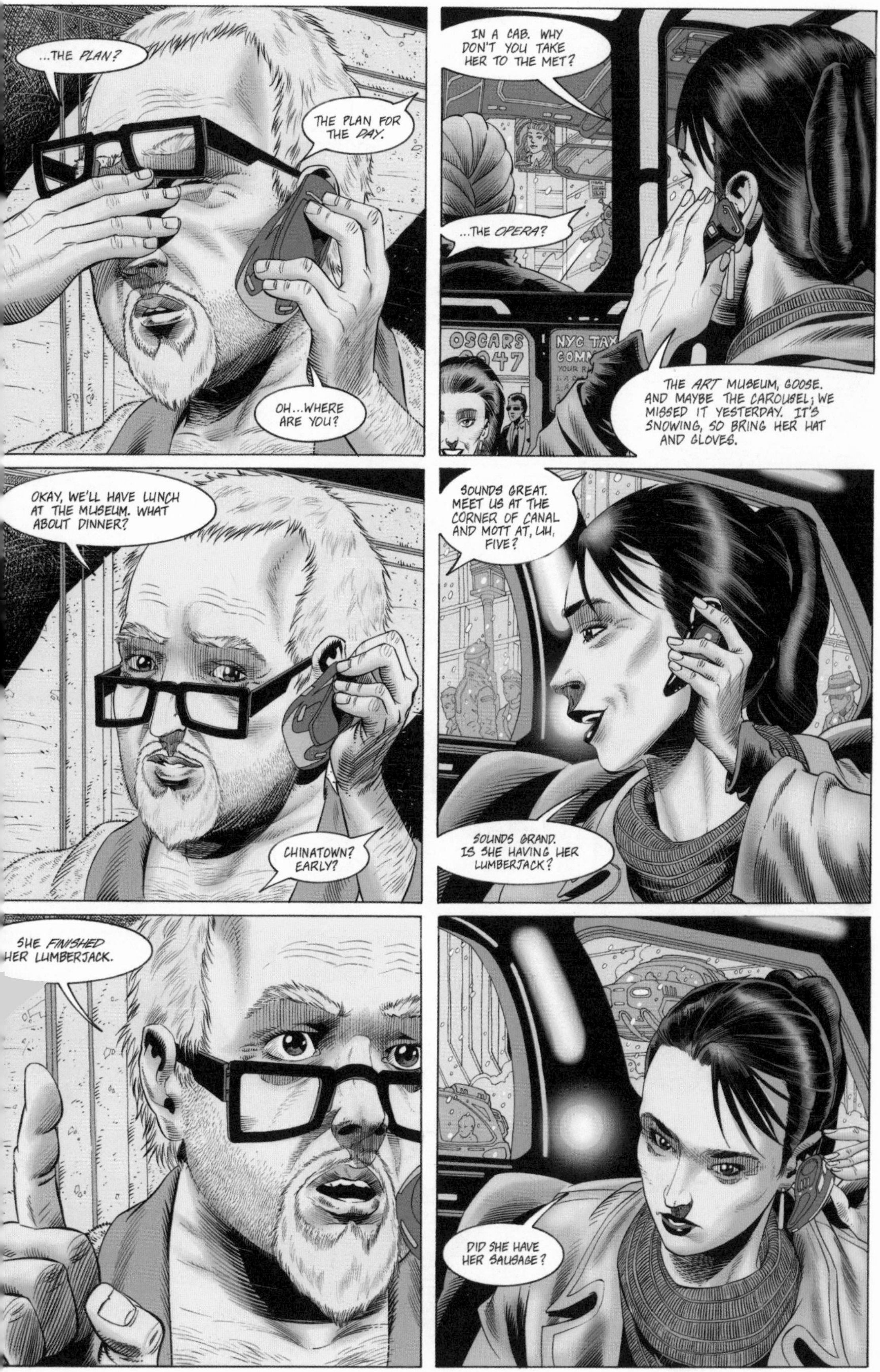
...THE PLAN?
THE PLAN FOR THE DAY.
IN A CAB. WHY DON'T YOU TAKE HER TO THE MET?
...THE OPERA?
OH...WHERE ARE YOU?
OSCARS 2047
NYC TAXI COMM
THE ART MUSEUM, GOOSE. AND MAYBE THE CAROUSEL; WE MISSED IT YESTERDAY. IT'S SNOWING, SO BRING HER HAT AND GLOVES.
OKAY, WE'LL HAVE LUNCH AT THE MUSEUM. WHAT ABOUT DINNER?
SOUNDS GREAT. MEET US AT THE CORNER OF CANAL AND MOTT AT, UH, FIVE?
CHINATOWN? EARLY?
SOUNDS GRAND. IS SHE HAVING HER LUMBERJACK?
SHE FINISHED HER LUMBERJACK.
DID SHE HAVE HER SAUSAGE?

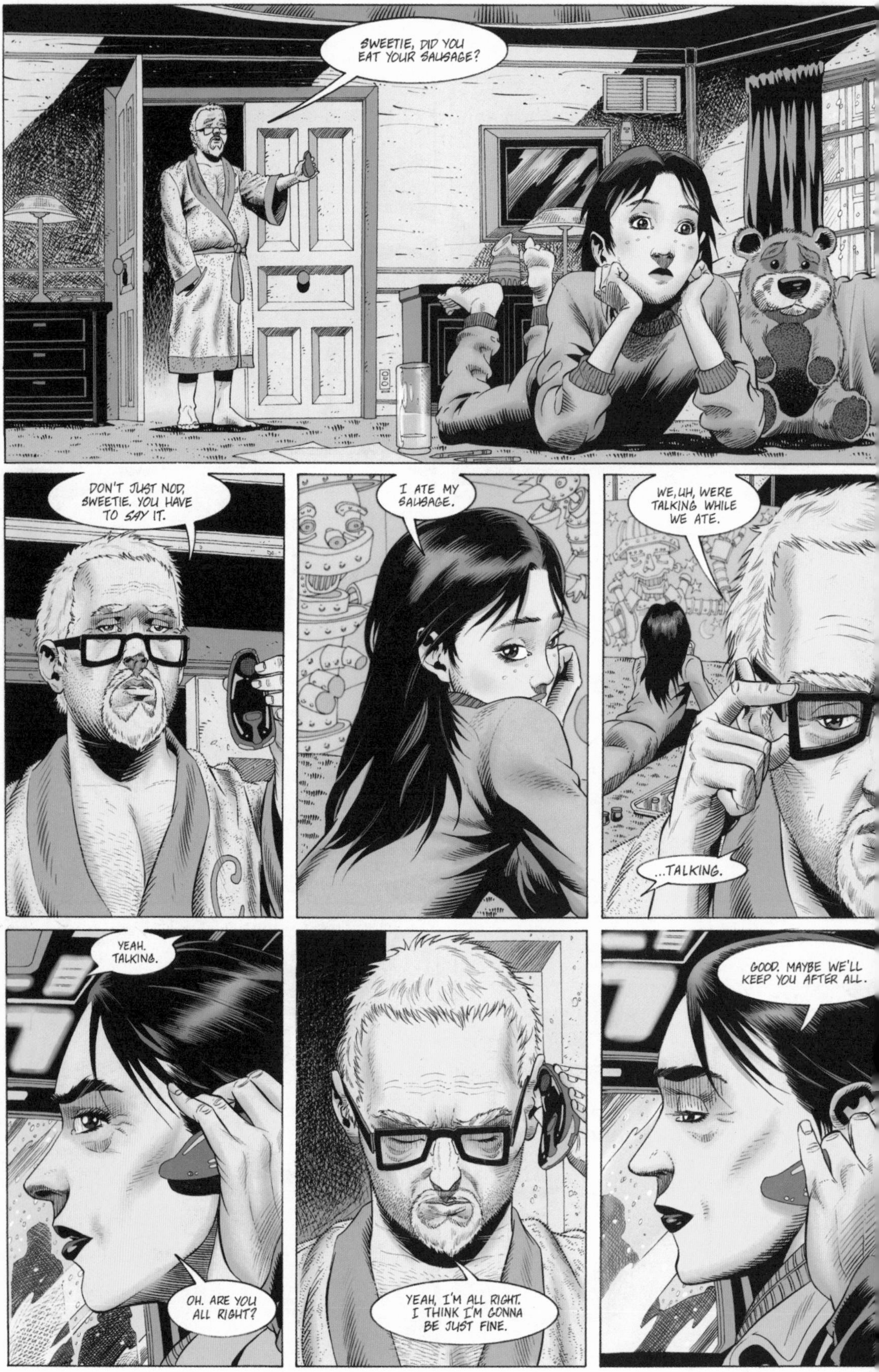
SWEETIE, DID YOU EAT YOUR SAUSAGE?
DON'T JUST NOD, SWEETIE. YOU HAVE TO SAY IT.
I ATE MY SAUSAGE.
WE, UH, WERE TALKING WHILE WE ATE.
...TALKING.
YEAH. TALKING.
OH. ARE YOU ALL RIGHT?
YEAH, I'M ALL RIGHT. I THINK I'M GONNA BE JUST FINE.
GOOD. MAYBE WE'LL KEEP YOU AFTER ALL.

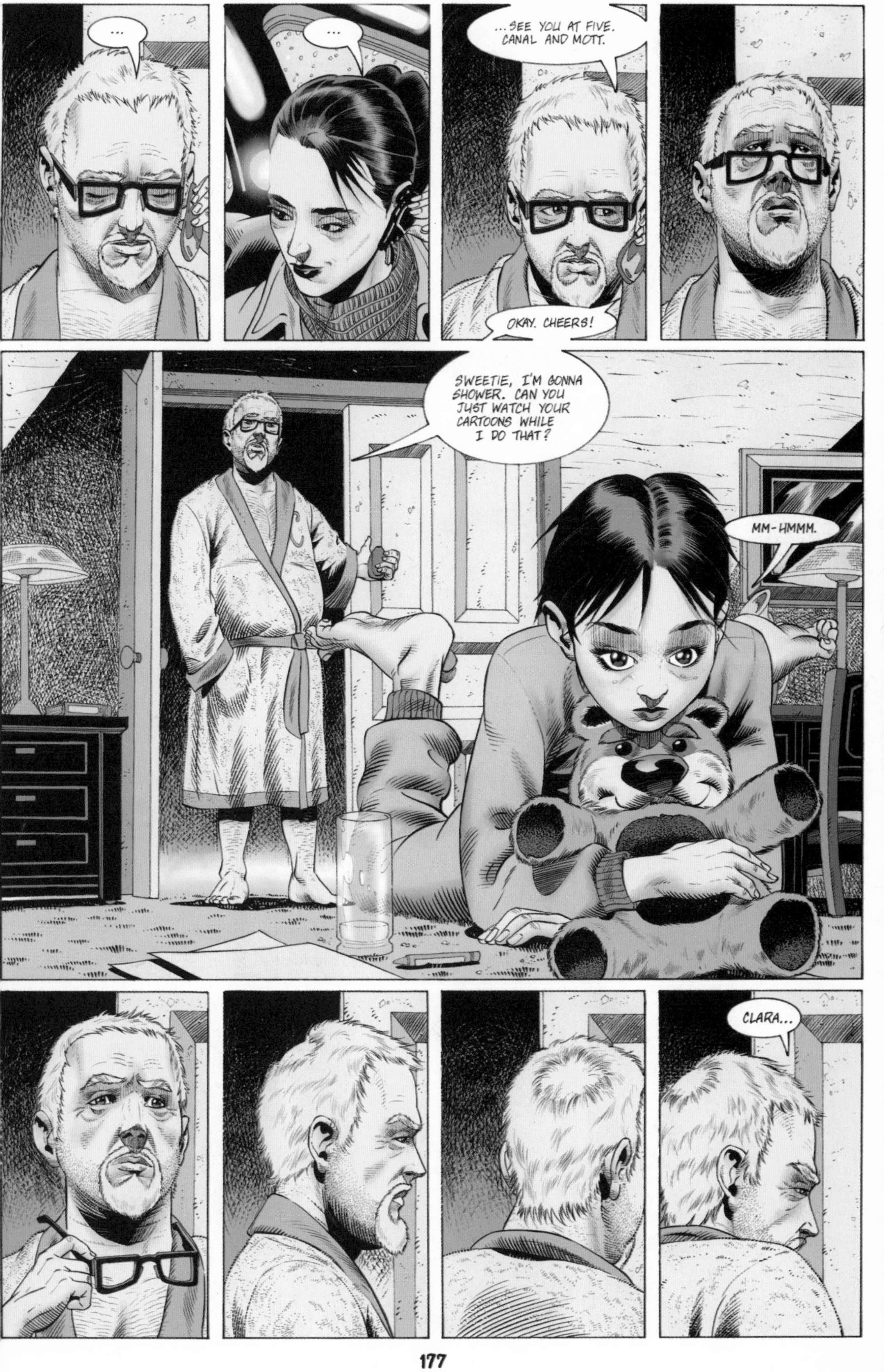
...
...
...SEE YOU AT FIVE. CANAL AND MOTT.
OKAY. CHEERS!
SWEETIE, I'M GONNA SHOWER. CAN YOU JUST WATCH YOUR CARTOONS WHILE I DO THAT?
MM-HMMM.
CLARA...

...MY FRIEND, THE ONE I TOLD YOU ABOUT... HIS NAME WAS MARC.

MARC LEPORE.

I WISH YOU COULD HAVE KNOWN HIM. HE WAS A GOOD GUY.

I KNOW HE WOULD HAVE LOVED YOU.

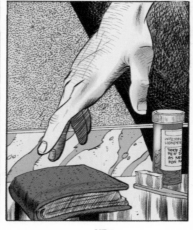

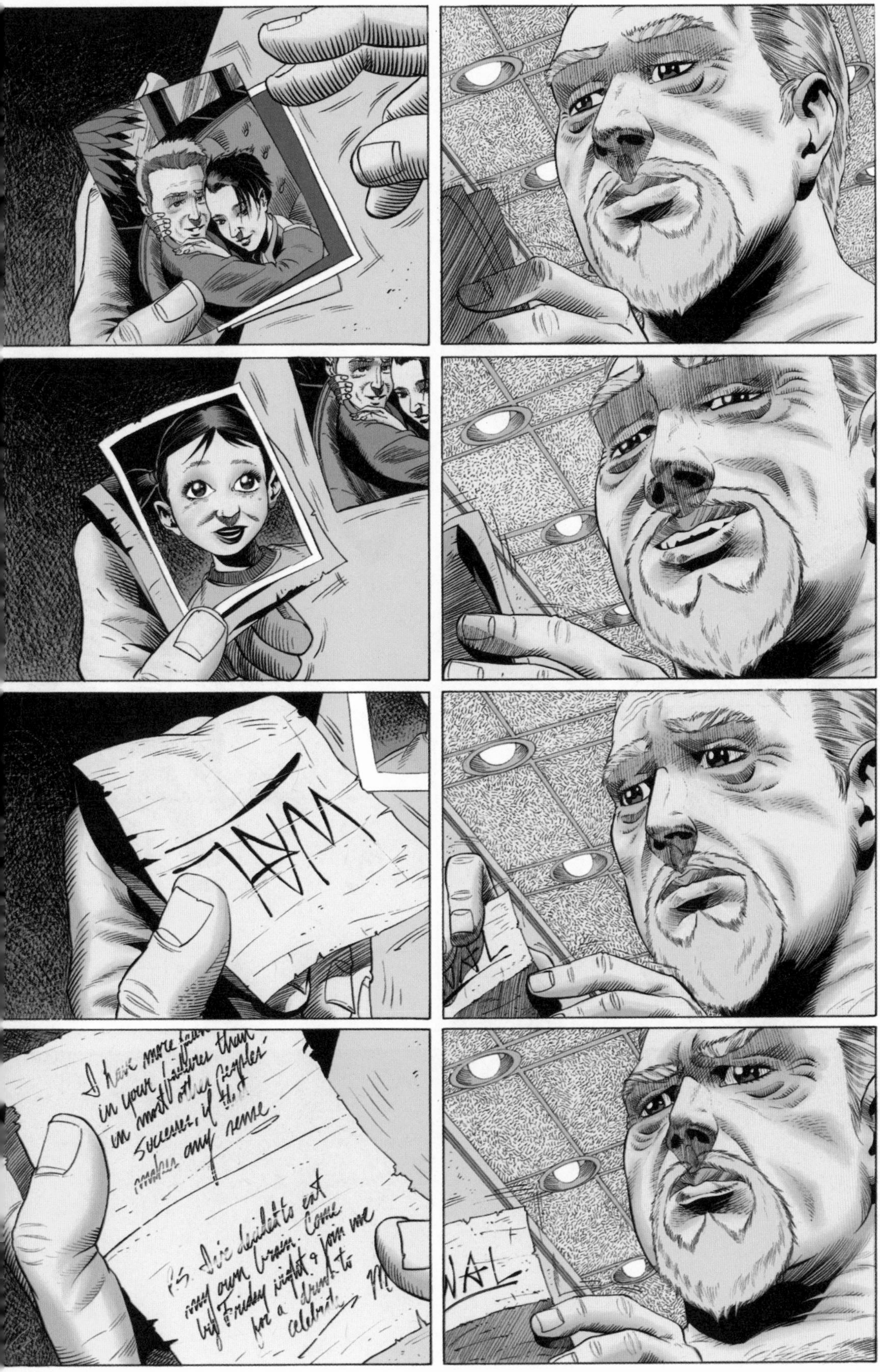
I have more
in your failures than
in most other peoples'
successes, if
makes any sense.
P.S. I've decided to eat
my own brain. Come
by Friday night & join me
for a drink to
celebrate

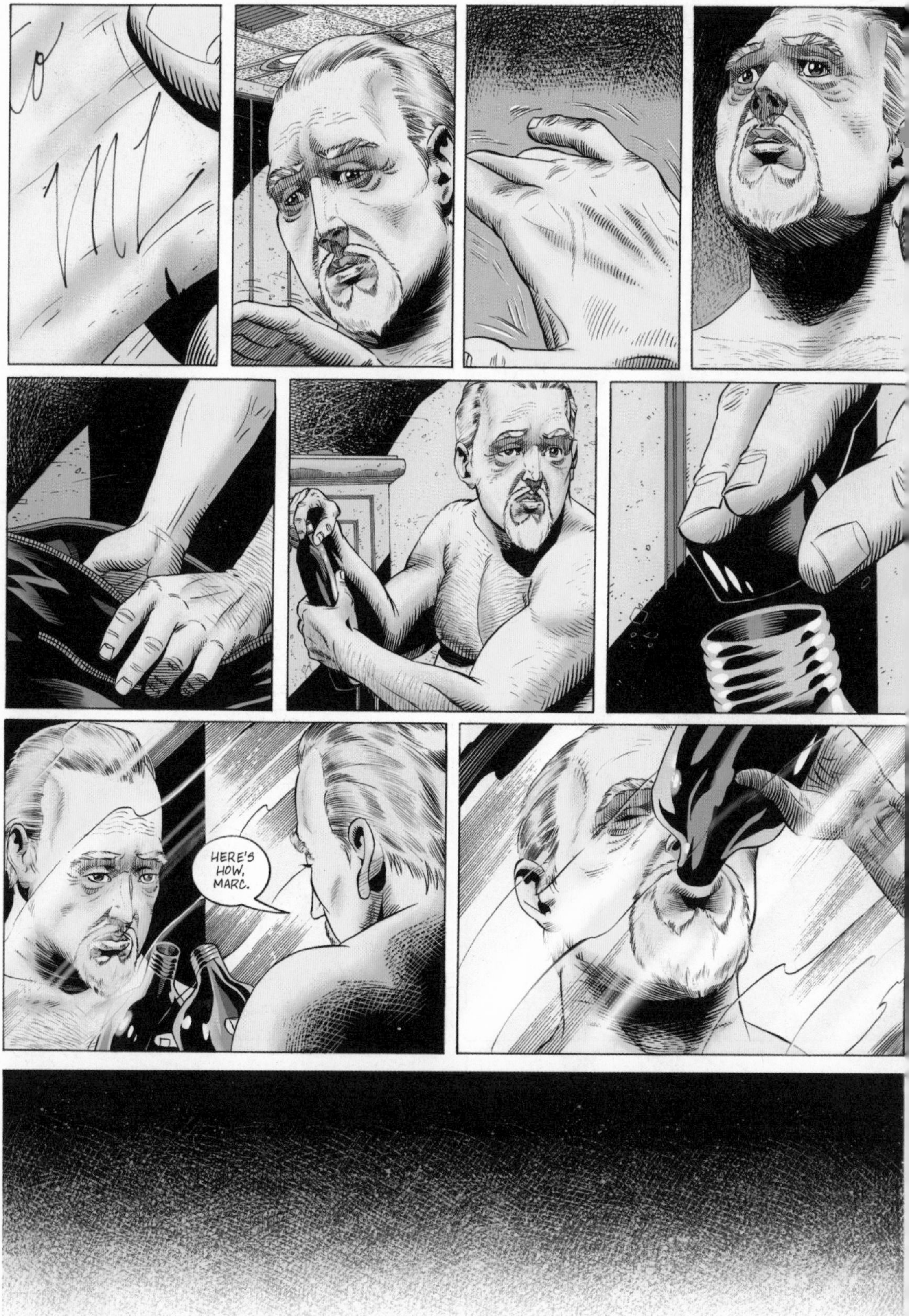
HERE'S HOW, MARC.

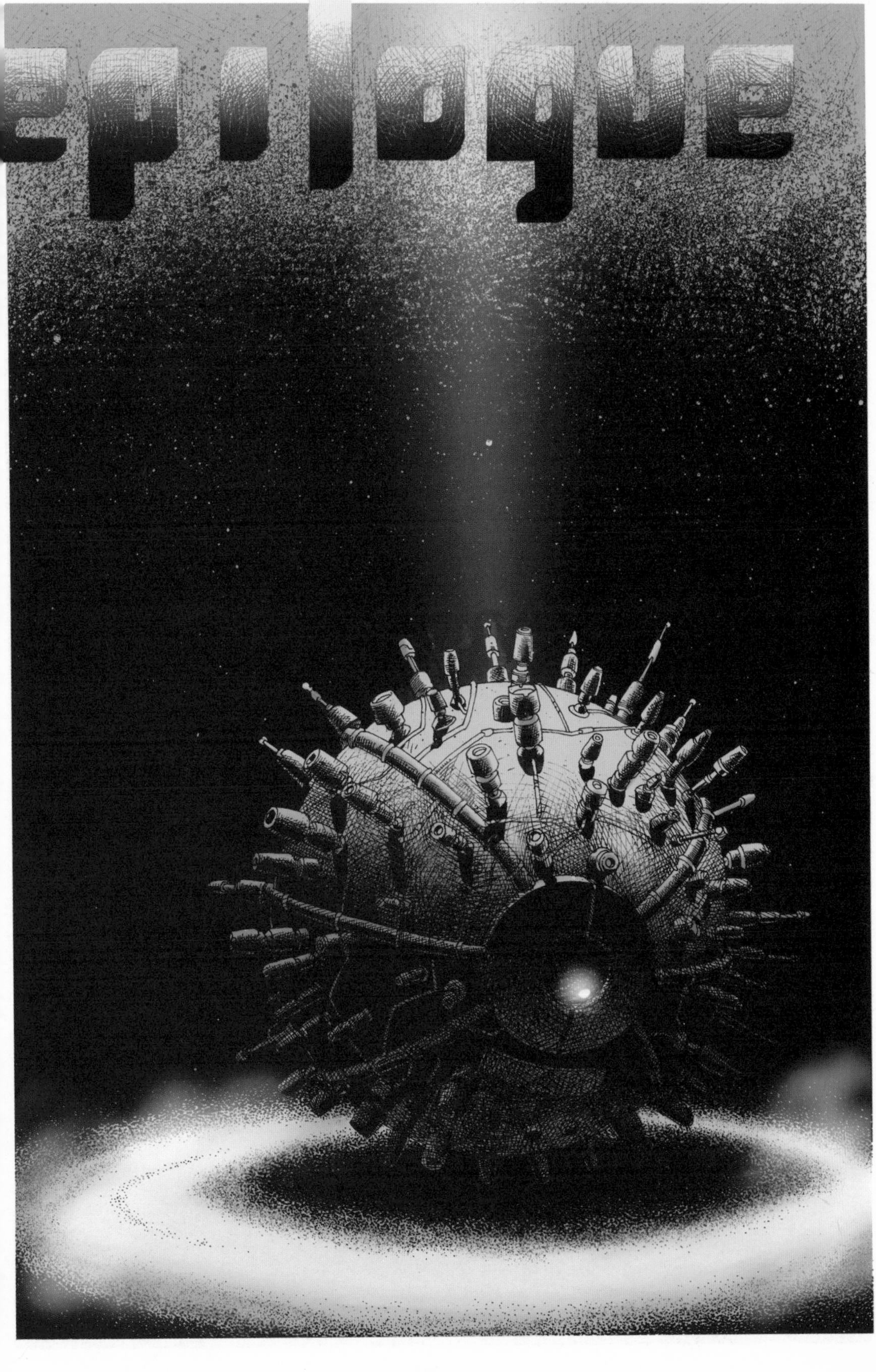
epilogue

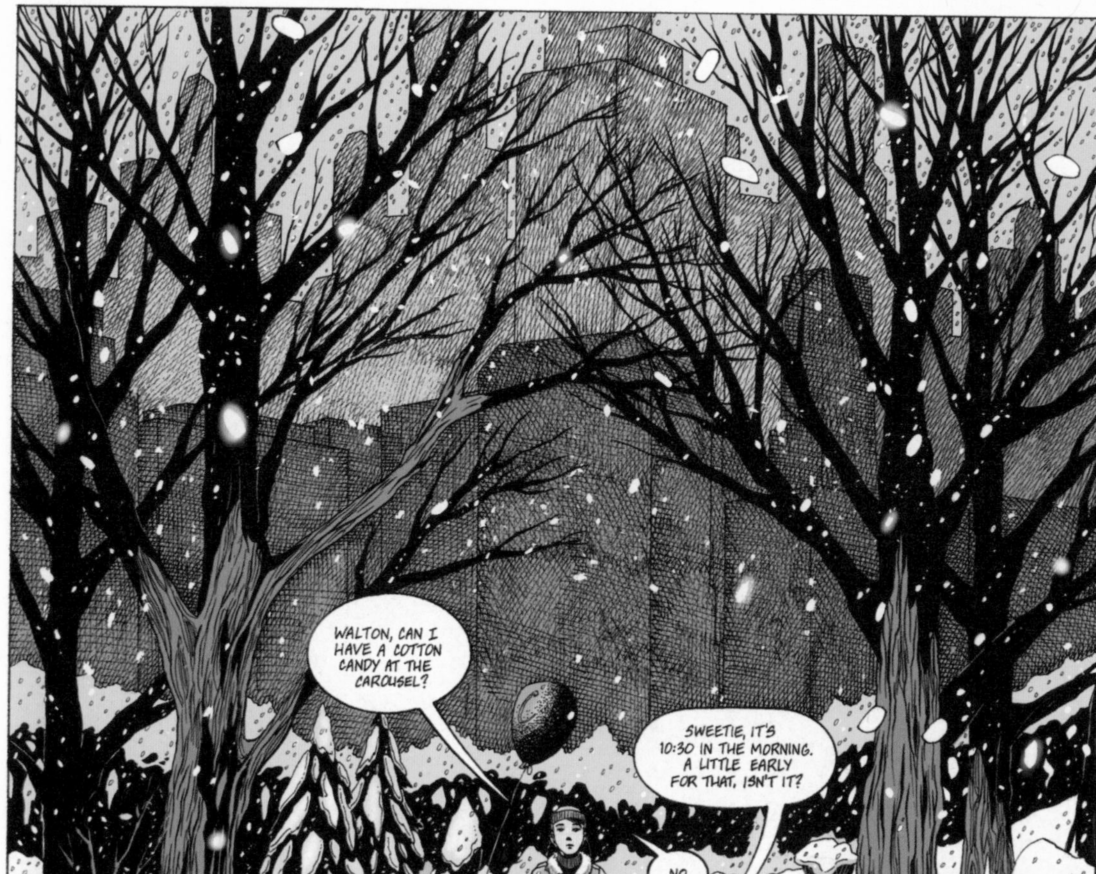
WALTON, CAN I HAVE A COTTON CANDY AT THE CAROUSEL?
SWEETIE, IT'S 10:30 IN THE MORNING. A LITTLE EARLY FOR THAT, ISN'T IT?
NO.

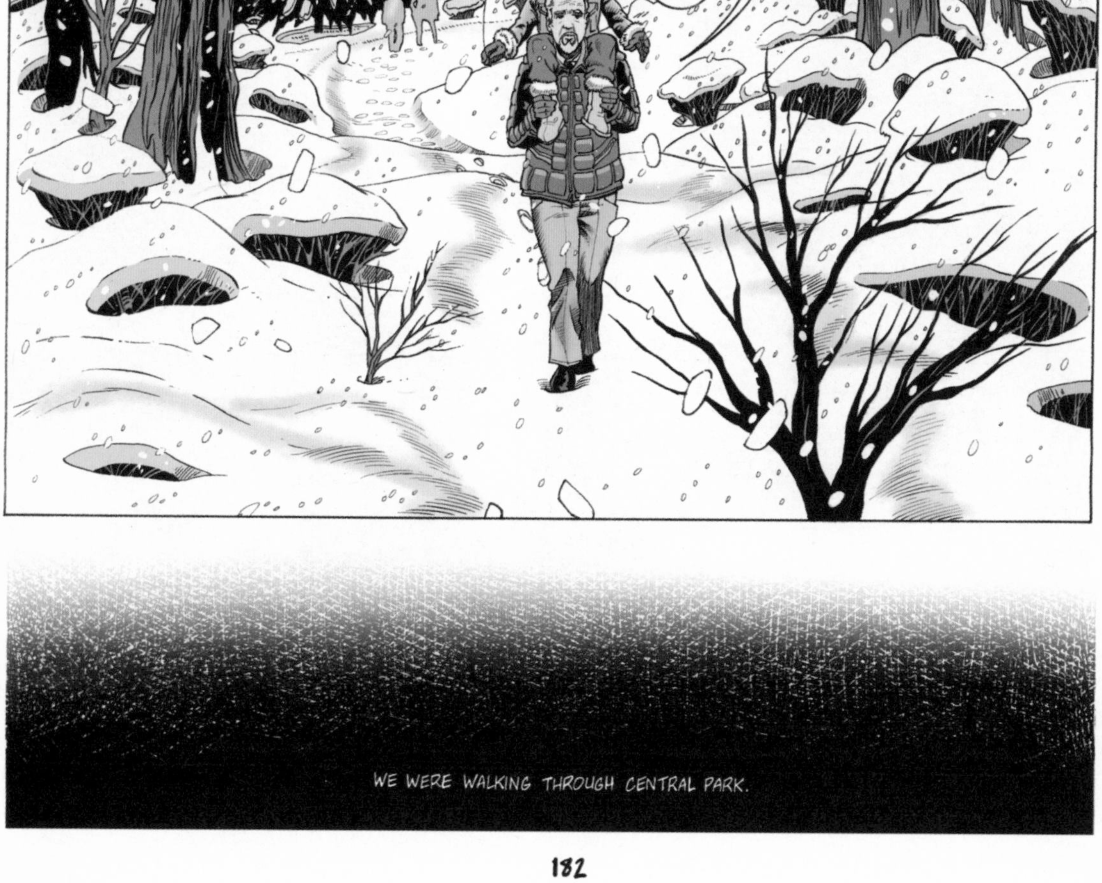
WE WERE WALKING THROUGH CENTRAL PARK.

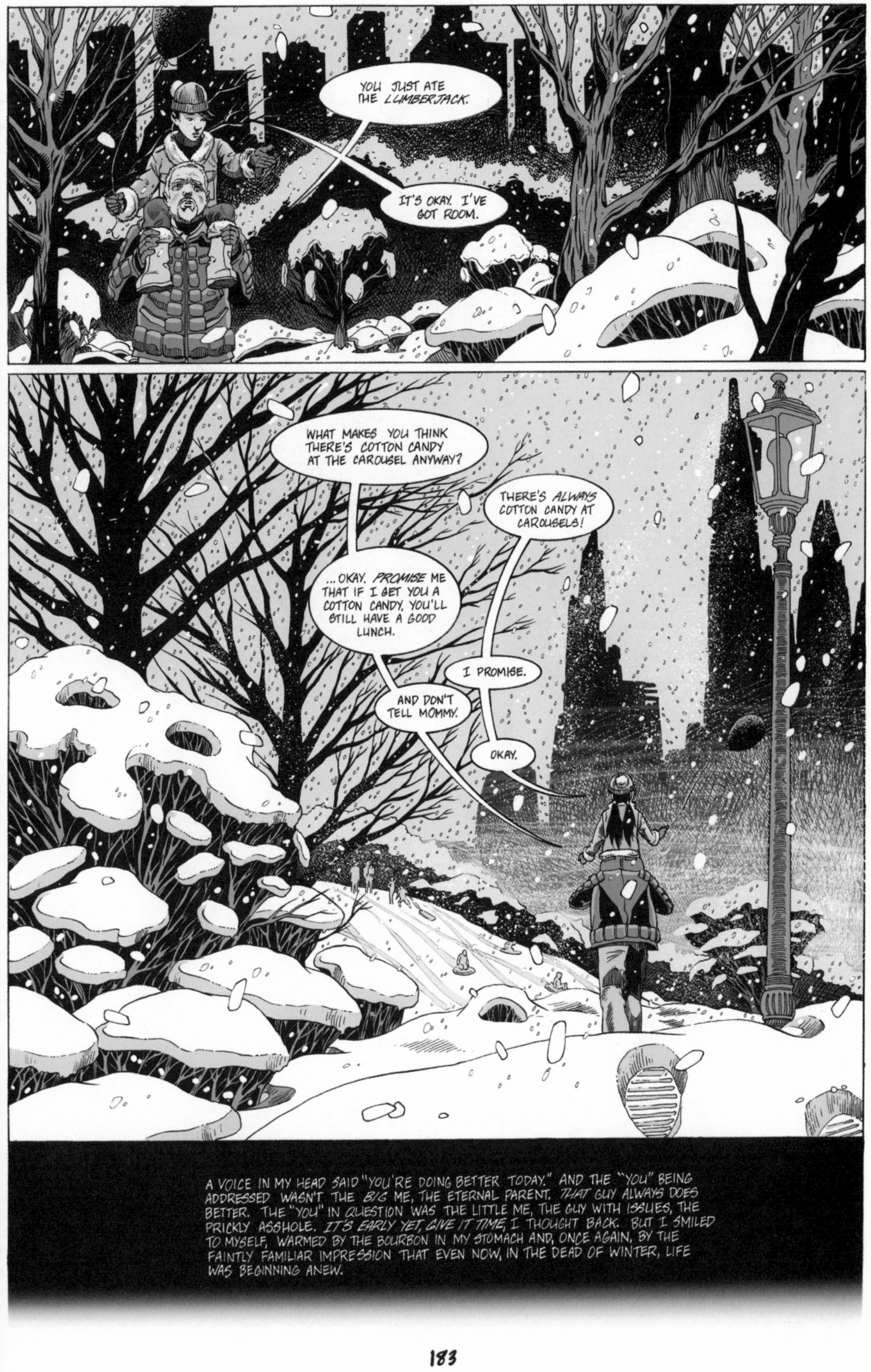
YOU JUST ATE THE *LUMBERJACK.*
IT'S OKAY. I'VE GOT ROOM.
WHAT MAKES YOU THINK THERE'S COTTON CANDY AT THE CAROUSEL ANYWAY?
THERE'S *ALWAYS* COTTON CANDY AT CAROUSELS!
...OKAY. *PROMISE* ME THAT IF I GET YOU A COTTON CANDY, YOU'LL STILL HAVE A GOOD LUNCH.
I PROMISE.
AND DON'T TELL MOMMY.
OKAY.
A VOICE IN MY HEAD SAID "YOU'RE DOING BETTER TODAY." AND THE "YOU" BEING ADDRESSED WASN'T THE *BIG* ME, THE ETERNAL PARENT. *THAT* GUY ALWAYS DOES BETTER. THE "YOU" IN QUESTION WAS THE LITTLE ME, THE GUY WITH ISSUES, THE PRICKLY ASSHOLE. *IT'S EARLY YET, GIVE IT TIME,* I THOUGHT BACK. BUT I SMILED TO MYSELF, WARMED BY THE BOURBON IN MY STOMACH AND, ONCE AGAIN, BY THE FAINTLY FAMILIAR IMPRESSION THAT EVEN NOW, IN THE DEAD OF WINTER, LIFE WAS BEGINNING ANEW.

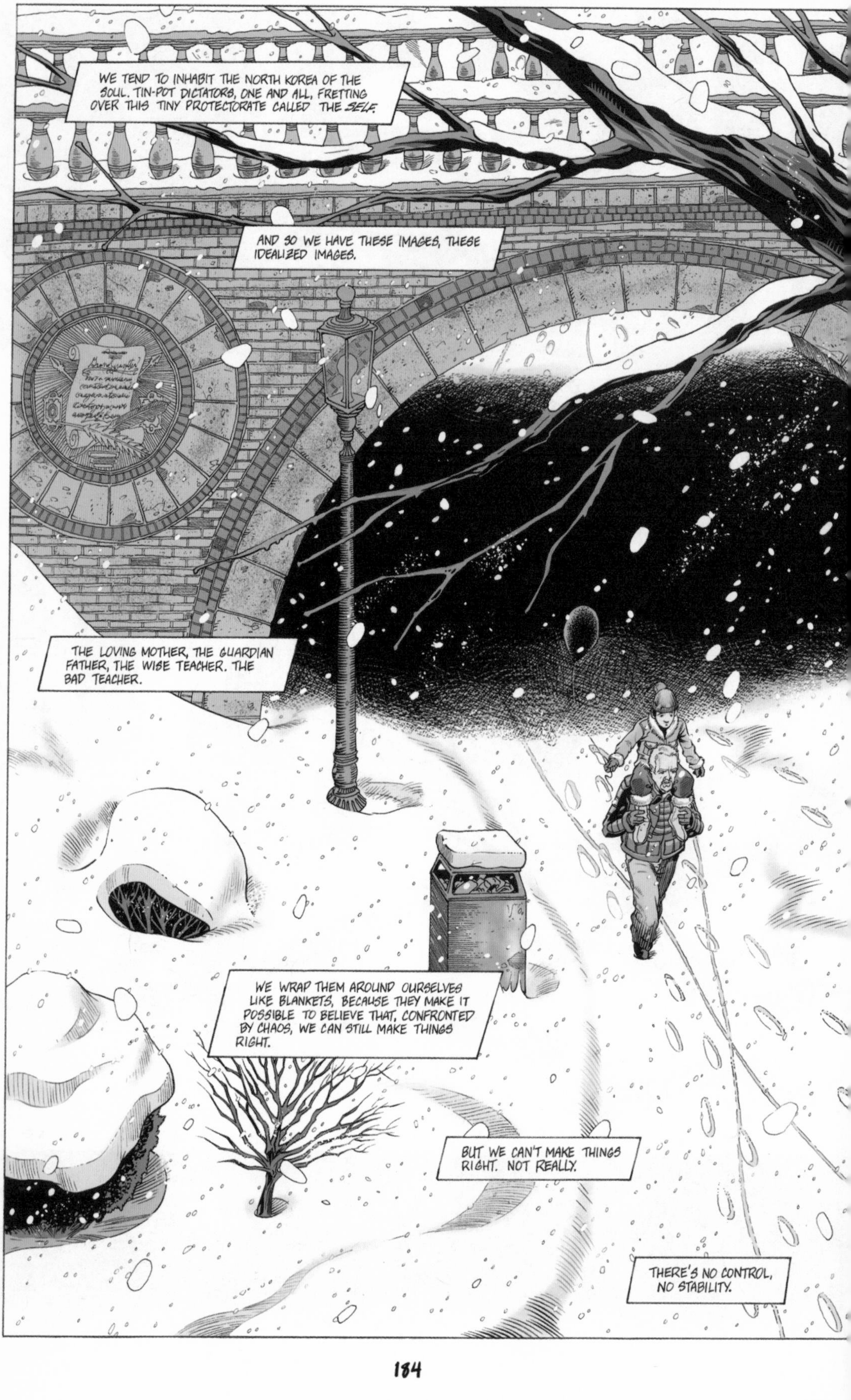
WE TEND TO INHABIT THE NORTH KOREA OF THE SOUL. TIN-POT DICTATORS, ONE AND ALL, FRETTING OVER THIS TINY PROTECTORATE CALLED THE *SELF*.
AND SO WE HAVE THESE IMAGES, THESE IDEALIZED IMAGES.
THE LOVING MOTHER, THE GUARDIAN FATHER, THE WISE TEACHER. THE BAD TEACHER.
WE WRAP THEM AROUND OURSELVES LIKE BLANKETS, BECAUSE THEY MAKE IT POSSIBLE TO BELIEVE THAT, CONFRONTED BY CHAOS, WE CAN STILL MAKE THINGS RIGHT.
BUT WE CAN'T MAKE THINGS RIGHT. NOT REALLY.
THERE'S NO CONTROL, NO STABILITY.

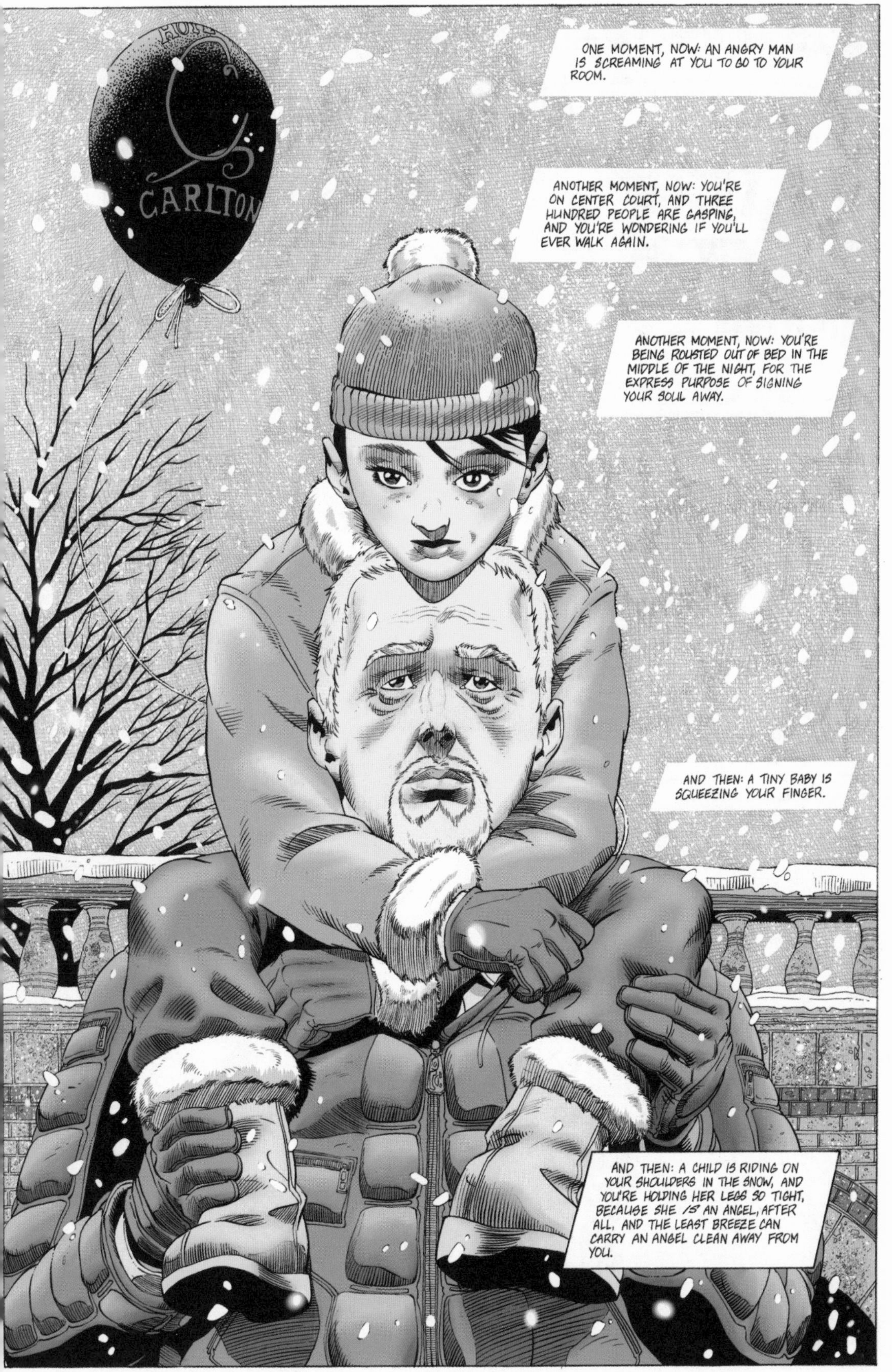
HOTEL
CARLTON
ONE MOMENT, NOW: AN ANGRY MAN IS SCREAMING AT YOU TO GO TO YOUR ROOM.
ANOTHER MOMENT, NOW: YOU'RE ON CENTER COURT, AND THREE HUNDRED PEOPLE ARE GASPING, AND YOU'RE WONDERING IF YOU'LL EVER WALK AGAIN.
ANOTHER MOMENT, NOW: YOU'RE BEING ROUSTED OUT OF BED IN THE MIDDLE OF THE NIGHT, FOR THE EXPRESS PURPOSE OF SIGNING YOUR SOUL AWAY.
AND THEN: A TINY BABY IS SQUEEZING YOUR FINGER.
AND THEN: A CHILD IS RIDING ON YOUR SHOULDERS IN THE SNOW, AND YOU'RE HOLDING HER LEGS SO TIGHT, BECAUSE SHE IS AN ANGEL, AFTER ALL, AND THE LEAST BREEZE CAN CARRY AN ANGEL CLEAN AWAY FROM YOU.

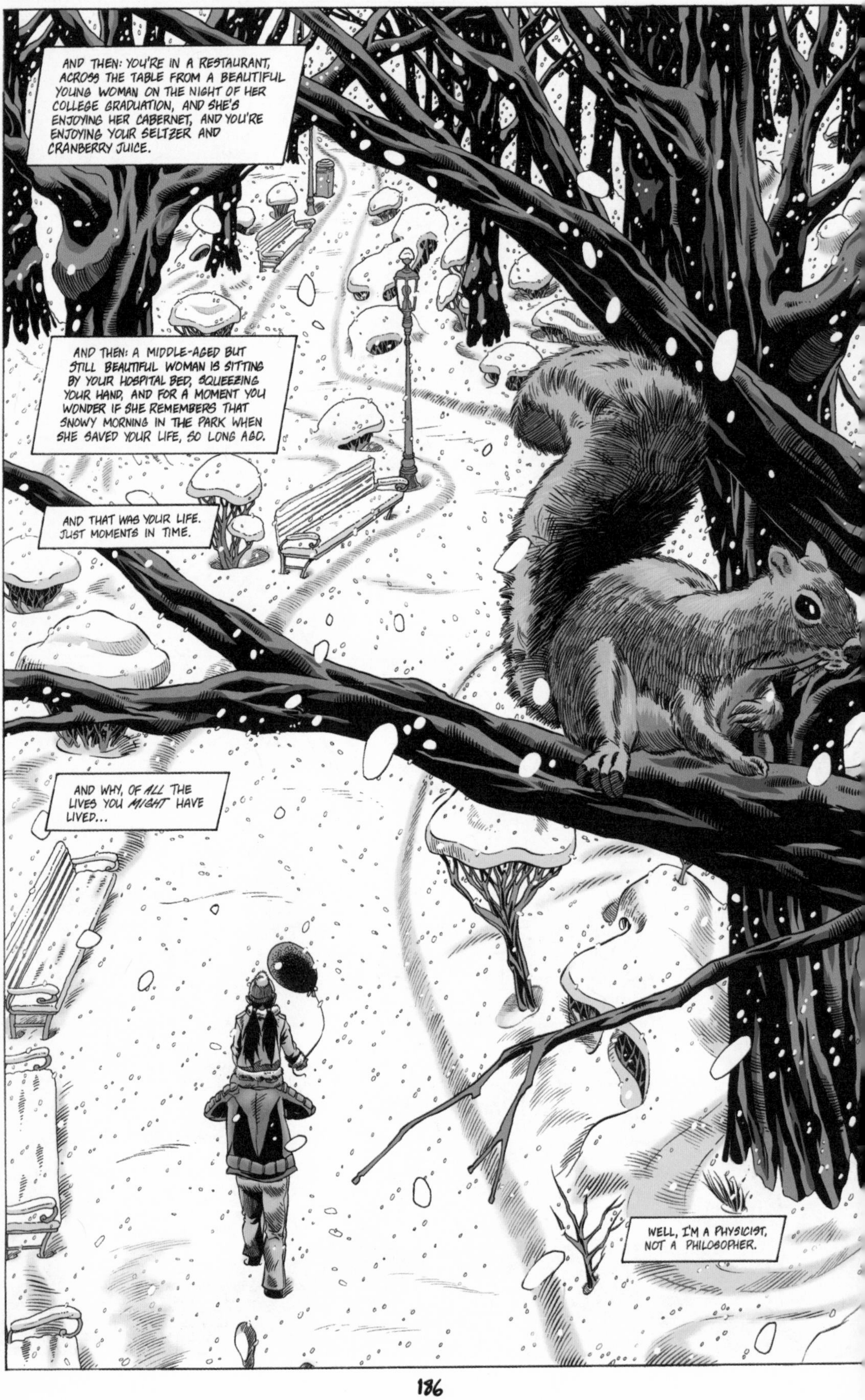
AND THEN: YOU'RE IN A RESTAURANT, ACROSS THE TABLE FROM A BEAUTIFUL YOUNG WOMAN ON THE NIGHT OF HER COLLEGE GRADUATION, AND SHE'S ENJOYING HER CABERNET, AND YOU'RE ENJOYING YOUR SELTZER AND CRANBERRY JUICE.
AND THEN: A MIDDLE-AGED BUT STILL BEAUTIFUL WOMAN IS SITTING BY YOUR HOSPITAL BED, SQUEEZING YOUR HAND, AND FOR A MOMENT YOU WONDER IF SHE REMEMBERS THAT SNOWY MORNING IN THE PARK WHEN SHE SAVED YOUR LIFE, SO LONG AGO.
AND THAT WAS YOUR LIFE. JUST MOMENTS IN TIME.
AND WHY, OF ALL THE LIVES YOU MIGHT HAVE LIVED...
WELL, I'M A PHYSICIST, NOT A PHILOSOPHER.

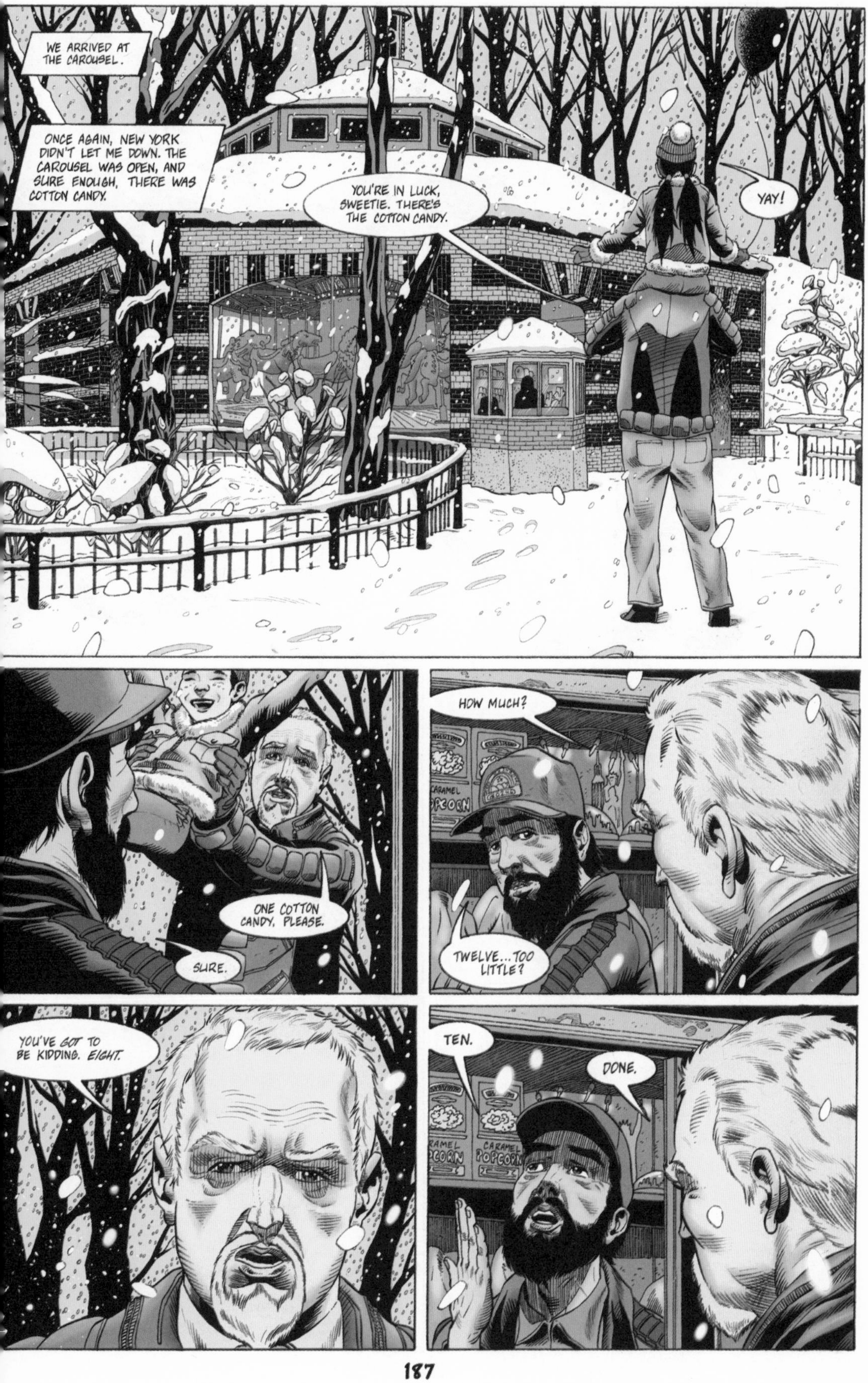

WE ARRIVED AT THE CAROUSEL.
ONCE AGAIN, NEW YORK DIDN'T LET ME DOWN. THE CAROUSEL WAS OPEN, AND SURE ENOUGH, THERE WAS COTTON CANDY.
YOU'RE IN LUCK, SWEETIE. THERE'S THE COTTON CANDY.
YAY!
ONE COTTON CANDY, PLEASE.
SURE.
HOW MUCH?
TWELVE... TOO LITTLE?
YOU'VE GOT TO BE KIDDING. EIGHT.
TEN.
DONE.

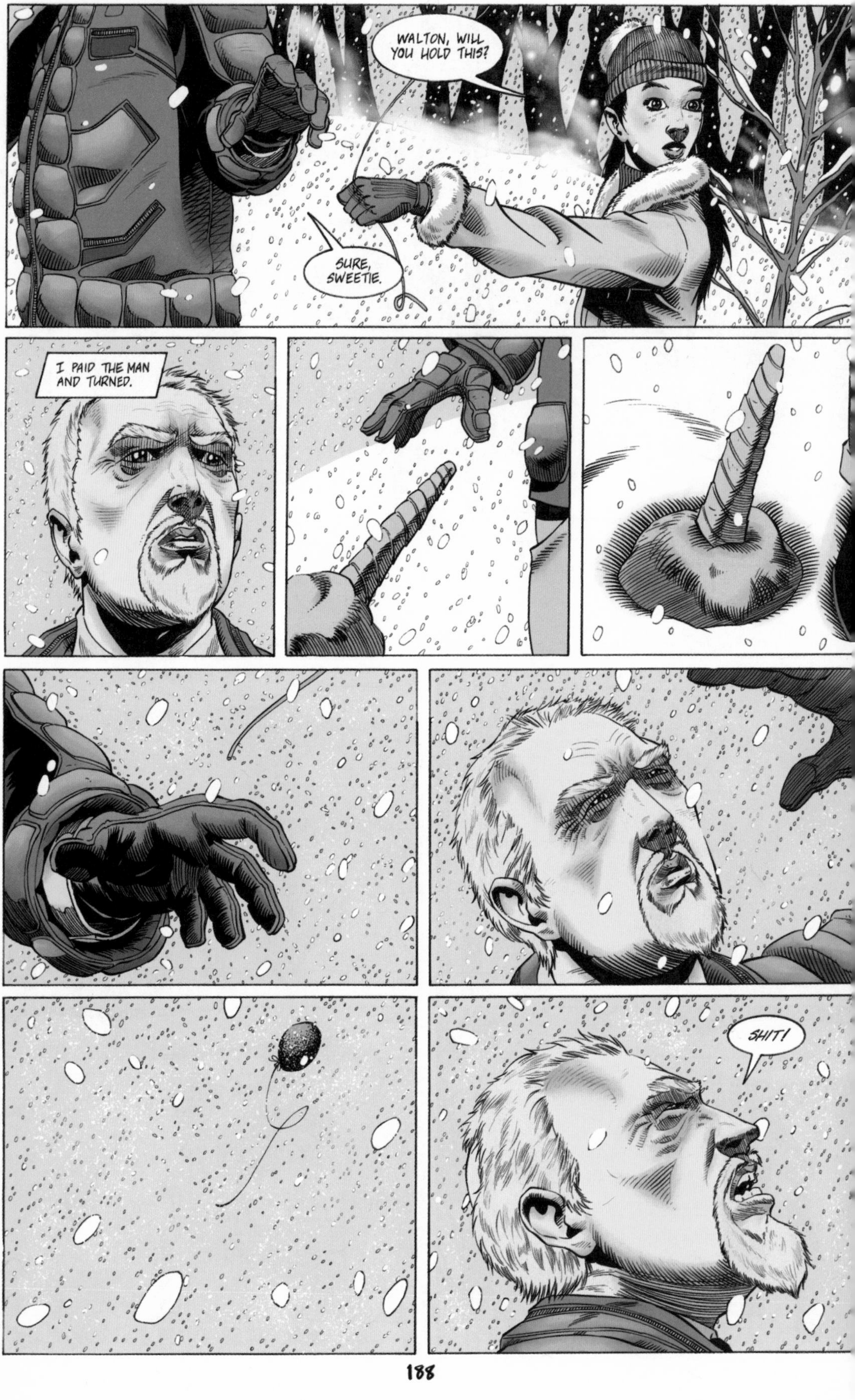
WALTON, WILL YOU HOLD THIS?
SURE, SWEETIE.
I PAID THE MAN AND TURNED.
SHIT!

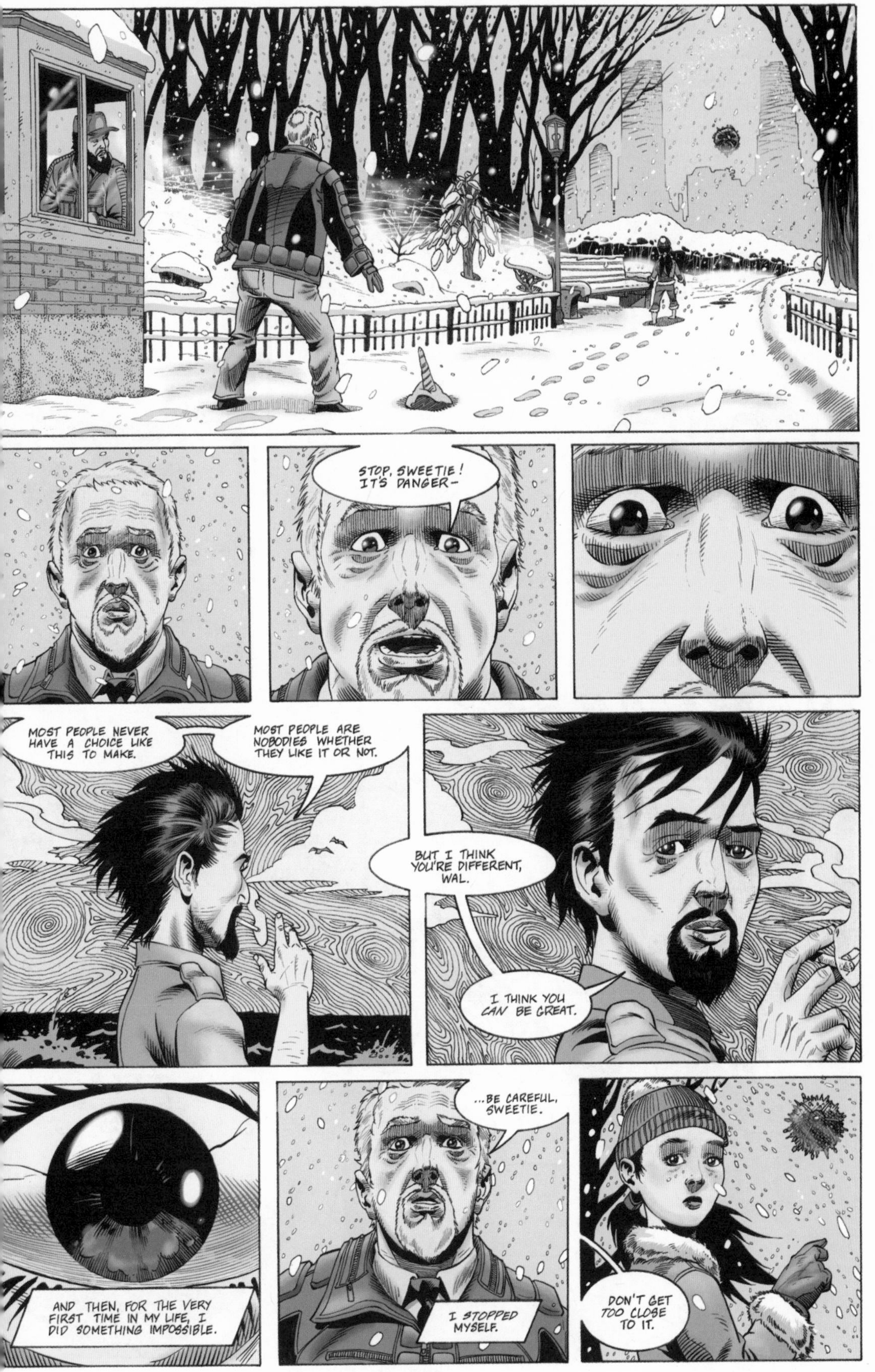
STOP, SWEETIE! IT'S DANGER—
MOST PEOPLE NEVER HAVE A CHOICE LIKE THIS TO MAKE.
MOST PEOPLE ARE NOBODIES WHETHER THEY LIKE IT OR NOT.
BUT I THINK YOU'RE DIFFERENT, WAL.
I THINK YOU *CAN* BE GREAT.
AND THEN, FOR THE VERY FIRST TIME IN MY LIFE, I DID SOMETHING IMPOSSIBLE.
...BE CAREFUL, SWEETIE.
I STOPPED MYSELF.
DON'T GET *TOO* CLOSE TO IT.

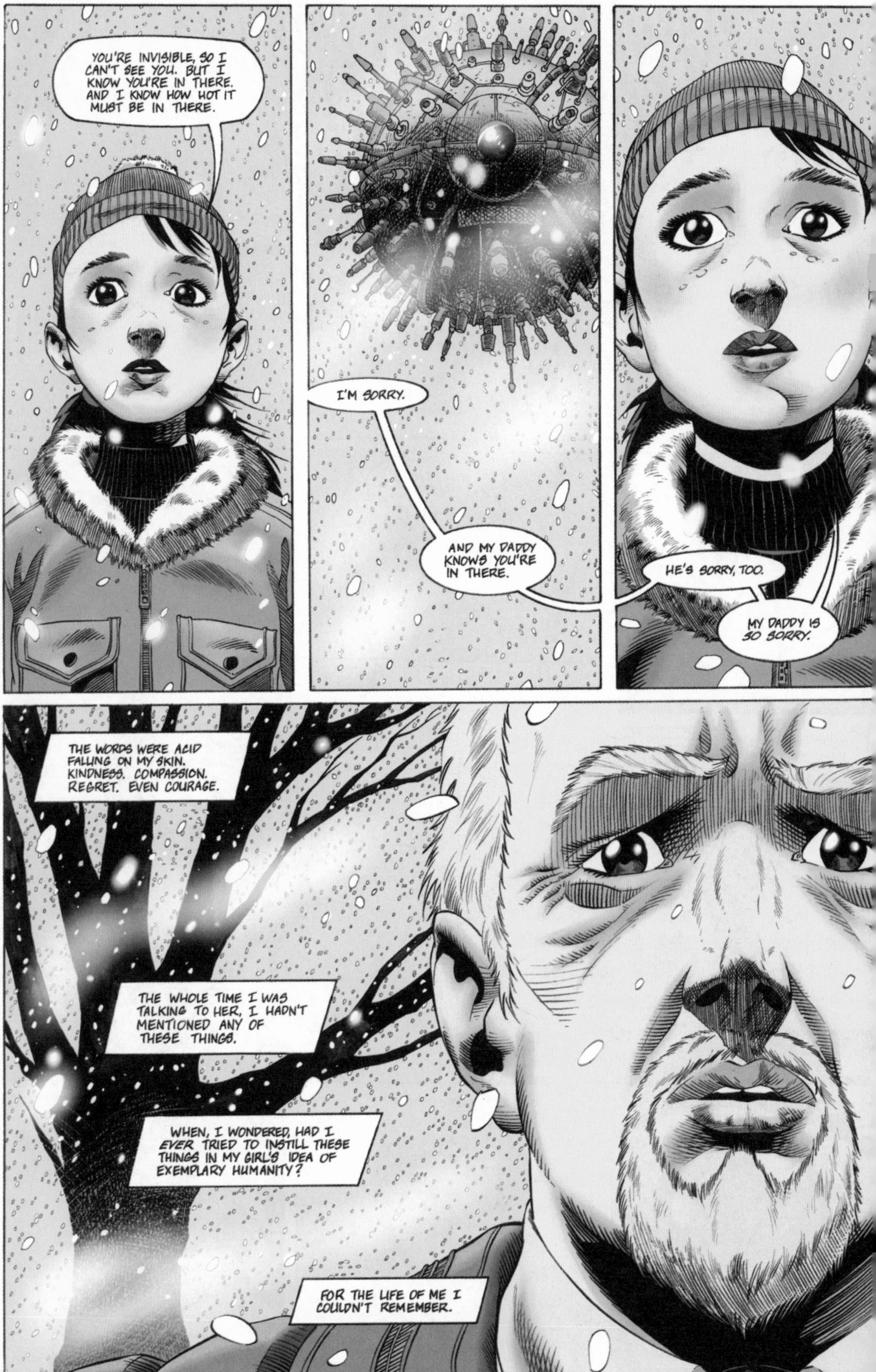
YOU'RE INVISIBLE, SO I CAN'T SEE YOU. BUT I KNOW YOU'RE IN THERE. AND I KNOW HOW HOT IT MUST BE IN THERE.
I'M SORRY.
AND MY DADDY KNOWS YOU'RE IN THERE.
HE'S SORRY, TOO.
MY DADDY IS SO SORRY.
THE WORDS WERE ACID FALLING ON MY SKIN. KINDNESS. COMPASSION. REGRET. EVEN COURAGE.
THE WHOLE TIME I WAS TALKING TO HER, I HADN'T MENTIONED ANY OF THESE THINGS.
WHEN, I WONDERED, HAD I *EVER* TRIED TO INSTILL THESE THINGS IN MY GIRL'S IDEA OF EXEMPLARY HUMANITY?
FOR THE LIFE OF ME I COULDN'T REMEMBER.

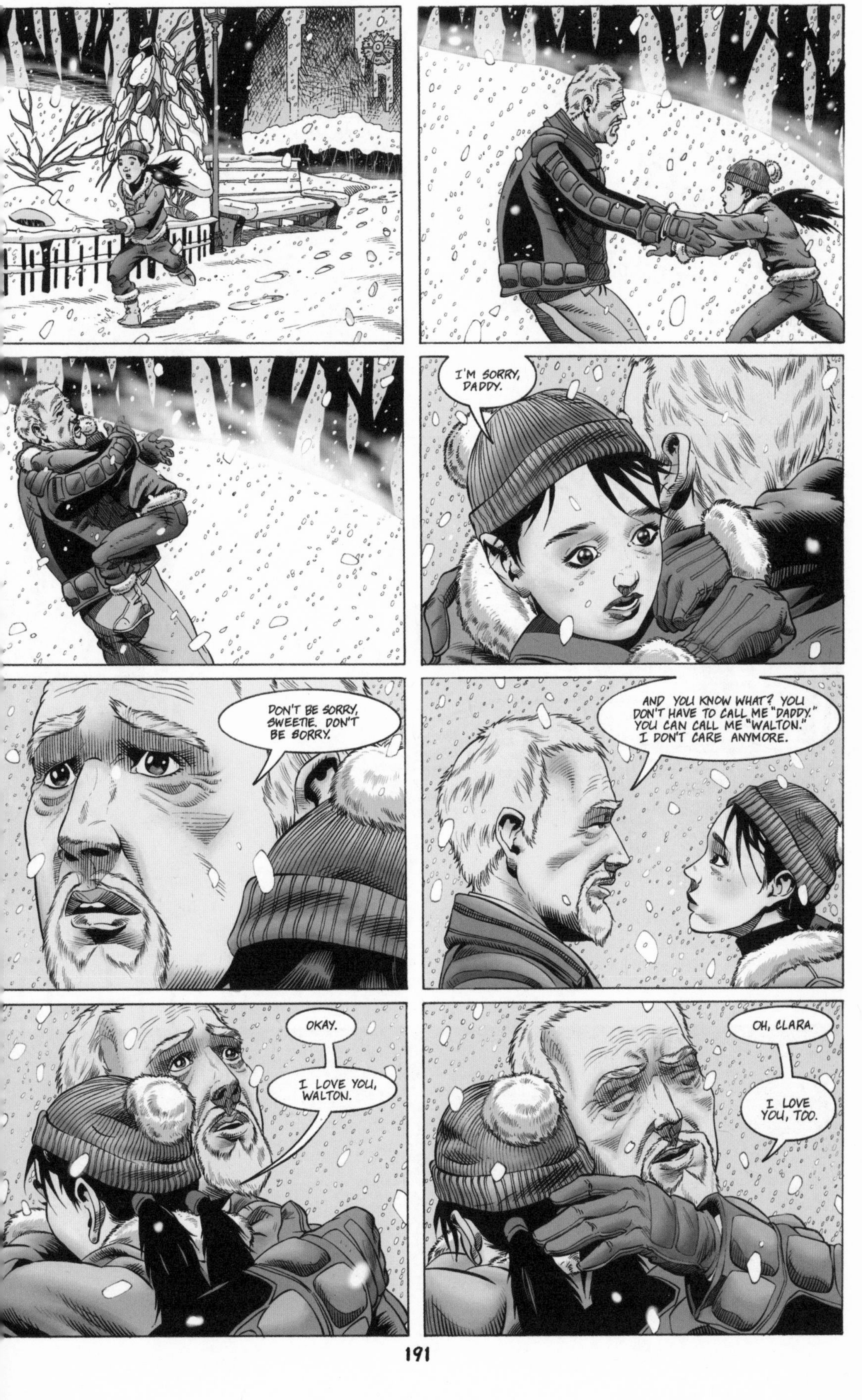

I'M SORRY, DADDY.
DON'T BE SORRY, SWEETIE. DON'T BE SORRY.
AND YOU KNOW WHAT? YOU DON'T HAVE TO CALL ME "DADDY." YOU CAN CALL ME "WALTON." I DON'T CARE ANYMORE.
OKAY.
I LOVE YOU, WALTON.
OH, CLARA.
I LOVE YOU, TOO.

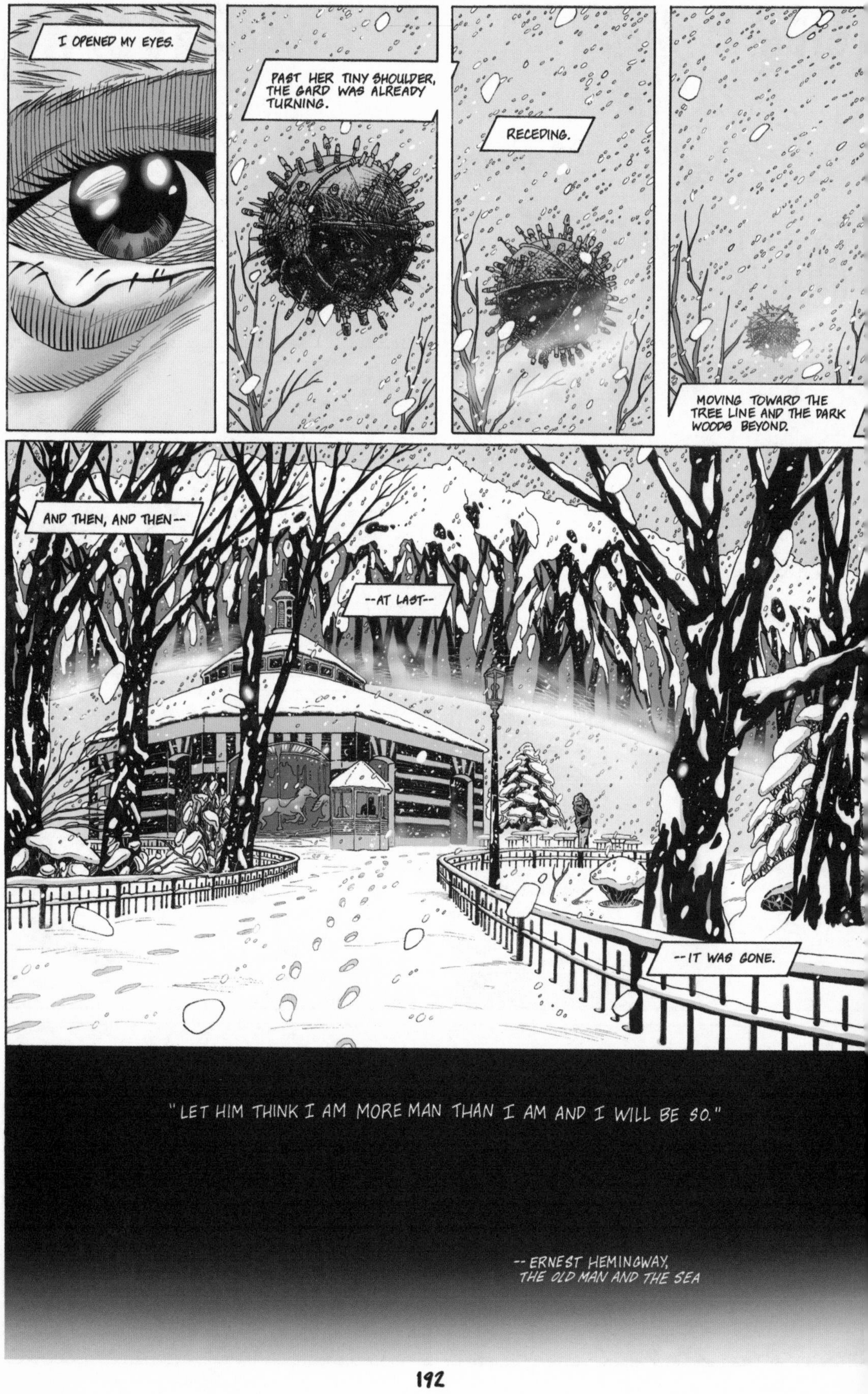
I OPENED MY EYES.
PAST HER TINY SHOULDER, THE GARD WAS ALREADY TURNING.
RECEDING.
MOVING TOWARD THE TREE LINE AND THE DARK WOODS BEYOND.
AND THEN, AND THEN--
--AT LAST--
--IT WAS GONE.
"LET HIM THINK I AM MORE MAN THAN I AM AND I WILL BE SO."
-- ERNEST HEMINGWAY, THE OLD MAN AND THE SEA

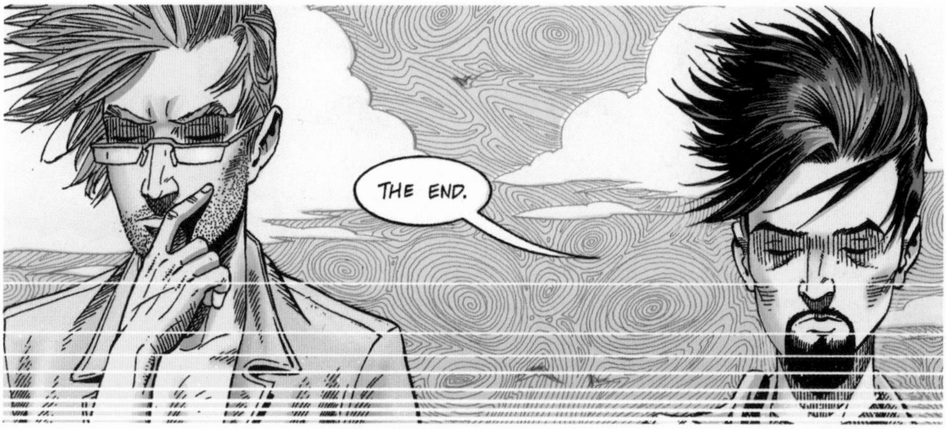
THE END.

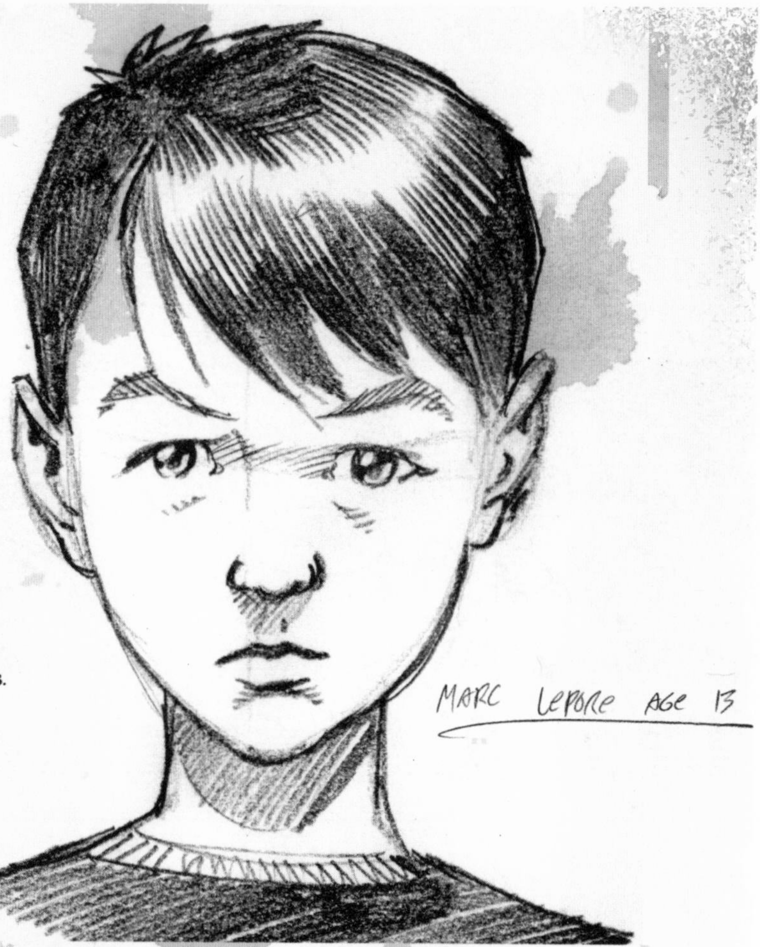
MARC Lepore AGE 13

MY PENCIL DESIGNS OF THIRTEEN-YEAR-OLD LEPORE AND HIS FATHER (FROM THE END OF CHAPTER THREE), COMPLETE WITH SPILLED COFFEE STAINS.

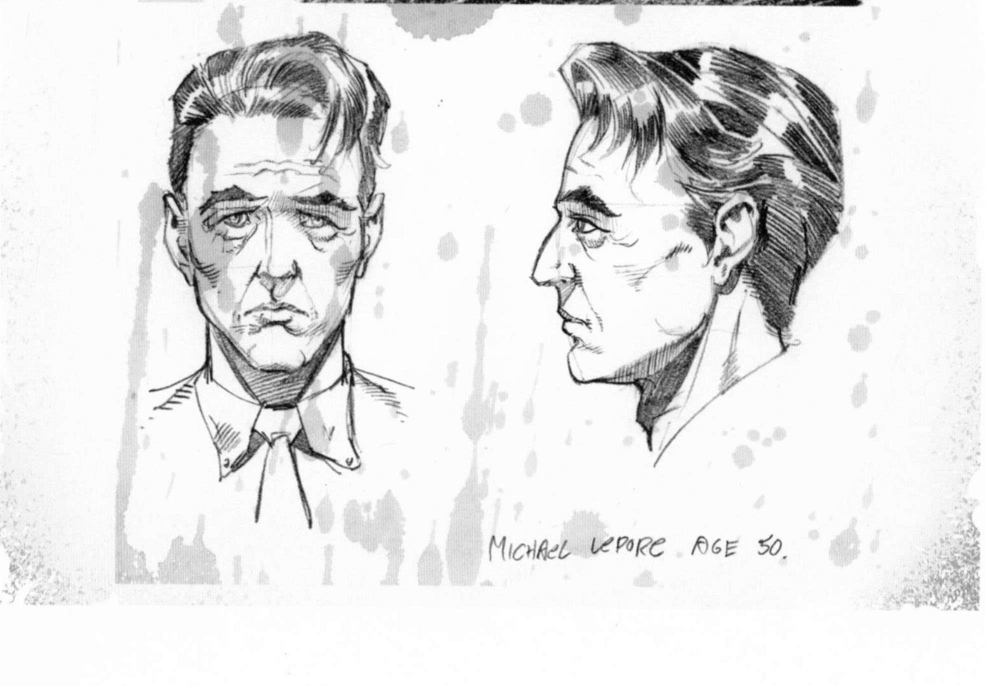
MICHAEL LEPORE AGE 50.

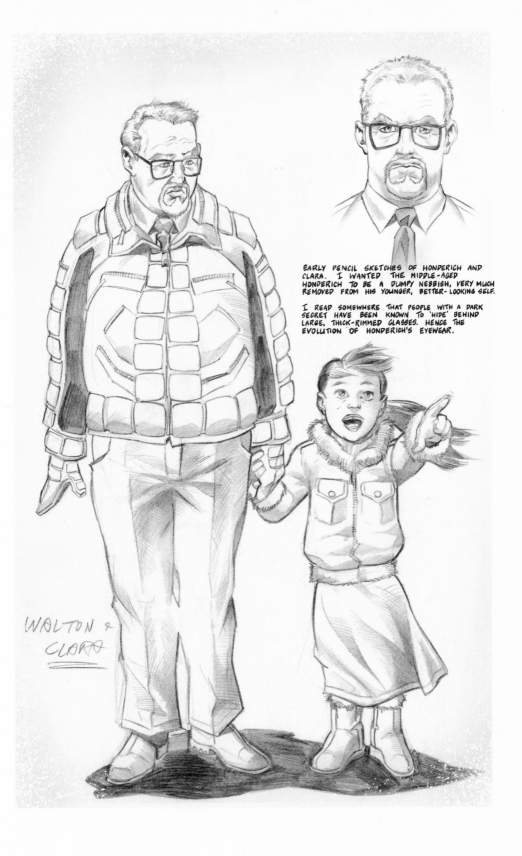

EARLY PENCIL SKETCHES OF HONDERICH AND
CLARA. I WANTED THE MIDDLE-AGED
HONDERICH TO BE A DUMPY NEBBISH, VERY MUCH
REMOVED FROM HIS YOUNGER, BETTER-LOOKING SELF.

I READ SOMEWHERE THAT PEOPLE WITH A DARK
SECRET HAVE BEEN KNOWN TO 'HIDE' BEHIND
LARGE, THICK-RIMMED GLASSES. HENCE THE
EVOLUTION OF HONDERICH'S EYEWEAR.

WALTON &
CLARA

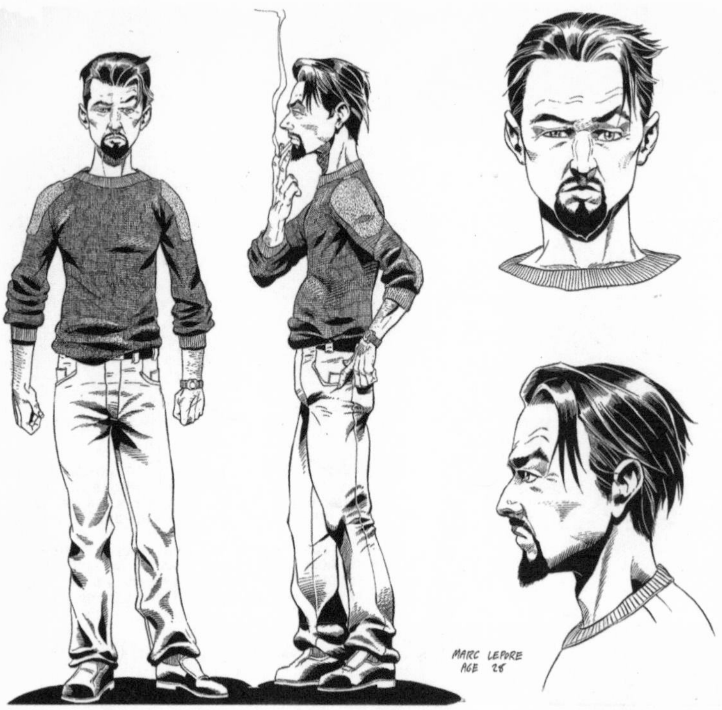

MARC LEPORE
AGE 28

MY MODEL SHEETS FOR LEPORE AND PIPER ALLEN-HONDERICH.

DOING THESE MODEL SHEETS EARLY ON IS CRUCIAL-- I HAD THEM BEFORE ME THE WHOLE TIME I WAS WORKING, TO KEEP THE LOOK OF THE CHARACTERS CONSISTENT.

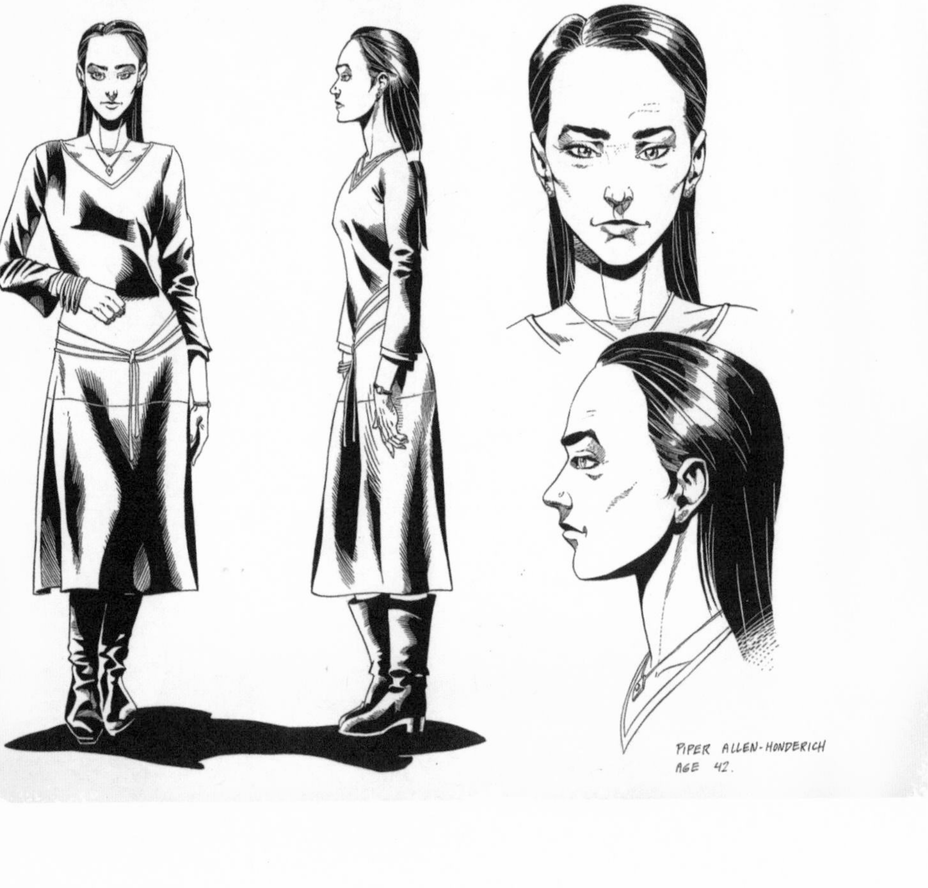

PIPER ALLEN-HONDERICH
AGE 42.

BUT THE FACT OF THE MATTER... ON HIS FEET.
MOM HAD TOLD
HE PROTESTED
THEN SHE WENT TO...
THEN WHEN I GET
NOPE, HE WORE
YEAH, I WORE
YOU'RE DEAD!
SO HE GOES AND
VIDEO GAME
HUNTER IN OPEN DOORWAY
MOM MAKING DINNER
WAL READING COMICS ON BED
140

BUT THE FACT OF THE MATTER... ON HIS FEET.
FAB NIKES
MOM HAD TOLD HIM.
HE PROTESTED
SHE INSISTED
HE RELENTED
FLIP FLOPS
FINE!
THEN SHE WENT TO
THEN WHEN I GET
NOPE, HE WORE
THEN WHEN SHE
YEAH, I WORE...
OH, IT MUST
TWO HOURS LATER
DID YOU TELL MOM
UH, YUP.
YOU'RE DEAD
SO HE GOES AND CONFESSES

BUT THE FACT OF THE MATTER IS: THIS KIND OF SHIT WENT ON ALL THE TIME WHEN I WAS A KID. LIKE THE TIME FIVE YEARS LATER WHEN HUNTER HAD POISON IVY ON HIS FEET.
MOM HAD TOLD HIM TO WEAR THESE RIDICULOUS-LOOKING FLIP-FLOPS TO SCHOOL SO HIS FEET COULD BREATHE.
HE PROTESTED THAT HE WANTED TO WEAR THE NEW NIKES HE'D GOTTEN FOR HIS BIRTHDAY.
SHE INSISTED.
HE RELENTED.
FIIINNE!
THEN SHE WENT TO WORK, AND HE WORE THE NIKES ANYWAY.
THEN WHEN I GET HOME SHE CALLS AND ASKS ME IF HUNTER WORE THE FLIP-FLOPS.
NOPE, HE WORE HIS NIKES.
THEN WHEN SHE GETS HOME FROM WORK, SHE ASKS HUNTER.
YEAH, I WORE THE FLIP-FLOPS. THEY REALLY SCREWED ME UP RUNNING THE 50-YARD DASH IN GYM, YOU SHOULD'VE SEEN IT!
OH, IT MUST HAVE BEEN SOMETHING.
TWO HOURS LATER IT OCCURS TO HUNTER TO ASK ME:
DID YOU TELL MOM I WORE MY NIKES?
UH, YUP.
YOU'RE DEAD.
SO HE GOES AND CONFESSES HIS LIE TO MOM.
140

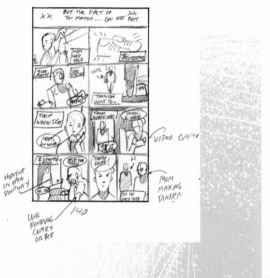

TOP LEFT: MY INITIAL THUMBNAIL OF PAGE 146. THIS IS 2 INCHES WIDE, 3¼ INCHES HIGH, ON BOND PAPER.

TOP RIGHT: 2ND, MORE INVOLVED ROUGH OF PAGE 140--3 INCHES WIDE, 4¼ INCHES HIGH.

LEFT: THE FINAL PENCILS OF PAGE 140, BASED ON ROUGH #2, 10 INCHES WIDE, 15 INCHES HIGH, ON 4-PLY BRISTOL BOARD.

12

LEFT: MY INITIAL ROUGH OF PAGE 12 (PAGE 15 IN THE ACTUAL TEXT)-- 2 INCHES WIDE, 3¼ INCHES HIGH.

RIGHT: MY 2ND ROUGH, 3 INCHES WIDE, 4¼ INCHES HIGH.

12

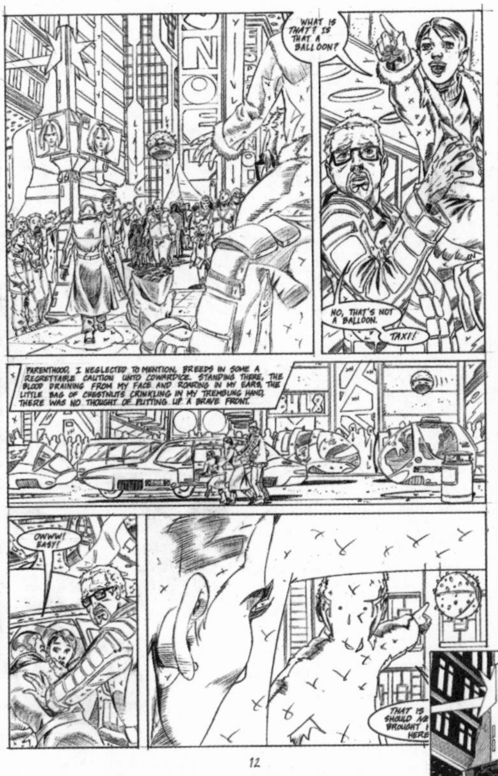
WHAT IS THAT? IS THAT A BALLOON?
NO, THAT'S NOT A BALLOON.
TAXI!
PARENTHOOD, I NEGLECTED TO MENTION, BREEDS IN SOME A REGRETTABLE CAUTION UNTO COWARDICE. STANDING THERE, THE BLOOD DRAINING FROM MY FACE AND ROARING IN MY EARS, THE LITTLE BAG OF CHESTNUTS CRINKLING IN MY TREMBLING HAND, THERE WAS NO THOUGHT OF PUTTING UP A BRAVE FRONT.
OWWW! EASY!
THAT IS
12

LEFT: FINAL PENCILS OF PAGE 12 (PAGE 15 IN THE ACTUAL TEXT). 10 x 15 INCHES, PENCIL ON 4-PLY BRISTOL BOARD.

RIGHT: FINAL INKS, DONE DIRECTLY OVER THE PENCILS, USING BLACK AND WHITE INK, A HUNTS 102 CROWQUILL PEN, AND VARIOUS RAPIDOGRAPH TECHNICAL PENS.

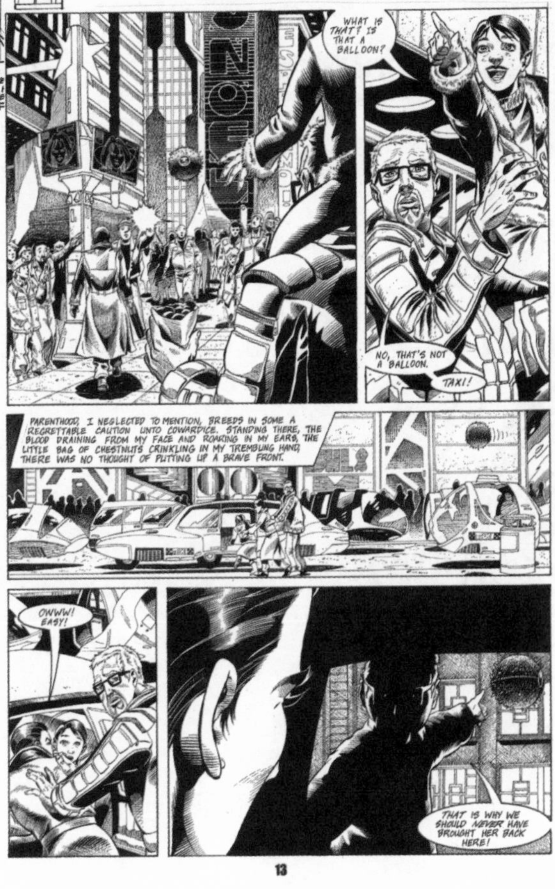
WHAT IS THAT? IS THAT A BALLOON?
NO, THAT'S NOT A BALLOON.
TAXI!
PARENTHOOD, I NEGLECTED TO MENTION, BREEDS IN SOME A REGRETTABLE CAUTION UNTO COWARDICE. STANDING THERE, THE BLOOD DRAINING FROM MY FACE AND ROARING IN MY EARS, THE LITTLE BAG OF CHESTNUTS CRINKLING IN MY TREMBLING HAND, THERE WAS NO THOUGHT OF PUTTING UP A BRAVE FRONT.
OWWW! EASY!
THAT IS WHY WE SHOULD NEVER HAVE BROUGHT HER BACK HERE!
13

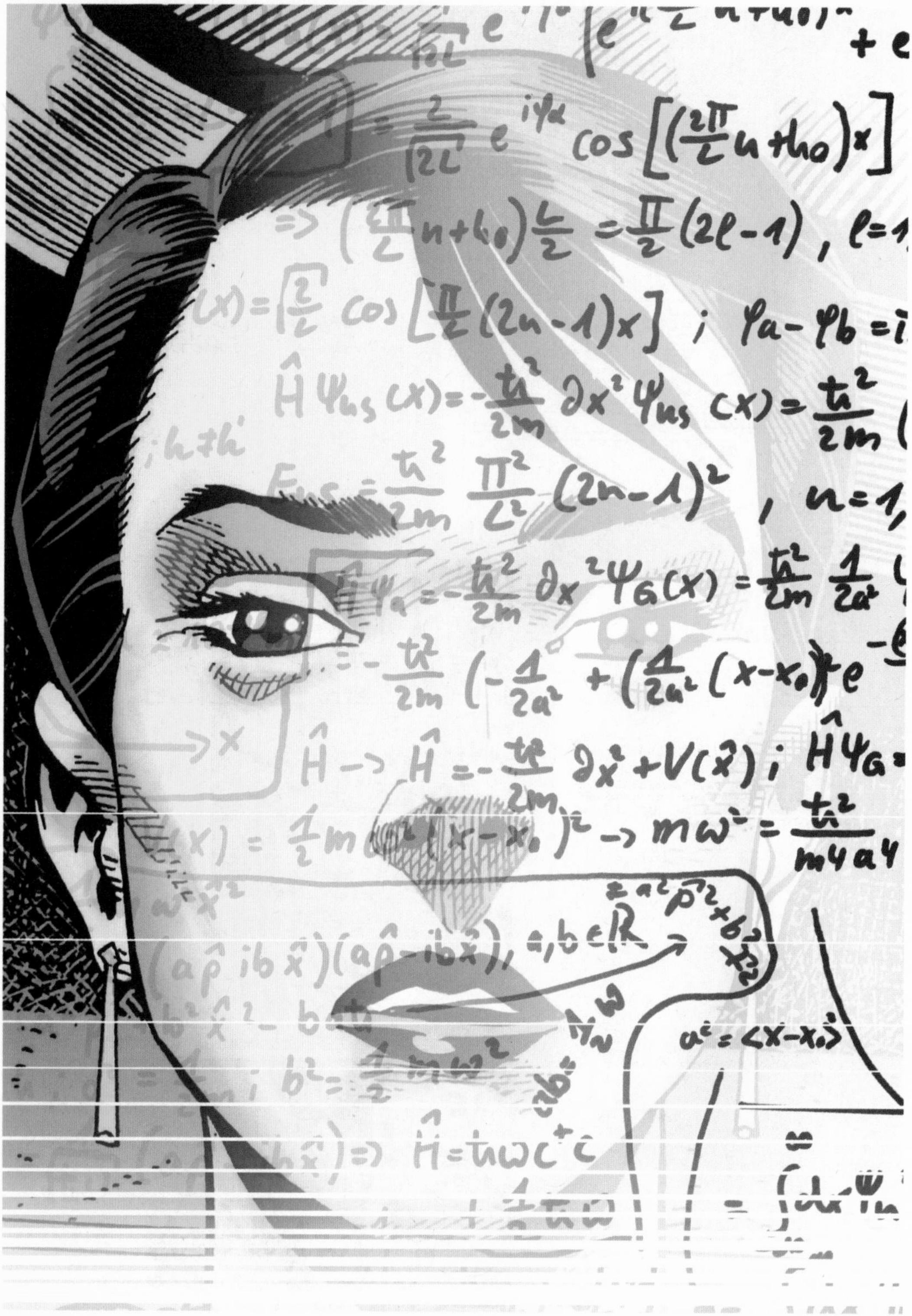

I'D LIKE TO THANK:

MY WIFE, JACQUELINE, AND MY KIDS, SCOTIA, DAGNY, AND LEE, FOR THEIR LOVE AND PATIENCE WHILE I WORKED ON THIS; JULIET CHING, JEROME SCHILLER, AND HOWARD WEBSTER FOR READING EARLY DRAFTS; JAMES PEACHEY FOR HIS TECHNICAL HELP AND ENDURING FRIENDSHIP; AMY GILES FOR HER INVALUABLE HELP IN THE PROCESS OF GETTING THIS PUBLISHED; MY AGENT, BOB MECOY, FOR FINDING THIS BOOK'S PERFECT HOME; MY EDITOR, DIANA M. PHO, FOR BELIEVING IN THE BOOK AND MAKING IT BETTER; PAUL LEVITZ, JIMMY PALMIOTTI, SHAWN MARTINBROUGH, AND JOHN JENNINGS FOR THEIR HELP WITH PUBLICITY; AND MY MOTHER, BETTY RAY WISEMAN (1942 - 2017) FOR HER LOVE, STRENGTH, AND EXAMPLE.

AND THANK YOU HARRY MARKOS -- FOR MAKING ME FINISH IT.

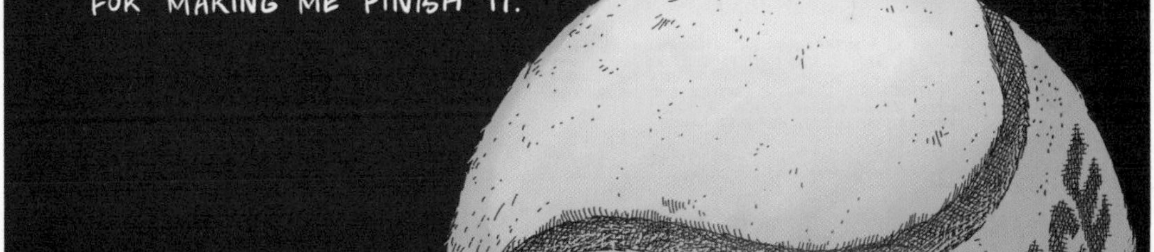
THE FURNACE

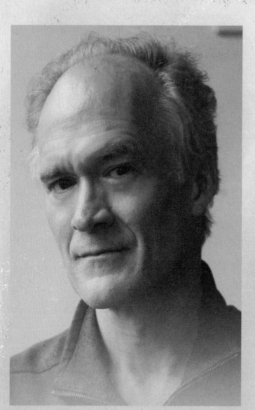

PRENTIS ROLLINS IS A VETERAN OF THE AMERICAN COMICS INDUSTRY, HAVING WORKED ON SUCH BESTSELLING PROJECTS AS *GREEN LANTERN: REBIRTH*, *GREEN LANTERN CORPS*, *DC ONE MILLION*, AND *BATMAN: THE ULTIMATE EVIL* (FOR DC), AND *NEW X-MEN* (FOR MARVEL). HE IS THE AUTHOR OF *SURVIVAL MACHINE* (STORIES), *THE MAKING OF A GRAPHIC NOVEL*, AND *HOW TO DRAW SCI-FI UTOPIAS AND DYSTOPIAS*.

HE LIVES IN LONDON WITH HIS WIFE AND THREE CHILDREN.

WWW.PRENTISROLLINSART.COM